THE FIRE THAT TIME

THE

FIRE

**TRANSNATIONAL BLACK RADICALISM
AND THE SIR GEORGE WILLIAMS
OCCUPATION**

THAT

**EDITED BY
RONALD CUMMINGS
NALINI MOHABIR**

TIME

**BLACK
ROSE
BOOKS**

Montréal • Chicago • London

Black Rose Books No. UU420

Library and Archives Canada Cataloguing in Publication
Title: The fire that time : transnational Black radicalism and the Sir George Williams occupation / Ronald Cummings, Nalini Mohabir, eds.
Names: Cummings, Ronald, editor. | Mohabir, Nalini, editor.
Identifiers: Canadiana (print) 20200345451 | Canadiana (ebook) 20200345885 | ISBN 9781551647371 (softcover) | ISBN 9781551647395 (hardcover) | ISBN 9781551647418 (PDF)
Subjects: LCSH: Sir George Williams University—Riot, 1969. | LCSH: Racism in higher education—Québec (Province)—Montréal. | LCSH: Student movements—Québec (Province)—Montréal—History—20th century. | LCSH: College students, Black—Québec (Province)—Montréal—Social conditions—20th century. | LCSH: College students—Caribbean Area—Social conditions—20th century.
Classification: LCC LC212.43.C23 M664 2021 | DDC 371.829/96071427—dc23

C.P. 35788 Succ. Léo Pariseau
Montréal, QC H2X 0A4
CANADA
www.blackrosebooks.com

ORDERING INFORMATION

USA/INTERNATIONAL	CANADA	UK/EIRE
University of Chicago Press	University of Toronto Press	Central Books
Chicago Distribution Center	5201 Dufferin Street	Freshwater Road
11030 South Langley Avenue	Toronto, ON	Dagenham
Chicago IL 60628	M3H 5T8	RM8 1RX
(800) 621-2736 (USA)	1-800-565-9523	+44 20 8525 8800
(773) 702-7000 (International)	utpbooks@utpress.utoronto.ca	contactus@centralbooks.com
orders@press.uchicago.edu		

For all the protesters,

in the spirit of collective liberation

CONTENTS

ACKNOWLEDGEMENTS

THE BOOK you hold in your hands is the result of many conversations, collaborations and networks of support. Some of these are individual, others institutional, others intergenerational. As co-editors, we are grateful to have been able to do this work together and in community. It would not have been as rewarding or meaningful to have done it alone. We do this work in the spirit of collective struggle.

From January 29 to February 11, 2019, coinciding with the historical dates of the student occupation of the Sir George Williams University's computer centre, a conference and series of events, *Protests and Pedagogy*, were organized at Concordia University, Montreal. Community members, faculty, staff, and students came together to commemorate the fiftieth anniversary of the Sir George Williams Occupation and to re-occupy the university with art workshops, roundtable discussions, and an interrogation of commitments to anti-racism, decolonization, and curriculum development. As part of these interrogations, a two-day academic conference extended space for meaningful dialogue to discuss the lessons of the protests (including, the ebb and flow of radical transformations, the development of Black community organizations, resistance, and sustainability of struggle, as well as legacies of loss and personal disorientation for those involved in the protest, and those whose horizons of possibility were threatened either by arrests, deportation, or police violence). We felt fortunate to have individuals travel from far and wide: Nancy Warner, Brenda Dash, Philippe Fils-Aimé, and Rodney John all accepted our invitations. We were also touched to see so many Caribbean academics whose work we admire also bridge distance to support us. We also want to thank those here in Montreal who have lived with the shadow of this history (Dorothy Williams, Liz Charles, Leon Llewellyn, Clarence Bayne, H. Nigel Thomas), and into the second generation. We also remember those who are no longer with us. We owe so much to all the contributors of this volume, but especially to Michael O. West who generously supported us with his keynote address at *Protests and Pedagogy*. Not only did our community pull together—including individuals, local community newspapers, consul generals of various Caribbean territories, and Caribbean community members in the literary and arts world, as well as the non-profit and private sector—they made the event possible.

This collection of essays emerges from the vital energy and commitments that held us during *Protests and Pedagogy*. We hope that this work provides a meaningful foundation for further sustained critical dialogue about Black studies and about decolonization across Canadian universities. A special thank you to all the contributors who immediately said yes to writing chapters for this volume and who responded generously to all our queries and questions about their work and about this history. We also want to thank Natasha Gordon-Chipembre, Sunjay Mathuria, and Kevin Lo who readily helped us with editing and designing this book.

Lastly, the book would not have been possible without Kaie Kellough, who first planted the seed with Black Rose Books, suggesting that it was time to revisit Dennis Forsythe's work. We wished to speak to, and with Forsythe, in person and intended to invite him to *Protests and Pedagogy*. Unfortunately, when we called his law office in Jamaica, we learned that he had passed only days prior. The renewed urgency of this work was immediately understood by Black Rose Books, an alternative and independent book publisher in Montreal, who first gave space to the protesters to tell their side of the story. Although we are beyond frustrated that the concerns raised by students in 1969 still continue, our goal is that this collection will strengthen their calls.

Sentences

A memory of the sound of snow. Montréal, February 1969/2019

i.

snow hisses down against a concrete backdrop

a film reel from 1969, grainy and fallible

memory of the national   media. camera

pans wide   students, migratory intellects

pace de maisonneuve boulevard

soft crackle   snow stutters in its uniform descent

       the students, pacing between winter and a future

in protest, black

and foreign in monochrome

       february, seem   lost. radical

youth, lost   languages i never knew

languages my who

might have spoken, become entangled   in a ship, my tongue can't

navigate, can't swim in their wake, they exert

a pressure in the place vowels press

      into the city's gray matter

moulding a concrete   sibilance   a density in the world

snow in the mouth   where phantom tongues once

      probed

      an urge strains behind this   silent moving thinking

a sinusoid repeating figure   an ostinato that

exceeds the individual   the movement of global capital

a student's intelligence   a resource that suddenly -

   sugar, rum, opium, people   revolts

   i might cry out

the names of languages known to   worlds carried in

vowel gourds   atop heads   where entire cultures

echo   ways of being consonants the bright ornament, the

beaded faces and parrot's   fluorescent coif, for which

there exist words in other créoles that may have   colored me into existence

before i swallowed snow

ii.

mouth open   a blizzard rushes in to fill

a story   the world and its objects dream

of their ideal   lolling green tongues

elisions, ellipses, suspensions, omissions, gaps

in the narrative and misdirections

misspellings of names and mistaken years

erasures and shifting borders, insurgent

latitudes met with resistance, geographies

hovering and reshaping to mirror the clouds

remembrances charging into fallacies, seeking the location of culture

which disappears into a period, white, falling at the end of dead seasons

lost steps, accidents of memory   shivering

while staring into the fluttering

     opacity that might conceal a maroon encampment or

guerillas, but instead it is just snow rising as reams of paper furl to the street

below, the concrete locked in ice, hardened like an attitude, a machine

whose drone, whose dirge is fed by white punch-cards, cards tossed

out the windows to flutter and freeze in the air, each one unique, digital

snowflakes turning, porous to light, and these are the gaps in our thinking

into which our marxist and post-colonial theories, fed by scholarships

in turn feed vocabularies, the places compassion is suspended and only

vexation and the practical desire to move the world, to push it faster

or slow its revolution on its axis, enters, the students sit at the feet of

cane stalks, sit at the feet of the enslaved and learn that snow

hisses down in sentences

IN MONTRÉAL'S Black history, we encounter two major incidents that were marked by fire. The more recent fire burned 50 years ago, in 1969, when Black Caribbean students and their allies occupied the 9th floor computer centre at Sir George William's University (now Concordia University). The occupation was carried out in protest against racial bias in grading: a bias exacerbated by the administration's negligent response to student complaints. The more distant fire was allegedly lit by Marie-Joseph Angélique, an enslaved woman, in 1734. That fire, perhaps a response to bondage and exploitation, may have been kindled by a desire for freedom that accompanied her from Madeira, Portugal, to New England, and eventually to New France, into whose territory she was sold in 1725. Her fire burned down much of Montréal's Port. This year marks the 285th anniversary of her death and the 50th anniversary of the Sir George Williams student occupation.

Caribbean history is animated by the figures of Nanny, Bussa, Toussaint, Cuffy, Quamina, Accabreh, and others who led and participated in uprisings against the plantation slave system, people who were considered, as Angélique was, to be enemies of the state, rebels, yet who came to be seen as the founders of independent nations. These figures are now national heroes. While nationalisms may commandeer the symbols and the narratives of freedom, they do not own the drive for freedom, respect, and self-determination. These properties trespass upon borders, span oceans, and sweep across centuries.

When I think about this, I cannot avoid considering whether, if Montréal was an island in the Caribbean, Marie-Joseph Angélique would be considered a national hero. Then again, the point of her fire, of our fire, is that it is not a hypothetical. It blazes with or without promises, official acknowledgements, titles, and honors. It does not require crowns or flags, medals of honor, uniforms, or other accoutrements. Fire is a force we have carried with us since our arrival on these shores, and which we continue to carry.

While both events, the 1734 fire and the 1969 occupation are unique, I would urge everyone to think of each one less as its own self-contained occurrence, and more as part of a tradition, part of a continuous fire. It is a fire that begets dub poetry, and roots and rebel music: work that thinks about how to be, how to survive, how to live with a world that is exploitive and oppressive, and how to transform it. But these traditions are more than that. Dub poetry speaks back in defiance, and in so doing fortifies the self and the community. By speaking out, as the students did in 1969, by speaking up for ourselves, we transform the world on an elemental level, the level of language, thought, communication, understanding, and possibility.

We ignite possibility.

Kaie Kellough
Montréal,
June 16, 2019

INTRODUCTION: THE FIRE THAT TIME

Nalini Mohabir and Ronald Cummings

> *Flame is our god, our last defence, our peril.*
> (Kamau Brathwaite)[1]

> *There is no more water to out the fire.*
> (Niney)[2]

FOR THOSE interested in activism, resistance, and liberation, the 1960s is a continuing source of inspiration, as well as deferred dreams. As seen in Black civil rights struggle in the USA, anti-colonial struggles in the Caribbean, Africa, and Asia, Canada's opening to immigration from the Global South, and the wider context of human rights struggles (including the women's movement and Stonewall uprising), the old order was shifting. Decolonization meant not only political independence, but a quest for dignity and respect denied under colonialism. Audre Lorde, in her essay "Learning from the 60s," written two decades later, argued that the "raw energy of Black determination released in the 60s…[was] still being felt in movements for change".[3] Lorde also acknowledged that as much as the 1960s was a time for revisioning a more just world, there were also significant errors made and cautions against romanticization. Nonetheless, if we accept that the struggles we face today emerge from the seeds of history, then the past also gifts us lessons about survival.[4] In the spirit of Lorde, we offer this collection of essays, reflections and conversations with unapologetic admiration for the courage shown by Black and Caribbean student activists of the 1960s. Yet this work is also done with more than a tinge of sadness at the way this crucial moment of transnational Black radicalism, connecting North America, Britain, the Caribbean and Africa has been largely overlooked in the present. We revisit this history to think about the provocations and possibilities of that time as well as ours.

The Sir George Williams University (SGWU) protest against institutional racism in 1969, along with the Congress of Black Writers[5] the year before, centered Montreal within global Black Power struggles of the 1960s. We have a rich sense of its national and international significance through the work of a number of writers, including Dionne Brand (1994), David Austin (2013, 2018), Michael O. West (2017), Rinaldo Walcott and Idil Abdillahi (2019), and others who have all noted its importance for igniting a sense of struggle and for transforming the lives of a generation of young Black people in Canada. As Dionne Brand puts it, the events at "Sir George Williams University had awakened the Black Power movement in Canada".[6] Black students from the Caribbean—many of whom had set their sights on a career in medicine that could contribute to the project of decolonization in their home countries—were enrolled in a prerequisite physiology course at SGWU. Despite being high-achieving students,[7] they were systematically failed by a young white (and by at least one account, conservative and unpopular) biology professor, Perry Anderson.[8] Anderson's discriminatory marking practices curtailed futures, both individual and collective. Mobilized and energized by the Congress of Black Writers in 1968, the students sought administrative avenues to address the pattern of racism experienced in the classroom.[9] However, the university stalled and then attempted to managerialize the complaints,[10] pushing the students towards direct action. In 1969, students, mostly Black, occupied the computer centre of the downtown university, located in the towering Hall Building, which held large IBM mainframes on the ninth floor. White allies took command of the faculty lounge on the seventh floor of the same building.[11] In a widely circulated image, students defiantly threw thousands of computer punch cards out the windows, which covered the ground like snow on a winter morning. Through the quintessential 1960s tool of protest, the sit-in, the aim of students was to hold the administration accountable to change, demanding, amongst other things, a fair hearing on discriminatory practices, and in the process, demonstrating the (still) urgent need for a Black Studies program.[12] A sign marked "liberated territory" claimed their territorial space locating SGWU and Montreal within a decolonial geography and an archipelago of Black liberation. (At the time several global south countries had gained independence or were engaged in independentist struggle and anti-colonial resistance).

After two weeks (Jan 29-Feb 11, 1969), riot police were summoned by the university administration to end the matter. The staircases and escalators were barricaded with furniture, to protect from siege, while the police encircled the building. The police entered, some with drawn guns, according to one first-hand account.[13] A fire quickly ensued, ripping through the computer centre, destroying it beyond recognition. The fire placed the lives of the occupying students at risk, although what was most frequently reported was the estimated $2 million dollar property damage.[14] Smoke from the Hall Building drew a crowd of white Montrealers, who gathered to see the students arrested and shouted racist slurs at those who had escaped the fire, as memorialized in the title of Dennis Forsythe's (1971) edited volume on the event. Several students reported severe

Fig. 1. Demonstrators walking on Mackay St. littered with debris, data cards and print-out sheets.

(photo credit: Canada Wide Feature Service Ltd). Source: Concordia University Records Management and Archives, I074-02-130.

Fig 2. This is Liberated Territory
(photo credit: The Gazette).
Source: Concordia University Records Management and Archives, I074-02-119.

Fig. 3. Damages cause by fire on the 9th floor of the Henry F. Hall building.
(photo credit: Bermingham Associates). Source: Concordia University Records Management and Archives,
I074-02-049.

beatings or torture by police.[15] Following the arrest of 97 students,[16] the students'
protest took on national and international proportions. Eric Williams, Prime
Minister of Trinidad and Tobago, through the High Commission, paid students'
lawyer fees and fines.[17] Politicians who had previously viewed educational
opportunities for international students as part of Canada's support to the
"Third World," now called for their deportation.[18] The RCMP systematically
searched the Hall Building, monitored entry through ID checks, and shut down
the offices of the student newspaper, *The Georgian*.[19] Protesters fell under
suspicion as Black Power activists, Maoists, or other 'rabble rousers' and some
were subject to state surveillance.[20] Five years after the crisis, through a merger
and "academic rebranding," Sir George Williams University became the
downtown campus of the newly named Concordia University.[21]

Dennis Forsythe, a Jamaican scholar studying and teaching sociology in
Montreal at the time of the crisis, countered the tendency to view this event
solely as a localized incident, and scaled up the protest to situate it within a
wider context of resistance to Canadian imperialist relations towards the

Caribbean. Canada held a relatively privileged place within the British Empire as a white settler colony, whereas the Caribbean were plantation colonies, built to extract labour and profits, including by Canadian proxies of empire.[22] Redpath Sugar Refinery in Montreal, for instance, began by importing sugar from the British West Indies. As we argue here, the inferno that ended the student occupation of the university's computer centre placed Montreal and the Caribbean not only within long-standing colonial relations, but also within a broader geography of Black resistance. Events in late 1960s Montreal had significant transnational implications. Guyanese historian Walter Rodney was expelled from Jamaica, after attending the Congress of Black Writers in Montreal, leading to the so-called "Rodney riots" in 1968 with protests against the Jamaican government's decision to ban Rodney headed by students at the University of the West Indies (UWI), Mona Campus. Following the arrest of SGWU student protesters the next year, students in Trinidad, at the UWI-St. Augustine Campus, mobilized into the National Joint Action Committee (NJAC) to support students in Montreal, and protest against Canadian interests in Trinidad, such as the predominantly Canadian local banks which hired only white or near-white employees. Students in Trinidad and Barbados also protested against Canada's governor-general, Roland Michener, who was on a goodwill tour (in the fashion of royal visits to the region, largely symbolic). It is this geography of resistance, and resistant knowledge, that we wish to theorize here, mapped through fire and through the concept of transnational Black radicalism.

The cause of the fire, which to this day remains officially unknown, becomes a shifting variable in accounts of the protest. David Austin (2013) describes the fire in vague terms: "At some point, amidst the mayhem and confusion a fire broke out".[23] Kiven Tunteng, writing in 1973, states: "we do not know for certain what had caused the fire"[24] refusing to attribute responsibility to anyone, although Michael O. West (2017) observes a conjuncture: "the arrival of the police coincided with [the] fire".[25] Dorothy Eber (1969) described the visible aftermath of the fire as a "burnt out ruin" and "charred mess", focusing on damage to university property, but again without direct attribution.[26] Brian Palmer's (2009) account of Canada's 1960s, suggests that the students torched the computer room.[27] By 2010, a narrative that students ignited the fire passed into institutional fact in at least one account,[28] even though one of the protesters, LeRoi Butcher (1971), questions the blame cast on students, by offering the following detail: "The police locked the back entrance and tied the door with a rope, and one must wonder whether the fire had anything to do with the students at all, for, with the treatment given to the students under arrest, one wonders if it was not meant for them to be killed".[29]

Eugene Genovese, a one-time Marxist historian of the American South,[30] also blamed the students. He taught at SGWU in the late 1960s and dismissively called the protest a "pseudo Freudian passion play" (deploying the colonial trope of excitable energies) and referred to the students as terrorists in the dedication of his 1971 book, *In Red and Black.* Curiously, the dedication is to the memory of the occupation—but not to the protesters—rather to his white liberal colleagues, faculty members[31] whom he viewed as the respectable voice of reason of the "American Left" in the midst of "nihilist perversions" of radical protest.[32] His statement occurred only a few years after he publicly welcomed a communist victory in Vietnam while teaching in the US, and suggests the discomfort that the "old left" felt with the shifting terrain of sixties social movements that foregrounded race (and indeed gender) through lived experience. Forsythe's work on the other hand was published the same year as Genovese's, and contained first-hand accounts and analyses by the protesters themselves (including Rawle Frederick, LeRoi Butcher, and Roosevelt Williams).

Between these two accounts of the event, both published in the same year but operating from polarized spaces (Forsythe from the space of transnational Black radicalism, and Genovese, an investment in white progressivism) we find two different roll calls of actors and contradictory analyses of the source of the fire. For our part, we are less interested in pursuing the firestorm of controversy behind what happened as a statement of historical fact (although some of the protesters have pointedly said to us, why would we endanger our own lives?). Instead, we wish to dwell on the interrogative imperative to explore the uses of fire, opened up between the two positions.

To do so, we turn to James Baldwin's classic text *The Fire Next Time* (1962), as the touchstone for any discussion on the social symbolism of fire.[33] Fire runs through his personal discourse and reflections. In "Down at the Cross," it is there in the sense of religious prophecy (of fire and brimstone), the fire of sexual tension, fire as torture and cruelty, fire as dynamic energy, and fire as the opposite of doubt (e.g., where there is smoke there is fire). A central question propelled by fire undergirds his essay: "Do I really want to be integrated into a burning house?" His writing notes the distortions, anxieties, and psychoses of white America at the thought of Black freedom, and attends to Black survival in the face of the violent resistance to integration. For this reason, his essay is read primarily within a U.S. national context. However, despite the turmoil of the 1960s U.S., Baldwin was also reflecting on a wider scale:

But in order to deal with the untapped and dormant force of the previously subjugated, in order to survive as a human, moving, moral weight in the world, America and all the Western nations will be forced to reexamine themselves and release themselves from many things that are now taken to be sacred, and to discard nearly all the assumptions that have been used to justify their lives and their anguish and their crimes so long.

Baldwin refused to accept the continuance of a colonial logic that held Western nations and its citizens as superior, anywhere in the world, and in his book inclusively gestures to the united struggles of colonized and subjugated regions of the world including Africa, the Middle East, and Latin America. He ends the essay with the resounding line: "God gave Noah the rainbow sign, No more water, the fire next time!" Baldwin's fire has a dual nature, becoming both a powerful call for radical change (implied is a hopeful note, that change is possible) and illuminating a warning.

The religious nature of the phrase, borrowed as it is from Black spiritual discourse and song, also resounds in the Rastafari call of "fyah" (as in "fyah pon Babylon!") which hails condemnation in a biblical sense (e.g., damnation of Western colonial systems). This sound and sensibility of damnation can also be heard in the dread music of the times. In 1969, for example, Desmond Dekker and the Aces' song "Isrealites" climbed the charts worldwide situating Black people and in particular Caribbean immigrants in diaspora as labouring in Babylon. The 1973 Wailers albums "Catch A Fire" and "Burnin" also vividly invoke the discourse of fire and Babylon and in a kind of way, might be heard, as part of the soundtrack for the times amplifying Baldwin's warning (about a decade before), about the burning desire for social change.

It is not surprising then, that fire also has a place of prominence in Caribbean discourse. As Kamau Brathwaite traces in his poem "Calypso," the Caribbean ("bloom of the arcing summers")[34] was birthed by shifting tectonic plates and volcanic eruptions. Fire is our history and geography; it is also synonymous with resistance. Bonham Richardson's *Igniting the Caribbean's Past*, an investigation into historical geographies of fire in the region, foregrounds the social meaning of fire. Unlike other regions of the world, where fire might signal an environmental history (e.g., wildfires), fire is a human geography embedded in plantation societies; fire is resistance, protest, survival, and punishment.[35]

As the founding site of what we have come to know as the Americas,[36] the Caribbean was where the world encountered each other, and colonizers imposed hierarchies of racial difference and domination, first through the decimation of the Indigenous population and brutalities of the Trans-Atlantic Slave Trade, and later through the bound labour of Asian indentureds, within European-controlled plantation systems. Natural landscapes were carved into monotonous patches of sugar cane through the forced labour of enslaved Africans. Plantation thinking (i.e., white supremacy) justified a coerced and controlled labour force on the basis of the time-sensitivity of processing sugar cane, which required burning the cane fields before harvest then quickly delivering the cane to the boiling house before it fermented. However, burning cane fields could quickly move "from being useful to becoming dangerous" as Richardson notes,[37] resulting in fears by the white minority that fire provided a cover for sabotage or rebellion. Thus, fire is rooted in geographies of the plantation system and Black diaspora histories as a signifier of possible revolt, threatening the white version of social order.

For enslaved populations across the Americas, fire was agency. Afua Cooper (2007) makes the case that Marie-Joseph Angélique, an enslaved woman in Montreal, deliberately set the fire which swept across the city in 1734 as an act of resistance.[38] Building on this history, Kaie Kellough, in his foreword to this volume, suggests that fire makes Montreal resonant as a space that transcends North American provincialism and highlights how Montreal's history of fire (the fires of 1734 and 1969) situates it in relation to the Caribbean. This volume asks us to recall Montreal's specific place within Black geographies of protest.

Fire also spread rapidly, for instance, during the Haitian revolution similarly destroying the infrastructure of white rule, e.g., plantation buildings and cane fields. As Richardson writes: "one can hardly conceive of ... a slave insurrection without a backdrop of flames" and accounts of fire in Caribbean newspapers perpetually carried a tone of underlying suspicion.[39] The orange glow of burning cane fields following the harvest provoked anxiety over either rogue or rebellious fires. These colonial suspicions continued until British Emancipation in 1834,[40] and were not without basis. The Christmas Rebellion in Jamaica, 1831, led by Sam Sharpe was announced with fire on the Kensington sugar estate in the parish of St. James. The estate was located on a hill, and fire served as a beacon for others to join the struggle for freedom, even as the rebellion was ended with brutal suppression. After 1834, the use of fire continued as a signal of celebration with torch light parades to mark Emancipation and the renewal of life and possibility, such as Trinidad's Canboulay (from the French, cannes brûlée) celebrations. However, such celebrations were opposed by colonial officials alarmed by exuberant "urban mobs," who reawakened memories of the Haitian revolution.[41]

A few years after Baldwin published *The Fire Next Time*, American cities (like Detroit, Chicago, Baltimore) burned in civil rights protest and urban rebellion. In short, fire marks the potential for radical societal transformation and unprecedented change. Fire, however, does not always kindle hope. Within the long history of slavery, colonialism and oppression, fire has also been a weapon wielded by those who uphold white domination. Angélique, for instance, was sentenced to be burned alive, but upon appeal, was tortured and hung.[42] Amongst the fighters for freedom in the Berbice Rebellion of 1763, five men were sentenced to death by "slow fire," not only as punishment but as a tortured warning to others who dared to consider revolt.[43] In the twentieth century, the burning crosses of the Ku Klux Klan were meant to terrorize the Black population of North America. They were searing spectacles of white supremacy. In the year of Baldwin's book, the Sixteenth Street Baptist church in Birmingham, Alabama was firebombed, killing four Black girls. The 1981 New Cross massacre in London, which occurred during the Thatcher-era of anti-Black and anti-immigrant racism, was a targeted arson attack on a birthday party which took fourteen young Black lives. This tragedy has been commemorated in verse by Linton Kwesi Johnson (2006) and Jay Bernard (2019). In Johnson's poem "New Craas Massakah" the tragedy and the terror of the time are captured in his reference to "di fyah owevah New Craas/.../kyastin dis shadow af gloom owevah wi life".[44] Bernard's collection *Surge* ends on a similarly gloomy note repeating the question "Will anybody speak of this/ the fire we beheld"?[45]

Yet the Black student protesters at Sir George Williams, despite the combustion of racism, exclusion, and violence they endured, believed institutions could change. The decolonial moment of the 1960s offered, as Lorde reminds us, a well-spring of hope and energy. This, as Rinaldo Walcott and Idil Abdillahi (2019) insist, is the gift the protesters gave to Canada, the ability think beyond the limitations of the nation and its institutions.[46] Their vision was one that saw Canada as part of the imperial world and thus as a space where decolonization was possible. They brought with them, on their geographies of migration, decolonial memories and analyses.

Despite a long history of entanglements in transatlantic networks of slavery and trade that historians like Afua Cooper document in this volume, Canada is often imagined outside of networked geographies of the plantation system. Indeed, if as we have argued here, these geographies are marked by associations with fire, then Canada's quintessential imaginative and literary construction as a land of snow articulates an opposite geography. Associations of the great white north, with purity and untouched land (a product of the settler-colonial imagination of frontiers) or a winter wonder landscape of leisure pursuits (such as skiing, hockey, and skating), are all far distanced from the histories of tropical labouring bodies. This geographical imagination is both a deliberate separation and an erasure of connections. Under colonial rule, one of the notions perpetrated by Western ontologies was that Western geography (temperate climate, flora and fauna, land use, etc.) was meaningful to all (e.g., the practice of marking time through four seasons). For instance, Kamau Brathwaite (1993) foregrounded the insidious nature of colonial pedagogies which lingered in the Caribbean even after Independence.[47] School children in the Caribbean were taught about snow through imported books, rather than about the surrounding local environment and landscape. Brathwaite shares a creative way in which one child reconciled this foreign geographic imaginary and made it her own. A school-girl wrote: "the snow is falling on the cane fields".[48] What if we were to learn from this girl-child and reconcile the submerged history of the so-called Sir George Williams "Affair" along similar lines? Kellough's poem "Sentences," that opens this volume, urges the reader to consider: "the students [that] sit at the feet of/ cane stalks, sit at the feet of the enslaved and learn that snow/ hisses down in sentences." What if the cane fields were burning in Montreal? *Cannes brûlées.* In other words, how might we take our cue from Brathwaite and Kellough, and locate Canada, not solely within a geography of snow, but rather an interconnected geography of fire, a networked geography of the plantation system that hails a transnational Black radicalism?

We use the concept of transnational Black radicalism to extend studies of Black Power analyzed through the lens of the nation-state.[49] This critical reframing allows us to emphasize multiple points of contact, connection and influence between the events that unfolded in Montreal in 1969 and the Caribbean, and allows us to trace this moment of struggle in a more expansive way. While others have examined Black Power and liberation movements across the Caribbean through international resonances, these efforts connect back to familiar circuits of geopolitical domination and relations, primarily, the US or the UK, largely excluding spaces like Canada.[50] The approach we offer here embraces what Rinaldo Walcott, in his critique of the centrality of nation to the Black studies project, has termed "a diaspora reading practice". For Walcott, such a reading practice might "disrupt the centrality of nationalist discourses...as it stands by putting on the agenda new and different positions and conditions for thinking".[51] He demonstrates the usefulness of this by engaging a provocative yet productive reading of Dana Inkster's film *Welcome to Africville* foregrounding queerness in relation to the story of Black Nova Scotia and Africville. This allows him to explore the multiple intimacies of Black queer diasporas in ways that refuse easy binary narratives of success, respectability or victimhood.

Instead, Walcott calls for keen and probing attention to how the "more difficult and intangible moments of interiority, sensibility, and political utterance play out in localized and transnational political alliances, desires, pleasures and disappointments".[52]

In thinking with Walcott, we note that the demolition of the Black settlement of Africville in Nova Scotia and the Sir George Williams University Protests in Montreal happened in the same year, 1969. Yet these events have been seldom considered together. While Africville indexes a relationship to land and thus in many interpretive frameworks becomes a way of understanding Black presence within the boundaries of the nation called Canada, the Sir George Williams protests might be read as a story of "transnational political alliances," of diaspora and even deportation. In many ways this unsettledness, that we signal, provides one way of engaging with and accounting for its often easy disappearance and absence from accounts and itineraries of struggle. But we also note how approaching this history through a framework of transnational Black radicalism holds space for multiplicity, dissent and divergences. If state narratives are embedded with demands for singularity, we contend that this alternative framework potentially provides an interesting positionality that allows for the indexing of multiple departures, intersections and relations. This story, and its impact, exceeds the Canadian nation state and its narrative-making processes and preoccupations.[53] This commitment to multiple locations and perspectives is evident in different ways throughout the chapters in this book. We read the contributions to this volume as offering us three particular ways of engaging histories and itineraries of transnational Black radicalism. Here we see different mobilities of people, the mobilization of ideas, and re-activations of time as central to the temporalities and spatialities of transnational Black radicalism. We map each of these briefly below.

Movements and Black Diasporic Mobilities

The opening chapters bring together a chorus of voices to engage remembrances of 1969. Gathered here are the narratives, voices and recollections of people directly connected with this history, whose own mobilities, often spurred by knowledge-seeking in rapidly changing times, provide insights into how one might encounter a Black radicalism in motion. Yet even as these conversations unfold across space, different orientations, in relation to gender, class and immigration, shape a varied understanding of how this story might be told. On the one hand this is a historiographical question, yet to simply characterize it as such misses the broader possibilities to map what this might tell us about difference and relation. As Walcott further reminds us here, we must "think really concretely about the stakes of the claims around 1969, because they are really crucial to how we even understand contemporary Black Canadian life beyond Montreal. In a sense, it is bigger than Montreal."[54]

The opening chapter sets the stage for the transnational but also the transgenerational dialogues that unfold throughout the rest of the volume. As Philippe Fils-Aimé tells us, drawing on the work of Walter Rodney and his critical-methodological practice of grounding—a practice of sitting with and learning from radical difference—"groundings is not just to hear, but to listen".[55] It is a commitment to a radical process of transformational dialogue. This is one of the aims of this work to facilitate different modes of telling but also to encourage different modes of listening to history. Yet the question of telling this story also depends on place. In this opening dialogue, we see voices from Montreal, Trinidad, Haiti and elsewhere in conversation, raising "conflictual convergences"[56] between a local Black community trying to survive within a hostile environment, and a group of international, even cosmopolitan, young people willing to take risks to confront structural racism and colonially-minded attitudes wherever they encountered them.

Similarly, the second dialogue that is included in this volume, the interview between Juanita Westmoreland-Traoré and Christiana Abraham, moves between Montreal, France and Trinidad and Tobago. It reminds us how, in that moment of political decolonization, radical influences and ideas were trafficked across old colonial borders. Juanita Westmoreland-Traoré, who is speaking for the first time in print about the trial against the students from her perspective as a young Black lawyer in the 1960s, narrates a transnational formation for her work and resistance. A Montrealer, Westmoreland-Traoré went to Paris for further studies in 1967 and became involved with the Student Nonviolent Coordinating Committee (SNCC) branch in Paris. The SNCC was a student-led, radical civil rights group which started in the US and was known for strategies such as sit-ins and freedom rides (challenging segregated interstate travel). When the events at Sir George happened, her cousin, Brenda Paris,[57] reached out to her, calling her back to Montreal to offer legal aid to the students. Westmoreland-Traoré's bilingualism and transnational experience, and connections to the Caribbean, served the students' defense counsel well. Her account of her experiences also reminds us of the embodied cost of freedom work as is illustrated in her moving account of working as part of the students' legal team and of travelling to Trinidad while being pregnant.

Amanda Perry's chapter "Montreal and the Caribbean Cold War: Reading Haitian and Cuban Connections" also offers another compelling portrait of a life lived across and against the logics of imperial border-making as a way of thinking about the complexity of the times. Her discussion focuses on activist Philippe Fils-Aimé, and uses his life story of migration and political organizing as one way of examining the horizons and enclosures that structured mid-twentieth century migration in the context of the Cold War. In returning to the archives of dreams (some achieved, some deferred) that are glimpsed in these life narratives, we focus on Black and Caribbean radicalism, not to romanticize the personal experiences within those fateful days, but to build upon key insights from work like Dennis Forsythe's PhD dissertation, *West Indian Radicalism Abroad* (1973) where Forsythe links West Indian radicalism in the diaspora to migration. Forsythe observed that the Caribbean diaspora has a reputation for radicalism. This is vividly depicted, for instance, in Philippe Fils-Aimé's narration of himself as "a lost soldier from a banana republic, [a] utopist with big dreams." Although migration policy privileged the "highly skilled" (e.g., university educated), and built expectations of "success", (quantified and calculated through a focus on remittances, economic investments, and flows of capital that connect migrations to countries of origins), transnational radicalism, is not so linear. Perry's chapter evokes multiple transnational settings for Fils-Aime's radicalism, which include crossings within the contexts of "the Duvalier dictatorship, the Vietnam War, and guerilla training camps in the Bahamas [influenced by the Cuban revolution]." In the wake of young radicals' aspirations for the meanings of decolonization, David Scott (2013) asks us to ponder how transnational movements might frame the character of Caribbean experience.[58] As Perry proposes bilingual activists such as Fils-Aimé, offer not only a "multiplicity of influences and transnational connections" but they also complicate the questions we might ask about the journeys of migration and exile. Perry suggests that these "ties to Cuba and to Haiti remain especially revealing" and necessitate "grappling with race as a structural phenomenon." Not coincidentally, Forsythe (1973) also observed that structural racism oriented Canada's relationship to Caribbean peoples, and thus Caribbean migrants become radicalized by the necessity of circumstances.[59]

The rich narrative resources that are evident in these opening chapters are also key to the later chapters by Raffique Shah and Alexis Pauline Gumbs. Both Shah and Gumbs combine memoirist prose and political observations to offer compelling narratives of revolutions in Trinidad and in Anguilla respectively. They also allow us to think about the intimacies that are a part of revolution-making. As Audre Lorde reminds us, "if there is one thing we can learn from the 60s, it is how infinitely complex any move for liberation must be."[60] In the case of Shah's essay, these relationships are about friendships across diaspora but also across the lines of race. Shah's writing allows us to think of the complex solidarities between Afro and Indo-Caribbeans as well as the transformative potential of these solidarities such as seen in the context of the Trinidad '70 revolution. In the case of Gumbs these intimacies are familial and inter-generational. Yet what Gumbs narrates is not simply a process of passing-on revolutionary stories, but rather her essay attends to a much more dynamic process of legacy and loss in which diaspora itself activates modes of disremembering. What is made apparent are the multiple and insecure ways in which each generation grapples with the process of making and finding inspiration and change.

The Mobilization of Ideas: Archives of Transnational Black Radicalism

While the chapters mentioned above focus on the movement and migration of people, a number of essays also focus on the practices and technologies that enable the circulation of ideas along various routes of transnational Black radicalism. Rupert Lewis, for instance, turns to an archive of letters from the late 1960s exchanged between himself (then a student at the University of the West Indies in Jamaica) and his sister Rose (then a student at Sir George Williams University in Montreal) to trace a memory of the time. The letters offer fascinating insight into events at Sir George, both before and after the protest, but they also place those events in direct relation to happenings at the UWI campus. As we encounter the index of dates that mark each letter, they produce a fascinating side by side unfolding that helps the reader situate events in Montreal and Jamaica relationally. The details in the letters also provide a rare personal glimpse into the political and intellectual education of one of the leading scholars of Black political thought in the Caribbean. During Lewis' time as a student, he was involved with *Bongo-Man* and *Abeng*, two of the leading radical Black newspapers in Jamaica in the era of Black Power and these letters are documents of those experiences. Lewis also recalls sending copies of *Abeng* and of *Moko* (another radical newspaper founded by the historian James Millette in Trinidad), to his sister in Montreal. His discussion reveals a dynamic network of radical publications and thinkers as well as a supply line of texts moving between Trinidad, Jamaica and Canada.

Among the many wonderful exchanges with Rose Lewis that are shared is one that also provides clues about the role music played as part of this community making process. In a letter written in the wake of the occupation in Montreal, Rose documents going to Toronto to attend a fund-raising fete to help fund the legal defense of the students who were charged. Her account points to the vital ways in which support was mobilized, by this community, beyond protests and picket lines. She also recalls the fete being raided by the police, demanding to see the IDs of the attendees. We recognize this as part of the mechanism of the state "surveillance of Blackness."[61] But then, she also describes the *afterwards*, dwelling for a part of her letter in the temporal space of utopian collectivity and solidarity of Black music and dance. After the police left, she tells Rupert, "a real cool thing happened. Someone put on the James Brown record, 'I'm black & I am proud' and ...everyone just went mad. Whether you had a partner or not you dancing." Much like the dread tunes which were climbing the charts at the time, these songs made people feel and perform modes and moments of embodied sovereignty as part of the politics of Black freedom. Rupert Lewis' chapter offers an intimate look into this time but also asks us to consider the personal letter as a technology of transnational Black radicalism in much the same way that Baldwin's *The Fire Next Time* asks us to meditate on the intergenerative potentiality of the epistolary form.

Whereas Lewis' chapter documents an experience of student migration to Montreal, Dorothy Williams's chapter addresses the tensions and relations between a Black Montreal community, living in a neighbourhood located adjacent to the university, and who had a long-term investment in finding ways to navigate the local, and the international students who were eager to confront and challenge the limits of societal institutions. For Williams, this becomes a productive tension lending to collaboration and a proliferation of community organs which provided news and commentary not available elsewhere in Canada. Her chapter also allows us to think about how these publications, that might be considered local, circulated elsewhere and thus became part of a transnational network of Black publications. For example, Williams, notes the numerous radical Black community newspapers that sprung from the SGWU occupation. One such example, the Montreal-based newspaper *UHURU*, is excerpted in Andrew Salkey's *Georgetown Journal* (1972). In the appendices, Salkey reprints *UHURU*'s expose on the imperial world view imparted to American Peace Corps volunteers. This was first published in *Uhuru* then reprinted in Guyana, by ASCRIA's (African Society for Cultural Relations with Independent Africa) *The Organ of the Cultural Revolution*, then later circulated in the diaspora by New Beacon, the first independent Black Caribbean press in London, UK. These transnational circuits of information became vital to informing analyses and actions outside of and beyond imperial networks.

In situating New Beacon Books within this transnational circuit, it is useful to acknowledge their important work in publishing the writings of Walter Rodney. Nigel Westmaas' chapter recalls Rodney as an energizing force in Caribbean Black Power circles. Westmaas, himself a long-time member of the Working People's Alliance of Guyana, the political party founded by Walter

Rodney, traces the development of Rodney's ideas and political consciousness through his early years in Guyana (where his parents were members of the then multi-racial party, the People's Progressive Party, and remained members even after the divisive split between Cheddi Jagan and Forbes Burnham), his time at the School of Oriental and African Studies (SOAS) where he would encounter students from around the world who lived the experience of colonialism, and his time in Jamaica, a Black majority country (with a smaller Asian and mixed population), and where he developed his praxes of "grounding." Westmaas suggests, as a result of these movements, Rodney developed a different ideological formation of Black Power, dissimilar to a North American Black radicalism. For Rodney, during this crucial post-colonial period, anyone who was "not white [was] black," suggesting a shared paradigmatic experience of colonial violence in one form or another.

That Westmaas, through his own praxes, shares a similar interest in departures from essentialist formations is not surprising given that he was schooled as a teenager through "bottom-house" classes with Rodney in Marxist ideology and Guyanese history. Even more remarkable is Rodney's course syllabus, which Westmaas has kept in his personal archives and shares with us in this volume as but one example of Rodney's multiple commitments to scholarship as activism. The 1977 syllabus, which featured modules on the environment, technology, historical periodisation, contradictions in capitalism, and class relations between capitalist and colonial societies geared towards a Guyanese working-class public, remains in Westmaas' possession (travelling with him to New York state), a reminder of the way Rodney's Black Power intellectual and ideological formations held transnational concerns relevant to the local, and retained special meaning for Guyana's working people.

A number of discussions in the volume attend to geographies routed through metropolitan spaces (Canada, the US, Europe). However, the chapters by Kirland Ayanna Bobb and by Ronald Cummings, much like Nigel Westmaas' work, offer keen attention to circulations through Caribbean space and time. Both Bobb and Cummings reflect on the significance of events at Sir George but then they also trace its ripples within and across the region. They also usefully examine spaces beyond the focus on Trinidad and Tobago that is seen in much of the literature on the Sir George crisis. In the case of Kirland Ayanna Bobb, she offers a rich and detailed discussion of Black Power in St Vincent and the Grenadines by tracing the formation and development of a number of local groups and situates these political formations within the historical context of decolonization. Her work, along with the chapters by Dorothy Williams, Rupert Lewis and Ronald Cummings, offers a rich index of Black independent publishing in the mid twentieth century and examines how these were part of a critical and political network of Black anti-colonial thought. Yet what she also observes and documents are the postcolonial anxieties about Black Power demonstrated by politicians in the region. Her discussion attends to this irony and demonstrates the state's investment in suppressing and policing of Black radical thought. Alongside this she also attends to the ingenious and unexpected modes of circulation of material and information. For example, she documents how news of the 1970 protests in Trinidad was distributed to St. Vincent and the Grenadines along and through trading routes between both territories. According to Bobb: "Trading was not limited to goods but extended to information. In fact, a number of Vincentians learnt about the Black Power movement and its ideologies, through this same trade whether it was via casual conversations or newspapers." Rather than a singular focus on territory, in Bobb's work, the Caribbean Sea itself is also invoked as a site of transnational relations and not just a means of travel and movement.

One notable point of intersection also emerges in the chapters by Kirland Ayanna Bobb and Ronald Cummings. Both authors each separately document and comment on a tour on which students at Sir George Williams University embarked in 1969 throughout the region. Bobb notes that the "aim of the tour was to bring clarity within the region about the Sir George Williams University Affair in an effort to respond to the propaganda that was circulating at the time." Cummings further examines this tour through a framework of marronage drawing on Antonio Benítez-Rojo's accounts of the circulation of revolutionary thought throughout the Caribbean archipelago, at an earlier historical juncture. As Cummings points out, through a judicious quote from Antonio Benítez-Rojo's *The Repeating Islands,* slave rebellions were ubiquitous and comprised not only battles and the burning of estates but also secret messages transmitted across islands and territories in ingenious ways. Cummings reads this as a formative part of the Caribbean tradition of radical transnationalism and marronage. Cummings's framework of transnational maronage offers a useful approach not only to understanding the students' journeys through the region but also the circuits of information carried through trade routes that Bobb examines in her chapter.

Re-activations of time: The temporalities of transnational Black radicalism

Whereas Cummings's work traces echoes and continuities between the past and the present, Michael O. West demonstrates how an in-depth attention to a particular historical moment can reap rich rewards. West's chapter takes as its framework, what he terms as, "the Worldwide Revolution of 1968." His attention to temporality as a structuring framework allows him to bring together a sweep of events and spaces; Montreal, the United States, Trinidad, Anguilla, Vietnam, Rhodesia and Biafra. We might understand his methodology here, in relation to the work of Phanuel Antwi and Ronald Cummings where they examine "keydates" as an analytical structure and " an organizing hermeneutic... for reimagining fixed projects (those of the nation, empire, identity, genre, geography and so on)".[62] Their work, in turn, also builds on Sylvia Wynter's essay "1492: A New World View"[63] where she engages with 1492 and the moment of Columbus' journey, as a world-making moment in sociosystemic, ideological, geopolitical and ecosystemic terms. West argues not just for an understanding of the significance of 1968 but also the particular significance of events at Sir George Williams University within the worldwide revolution of 1968. He notes that "the Sir George Crisis was not just a Montreal or Canadian affair; it was also an incident with world-historical dimensions and implications." We might also note additional connections between the writing of Wynter and West. Wynter is well known for her use of the long essay as a critical genre. Similarly, Michael West has likewise used the temporal-spatial structure of the long essay to great effect in his investigations of the Sir George Affair. His 2017 essay, "History vs. Historical Memory: Rosie Douglas, Black Power on Campus, and the Canadian Color Conceit" was published in two parts in the journal *Palimpsest*.[64] West offers another long essay here. We felt that it was important to publish the essay in its entirety in this volume. Its transnational scope, which is mentioned above, is part of its compelling force as a long essay that demands to be read in full. The essay is also compelling for other reasons. There are also resonances of James Baldwin in West's meditation on fire. Like Baldwin, West turns to Black religious discourse as a compelling source of thought, symbolism and rhetoric. These elements make the essay alive with the cadences and moral imagination of the Black sermon asking us to consider the apocalyptic and the transformative force of fire.[65]

The essays by Océane Jasor, Afua Cooper and David Austin also reflect on the temporalities of transnational Black Radicalism. They engage re-activations of time to ask us to think through the rubrics of history and history-making. They also ask us to consider what we might *do* with this history, although in each instance the provocations, interventions and conclusions differ. If decol-onization, both at home and abroad, pushed young Caribbean people from middle class backgrounds into a radical confrontation with "the whole social structure [of] white values and white behaviour patterns",[66] then Océane Jasor's chapter asks us to consider the relation of Black radicalism to feminist praxis during the SGWU occupation. Her work offers a crucial intervention into a protest that has been under-theorized in relation to gender, despite the presence of formidable women, like Anne Cools, who were not afraid to risk prison in the struggle for Black liberation.[67] Through a repositioning of women's participation in protest, Jasor asks: how might we identify a radical diasporic feminism when protesters themselves may not identify with feminist subjectivities, rendering their own feminist praxes "un-visible" in the present? In the context of a conversation with women protesters, a younger audience locates a submerged feminist consciousness in their concerted actions (such as collecting funds to support the students' legal defence) raising important questions about the ways in which Black radical feminist practices are made visible not only through a transnational mapping (a re-routing through Caribbean feminism), but also through intergenerational interventions which seek to make the un-visible and unremarked visible.

While Michael West's discussion focuses on a particular historical moment, Afua Cooper's chapter offers us a sweeping view of time, from the seventeenth century to the present. Her intervention additionally represents a twofold call to action. Firstly, she advances a call for reparations for African diasporic people in Canada, and secondly and specifically, a commemoration of the SGWU protest and its aftermath. While calls for reparations are not new, and have experienced a vigorous renewal with the establishment of the Centre for Reparations Research at UWI, they are seldom heard in Canada. Cooper provides a chronology of anti-Black racism in Canada to remind us of the debt Canada owes Black people and to puncture any nationalist imagination of benevolence and goodwill. Her discussion takes us through painful moments including (but not limited to) slavery, networks of capital and commodities that linked Canada to plantation colonies, segregation, exclusion, and police violence. It is a litany of evidence demonstrating the need for reparations and commemoration of Black life in Canada. Her evidence is mounted against a deep resistance embedded in the psyche of Canadian whiteness that hinges upon amnesia, i.e., slavery did not happen in Canada; deflections that discrimination happened "long ago" (eschewing the everyday practices of anti-Black racism that exist in the present); or happened elsewhere as if racism stops at policed borders; or is fearful of "creating division" (i.e., losing the social hierarchies of racial dominance that structure Canadian society). Temporalities of transnational Black radicalism teach us that the past circulates in the present. If we not simply hear echoes, but rather listen attentively, the past presents an ethical demand. Thus, Cooper ends her chapter with a challenge to Concordia University to make amends for its actions during the SGWU occupation. This is not a call for university administrators and board of governors to showcase good intentions, but rather a demand for the university to take responsibility for a violence underpinned by colonial dynamics.

David Austin's afterword closes the volume, fittingly on a personal note about the significance of Black radical histories to his own life. In a retrospective return to the moment of his own political awakening, he recalls Toronto's Third World Books and Crafts store, where he not only encountered the works of Black intellectuals, but met individuals in person, including key figures from the 1968 Congress of Black Writers such as Raymond Watts and Robert Hill. Bookstores, living rooms, roti shops—these are the personal, intimate spaces where the lessons of transnational Black radical histories are passed onto the next generation. However, Austin also offers a critical re-examination of Black radical thought circulating at the time (such as an emphasis on great African kings and queens, without recognition of subjection and slavery), or particular forms of Black masculinity, propped up by homophobia. In addition, he asks us to not simply identify with romantic notions of resistance, but to ask ourselves about the implications of the SGWU protest in the present moment. What is the work of remembering this time of dissent and protest?

Conclusion

The Sir George Williams occupation, occurring, as it does, at the end of the 1960s, is an important event for understanding the transformative will that marked the decade. This can be seen in the protests across the UK, France, the US, and Canada as well as in the interconnections between anti-colonial efforts and the contemporaneous decolonizing struggles in the Caribbean and in African countries, such as Nigeria (eg., the Biafra War), or Rhodesia. By bringing these events into relation, under a framework of transnational Black radicalism, different connections come into view more apparently, depending upon how one enters the analysis. This volume brings together a range of voices thinking about some of these convergences, connections and intersections to remind us of some of the lessons that we might learn from the 1960s.

NOTES

1   Kamau Brathwaite. "Prelude", *The Arrivants*. (Oxford University Press, 1973).
2   Winston "Niney" Holness, "Blood & Fire." Big Shot, 1971.
3   Audre Lorde. "Learning from the 60s", *Sister Outsider*. (New York: Crossing Press, 2007), 138.
4   Ibid.
5   The Congress of Black Writers (October 11-14, 1968) brought together young Black activists, leaders, and luminaries, such as CLR James, Stokely Carmichael, Miriam Makeba, Walter Rodney, Tim Hector, Raymond Watts, Robert A. Hill, Richard B. Moore, Franklyn Harvey, Rocky Jones, and Rosie Douglas. It was held at McGill University and brought together

students from both McGill and Sir George Williams Universities. For more on the Congress, see David Austin's *Moving Against the System* (2018).

6   Dionne Brand. *Bread Out of Stone*. (Toronto: Coach House Press, 1994), 67.

7   We have a sense of their ambitions if we look at the achievements post Sir George. Rosie Douglas, one of the leaders of the occupation, became head of state of Dominica (2000). Ann Cools, also one of the leaders, was arrested along with Rosie Douglas. She became a Canadian Senator. DeLisle Worrell, who received a PhD from McGill, and contributed a seminal chapter to Forsythe's book, went onto become a governor of the Central Bank of Barbados. Rodney John, another protester, now based in Toronto, attained a PhD in psychology. Valerie Belgrave was a published novelist. We could go on.

8   Eugene Genovese. "By Way of Dedication" in *Red and Black: Marxian Explorations in Southern and Afro-American History*. (New York: Pantheon Books, 1971).

9   In personal communications, Rodney John, one of the complainants, stated that a Syrian-Caribbean student was the first to warn him and others about Perry Anderson's racism. On May 5th, 1968, eight students came forward—Rodney John, Terrence Ballantyne, Allan Brown, Wendell Goodin, Douglas Mossop, Kennedy Frederick, Mervyn Philip and Oliver Chow ("the first six students were West Indian and the last two students were East Indian and Asian, respectively")—and held a 3 ½ hour long meeting with university administration to discuss the charges of racism, with little progress (Richter 2011; "A Chronicle of Events" January 28, 1969). On January 10, 1969, the six Black students (Rodney John, Terrence Ballantyne, Allan Brown, Wendell Goodin, Douglas Mossop, Kennedy Frederick) issued a signed public declaration accusing Anderson of racism ("A Chronicle of Events" January 28, 1969).

10   For a sense of managerial and administrative processes from the students' perspective, see the famous "Black Georgian" special issue of SGWU student newspaper dated January 28, 1969.

11   Valerie Belgrave, "The Sir George Williams Affair," in Selwyn Ryan and Taimoon Stewart (eds.), *The Black Power Revolution of 1970: A Retrospective*. (Kingston: University of the West Indies Press, 1995), 127.

12   The students had started an informal Black Studies program prior to the occupation (see *The Georgian*, January 21, 1969, p. 6). This was the first program of its kind in Canada; however, despite the occupation's spotlight on Black radicalism, the wider student body at Sir George Williams University (SGWU) remained "...unresponsive, apathetic, uninterested..." (see Phil Griffin, "SGWU and the Black Studies Program," *The Georgian*, February 7, 1969, p. 1). For the Black Students' "statement of position" regarding investigation and hearing, see *The Georgian*, January 28, 1969, p.1).

13   LeRoi Butcher, "The Anderson Affair," in Dennis Forsythe (ed.), *Let the Niggers Burn: The Sir George Williams University Affair and its Caribbean Aftermath*. (Montreal: Black Rose Books, 1971), 96-97. Leroy (aka LeRoi) Butcher was a Black student at SGWU at the time.

14   "Montreal Jury weighs case." *New York Times*. March 11, 1970., p.10.

15   Butcher provides detailed accounts of Montreal police brutality against the students, including cigarette burns, beating around the genitals or head, being forced into the burning computer centre, and an attempt to grind shards of broken glass onto a student's body. ("The Anderson Affair"), 98-99. Eighteen year-old Bahamian student Coralee Hutchison was allegedly hit on her head by Montreal police, and died shortly of related injuries (Austin 2013), 136-137. Accounts of police violence are corroborated in film Ninth Floor, directed by Mina Shum (NFB, 2015).

16   "A Breakdown." *The Paper*. February 17, 1969, p.7.

17   Belgrave, Valerie "The Sir George Williams Affair." (1995), 131.

18   See McCartney "Inventing international students" 2016, 15.

19   "RCMP cases Sir George." *McGill Daily*. Thursday Feb 20, 1969, p.1.

20 See David Austin. *Fear of a Black Nation: Race, sex, and security in sixties Montreal*. (Toronto: Between the Lines, 2013), 26, 124. Also see Martel "Riot at Sir George Williams," 98.

21 "It may be safely assumed that one important, if unstated, reason for [Sir George Williams University's merger with Loyola College] was an attempt to overcome the trauma of the crisis and the accompanying scar it left on Sir George. The adoption of the new name [Concordia University] was an exercise in academic rebranding, an attempt to efface the Sir George brand, which was seen as having been tainted by the crisis of 1969" (as stated in West 2017, 85).

22 These proxies of empire are named as Canadian bauxite, banking, insurance, and manufacturing companies, as well as real estate and tourism investments in DeLisle Worrell's chapter "Canadian Economic Involvement in the West Indies" (Forsythe 1971).

23 David Austin. *Fear of a Black Nation*. (Toronto: Between the Lines, 2013), 135.

24 Kiven P. Tunteng, "Racism and the Montreal Computer Incident of 1969." *Race* 14, no. 3 (1973): 238.

25 Michael O. West, "History vs. Historical Memory Rosie Douglas, Black Power on Campus, and the Canadian Color Conceit." (2017), 193. Also, West offers further meditations on the fire in his chapter in this volume.

26 The "burn out ruins" are pictured in the insurance claim photos held in the university's archives, which focuses on damage to and loss of property (approximately $2 million dollars).

27 Bryan D. Palmer. *Canada's 1960s: The Ironies of Identity in a Rebellious Era*. (Toronto: University of Toronto Press, 2009), 286.

28 Wes Coclough, "The Henry Foss Hall Building, Montreal: From Riots to Gardens in Forty Years." In *Montreal as Palimpsest III: The Dialectics of Montreal's Public Spaces*, edited by Cynthia Hammond. Department of Art History, Concordia University, 2010. https://cityaspalimpsest.concordia.ca/palimpsest_III_en/papers/Colclough.pdf

29 LeRoi Butcher. "The Anderson Affair." In *Let the Niggers Burn: The Sir George Williams University Affair and its Caribbean Aftermath*, 97.

30 Douglas Martin. "Eugene D Genovese, Historian of the South, Dies at 82." New York Times. Sept 29. 29, 2012. LeRoi Butcher refers to ""professed "Marxists"–who supported and advised the Administration. Today some of these professors no longer work at Sir George…" which might be in reference to Genovese (Butcher 1971, 92)

31 The individuals named were Alan Adamson, Charles Bertrand, Sanford Elwitt, A. Norman Klein, Aileen Kraditor, John Laffey, and G. David Sheps. Alan Adamson, a historian of British Guiana, was appointed by the university administration to be chair of the hearing committee, however Black students opposed his appointment. See their "Statement of position," in *The Georgian*. January 28, 1969. The hearing proceedings are held in Concordia University's institutional archives.

32 Eugene Genovese. "By Way of Dedication" (New York: Pantheon Books, 1971), iv.

33 James Baldwin. *The Fire Next Time*. 1st international ed. (New York: Vintage International, 1993).

34 Kamau Brathwaite. "Calypso", *The Arrivants*.

35 Bonham C. Richardson. *Igniting the Caribbean's past: fire in British West Indian history*. (Chapel Hill and London: University of North Carolina Press, 2004).

36 *Universalis Cosmographia* (Martin Waldseemüller, 1507) was the first map to use the term "America," erasing indigenous populations from "new world" cartographic history.

37 Bonham C. Richardson. *Igniting the Caribbean's past: fire in British West Indian history*, 21.

38 Afua Cooper. *The hanging of Angélique: The untold story of Canadian slavery and the burning of Old Montreal*. (Athens: University of Georgia Press, 2007).

39 Bonham C. Richardson. *Igniting the Caribbean's past: fire in British West Indian history*, xii.

40 Emancipation occurred in British colonies, including the Caribbean and Canada, in 1834. In French, Dutch, Spanish, Swedish, and Danish colonies it was later, as it was in the US and Brazil.

41 Bonham C. Richardson. *Igniting the Caribbean's Past: Fire in British West Indian history.*

42 Afua Cooper. *The hanging of Angélique: The untold story of Canadian slavery and the burning of Old Montreal.*

43 Marjoleine Kars. *Blood on the River: A Chronicle of Mutiny and Freedom on the Wild Coast.* (New York and London: The New Press, 2020).

44 Linton Kwesi Johnson. *Mi Revalueshanary Fren: Selected Poems.* (Port Townsend, Washington: Copper Canyon Press, 2006), 52-57.

45 Jay Bernard. *Surge.* (London: Chatto and Windus), 2019.

46 Rinaldo Walcott and Idil Abdillahi. *Black Life: Post BLM and the Struggle for Freedom.* (Winnipeg: ARP Books, 2019).

47 Kamau Edward Brathwaite. "History of the Voice". In *Roots*, 259-304. (Ann Arbor: University of Michigan, 1993).

48 Ibid., 264.

49 Quito Swan. *Black Power in Bermuda: The Struggle for Decolonization.* (London: Palgrave MacMillan, 2009); David Austin. *Fear of a Black Nation: Race, sex, and security in sixties Montreal.* (Toronto: Between the Lines, 2013); Ryan, Selwyn and Taimoon Stewart. *The Black Power Revolution of 1970: A Retrospective.* Port of Spain: University of the West Indies, 1995.

50 Kate Quinn (ed.). *Black Power in the Caribbean.* (Gainesville: University Press of Florida, 2014).

51 Rinaldo Walcott, "Outside in Black Studies: Reading from a Queer Place in the Diaspora," in E. Patrick Johnson and Mae G. Henderson (eds.), *Black Queer Studies: A Critical Anthology.* (Durham: Duke University Press, 2005), 90-91.

52 Ibid., 98.

53 Readers might note for instance some key figures like Rosie Douglas and Anne Cools who were central to events at Sir George are not discussed in great detail in this volume. Both Cools and Douglas were arrested and served time in prison for their roles in the Sir George Crisis. Two reasons account for their relative absence here, which are important to state. First the framework of transnational Black radicalism in which we situate our intervention aims to move beyond state narratives and frameworks. Both Douglas and Cools became prominent politicians. Rosie Douglas was Prime Minister of Dominica from February 2000 until his death in October 2000. Ann Cools was a senator in the Canadian government from 1984 – 2018. She was the first Black person to be part of the Canadian senate. There have also been excellent critical-biographical essays written about them by leading historians. Michael West's two-part essay on Douglas is a sustained and forensic examination of Douglas' participation in the protest. David Austin's (2010) essay "Anne Cools: Radical Feminist and Trailblazer?" is an excellent examination of Cool's life and work. In this volume we are interested in how transnational Black radicalism might help us to see some of the fleeting, shifting but useful interconnections or what Rinaldo Walcott calls "transnational political alliances," that shape this history.

54 Rinaldo Walcott, see chapter "Fifty Years Ago" in this volume.

55 Philippe Fils-Aimé, see chapter "Fifty Years Ago" in this volume.

56 M. Jacqui Alexander. *Pedagogies of Crossing: Meditations on Feminism, Sexual Politics, Memory, and the Sacred.* (Durham and London: Duke University Press, 2005).

57 Brenda Paris in discussion with editors, November 2019.

58   David Scott, "On the Question of Caribbean Studies." *Small Axe: A Caribbean Journal of Criticism*. 17, no. 2 (41) (2013): 1-7.

59   Dennis Forsythe. *West Indian Radicalism Abroad*. PhD dissertation. McGill University, 1973. Another example of structural racism fostering Black radicalism is the Black Action Defence League organized by Caribbean immigrants in 1988 to combat police violence in Toronto.

60   Audre Lorde, "Learning from the 60s."

61   Simone Browne. *Dark Matters: On the Surveillance of Blackness*. (Durham: Duke University Press, 2015).

62   Phanuel Antwi and Ronald Cummings, "1865 and the Disenchantment of Empire," *Cultural Dynamics* Vol. 31.3 (August 2019): 162.

63   Sylvia Wynter, "1492: A New World View," in Vera Lawrence Hyatt and Rex Nettleford (eds.), *Race, Discourse, and the Origin of the Americas*. (Washington, DC: Smithsonian Institution Press, 1995).

64   Michael O. West, "History vs. Historical Memory Rosie Douglas, Black Power on Campus, and the Canadian Color Conceit." *Palimpsest: A Journal on Women, Gender, and the Black International* 6.1 (2017): 84-100.

65   See Anthony Bogues *Black Heretics, Black Prophets: Radical Political Intellectuals* (Routledge, 2003) for an examination of the intersections of Black history, philosophy and prophecy. Also see Hortense J. Spillers, "Martin Luther King and the Style of the Black Sermon" *The Black Scholar*, (1971) 3:1, 14-27,

66   Dennis Forsythe. *West Indian Radicalism Abroad*, 325.

67   Anne Cools served four months in prison for her role in the "Sir George Williams Affair." Rosie Douglas served eighteen months.

Fifty Years Ago: Reflections on the Sir George Williams University Protests

Clarence Bayne, Brenda Dash, Philippe Fils-Aimé, and Nancy Warner

THIS CONVERSATION was convened as part of the *Protests and Pedagogy* conference at Concordia University in February 2019 to mark the 50th anniversary of the Sir George Williams University student protests. In the script included here, each of the participants introduce themselves and talk about their respective roles as well as their memories of the period and of the protests. They offer an important glimpse into the ideological, social, political, and personal stakes of the protests. However, the question of the terms of memorializing and narrating the protests also emerges strongly here. While they each, along with the various contributors to this book, agree that the protests should be remembered, there were differing views, presented at the table, about how to narrate it. There emerges a rich conversation that sets the stage for further historiographical work on this important event in Black Canadian history. We have also included in this discussion some of the questions and comments from the audience (such as comments by Rinaldo Walcott, and Carol Marie Webster). The inclusion of these comments further points to the collective work of remembering that the gathering occasioned as well as the dynamic of dialogue that enlivened this gathering.

Philippe Fils-Aimé: The subject is about protests and pedagogy. I think that I have to be on the subject, but you too, who are here, must also be on this subject. And if we are speaking about pedagogy, I recall the memory of the greatest pedagogue that I have ever met, Dr. Walter Rodney. Walter Rodney was actually a key figure at Sir George Williams University. Not necessarily by his physical presence, but Dr. Rodney gave us young Black militants a fantastic tool that I must share with you, and I urge you to participate with me in a little exercise. It's called groundings.

Groundings, you would say, is not simply to hear but to listen. And the best position when listening is to be very close to shorten the distance between mouth and ears. So, I am asking everybody here who is sitting in the back to come closer and feel my breath. I have some things that are very intimate to tell you. I am not going to give you all a long speech, but I will simply share with you some little thoughts that are in my mind.

The first thing, I will mention is the beautiful sister who died in this thing. Her name is Coralee Hutchison.[1] She is my hero. I am going to also make a few comments on the question of the fire at the computer centre. I will tell you things that I have never said or mentioned. I had to come here for them to come in my mind. Wanting to fit into history, we sometimes do not tell things as they were because we don't want to look bad.

To understand Sir George, you have to look at it first as a saga. It is the saga of a group of West Indian intellectuals who had not been here more than five years. Out of the blue, these negros came to Montreal from different backgrounds and they started a study group. The head of the study group was a man named Alfie Roberts.[2] He introduced us to the philosopher called C. L. R. James. This philosopher guided us through the whole confrontation, and even after. This old man is the real mentor of the struggle at Sir George because not a day had passed when we were not in contact with him, sharing our revolution with C.L.R. James.

Now, how did we accomplish that? There was an agreement made for the upkeep and the safety of computer centre. That was negotiated by Alfie Roberts. He was a long-time Marxist companion of C.L.R James. Now, I do not know the content of this agreement nor do I know everybody that was involved. However, I can confirm that inside the administration there were some Marxist-Leninist individuals whom Alfie had been in exchange with for a long time before the riots happened. One of the results of this agreement was that, we had some white boys who would come to the centre and make sure the computers were in good shape, that the temperature was okay and we also got some connections, that allowed us establish telephone contact with the whole of planet earth. So, we had a fantastic deal. We did not question it. Were it not for these new technological tools, we would not have been able to have daily talks with Stokely Carmichael, James Forman,[3] with the guys in London, with some universities in Africa, universities in the West Indies, labour movements in South Africa, all the campuses in the U.S. and Canada. Nor would there have been this international reaction when we were arrested.[4]

Some people say that we were hot-headed West Indians. But we had intelligence in the computer centre. You would be surprised how organized the leadership was. We would get advice from very experienced people like C.L.R James. He had lived through a lot. He would say, "look, this is what's happening. This is what you must watch out for." Even how one should deal with mounted police and the intelligence agents, he was the one who gave us cues. When he would say "this thing will happen," that is exactly how things happened. Let me tell you that we had predicted that if we did not have international support, we were going to be arrested and put somewhere for the rest of our lives.

I have another thing to say. This agreement is related in some way to the question of the fire. I have some intuition, a hypothesis I share with others. I am glad that there will be research which will be made into available data. As we were in jail, I had a chance to talk with Rosie Douglas. I said, "Rosie, did you set this fire?" He responded "Phillipe, I must tell you that I didn't have to." I said, "who did it?" He says "well, there was a guy that was faster than us, more devoted." This guy, all that we could gather, was that he was a devoted anarchist, or he at least appeared to be as such. This fellow that I speak about, he had talked with Rosie and he had told Rosie that, "he is ready to volunteer." This fellow had some friends inside the university. He mentioned some professor who was in the anarchist movement with him that had a high position and a few others. I did not really pay interest to that narrative.

The connection I want to make is this. I have come to ask myself. When you buy a computer now, how long does it last? One year? Six months? It is obsolete. That's now. In those days when all of these technologies were experimental, how long were those computers made to last? The question was raised. Rosie said look, we must not get into that because if it turns out, that we had been out-maneuvered so that we helped to renew the computer systems in the university, we would look ridiculous in the face of our international supporters. So fear of ridicule made it so that we never dwelled too much on the question at hand. Rosie decided that he would take the responsibility because the fact is that in the computer room, he was the commander-in-chief. He told me, "look man, I was the captain of the boat, the boat goes down, I go with the boat." That was Rosie.

Clarence Bayne: My name is Clarence Bayne. I was at the university as a lecturer back in 1966. I was also one of the two Black professors on the initial committee set up to investigate; to hear the charges and the defense of students versus professor, to collect information and to come up with some sort of solution to the problem. That was a no-starter almost from the beginning. In one situation I was confronted by four of the students. Let me put it this way, we were are all from the Caribbean and I wasn't always a professor, and the altercation was one which led to a compromise of my position on the committee. So, I withdrew from the committee because I didn't want to be judge, jury, analyst, and protagonist all at once. From thereon I was outside of the proceedings until events rolled out of control.

I have more questions than I have an analysis to make. There were at the universities at the time, McGill, Concordia (or Sir George at the time) and University of Montreal, probably about 150 Black students. And of those 150 students, there were only three students, that we could identify, who were from the Little Burgundy area. The Little Burgundy area accounted for about 90-95% of the Black population living in Quebec. In fact, the 1960 census put the population in Montreal at 6,000, most of whom lived in the Little Burgundy area.[5] This was a matter of concern to many of us. But I mention this to indicate to you that the Caribbean and African student population was a very small part of the Black population, but perhaps the most vocal. In addition to that, it was external and its interests were external interests. They were not accountable to the Black community. They were accountable to the countries from which they came. And this has to be understood because we hear expositions about this event and the impact that it has and its importance, and all the rest of it. Fifty years later, as I listen, I begin to understand the kind of reaction that I got from so many of the Black persons living in Little Burgundy. As a Caribbean person living in Montreal and being at the university, I was, not exactly told in those terms, but I was generally reminded that I was basically foreign to the community. I took exception at the time, but as time went by I looked at these events and began to understand.

In 1960, there were 6,000 blacks living in Little Burgundy. By 1974, there were 49-50,000 Black persons living in Montreal.[6] I am sure that the 6,000 Blacks living in Little Burgundy were not that fertile. So, it was essentially a massive, overwhelming increase in the population from about 1960. From the 1860s to 1960s you have not a complete reversal, but a liberalization of the Immigration Act. 1963 terminated a period of keeping Black people out of Canada.[7] Economic conditions were changing at an incredible rate and the population was too small to accommodate the growth. That helped to loosen up the immigration policies towards immigration from the Caribbean. In spite of the fact that there were labour supply needs, it wasn't all that straight forward. I'm just giving you these details to let you know that when we took the action that we took, justified as it may have been, it was taken by 150 students inside the universities, inside the security of the university. Outside in the Black community of Montreal it was not received always with the ease that we sometimes like to say. So my question is, what contribution did the Sir George Williams "happening," as I called it, have, apart from the obvious contribution in terms of impact internal to the university? Did it create institutional arrangements outside of the university in the core of the Black community that were not already taking place prior to events? I pose that question. We can explore that as we go along.

Brenda Dash: I'm Brenda Dash and I was one of the persons arrested on February 11, 1969. It's mind blowing to know that was 50 years ago and I can't believe that 50 years later we would be discussing this with people who care and who are interested in this topic. It is very gratifying because one of the things that happens with protests is that they are very exciting and hot in the moment, but then the interest dissipates and it wanes. The main thing I think with a protest is you've got to move the ball forward. You may not be going in for that touchdown, but move the ball forward. Those who come behind, it is their job to do likewise. In that regard I think that is what we did, though that is not what we started out to do. All we started out to do was get six, seven students fair grades from one professor.[8] That's all we were doing. We had no idea that it would mushroom into this gigantic thing that changed all of our lives forever. In a reasonable atmosphere, this is an issue that should have been concluded in 24 hours or a week. Let's have a hearing, let's hear both sides, let's conclude, let's move on. But it didn't happen that way. The offended students were not given the proper respect that they should have gotten. The temperatures were rising and they were gathering momentum because other people agreed, "well, that's not right. You can't do this." One thing led to another and we ended up in the computer centre.

The one thing I do want to say is that I went to see *Blackout*.[9] In the play, they talk a lot about the people that were outside of the computer center. When this was happening, the riot police were there, other people were there, people who didn't know what was happening during the night and were coming to work and school and who were discovering the circumstances. There were some offensive things being said.[10] But what I do remember distinctively is being inside the computer centre particularly when the riot police showed up. It was not their intention, but it bonded us together so much more than we could have done on our own. Suddenly we were trapped in this set of rooms that were barricaded, locked, and with a fire going on somewhere down the hall. What are we going to do? We never turned on each other and I think that's our biggest accomplishment. Perhaps that's the energy that lives today. That we bonded, we became closer because in actual fact, everybody in the computer centre didn't know one another particularly. There were students, there were community people such as myself; I wasn't a student at that time. I lived in the community and I supported the sit-in as many people did. After work I would come by everyday and spend a few hours. We would have talks about what happened that day and what was new, and if we were making any headway with the administration. I never overnighted there but the particular evening of February 10, we were told, "everything is okay and everything is going to be arranged."

We were going to have an agreement. People like myself would say, "Let's stay over. Let's clean up because we don't want to leave a mess." That's what we were doing and to our surprise, here came the riot police. We were played. In that process we learnt a lot of things about ourselves, about each other, about protest, and I think it forced us to grow up really quickly because there were a lot of things that happened as a result.

There were 97 people who were arrested. There were nationals from various countries. So now you have various governments and their consulates involved. I think it was ten students from Trinidad, some from Grenada and some from Jamaica. Then there were those of us like myself who were born and raised in Montreal. The West Indian students were the focal point, but there was a lot of support by local students, not necessarily Black students; there may have been more white students than Black students in that sit-in. A lot did happen and it was a unique event. Like I said, it changed my life and I'm sure it changed the lives of everybody there. Many of us are no are longer on this side of the dirt. We've had many people who have gone on to other terrific things, but I am very awestruck and moved that it is of interest to anyone, particularly to people still living here and still trying to get things right.

Nancy Warner: My name is Nancy Warner. I was born in Montreal. My grandparents came from the Caribbean between 1915 and 1920. At the time of the Sir George affair, I was a student at McGill. I was not arrested on February 11. I was one of the people outside of the Hall building on that day. I was, in retrospect, part of what I see as a community of Black young people the core of which was based around Sir George and McGill students. I think the two communities of students were one community for the West Indian students. There was a small handful of Black Canadian students at McGill and Sir George. We were very much attached to this majority West Indian student community, and then there were other Black people of our generation who were working people, even a couple of high school students. There was a community of Black youth that had formed.

My purpose here is to share memories. I was a teenager at the time. I was not an organizer or in any kind of leadership position. I am hearing things from Brenda and Philippe, stuff that I didn't know at the time. I was around the periphery. What I also wanted to say was that in telling this story, there was before February 11, there was the day of February 11 and then there was after February 11. It was a period in the history of the Black community of Montreal. And I do remember very clearly that after everything exploded, we on the outside, many people, took interest in what was happening to these Black students at Concordia. For example, people of my generation and my parents' generation, we saw a face of Montreal we had never seen before. The sheer hostility, the racism, the things that were said to people at work or to people who had nothing to do with Sir George. My mother went to work and people said things to her. What we thought were the rules of the game, rules of due process, of people being treated like they had some kind of civil liberties, they were dashed. The stories that we heard, it was just like, "can this happen? Yea, this is happening." It's really happening. Police did beat people up. That's not a rumour. They threatened people. That radiated out into the entire Black community. At least for people of that generation and even for others.

Brenda: I think also that what was important was that the affair engaged the community because now you had people reacting. They're not a parent or friend of one of the students. They're just reading the papers, getting an opinion. "They're guilty. They're not guilty." "The poor students," or "they're rabble rousers." Even more than the West Indian students, I was really getting it because people knew me, and my family was very well known in the community. My mother was very active in the community and my father was a labour organizer. Some people would say, "what are you doing with those crazy students? Are you crazy? What are you doing? Get away from them." I cannot tell you how many conversations happened. They knew me from church, or maybe I went to school with them. And then there were others saying, "She's fighting for our rights." So it did really wake up what was an otherwise sleeping community. It woke everybody: white people, Black people, students, grandmas, everybody. Everybody was in the action and everybody had an opinion.

I can tell you that when we were in jail, we were there for a long time, we were there for about two weeks. They denied us bail because they could. Actually, again they did us a favor because now we were there, we were getting to know each other. We had nothing to do but to talk. They separated us from the general prison population because they were afraid that we would get the prisoners to protest with us. They separated the women. I think they did the same for the men. And the regular prisoners, they would see us coming and going into the lunch room and so forth, and when we would walk by their cells they would yell cheers at us. One of the things they did, and maybe this was a mistake on their part, was that we used to get the newspapers. It was of great interest to us because we wanted to know what was happening on the outside. It really was the outside that was feeding us and giving us courage, giving us strength. Their endorsement that made us feel, "yes, we're right" and we should not quit or feel cowardly because of the weight of the government, which was now starting to come down on us. So maybe it was the second or third day, there was a protest not unlike what we do today (protesters still use placards). On the front page of the *Montreal Gazette* was a woman with a placard saying, "Free the Students" and it was my mother. I was so proud of my mother. The others around me were like, "Wow! That's your mother?" I said "Yes. And I guarantee you that she'd never been at a protest before in her life." She was a fighter.

Nancy: I'd like to add some of my memories of that time as well. What happened was that people who had no connection whatsoever with the students, every Black person, was sort of put on the spot to have an opinion, to justify to strangers. It was the news of the day. My mother's white co-workers were like, "what's going on with those students? What were they doing?" They wanted her to explain. It touched all parts of the Black community. I don't know if we mentioned that in 1969 this was a very small Black community. I remember in the early 60s that if I went downtown with my mother to go shopping, she spoke to every Black human being she saw by name; she knew everybody. We had one church for many years.[11] All the Black people in the community went to that church. We were small and it was a community where previous generations had relied on themselves to build what they could for themselves like the church, like the Negro Community Center, like the Coloured Women's Club of which Mrs. Dash (Brenda Dash's mother) was the President and a foundational member. This small community was not used to being in the limelight, not accustomed to bringing attention to itself. If you bring attention to yourself, you make it bad for everybody else. That was the mentality. And in one day, and a few weeks after, all of that was blown up. People were living their lives from one day to the next, then everything changed. And it never went back to how it was before.

I remember that those of us who were on the outside, the meetings started the very next day, February 12. I remember there was a group of students at McGill, there was a February 11 defense committee. That started the same day, on the sidewalk. People were raising funds. A friend of mine, Marguerite had the postal box and she was getting the cheques in the mail, and she also received excrement, an envelope with excrement in it. Hate Mail. So this all started within hours. I remember we had meetings, the young people, at the UNIA Hall. We were galvanized, the people of this generation. Sir George, McGill, Montreal High, people were not going to school at all. If you were in your late teens, twenties, if you were between sixteen and thirty-five in those days and you were Black in Montreal, you were touched by this.

Clarence: There's another aspect to the position that the students took. The newest West Indian immigrants thought they brought revolution to Montreal and to the Black community. That was basically incorrect. It was a hijacking of a story of the resident radicals in the community, which did not please them at all. For instance, the West Indian students came to Montreal in the late 50s, early 60s. The Negro Theatre Guild existed since 1942, long before we came here. They were not just doing white theatre. They weren't just doing Shakespeare. They were doing American, Black theatre. Then the Montreal Citizenship Association came into being, albeit on a moderate level, to integrate Blacks into society and to fight for their rights and freedoms and for employment in 1966. The Colored Women's Club was here since 1902. They weren't exactly quiet, calm people either, although they did not necessarily promote revolution in the sense of the justification of violence *à la* Stokely Carmichael or the Black Muslims. This is not to say that violence cannot be justified in certain circumstances. But the movements of that time, prior to the students, was more along the lines of Gandhi or Martin Luther King type of resistance. If you look at a chart of the organizations, you can see where the Negro Community Center essentially had created a whole set of organizations that are now the modern organizations carrying forward community work in Montreal, albeit under great financial stress. They created the Black community associations. They were not always very happy about these West Indians. I remember having to go down to the church with Dorothy Wills from Dominica, who has made a significant contribution to the Black community here, to have to speak to Reverend Este and the people of the church and say, "Look. Okay, you don't agree with what they are doing but the reality is that this has come about like a flash flood and we can't leave them out there hanging. The best you can do is to say nothing about how you feel." They agreed with us. So the story told for the last fifty years is not being told in a way that gives true credit to all the players in the game. Basically, it has been a hijacking by the radical left who were much more active.

Rinaldo Walcott: I want to say something really briefly. I want to challenge Clarence a little bit around the idea that somehow a radical left has hijacked the story. By the time Martin Luther King is assassinated, you would be reading him as part of the radical left. For instance, when he goes to Chicago for the garbage people's strike and so on. I think we have to be careful to make a distinction between folks on the left who do certain kinds of scholarship, who have gone into the archives, doing the hard work of recovering this story and placing it in a context that begins to allow us to understand how Black life unfolds in this country. I don't know if you were pointing to David Austin's work in particular in making that claim, but I think David has done something important, and Michael West has done something important in bridging the way in which we see the Sir George Affair as linked to a range of other things that were happening in Montreal and Toronto and around the world such as the C.L.R. James reading groups, the Black Writers Congress, the emergence of Austin Clarke as a writer and thinker, on the conservative side of things but sometimes moving into (under pseudonyms), a certain kind of Black nationalist rhetoric—he is a Fanonian after all. I just want to pause and think really concretely about the stakes of the claims around 1969, because they are really crucial to how we even understand contemporary Black Canadian life beyond Montreal. In a sense, it is bigger than Montreal.

Philippe: There is one point that I want to make. I think it is true that we, Black radicals, we did not know enough about the local Black community. We did not know because they did not give us signs of existence. I remember that one of the first actions that we did as a group was to address issues concerning West Indian domestics. I remember the action. It was a military action with an objective to liberate the passports of some domestics. There was this Black landlord who would rent them houses at high prices. He would have their passports; he would abuse them sexually. In those days it was like, "look, this is bad. We should do something about it." The ideological talking and definitions was someone else's job. We said, "Let's be practical. Let's deal with this concrete situation of oppression."

You remember when I started to speak here today, I talked about the saga of these West Indian radicals? I still stand by that. However, I'll add one thing. If you have not read David Austin, and you have not heard Professor Michael West, you will not understand that saga because what these people do is to put the saga in perspective. The broken silence was not just the work of these Black hero figures. We are not heroes at all. It was simply circumstantial in that we happened to be there when there was a global moment that was taking place. We rode the wave. We got to understand the wild horses of the time and we rode on it. If people like Anne Cools, Alfie Roberts, even Rosie Douglas at times and C.L.R James had not taught me about the dynamics of dialectics, I would have never thought that philosophy was something so powerful. There was, of course, Mao Tse Tung, Lenin and all of that. However, it was through the study group that I understood the power of dialectics. This is what allowed us to mobilize. For example, one hardly speaks about the fact that half or more of the students that were in the streets were French Canadians. The funny thing is this, you have English speaking students and French speaking students fighting alongside and shoulder to shoulder against the police. A few months after they will be in confrontation because the same guys who are there in solidarity with the Blacks, the French guys start their own McGill-Français operations. I think that this is a very important thing to study in this period, by understanding the Sir George altercation as a microcosm of what was happening in the society. The RCMP has said that there was a conspiracy among international movements at the time and they were scared of it. Damn right they were!

My role in the Congress of Black Writers was to network with different people. I don't know the fullness of it but I know, for instance, that the *independentistes* did some dealings with the FLQ. I know that the West Indian people, the Jamaican guys, they had some talks with Haitian members of the opposition. Some of the weapons that managed to pass through went to Jamaica. These were solid links that took place. The next time peoples of different nations come together, it will be explosive. You will not believe what it can do.

Nancy: I know our time is almost up, however, I wanted to just follow on what Clarence Bayne has said about the story being hijacked from a standpoint of pure sociology and psychology. Long before February 11, long before I had heard the name Perry Anderson, long before the protest had arrived, I was walking along the corridor and I recognized a fellow who was a student from Sir George. He was Trinidadian. And I said, "Oh, did you transfer to McGill?" He said, "No. I'm taking a course here." He wanted to go to med school and he needed to get a good grade in this course. The professor giving the course was well known for not giving good grades to Black people. In order to preserve his chances in life, the student decided to come over to McGill. These original students were not radicals. These were middle class people hoping to join the professional classes of their society, people wanting to go to medical school. The response of the institution was such that it brought together people who were already sensitized in a certain way. Let me remind you that if you were twenty in 1969, everybody was reading Fanon's *The Wretched of the Earth*. It was all over the place. People were reading Mao Tse Tung's *The Little Red Book* and quoting from it.[12] The French people in Quebec, I cannot overstate to you, what ferment they were in during 1969. This is a year before 1970. The FLQ was around and active. At the same time, so was the anticolonial movement. The countries in the Caribbean and Africa were just starting to get their independence—they were five or ten years into independence. Kwame Nkrumah was another name. He had a book out and people were going around quoting from Nkrumah.[13]

These middle-class students trying to live life, come up against the system and the institution does its thing. When it moved outside of those original six students, it touched people like myself. I was not an organizer. I did not know the word dialectics as yet. I had heard of Frantz Fanon, yes, dialectics I had not heard. In the period of time where people of that generation were protesting English domination of Quebec, we were just learning to appreciate that it was okay to have kinky hair. In 1969, it was a big statement if a Black woman did not straighten her hair. The people were questioning capitalism. There were several things that happened before the occupation of the computer centre and those seeds fell on fertile ground, even for people like me who were just regular people living in Montreal. I remember very clearly that when students were marching along, the phrase at a lot of demonstrations was, "*Ce n'est que le début, continuons le combat!*" And that means, "it's only the beginning, let's continue the struggle."

Carol Marie Webster: I want to thank you all for graciously contributing to this amazing moment. I am learning. I sit here as a student as I learn more about the Sir George Williams affair. I also want to question or at least explain what I believe I am learning at the moment. I am learning that in Montreal at the time, the community of African diasporic peoples who lived here had learned a way of living and surviving that was on the quiet. But on the quiet did not mean silent. They were building institutions and creating spaces for, not only survival, but thriving in a surrounding that was not conducive to Black peoples' survival. Somehow they had found cracks in the infrastructure to build solid things, things on which people could live. That's what I am learning. So there is a type of protest and a particular kind of pedagogical strategy for survival, existence and growth that was already in the play when the Sir George Williams Affair happened. I am also learning that these students were not setting out to create some radical left movement. They were trying to get the grades that they felt they deserved. "That's it! My grade is wrong. I have worked hard. I have answered the same questions that my non-Black counterparts have answered in strategically the same ways, and I am not getting the A which this individual got. The A is not appearing on my transcript, on my test scores." They were not attempting to create a radical left. I am learning that in the process the structure of the institution put them in a position that they had to push back and that they did not pushback alone. They pushed back with allies from within the Black community, but also white and Asian allies who also understood that there was unfairness in the ways in which the grading process had taken place, and so they stood alongside them. That's what I am learning. But I am also learning that within this there was a Black revolutionary temperament that allowed this program to be pushed forward in a particular way that allowed it to speak not just for what was happening in Montreal at the time, but to speak for and to speak to an international wave that was going on. It is difficult, I suggest, to get at any one of these spaces, these multiple intersecting strategical spaces, these pedagogies for living and survival without calling them protest. Because, if that living on the silent, that living and succeeding on the silent was not protest against a society that has said you should not be able to live and survive here and that would have us fail, I don't know what is. The radicalization needed to happen in order, it appears, for survival and for us to reach this very historical moment where we are able to unpack something of this because it became poetically and politically visible.

NOTES

1   Several protesters believe that Coralee Hutchison's death, one year after she participated in the Sir George Williams protest, was the direct result of health complications related to her experience of police brutality. See: Austin, David. "All roads led to Montreal: Black Power, the Caribbean, and the Black radical tradition in Canada. *The Journal of African American History* 92, no. 4 (2007): 516-539.

2   Alfie Roberts was born in St Vincent and the Grenadines. He notably came to regional fame as part of the West Indies cricket team where he played alongside legendary players such as Sir Gary Sobers and Sir Everton Weeks in the mid 1950s. At the time of his selection, he was only eighteen years old and one of the youngest players ever to play international cricket. In 1962, he emigrated to Montreal to attend Sir George Williams University and in 1965 teamed up with Robert Hill, Rosie Douglas, Hugh O'Neale, Ann Cools and others to constitute the group of West Indian intellectuals, referenced here by Philippe Fils-Aimé, that would be instrumental in organizing a series of conferences that would host leading West Indian thinkers like CLR James, George Lamming and Walter Rodney in Montreal. Roberts' work was not only important regionally but also across the diaspora including Ghana, Tanzania, Uganda, Libya, Cuba, and Martinque. He died in Montreal in 1996.

3   Both Stokley Carmicheal and James Forman had been participants in the Congress of Black Writers in Montreal the previous year.

4   The students' protests received coverage in Trinidad, St. Vincent, Barbados, Jamaica, the US, and the UK among other places.

5   The first time "visible minority" was used in the Canadian census as a category separate from ethnic origin was in 1996. The census for the Montreal Metropolitan area in 1961 and 1971 lists population by ethnic origin, indicating birthplace but does not provide details on the Caribbean. For these reasons, it is difficult to ascertain the size of Black population, however, historian Dorothy Williams (1989: 65) estimates that the size of the local Black population at the time was approximately 7,000.

6   As noted earlier, it is difficult to estimate the size of the Black population during this time; for the decade of the 1970s, Williams (1989:86) cites estimates ranging from 15,000 to 100,000 persons.

7   Immigration regulations introduced in 1962 represented a watershed moment when overt racial discrimination was removed from Canadian immigration policies.

8   The six students who filed the complaint were Terrence Ballantyne, Allan Brown, Kennedy Frederick, Wendell Goodin, Rodney John, Douglas Mossop.

9   The play "Blackout" was staged by Tableau D'Hote in February 2019 in the D.B Clarke
     Theatre at Concordia to mark the fiftieth anniversary of the computer protests.

10   LeRoi Butcher recalled a hateful crowd gathered on the street chanting "Burn, nigger, burn"
     (Butcher, 98).

11   Union United is Montreal's first Black church, established in 1907.

12   For a further discussion of the impact of these volumes on political and social thought of
     the time, see Michael O. West's chapter in this volume.

13   See Kwame Nkrumah's *Neo-colonialism: The Last Stage of Imperialism* (1965).

A Trial to Remember: Memories of the Sir George Williams Court Trials

An interview with Judge Juanita Westmoreland-Traoré by Christiana Abraham

Introduction

THE YEAR 1969 has become known for one of Canada's largest student protests. That year, students at Sir George Williams University (now Concordia), occupied the university's computer centre and faculty lounge to protest racism in the classroom.[1] Prior to this, six Black students from the Caribbean lodged a complaint to the university that their biology professor was deliberately failing them because of the colour of their skins.[2] The lack of concrete action by the university led to an escalation of student action and the occupation of the ninth-floor computer lab and faculty lounge. After two weeks of protracted negotiations with the university administration, police stormed the occupied floors early in the morning of February 11, 1969, and violently arrested ninety-seven students.[3] This was followed by lengthy court trials resulting in a negotiated settlement, fines, and in some cases prison sentences and deportations.

I became involved in researching this event in 2018 as part of a group of faculty and staff at Concordia University who took on the work of commemorating the fiftieth anniversary of these protests with a series of events entitled *Protests and Pedagogy*.[4] My task involved curating an archival exhibition. This required extensive research and community memory work.[5] During numerous engagements with community members who were involved with the protests fifty years earlier, we discovered a network of actors, including many women who had not been given specific attention in the coverage of this event. In these interactions, one of the recurring names was that of Juanita Westmoreland, one of the attorneys involved in the famous trial of the students. I was familiar with the name, and my curiosity led me to articles, and oral histories where a fascinating, formidable character emerges in the shadow of the Sir George Williams Affair.

Back row: Robert Lemieux on the left, Juanita Westmoreland in the middle, Valerie Belgrave on the right. Meeting with students from the Trinidad 10 group during the trial.
Source: *Uhuru*, vol 1 no 15 Feb 02, 1970, p.1

Juanita Westmoreland was the only Black, female lawyer involved in the legal team that defended the students following their arrests. Westmoreland assisted the main defence team led by Bernard Mergler. This was her first court case as a young attorney, and it would have major implications on her life and the illustrious career that followed. This article revisits the complex drama of the court trials more than fifty years ago through an interview with Juanita Westmoreland where she sheds light on some previously unknown aspects of the process.

About the Trials

The trials that followed the arrests took place from 1969 to 1970 and have been described as among the most notorious trials in Canada at that time. It attracted extensive local and international press coverage and was an international event involving forty-six foreign students, most of whom were from Caribbean countries whose governments had provided bail money for their nationals and whose diplomats attended the hearings. Bail hearings for the students began on

February 18, one week after their arrest. In a detailed account of the hearings, Dorothy Eber, spends much time on the appearance of the accused students at the courts, "with their extraordinary story, their youth and striking appearance." She also notes the introduction of a young Black lawyer, Juanita Westmoreland to the court:

> At the moment, I am not aware of this young lawyer's existence but early in the ....enquete, Judge McMenemy suddenly stops proceedings and says he understands an attorney has been prevented from entering the court. Mergler rises and introduces Juanita Westmoreland, an attractive girl in her middle twenties who was obviously mistaken for a student. Mergler explains Miss Westmoreland graduated in law three years ago but is not on the roll since she went immediately to Paris where she is working on her doctorate. She will assist with the case he says.[6]

Mistaken for a student herself, Westmoreland, as a young, Black woman, experienced first-hand the racial tensions related to the case as she was first denied entry to the court and admitted after protestation. This experience enabled her as an attorney to, "put herself in the students' shoes" so to speak.

On February 19th, the first group of students (fifty-one) were granted bail. Five of the foreign students deemed Black power ringleaders, were denied bail and sent back to prison.[7]On March 05, 1969, bail was granted to the remaining five foreign student leaders, amounts were set from $5,000 to $15,000.00 in the case of Rosie Douglas.[8] All foreign students were ordered to surrender their passports or visas.[9] In addition, all students involved were suspended from the university and ordered to keep away from its vicinity.[10]

By September 02, 1969, arraignment on indictments for the accused began. The trial for ten students from Trinidad began on January 19, 1970 and lasted nine weeks. Twelve charges were laid against the students, many of which were conspiracy charges, and another for the grave charge of arson.[11] Six juveniles tried in juvenile court were found guilty of mischief, for which they were declared juvenile delinquents and their parents fined $500.00.

In his autobiography, Fred Kaufman, special council engaged to lead the case for the crown, describes the trial as difficult involving many skirmishes between the Crown, the court, and the defence.[12] Jury selection, according to Kaufman, emerged as a major point of contention when the defence rejected many of the initial jurors. The judge then issued a writ that urgently empowered the police to find persons to complete the jury. Squads of police gathered English-speaking persons who they deemed fit, to complete the jury, all of whom were white middle-class men from Montreal's financial district.[13] This prompted public comments by Westmoreland at the time, on the systemic racism laid bare by the jury selection for the trial:

> No one can say that the fact that all of the ten accused are black is a co-incidence. We maintain that they cannot have a fair trial unless there are also black people on the panel from which their jury will be chosen.[14]

Jury deliberations in the case lasted four days with frequent calls for transcripts or explanations from the judge. After a verdict was rendered, the judge swiftly delivered a judgement that included fines. Following the trial of the Trinidad Ten, two other trials were held for three student leaders who refused to accept settlement. These ended in fines and prison sentences of up to two years.

Westmoreland's participation in this trial is significant. She describes her participation in the process as a baptism by fire, an effective training ground that solidified a legal social consciousness that marked her career for the many decades that followed. The trial set her on the trail-blazing path of legal practice in human rights, community work and humanitarianism. In the 1960s environment where opportunities for Black female professionals were rare, her task was that of literally breaking down systemic barriers. And that she did. She became the first Black dean in the faculty of law at a Canadian university,[15] the first Chair of Quebec's Council on Cultural Communities and Immigration, the first Black Canadian Human Rights Commissioner, and the first Black judge in Quebec's provincial court. In the decades that followed the trial, Westmoreland rose to the forefront of legal practice in Canada as a fierce fighter for equality and racial justice for which she has been recognized through many awards and accolades.[16]

In this first-of-its-kind interview, Westmoreland walks through some of the behind-the-scenes details, offering insights and interpretations of the defense strategy. She lays out the rational for the test case on the Trinidad and Tobago students as the first case to be heard in the courts and she walks us through some of the finer points of the negotiated settlement. Her reflections on the legacy of the case within the legal landscape of Canada is also elaborated. She also offers a vivid description of her return to the Caribbean with the students after the trial had ended. As this interview demonstrates, Juanita Westmoreland, the woman, and legal icon, emerges as a force who should not be relegated to a footnote of this history, but one to be foregrounded in a renewed, Black-centered, grass-roots revision of this important event.

Christiana Abraham(CA): Thank you so much for sharing your time and thoughts with us on the Sir George Williams students' protest. Can you introduce yourself for some who are not familiar with who you are?

Juanita Westmoreland-Traoré (JWT):I'm an African Canadian born in Montreal. My parents are both from Guyana, and I was raised by my grandmother and my dad. My dad, who was very affectionate, treated me as someone who could work hard. They were both from Guyana and successful. My father loved me and encouraged me, and put the emphasis on education. He was a community person as well as someone who was involved with the debating society and the Negro Citizenship Association and all those activities in the community, at that time. So that was my background. And both my grandparents were religious. One Catholic and the other Protestant with the Gospel Hall brethren.

After finishing a classical education at Marianopolis College, I got my BA. Then, I went on to University of Montreal and did law. It was a good idea because I was able then to become more acquainted with the French speaking community in Montreal and those in the legal profession. It was a direct way (if you want) of immersion, because I had to really learn my functional French when I was at the University of Montreal. Then, I decided to study overseas in Paris, and came back as a teacher. I taught at the University of Montreal for years and moved to the University of Quebec in law. There again, I made a lot of contacts and I was involved with a lot of community organisations. Then, finally, I was in practice with my office. I called it a community practice. I was appointed first chair of the Quebec Council on cultural communities and immigration by Gérald Godin (under the Parti Quebecois government).

And next on to Ontario. That was a big step after much consideration. I was very committed to employment equity and affirmative action programs. This was an opportunity to work and exercise some leadership in that area at the very beginning of the process. So, I went to Ontario and stayed there for ten years. When the coalition government changed, the government decided to eliminate the process of legislation and the commission that was set up for employment equity. I was then recruited at University of Windsor and became Dean of the law school. So, I usually say that I'm characterised by occupational instability: public sector, private sector, as well as non-governmental. I did a lot of work with non-governmental organizations. I was involved with women's organizations and international organizations. It was time consuming but very fulfilling. I had my family, I mentioned my parents, but I had two sons. Unfortunately, one of my sons just died recently. My husband was overseas, and therefore I am also familiar with working as a mother with principal care of her family but I had a lot of family support. I lived in an extended family.

CA: How did you get involved with the Sir George Williams students protest in 1969?

JWT: I was overseas at that time. I was studying in Paris in 1967. And I was involved with friends of the Student Nonviolent Coordinating Committee in Paris, and not very much in touch with Montreal, except for my family. And then one of my cousins called me, in crisis. I remember taking the call and calling back at a payphone. She tried to explain what had happened, but mainly said, "you know, you have to come, you have to come." It wasn't even a decision, I had to be with my community and the students in particular. And so, I just came to Montreal and when I got here, I got in touch with those people. They said that a team of lawyers had been formed because the students were all incarcerated that time. They were awaiting bail.

There were ninety-seven students arrested. Trucks of students at the Youth Court. But I was involved with the students who were tried as adults. And with Mr. Mergler, we met the students and prepared their defence. Robert Lemieux, Bernard Mergler, and myself were the main defence team.[17] Some students had their own lawyers, whom we contacted and who we worked with together, but we were the lawyers responsible for the group of students.

So, the first case that went forward (that Mr. Mergler negotiated in terms of the timing of the cases and how the charges would be presented) was, as we called them, 'The Trinidad Ten'; the students from Trinidad. That was the main case I was involved with. It was a jury trial.

CA: I imagine your return to Montreal had to do with your involvement and interest in the community but was it also because you, yourself, were a student as well?

JWT: Yes, I was a student overseas. But I had done my bar exam before leaving because it was my conviction that if I didn't do the bar right away, I would never get it done. I didn't take my oath; I went overseas immediately but I had passed my bar exam. And so, when this happened, I was told I'd have to wait three months when I came back. That's the regulation of the bar before you can swear your oath; so, they could do whatever private checks they needed to do. When three months rolled around, I took my oath and became a full practising attorney.

When I arrived, I went straight to municipal court because the bail hearings were being held before Mr. Justice McMenemy. I didn't know the students except one or two who were originally from Montreal.

But it was like electricity. It was just a moment we'll never forget. When I entered the court, you never would imagine seeing the whole courtroom filled with accused and all of them were principally Black students. There were some students yes, from the white community. The younger students were at youth court; they were more of the majority community; white students. I don't remember how many Black students were in youth court, but the main group, the adult students, were Black students. I've never been in a court to see the court just packed with people sitting there who were accused and who were Black students.

CA: What was Montreal and Quebec like then?

JWT: I imagine there was a smaller, Black community. The community was relatively close-knit. People knew each other. And the people who were living and working in Montreal, were mainly working at entry level positions. There weren't very many people in the Black community at that time who were working in offices.

So, some of the men worked as railway porters, and many of the women worked as housekeepers, that's where the openings were for them. And many of the women had responsibilities as head of families, because it was very difficult for them to sponsor relatives. Immigration was basically shut to Black people except from 1967, when they began with a new point system as opposed to simply countries of origin to allow people to immigrate to Canada. [18]

So, it was a fragile community, but I would say a close-knit community. And obviously, a community that was also marked by the racial discrimination that was prevalent at that time. It was only in 1975 that the Quebec Human Rights Commission was created and became functional in 1976. So, there wasn't that much recourse.

And I know I had one of the first cases. I went to defend a woman who was a nurse and her son was recently a federal deputy. This nurse, Baylis, decided to make a complaint. And it went to the federal commission. She went to the provincial commission initially because she had applied for a position, she was told was open, when she got there (the Queen Elizabeth hotel), they refused and said the position had been taken. Her roommate was a white woman. And when the roommate went, she was offered the position. The position was still open. That was just so crass. But she did have the courage and her ability to make that complaint. And when we went, it was just amazing how they were totally unprepared. Under the Discrimination Act legislation, there was no discrimination allowed in hotels, motels, and campgrounds. In the end, after going through all levels, the hotel claimed that we had the wrong jurisdiction. If we're federal, it would have to go back to provincial because it was tied to the industry; it was employment legislation, as opposed to service. This was an attempt to squash proceeding.

But further down the road, Miss Baylis went to another lawyer in Montreal, and they did proceed. She was successful in her complaint. But those were the conditions people were facing. Working women, working double duty in people's homes, often as live-in housekeepers, and then having to come home and do the same work with their family while being separated from their partners and facing discrimination in everyday life.[19] It was a difficult situation but at the same time there was a solidarity within the community.

CA: What was the influence of the broader Civil Rights Movement on the Black community?

JWT: One of the things that was happening in Quebec was the movement towards sovereignty, the independence movement.[20] And, there was some communication between the leaders in the Sir George Affair and the people who were organising around Quebec's independence. That was an important question, because a lot of times when the students were arrested, it was just one broad sweep. There were people from the independence movement and people in the FLQ security events who were arrested, and then detained again.[21] It was a time of political movements and international activities, people were travelling. At this point, there had just been the Black Writers Congress in Montreal.[22] So that too served to be a time of reflection, study and discussion around political regrouping and a call for people of African origin around the world.

CA: What can you tell us about the charges that the students faced?

JWT: Initially, there were twelve charges against the students. They were charged with the basic, substantive act of mischief by destroying equipment in the computer room, and in the professors' lounge. They were charged again with conspiracy to destroy and conspiracy in both places. And then, they were charged with conspiracy and substantial offence to mischief by destroying the computers, and by depriving professors of the use of the faculty lounge. And then there was a substantive accusation of arson.[23] So, in all there were twelve charges against the students at the 'Trinidad Ten' trial before the jury. We call it 'throwing the book at them'.

CA: What was your role in the process?

JWT: I was one of the three lawyers, and Mr. Mergler asked me to do an assessment of the evidence. So, as the trial was proceeding, the witnesses were coming in, including the different police officers and some of the people who were responsible for providing evidence that was submitted by affidavit and so forth. I was asked to help analyse and marshal the evidence.

It was quite focused. Robert Lemieux did pleadings arguments before the jury in terms of what the impact was on the students. He also outlined what the whole idea of conspiracy trials are and how indeed, conspiracy trials are political trials, and what outcomes can be expected. And Mr. Mergler was very effective in terms of talking and pleading about the quality of the students that were before the court, about the charges that were against them, and about their commitment to principle: the principle of fair treatment and equality. The fact that they were students and that their countries were depending on them.

It was a well-coordinated defence strategy to the result that eleven charges were dismissed by the jury, all the charges, except one. One charge after the trial was that the students were found there. They couldn't have been there just by accident, so the charge of conspiracy to deprive the university of the use of the computer centre was upheld but it wasn't substantive. And it wasn't the other charges of destruction or arson. Two students were acquitted, as I remember, because their identification had not been properly achieved.

CA: To your knowledge, how involved were Caribbean countries or their representatives at this stage of the affair?

JWT: When the students were arrested, the embassies were contacted by the parents. The parents panicked, obviously, because their children had come to study and to complete their education to return to the different nations in the Caribbean, to carry out their future responsibilities. And here, they were in jail, it was just an aberration. So, the ambassadors from Trinidad, Jamaica and other Caribbean islands arrived, and I think this was something that gave an impression to the court.

It wasn't just students who the court may have thought of as acting beyond their basic duties to study. These were persons represented by foreign diplomats who were very much present in the court. In fact, the governments of these countries posted bail and, so they were directly involved. And the students had obligations to attend. The bond money, which was set at a very substantive amount, represented tangible support of the students, an investment to know that the money wouldn't be confiscated.[24] People from the embassies were present almost daily. Perhaps not all the embassies, perhaps some embassies were represented by others but on appointed days, ambassadors were there. I remember at the bail hearings initially and then when the case was going on, it was the embassy people from Trinidad.

So, the parents were behind this, it is true. And this is what Mr. Mergler argued: "these are the future leaders of their country they carry a responsibility. You have to understand that they are not just here as individuals."

CA: What can you tell us about the trial?

JWT: The Crown were ad-hoc crown attorneys led by Fred Kaufman who became the appeal court judge.[25] It was an ad-hoc prosecution really, an ad-hoc mandate that was given to Fred Kauffman at the trial as opposed to the bail hearings. But at the trial, his office had an ad-hoc mandate from the government to do the prosecution. At the preliminary inquiry it was Claude Rush Shapiro who had that mandate. But at the trial there was discussion with these lawyers, and they decided that the Trinidad and Tobago trial would be like a test case for the students.

It was decided as a matter of strategy that because the evidence was somewhat similar for those ten students, and obviously they were all from the same country and the embassy was there to support them, that evidence could be marshalled, and they could be grouped together for their trial.

Now, among them, there may have been somebody like Kelvin Robinson.[26] There may have been more evidence against him like in terms of police identification, or what not. But as I said, for some of the Trinidad students who were on trial, there was no evidence in terms of identification. They were there, but they have to be identified by the police or through evidence, at least in terms of some of the substantive accusations against them. So, it was felt that the evidence against them was rather similar. It wasn't the strongest evidence and it wasn't the weakest evidence and so, it could be a collective trial. And for the Crown, they weren't envisaging ninety-seven separate trials. So that was the position, although the accusation of arson is very serious.

When the case note came about and the evidence was put in, we analysed the evidence. The other evidence concerning our ten students was not beyond reasonable doubt. Except for the fact that they were there.

They were taken aback, I think, by the strength of the defence attorneys, and also the presence of the students. You could see from their presence that they were very much aware. These were university students, and it couldn't help but affect the juries.

The jury dismissed eleven of the twelve charges. They were found guilty for one charge of conspiracy to occupy the computer centre. The terms of the final judgement that included fines was negotiated between the defence and the court.[27]

So, the idea was, with the consent of the embassies, that the fine could be paid from the money that was deposited for the bail. And when the other students came to trial (except for Rosie Douglas, Brenda Dickenson-Dash, and Anne Cools), the Crown basically relied on the evidence that had been made in the case of the 'Trinidad Ten' except for identification, obviously. And they didn't want to redo the trial. There was a possibility that the lawyers then could discuss among themselves and agree that if the students admitted that they were present, which they were, then, there could be a negotiation per sentence similar to that of the students from Trinidad.

But the three accused, as I said, did not agree to that. As a matter of principle, they decided that they would not make that affidavit, and that they would go to trial, which they did, but I was not one of their lawyers.[28]

At that time, I was still going back and forth between Paris and Montreal when I wasn't at trial or going to trial or preparing trial and so forth. From time to time, I did go back to Paris, to try and complete my year. I got married in 1969, in December. And I had a baby boy, my eldest boy, and my husband was living and working in Paris. I wanted to be in Paris when my son was born, but I was coming back and forth for the child. So, I have some solidarity with women in these shoes. We live it.

CA: You mention the Trinidad Ten and the other Black students, so what happened to the white students (because there were more white students than Black students) who had been arrested?

JWT: Well, for the white Canadian students, at the bail hearing we represented the vast majority of the students. For some of the white Canadian students, obviously being here with their parents, their parents could hire lawyers for them. So, the lawyers would communicate with the Crown office.

CA: After the Trinidad and Tobago test case, were the remaining students let go?

JWT: No. After the Trinidad and Tobago trial, the other students, except for the three that I mentioned earlier (Brenda Dickinson-Dash, Rosie Douglas, and Anne Cools), decided that they would take the advice to plead guilty to being present or to make an affidavit saying they weren't present. And then on the strength of that affidavit, the Crown would offer a fine. The students in turn, did have the conviction of conspiracy to occupy the computer centre.[29]

CA: I've read of how exciting, how electric the atmosphere around the trial was. What was it like as a lawyer going in every day to this kind of atmosphere in Montreal?

JWT: I think it was challenging, that would be the word. I was deeply involved, in the sense that I felt I was a part of the student group. You can understand that. I didn't know most of the students because I was coming from Paris, I hadn't studied with them. I had studied in the French milieu. But I was a Black student and this was my home, Montreal. And so, as I did my work in a team, it was not just work, in the sense of doing the research and assisting with the analysis, and helping in whatever way to gather defence material, but it was a commitment that I had to further rights to equality.

I felt that they had been accused as a group on the basis of actions that occurred. They had been there to protest what they considered unfair treatment at university. That's why they were in the computer centre because there were students who made a complaint that their evaluation by a professor had been unfair. And the university had agreed to set up a hearing committee, but the composition of the committee and the process concerned the students.

They asked that the hearing committee be expanded to include some Black professors, and also that the professor be sanctioned. So, they were there to protest an allegation of racism, on behalf of the six students who were complainants. And that was their basic purpose. So, there was no question that I would not be party to that defence and that I would provide whatever skills I had.

At the time, there was only one other Black attorney in Montreal, that was Fredrick Phillips, who was my uncle. And he decided not to be a lawyer for the students. And so, at that point, I was the only Black lawyer. But as I say, there were other lawyers such as Robert Lemieux and obviously Mr. Mergler, who worked very astutely, and very diligently to defend these students.

CA: Tell us a bit about the students that you were representing?

JWT: There were some couples among the students. One was Valerie Belgrave and Teddy Belgrave. You know, it was a remarkable thing that there were also women arrested. There was also Glenda Edwards. She was also one of the students. And I think she became a lawyer when she went back to Trinidad. But while the women were on trial, I don't remember socialising so much as being in group meetings.

Among the general group as opposed to just the Trinidad and Tobago students, I remember Philippe Fils-Aimé. Philippe found himself in another trial. He kept Mr. Mergler busy. They were denouncing the Duvalier regime in Haiti and he was arrested because he had taken down the Haitian flag or something of that nature and Mr. Mergler had to rush off to represent him in another court room. But he was acquitted. Mr. Mergler had the brilliant idea of pleading that it was too petty an affair to be prosecuted criminally. And he was acquitted on that. But Philippe wasn't happy that it was qualified as a petty affair.

I remember another incident. This was in municipal court. It must have been during the bail hearings. Mr. Shapiro was the attorney. The bail hearings went on and on and on, because there were all these students. That morning, the students prepared what they called 'a gift' for Mr. Shapiro. And as he came in, they presented him with this big box. He was taken a back; he didn't expect the students to be giving him a present, like a big hard box. When he opened it, it was a voodoo doll with a hard pin going through the heart of this doll. Right away he ran to the judge. And when the trial started, he got up before the judge and said that he'd been the object of a threat to his life and wellbeing. And of course, the students are just sitting there observing. You know, these were things that you could expect because it was a lot of young people. And Mr. Mergler stood up and said, "Well, Your Honour, I would only say that this was not something that was intended to harm my good friend, but basically it was for his wellbeing."

But during the trial, there were also very tense and intense moments. The accusations were heavy. These were students coming from overseas and there was a lot of media involved and a tremendous amount of work to be done.

I was very fortunate to begin my active professional career as a lawyer with Mr. Mergler and Robert Lemieux. We worked late into the night. Mr. Mergler worked, I'd like to say, 24 hours but that's not physically possible. But just managing that large number of students' cases and the number of accusations and the fact that it was institutional in terms of Sir George, the embassies, and the other ad-hoc attorneys. It was very, very challenging, and all-encompassing. Mr. Mergler had tremendous experience. Robert had been working also with Mr. Mergler on these cases.

But those accusations were my first experience in court. Initially I was a junior, because I had been sworn in (I wasn't articling), but it was my first case. I guess I had confidence because I had worked in different positions and I had been involved overseas, not at the level of a lawyer but at a level of helping to organise when representatives of the American Civil Rights Movement came through Paris. There were groups such as the 'Circle of Friends' who organised activities and the unions who organised activities. We would be the liaison with these people who would come. And so, we had a commitment. These were historic times. And we felt the weight of community responsibility and the necessary need to bring about change through individual commitment and sacrifice. While I wasn't one of the accused, I certainly understood why they were there. So, we worked very hard.

CA: We are aware that there was a negotiated settlement at the end of the trial. What was your role in these negotiations?

JWT: Yes, I was part of a group. It would have involved Mr. Mergler, who would have been principally involved in those discussions and Robert was present. Mergler had the experience, the expertise, and knew the different cases, although they weren't being looked at individually. Except that the bail money was different. It was higher for some, as opposed to others. So, there had to be some discussion at that level.

CA: And why so? Was it because of the perceived flight risk for the foreign students or systemic racism?

JWT: The evidence against certain students was stronger and more copious than against others. Like I said, two were totally acquitted. But for others, there was more evidence in terms of identification, what they had obtained from potential witnesses.

Some of the students, Williams, I think, had been one of the initial complainants. He had been acquitted. But there were some roles that were distinguished among the students, or some may have been observed at the time of the incident. So that would have made a differentiation in the amount of the fine, but that was negotiated in the amount of the bail that had been deposited.

CA: Is this case important to the legal landscape of Canada? If so, what does it teach us?

JWT: We consider it to be extremely important. I don't know that there was a precedent in terms of a trial of a political nature involving international students, and then you put that in the context of the Civil Rights Movement. It was during this context of the 1960s. This was basically a student sit-in, an occupation to protest the alleged discriminatory treatment that the students were suffering. So, it was a human rights case and it was regarded as such by the team. The media latched on to it because they saw the sensationalism, if you wish, of the computer centre being destroyed.

When they evaluated the financial amount of the damages, they weren't thinking of the impact on the students' future and their studies and possibly their expulsion from Canada, but they were looking at dollar signs, two million dollars involved, and it was the first time such a thing had happened. It was on the news across North America. So, in the proceedings, the ad-hoc attorneys were aware that the case was very much mediatized and the accusations were of conspiracy. Conspiracy always brings an aura of political action against certain groups. We don't always, in law, frame it as a political case, but when it has to do with individuals and their rights against the state, I characterise it as a political case and the need to make a political defence.

And these students we were defending, were students from one nation, Trinidad and Tobago, but many of the Caribbean nations were involved. And, I believe there was also a student who was American, who may have been among the minors. And there was real concern about their security, welfare, or deportation among other things.

So, this was an experience of a political case with international impact in terms of the Canadian government and its diplomatic relationships.

In terms of conspiracy cases, I believe that it is significant that the jury considered the question whether there was the intention for students to be there for a reason that was a guilty reason. This was a decision being given by a jury that the Crown did not fulfil that burden of proof. They didn't prove clearly that the students had been there for criminal purposes because it involved the negotiation of a settlement around these complaints that were pending before the university committee.

The university had entered into a negotiated process with them and the students were students of the university. These were all factors that were relevant. So, in terms of deciding the case of conspiracy in a political context, this is obviously an important case. And the other thing is that when the case goes before a jury, the jury does not articulate its reasons. The jury simply says, 'guilty or not guilty'.

It was not a case before a judge where the judge will elaborate his ruling and we can look back and explain why the sentences was as it was. In this case, the sentence was already negotiated between the Crown and the defence, so that it's hard to say that lawyers or individuals can look up the case and find the judgement and then plead the judgement and the reasons for judgement because of the jury trial.

There was another case in which I was not the attorney. That's the case of Rosie Douglas, Brenda Dickenson-Dash, and Anne Cools. They went to trial.

I think it was a jury trial. But I wasn't involved. And if it were a jury trial, it would be the same matter. Sometimes lawyers may say, "well, we'll use the case in terms of what is the range of sentencing for these accusations in these circumstances these accused are relatively similar." But it was really exceptional.

It was an exercise in calling an institution on human rights charges in a very charged social and mediatized atmosphere. So, for lawyers and their trainees, it is a very significant trial.

In terms of the sudden new judicial precedent, I'm not sure that there are specific points of law that can be turned to now. As I said, the students received bail, they were all from overseas. Because they were being treated as a group because of the numbers I guess the bails were set according to certain blanket criteria. And once they were set for one group then that was used more or less as a standard for others. Some were bailed for significantly higher for those students for whom there was more evidence, but generally speaking, it was negotiated in terms of groups.

CA: You have spoken before about the return of the students to the Caribbean. Can you share your experiences of this return?

JWT: The students asked me to accompany them back to Trinidad. There was an uprising in Trinidad and Tobago and so the country itself was in the throes of political tension, and here were these students coming back from the Sir George event.[30] Many of these students came from families that were well-known and their parents were concerned.

Now, they asked me to accompany them because they wanted to make sure that when they returned, they would be able to justify the fact that they had acquitted all their responsibilities here in Canada and that they would not be the object of any detention or interrogation when they return to Trinidad. And if so, that I would be there to give firsthand information about what exactly had occurred and what was the status of the students and whether they had any remaining conditions, which was not so.

So, I did return. Perhaps because it seemed to me to complete my mandate. And it was (shall I say), a bit different on my part in as much as I was six months pregnant at that time. But they asked me, and we thought about it, I would be travelling together with them, so I agreed to go. It was just after the trial because they did not remain in Canada much longer after the trial.[31]

I remember being on the plane with the students and there had been an alert. The police agencies informed Trinidad and Tobago that the students would be travelling. And they re-routed the plane that we were in, so instead of going to Trinidad and Tobago it was re-routed to Barbados. Obviously, this created concern. I think we sat on the tarmac in Barbados; we didn't disembark for about three hours. And time was passing and apparently, they were removing aeroplanes from Trinidad and so forth as the students were going to be landing. This was all hype.

We eventually continued our journey. The students had asked me about documentation that they may have been travelling with. And they were concerned that they would be interrogated, or materials might be seized. I was basically giving them my considered opinion that they were students and that they were taking some of their materials with them, and that there was no reason for censorship. They had materials used for their studies (mainly books about political philosophy), and what not. I wouldn't be a lawyer in Trinidad. They would have to have lawyers from that jurisdiction. But I would be able to provide the basic information as to what had occurred in Canada. So, we were quite tense after waiting in Barbados for a number of hours. It was getting dark and we were concerned that we may not even get to Trinidad. And there was the issue about possible detention when they arrived in Trinidad.

Finally, we took off and we arrived in Trinidad, a short flight later. The amazing thing is that when we landed it was still twilight. As we disembarked, we could hear the drums. There was drumming. And because we were in the airport, which is a broad open space, the earth was vibrating. There were no other interfering circumstances. It was the most overpowering, overwhelming experience to see the sun setting and to hear the drumming. As we moved closer towards the airport, we could see the drummers, and we could see the people who had gathered. My goodness, a crowd of people! And at first, relatives didn't disengage themselves to come forward, to meet the students, it was just a sea of humanity there at the airport, cradled against the sunset, there to welcome the students.

The students had been living this horror for, I would say a year, the anxiety, being under bail and conditions and away from home, out of studies, everything had been put in jeopardy with regard to their life plans. And here they are, now, resuming their humanity and the respect and love of their parents, and the welcome of their country. It was just overwhelming.

It was something that I hadn't expected to experience. I was going on a mission because I had been involved with the students over this time and got to know them and appreciated the work that we had done together. But it was my first visit to Trinidad. My parents were from Guyana. I had been to Guyana when I was six years old. I hadn't been back since then.

So, these relatives, basically the citizens of Trinidad, came out to welcome their returning sons and daughters. That's what it was. They were like, "we're here for you, and believe you, we love you, you're home." And the students were just overwhelmed because they had been expecting very difficult circumstances.

As we were getting closer to the customs offices, parents were coming out and the officers allowed them to go through. They didn't even say, "show us your passport, show us your vaccination" or whatever. We just walked right into the country. It was totally unexpected.

And parents, friends, and people who had been following the case against the students, came to hug and welcome the students. And the students at that point, could relax and feel, "you know, we're here, we are home and we're safe and what we stood for mean so much for the people that we're here with."

So, there was no question of going through their bags or seizing documents. They kept me busy while I was there, going to small meetings and what not to greet people, and also on one or two occasions with the movement that was taking place in Trinidad. But I had to tell them, "believe me, I'm pregnant, there is only so much I can do."

Because of the nature of our participation as the defence team and the respect we had toward the students, to travel with them, to make sure that they wouldn't have on-toward scrutiny or hardship and have to wait because they couldn't get the necessary papers they needed, that was the purpose of me going. But it did allow me to experience this re-uniting with the homeland and the respect that they enjoyed as relatives, friends, and citizens. That was so precious.

CA: Thinking back, what do you think is the biggest misconception about this protest all these years later?

JWT: I guess, I resent the fact that in some instances it's reduced to the damage to computers. It's as if in the system that we live in, property is more important than respect. These students who came here to study, confided their future in this institution and to be evaluated like all of the students. They were not asking for any privilege or special treatment but just to be treated as others and to be able if they felt that they had been the object of mistreatment to bring their complaints to a body within the university that would provide an equitable recourse.

That is what it was about. And it became broader because the Black community in Montreal understood that these students were alleging that they had been treated differently because of their race. And the community in Montreal understood that very well. At that time, people lived basically in reserved locations in Montreal, and their employment was restricted, and their remuneration was inferior. And the immigration system was telling them they were undesirable in the sense of restricting the possibility of bringing relatives and family. So, there was necessarily an identification.

And some of these students were from homelands that were the same as some of the members in our community. It's true in our community at that time a large number of Black people were coming from the Maritimes, and Black people, not a large number but a significant number, coming from the United States who became the porters on the Pullman trains.[32] It was a small community, but a community that was very sensitive to solidarity in the sense that they knew discrimination. Many had lived and were living it and could sense the disarray of students who were coming from other countries who were young and who had not necessarily had the experience of discrimination because of their race and colour.

So, the community was very much affected by this. And the trial against the students became a real media event. But the knowledge of the general population in Montreal was conditioned by what they read in the newspapers and what they saw on February, 11th, when the arrests took place. And so, there was a definite hostility by the majority population in Montreal and there were very racist statements made unabashedly. You've probably heard some of those things that affected the Black people who lived in Montreal like, "burn the niggers!" Who would ever think that such statements would actually be expressed?[33] People were not naive; they knew that they were looked upon in a discriminatory way and considered to be inferior and intruders in Canada. Except on another level, their services were very well sought after as home makers and so forth. But in terms of having equal status, that was a different matter. So, they identified at that level with the students, although some of the members in the community were concerned that the action of the students would reflect upon them negatively. And so, they were critical of the students' stance in terms of the sit-in at the computer centre or the faculty lounge.

The faculty lounge was basically occupied at the call of the George Williams Student Centre. So, the majority of the students who were standing in the faculty lounge in support of the students who are in the computer centre, were white students from traditional Montreal families, or mainstream Canadians. That part doesn't come out so much in the materials. What comes out is 'burn the niggers', and 'destruction of the computers', and 'this is not their country, they should go home', 'send them home'.

But the students when they returned home, were welcomed. Some I understand became doctors. Rosie Douglas became Prime Minister of Dominica because you know he always was a political being. And some became engineers. They did fulfil the promise that Mr. Mergler talked about. He could see it in them, and he knew that these young people were here for a reason as their forefathers. I should say mothers, but in those days the mothers didn't necessarily have the same opportunities. This was the promise that they fulfilled.

And Valerie Belgrave, bless her soul she's passed on now, but she was such an artist and a writer. She wrote novels, she was very successful, she did annual exhibits, she travelled with her paintings across the United States, came to Canada from time to time. But, the students paid a price. At the same time, they raised awareness and consciousness not only of the discrimination but the lack of recourse and, of the limitation of the recourse. What allows the discrimination and oppression to continue is when people are not held accountable.

CA: What do you think are the most important lessons from the 1969 events that this generation must pay attention to 50 years later?

JWT: I do believe that politics is everything. In other words, if you do not take care of politics, politics will take care of you. And I am not talking about politics in terms of political parties, I am talking about politics in terms of being involved in the political process. So, it's very important that we see our role and we commit to carry our weight in this world. Because, what we do influences the experiences of others and the life condition of others in this world. My most ardent desire would be that people have a perspective first that includes the perspectives of young people, who we say are our future, but who understand what's facing them.

NOTES

1   UHURU, "Still no justice," 1970; David Austin, *Fear of a Black Nation: Race, Sex, and Security in Sixties Montreal* (Montreal: Between the Lines, 2013).

2   Dennis Forsythe *Let the Niggers Burn: The Sir George Williams University Affair and its Caribbean Aftermath*, ed. David Forsythe (Montreal: Black Rose, 1971).

3   Ibid; UHURU, "Still no Justice,"1970.

4   Protests and Pedagogy was a two-week series of events, presentations, workshops and community activities commemorating the fiftieth anniversary of this protest. It was organized by a collective of faculty, staff, and students from Concordia University and community representatives, from the Black and Caribbean communities in Canada.

5   Christiana Abraham, "Critical Curating as Decolonial Practice: Protests and Pedagogy: Representations, Memories and Meaning. Anatomy of an exhibition," *TOPIA* (2021): Forthcoming.

6   Dorothy Eber, *Canada meets Black Power: The Computer Centre Party* (Montreal: Tundra, 1969), 151-152.

7   These included Rosie Douglas from Dominica, Ian Belgrave and Kelvin Robinson from Trinidad, and Kennedy Frederick from Grenada.

8   LeRoi Butcher, "The Anderson Affair" in *Let the Niggers Burn: The Sir George Williams University Affair and its Caribbean Aftermath*, ed. David Forsythe (Montreal: Black Rose, 1971), 76-110.

9   Roosevelt Williams, "The Myth of White "Backlash," in *Let the Niggers Burn: The Sir George Williams University Affair and its Caribbean Aftermath*, ed. David Forsythe. (Montreal: Black Rose, 1971), 123).

10   Ibid, 129.

11   Butcher, "The Anderson Affair"; Fred Kaufman, *Searching for Justice: An Autobiography*. (Toronto: Osgoode Society, 2005).

12   Ibid, 161.

13   Women were not allowed of serve on juries in Quebec at that time.

14   UHURU, "Still no justice,"1970.

15   She was Dean of Law at the University of Windsor from 1996-1999.

16   For more on Westmoreland's recognitions see: Hill, 2020.

17   Bernard Mergler and Robert Lemieux became well-known civil rights lawyers in Montreal. Lemieux represented the FLQ following the October Crisis in 1970, and Mergler was the mediator between the FLQ and the government.

18   Canada introduced a point system in its immigration policies allowing independent migrants points in specific categories related to their ability to settle successfully in Canada.

19   Many of these women were linked to the West Indies Domestic Scheme implemented by Canada in 1955, an immigration program that targeted women from the Caribbean to migrate to Canada as domestic servants. Black women from the Caribbean and elsewhere were settled in Canada long before the introduction of this scheme. However, most worked as domestic workers as this was among the few work options offered to Black women at the time.

20   The Quebec Independence movement emphasised the separation of the French speaking province of Quebec as a sovereign country on an equal basis with English Canada. This movement was at a peak in the 1960s, led by Quebec Nationalists to counter the domination of Quebec within the Canadian Federation.

21   The (FLQ) Front de libération du Quebec, described as a separatist para-military group, was involved in several high-profile, violent events including bombings and kidnappings in the late 1960s and 1970s in Quebec. The day following the students arrests, Montreal was rocked by the bombing of the Stock Exchange (see Eber, "Canada meets Black Power," 1969). During police raids of suspected FLQ militants, some of these students awaiting trail would again be arrested.

22   The Congress of Black Writers took place at McGill University in 1968 and brought together important global thinkers of the growing Black power movement, civil rights, pan Africanism, among others (see Forsythe, 1971; Austin 2013).

23   For these substantive charges such as arson, the students faced steep sentences including life in prison (see Kaufman, "Searching for Justice," 61; Eber, "Canada meets Black Power, 7).

24   Bond money for these students were set from $1,500 - $15,000.00 (see Butcher, "The Anderson Affair,"104).

25 Ad hoc is a legal term to refer to lawyers appointed for a specific purpose. Kaufman and his team for the Crown were criminal defense attorneys who were specially appointed (ad-hoc) for the trial. (See Kaufman, "Searching for Justice," 159).

26 Kelvin Robinson was among those considered student ringleaders who were charged with multiple offences and initially denied bail for up to three weeks after arrest (Eber, "Canada meets Black Power," 163).

27 Similar negotiations on fines and conditions were also conducted during the bail hearings earlier on in the process.

28 The trial for the ten students from Trinidad was followed by two separate trials: One for Brenda Dash and another for Rosie Douglas and Anne Cools. Dash was fined $2000.00 while Douglas received a sentence of two years plus $5,000 fine and Anne Cools: six months jail sentence and a $1,500.00 fine (Kauffman, "Searching for Justice," 163).

29 After the jury decision, a settlement was negotiated between the court and defense. Kaufman describes the swift judgement after the case that saw fines ranging from $1,000.00 - $ 1,500.00.

30 These events are detailed by Victoria Pasley as a series of violent demonstrations that "rocked the island" of Trinidad in 1970 when young people took to the streets to demand equality and access to opportunities for Blacks. This was at the height of the Black Power movement in the Caribbean. The Government responded with arrests and a state of emergency (see Victoria Pasley, "The Black Power Movement in Trinidad: An Exploration of Gender and Cultural Changes and the Exploration of Feminist Consciousness, *Journal of International Women's Studies* 3, no. 1 (2001):24-40.

31 As part of the settlement the judge recommended that the immigration department consider deportation for the foreign students (Kaufman, "Searching for Justice," 163).

32 The Pullman trains offered sleeping-car travel to passengers across Canada. It employed mainly Black male porters from the United States and Canada to serve travellers' every need. This position was one of few opportunities for Black men in Canada at the time.

33 As the Hall building of the Sir George Williams burned on February 11, and while the students were being arrested it was reported that crowds of detractors on the street below were heard chanting "Let the Niggers burn" among other racist chants (see Butcher, "The Anderson Affair," 97). Similarly, racist chanting surrounding the court was also reported during the bail hearings and trials (see Eber, "Canada meets Black Power," 7).

The Sir George Williams Affair: A Watershed in the Black Press

Dorothy W. Williams

THE ENERGY and ideology of the students that had been maturing throughout the 1960s was tested during the Sir George Williams Affair.[1] For Montreal's Black community, this was the watershed event in the post-war era. The affair, and its aftermath was the demarcation of before and after institutional strategies. The Sir George Williams incident signalled a new focus for Black youth. It was their rallying cry for activism to achieve new institutional goals, and socio-political impact to mitigate the effects of racial animus and disadvantage. Nevertheless, the incident made the Black community as a whole feel more vulnerable because it engendered the feeling that they could be endangered or that the students' agenda, without consultation, was defining the needs of the established community.[2]

Thus, the Sir George Williams incident and its aftermath, made residents more aware and less apathetic. It forced the community to look inward at the extent of its own problems and consider changes that many considered 'radical'.[3] One such radical move was the emergence of new forms of institutional structures and expressions.[4]

Moreover, the crisis generated a lot of sensitization within the Black community. It brought a group of West Indians, who normally would not have become involved in the community, together with a group of Blacks Canadians (who normally would not have become involved with West Indians), and for a while it allowed things to happen collectively. For instance, as this "student event" picked up steam, Blacks (as well as whites) worked together during those few days of the occupation to get food and supplies to the students. This co-operative activity laid the groundwork for the reconstruction of a cultural renaissance, such as the new sense of Black awareness and pride.

There were local changes as well that had significant impact. First, the Sir George Williams Affair made the dominant society aware that, along with foreign students, there was a Black community with deep roots in Montreal. Second, the Sir George Williams Affair achieved the same goal for the Black students on campus, who became aware of the Black residential community. Having been isolated from the community with their lives revolving around the campuses, these Black students were not fully aware of the deep roots of the settled community just below the hill. Thus, when they needed support, they reached into a community they knew little about. They began to examine what was happening in the small Black community, ensconced not more than 10 minutes away from Sir George Williams University (SGWU).

Once aware, students worked to establish new organizations to represent the interests of the local Black organizations. They began to demand changes in the old community structures and institutions that they believed were ineffectively serving the Black community.[5] There was also a push toward creating umbrella organizations. On the one hand, this reflected the institutional centralization which was occurring throughout the social service system in Quebec. On the other hand, these new forms of association were also an outgrowth of the community dispersal.[6]

For many in the Black community, the incident was a tumultuous and painful event with a lasting, negative legacy. For others, it was an opportunity for renewal, re-focusing and rupture, best described as 'in with the new and out with the old'. In retrospect, renewal was most evident in a reinvigorated print culture that sprung from the Sir George Williams Affair. Indeed, the resurgence of Black print culture in the Black community became the means of transmitting the ideals and aspirations that subsequently emerged.

There had been a print culture before the Sir George Williams Affair. The first Black newspaper, *The Free Lance* began publishing in Montreal in 1934.[7] From its demise in 1938 up to 1969, Blacks in Montreal had produced just nine periodicals. After the Sir George Williams incident over 200 titles have been published.[8] Specifically, my focus below will be just those titles that emerged between 1969 and 1974.

As the 1960s closed and Montreal entered a new era of exchange with its Black residents, the Black press became an important mediator. It was significant because of the role that the Black press played in education of the individual, while simultaneously creating a community consensus around strategy and tactics. Most important was controlling the message. The press that arose immediately after the 'incident' attempted to counter the mainstream version of events in the city's papers during the court proceedings, and the events leading to sanctions and incarceration of the protesters.[9]

The Black press also became a platform to demand radicalization in public spheres, particularly in education. The Sir George Williams Affair had made evident, writ large, the fact that the Black presence in the city's universities was overwhelmingly made up of foreign students. This led to an examination of the systemic barriers that mitigated the educational success of the city's Black youth.

BULLETIN NO. 2. February 22nd, 1969.

BAIL AS PUNISHMENT

To the Black population of Montreal, the events since February 11th constitute a rude awakening for us from a rather pleasant dream in which Montreal, indeed Canada, was characterized as a place where deep-seated racist tendencies did not exist; now we see all around us the manifestations of all the symptoms of a society filled with hatred towards Black people as a group.

We are particullarly interested in the use of bail as an extension of the hysteria and an expression of latent racism.

The decision to grant bail or not is usually and legally based on the probability that the individual will show up at the trial and not on whether he is guilty or innocent, or on the part he is alledged to have played in the incident.

We submit that the amount of bail levied is excessive and out of all proportion to the nature of the alledged crime and the character of the individuals being tried - they are afterall students, not hardened criminals. Unless the aim is to deny them their basic rights, we judge that bail which exceeds its proper function is punitive and denies the individual of his rights.

We deplore such prejudiced behaviour and submit that it should still be possible for any man, regardless of his race, colour, creed, or place of origin, to have a fair trial, and to be considered innocent until PROVEN guilty with all that this implies.

The principle that every person should have the right to a fair trial leads us to raise this issue of the excessive nature of bail and to commend to the public in general the need for their support of the Defense Fund so that no person should be denied justice because the cost of justice may be beyond his reach, whether we think the person is guilty or not.

HARASSMENT OF DEFENDANTS' SUPPORTERS

Several points about the way the hearing into the events of February 11th is being handled lead us to wonder whether justice will be done and an attempt made to examine the case on its merits.

Prominent among the apparent irregularities are the determined efforts which have been made to exclude blacks from the courts, and the attendant harassment and elaborate security arrangements at the courts.

Fig. 1. February 11th Defence Committee Bulletin, February 22, 1969

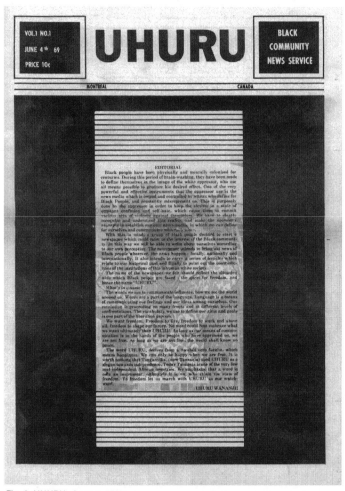

Fig. 2. UHURU, June 4, 1969

The Black press also became a platform to foster community education.[10] The newly emerging Black identity in Montreal, of the late 1960s into the 1970s, had yet to be claimed by the thousands of newly immigrant Blacks. It was the Black press that attempted to answer the question: who are 'we' in Montreal? The Black press became a dynamic interlocutor for Montreal's post-war community, one that had been forced to disperse throughout the island. Thus, the Black press kept a diffused population in touch with different parts of the city. Through this press, the Black individual's lens broadened beyond their local neighbourhoods. Indeed, Black readers learned about the world-wide struggles

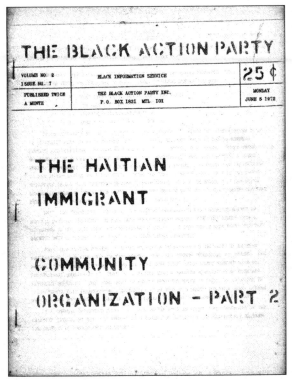

Fig. 3. The Black Action Party: Community
Information Service, February 1971

of international liberation. The drumbeat of Africa's struggle to attain self-autonomy and even the political independence of Caribbean island-nations were often covered. Through the pages of the Black press, historical and present-day Black heroes were introduced. Youth were encouraged to emulate new role models. Moreover, the concepts of Blackness and Africanisms were debated and assimilated. Finally, the writings of the Black journalists made clear that the Sir George Williams Affair had demonstrated the tenets of the Congress of Black Writers and the perspectives of the Caribbean conferences that had taken place at Université de Montréal, McGill, and Concordia in previous years.[11] The following section introduces the first nine serialized papers that arose out of the SGW crisis.[12] Each item is a quick snapshot of the origins and the intent or mission as framed by Black 'radical' journalists.

In the immediacy of the crisis, the Black students' first paper the, *February 11th Defence Committee Bulletin,* was published. The date signified the students' resolve to counter the police's racial profiling and to fight the onerous legal conditions that resulted from the protest at Sir George Williams University, on February 11th, 1969.[13] As the confrontations unleashed racial backlash, Blacks felt it was imperative to be observers, to report on what they saw, to educate the broader non-student population about the wheels that grind slowly in the justice and penal systems and to bring context to the unprecedented abuses. This was the first student-based publication that dealt with the impact of the Affair. The *February 11th Defence Committee Bulletin* eventually morphed into *UHURU*.

When *UHURU*, which means freedom in Swahili, hit the streets on June 4, 1969 (almost four months) after the Sir George Williams Affair, it caused a stir in calling for Black solidarity. It was a bi-monthly tabloid sized paper initially funded by the investment of several individuals. The content of *UHURU* was decidedly anti-white supremacy while extremely Afro-centric in its orientation. Each issue was replete with African history and Black studies on a national and international scale. This included articles and editorials about symbols of Blackness, what it means to be 'Black', and tips on how to shed one's 'whiteness'. Suffice it to say, the major objective of the paper was to "develop a political level of consciousness based on Pan-Africanism."[14] Educator, Roy States remembers how valuable *UHURU* was after the 'incident':

> If I were to tell you the story about that newspaper now it would probably be mild, but I wrote about it the night the paper was born, and I have all the feeling and the excitement. Everything was shown in that document. Even though white people couldn't read it, it disturbed them. You'd see young Blacks telling White people, 'Oh no it is not your paper. Only Black people could buy this paper'.[15]

UHURU also functioned as an internal watchdog by analyzing community activities and the institutions that served Black readers. *UHURU* almost became a buzzword as students fanned out in the streets and campuses, selling the paper to Blacks while engaging in debates on the street corners. The paper's headquarters on St. Antoine Street became another meeting place for students to hang out. More importantly, *UHURU* functioned as an informal clearing-house of student related events and of the on-going judicial process of the students undergoing prosecution. The work to keep the SGWU issue alive had very real objectives, particularly for the foreign students who had been involved in the protest. They lost their visas and/or passports, had no status and could not legally support themselves with work.[16]

Fig. 4. The Black Action Party, 1971

Fig. 5. The Black I, March 1972

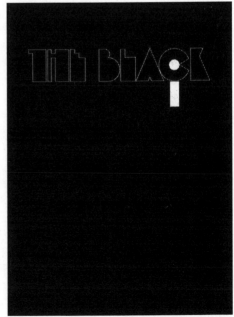

Fig .6. African Voice, March 1972.

Fig .7. Black Voice, September 1972

Many of the same students were also suspended from the university and could not pursue studies elsewhere as the university refused to issue their records to other universities. Without student status, the support from their country of origin was put into jeopardy, forcing many to leave.[17] Due to the charge of racism and the extreme treatment by Canadian authorities throughout the entire affair, these students believed that SGWU was a significant international event. They expected support from their home countries, but this was not the case. Thus, many articles of *UHURU* castigated the colonial dynamics of the Caribbean nations (vis-a-vis Canada) and tried to explain why the various Caribbean governments threw their weight behind the actions of the SGWU administration, the Federal government and/or behind the Canadian judiciary.[18]

As 1969 progressed, many of those who had worked on *UHURU* moved on. Some students returned to the United States, the Caribbean or to other jobs. As the core of militants left and the fervent militancy waned, *UHURU* ceased on November 9, 1970. *UHURU* was considered the quintessential organ of the Black ideological movement in Montreal, yet it could never have been

Fig. 8. The Black Student
Voice, March 1973

institutionalized within the mandates of other Black organizations. Though it folded, it was not long before Black institutions responded to fill the void.

The Black Action Party: Black Information Service was launched in February 1971. This post-Sir George paper came out of the Negro Community Center. Its impetus came from Sir George students in the Caribbean Society which was a small social club on campus. After February 11, their aims and energies moved in a definite direction — some would say they radicalized in order to counter the adversity they now faced.

The Caribbean Society evolved into the Black Students' Union. Off-campus, in the heart of the Black community, they produced 20 issues of *The Black Action Party*. It had community impact because it questioned not just aspects of the dominant society, but Black institutions that supported the status quo. One article, "Quebec Black United Front," focused on multi-organizational efforts around police racial profiling.[19]

The Community Information Service which promoted *The Black Action Party Bulletin* in *Cote des Neiges* was an arm of the Black Action Party. Pushing for a self-reliant community, *The Black Action Party Bulletin* focused on two questions: what does increased self-reliance mean? and what would such increased self-reliance consist of? The Bulletin lasted for eleven issues. Then it found itself without a home due to its building being expropriated. Volume two, issue eleven of the bulletin, "Towards Self-reliance," was a manual on how Montreal's Black community could control its own institutions and services.

The Black i began publishing in March 1972 and although they only had two issues, The Black i had a profound impact. It remains one of the most highly cited Black publications from that period. Its all-black cover made it very clear to the reader that the focus was the Black experience. Readers got a sprinkling of literature, sports, education, politics, and history. The article, "Black Power: Shadow and Substance" was a review of an interview of African American activist, Stokely Carmichael on Black goals in the Civil Right Movement.[20]

Just over two years after the arrest of the Sir George students, on March 28, 1972 a group of Blacks put together a bulletin called African Voice Organ of the Progressive Study Group. Despite the gap in time, their masthead included an A-K 45 rifle, ensuring that they would be taken seriously. They strove for revolution in Africa and Canada. The rifle's graphic signaled that their words were radical, and their focus was on collective and political change. The very first article was titled, "The Political Manifesto of the African Progressive Study Group."

Out of the Cote des Neiges Project, Leroy Butcher and other Black activists issued The Black Voice in May 1972, to focus on Project news. Most articles tackled racism, youth issues, local politics with a view to history, thanks to the input of Roy States. The issue depicted here, advanced youth activism. "Black Left Seeks Unity" covered Black delegates attending the Black Worker's Freedom Convention in 1972.[21] This article ended with a call for Blacks in Montreal to move away from their typical social-welfare organizations and create ones that foster political and economic power.

Just over three years after Sir George, students looked around and were discouraged. In their eyes, the promise of community reform after the incident had stagnated. Black students from high schools, CEGEPS, and universities reached out to each other to create a new vehicle to advance youth and education issues. This nascent island-wide Black Student Union needed support. Thanks to the active intervention of the Cote des Neiges Project, The Black Student Voice was printed.

The students introduced themselves to the community in a strongly-worded mission statement that spoke about their distinct educational focus: "This is the first attempt by a collective body of representatives of high school and universities to bring to the attention of the community, the problems and

Fig. 9. Focus Umoja, November 4, 1974

viewpoints of Black youth and also to develop a constant means of getting information to the community...It is part of a proposed means of bringing together the school and the community in the hope that by the first hand (sic)knowledge of what is happening Black parents will begin to take an active part in the struggle to make education relevant to the needs of our community. It is also designed to be a means by which Black youth and the community can begin to understand the way in which education is being used against people, so that by this understanding, no longer will they turn off from the process of learning but rather will be in a position to master the process and use it for the benefit of their community and the oppressed segment of mankind."[22] Despite this resolve, student energy and transient lifestyle stymied their long-term effort to enact change. *The Black Student Voice* survived for just a few issues.

With the demise of *UHURU*, the community was left without a press. NCC staff member, Carl Whittaker, initiated the idea to produce a monthly. With the help of one of the students from *UHURU*, *Focus Umoja* began publication November 1, 1974. The Black serial in the city was reborn out of a need to educate a Black constituency that now numbered in the tens of thousands. *Focus Umoja* became the voice of the Black Community Central Administration of Quebec, (BCCAQ). This was an umbrella committee with a mandate to oversee, manage, and promote activities within seven English-speaking Black institutions.

While familiarizing the whole community with the BCCAQ and its operations, *Focus Umoja* was a local community magazine that covered aspects of community life. It emphasized culture, politics, and especially education. The tone of *Umoja* was less strident than *UHURU*. It was not Pan-Africanist, nor anti-White. Yet, many saw *Focus Umoja* as a descendent of *UHURU*, because where 'Uhuru' meant freedom, 'Umoja' was defined as unity. Both were vital to the propagation of Black community-ness. Indeed, unity was the integral concept that the BCCAQ promoted.

In a major 2006 study of Black serials in Montreal, these early, post-Sir George periodicals stand alone in the history of the Black paper in Montreal. It has been shown that over 50 percent of Montreal's serials were mandated to help Blacks "identify with the norms, values, and appropriate behaviors of the dominant society."[23] Significantly, these student-driven papers ran counter to that trend. Rather, these journalists used the press to debate, espouse, and elucidate a new Black identity and a new set of values with an eye to local change and Pan-African solidarity. For a brief time, these post-Sir George papers served as definers of Black culture. In doing so, the watershed moment that was the Sir George Williams Affair became a fulcrum to promote and normalize radical thinking of Blackness within Montreal.

NOTES

1   The literature on the Sir George Williams Affair has become quite voluminous. Dennis Forsythe, ed., *Let the Niggers Burn: The Sir George Williams University Affair and its Caribbean Aftermath* (Montreal: Black Rose Books, 1971); Dorothy W. Williams, *The Road to Now: A History of Blacks in Montreal* (Montreal: Véhicule Press, 1997), 120-122.

2   Comments from interviews about the Sir George Williams Affair, *The Road To Now*, 1997, 122.

3   For some, the mere teaching of Black history, Blackness, and espousing of Black Power was radical.

4   See Williams, *The Road to Now* (122) for an outline of the emergence of student-created post-Sir George Williams Affair organizations.

5   Ibid., 122-138.

6   To understand the impact of Montreal's urban renewal on the dispersion of Black households within the historical Black district, see Dorothy W. Williams, *Blacks in Montreal, 1628-1986: An Urban Demography*, (Cowansville: Les Éditions Yvon Blais, 1989).

7   Dorothy W. Williams, "The Free Lance," *History of the Book in Canada/Histoire du livre et de l'imprimé au Canada, vol. III (1918-1980)*. eds. C. Gerson & J. Michon (Toronto, University of Toronto Press. 2007).

8   Dorothy W. Williams, "*Sankofa*: Recovering Montreal's Heterogeneous Black Print Serials," (Ph.D. diss., McGill University, 2006). Specifically, my focus in this paper will be just those titles that emerged between 1969 and 1974.

9   The best analysis of the local press coverage of the Sir George Williams Affair can be found in Roosevelt Williams, "Réactions: The Myth of White 'Backlash,'" in *Let the Niggers Burn: The Sir George Williams University Affair and its Caribbean Aftermath*, ed. Dennis Forsythe (Montreal: Black Rose Books, 1971), 111-120.

10   One of the critical legacies in the city from the Sir George Williams incident was the resultant Black relationships, concessions, and partnerships that arose within the educational sector. The Black press questioned the lack of Canadian-born students in local universities. Student activists began an earnest debate/campaign directed, not at increasing foreign enrollment, rather, elevating the achievement of the city's Black youth. See Williams, *Road*, 123-126.

11   David Austin, *Fear of a Black Nation: Race, Sex and Security in Sixties Montreal*, (Toronto: Between the Lines, 2012); Sean Mills, *The Empire Within: Postcolonial Thought and Political Activism in Sixties Montreal*, (Montreal: McGill-Queen's University Press, 2010); David Austin, *Moving Against the System, The 1968 Congress of Black Writers and the Shaping of Global Black Consciousness*, (Toronto: Between the Lines, 2018); Denis Forsythe, "The Black Writers Conference: Days To Remember," in *Let the Niggers Burn: The Sir George Williams University Affair and its Caribbean Aftermath*, ed. Dennis Forsythe (Montreal: Black Rose Books, 1971):, 57-74.

12   All serials illustrated in this section come from the author's personal archives.

13   For a detailed chronicle of the painful and disturbing events at Sir George Williams University on February 11, 1969, the final day of the student occupation, see LeRoi Butcher, "The Anderson Affair," in *Let the Niggers Burn: The Sir George Williams University Affair and its Caribbean Aftermath*, ed. Dennis Forsythe (Montreal: Black Rose Books, 1971), 96-102.

14   "Focus on UHURU," *UHURU* 1, no. 12 (December 8, 1969): 4.

15   Williams, *Road*, 136-37.

16   For the extent of the judicial push-back see: LeRoi Butcher, "The Anderson Affair," in *Let the Niggers Burn: The Sir George Williams University Affair and its Caribbean Aftermath*, ed. Dennis Forsythe (Montreal: Black Rose Books, 1971), 121-127. The violence and extra-judicial activities by the authorities, against the students, led to Black fundraising efforts, pro bono legal support and other direct community support.

17   Initially the judge ordered several deported. Williams, *Myth*, 123, 127,135.

18   Ibid., 131-138.

19   "The Quebec Black United Front," *The Black Action Party* 2, no. 6, (May 18, 1972), np.

20   Anselm Clouden, "Black Power: Shadow and Substance," *The Black i* 2, no. 1, (June 1973): 16.

21   "Black Left Seeks Unity," *The Black Voice* 1, no. 5, (September 1972): 5.

22   "What is this about?" *The Black Student Voice* 1, no. 1, (March 1973): 1.

23   Dorothy W. Williams, "Sankofa: Recovering Montreal's Heterogeneous Black Print Serials," (Ph.D. diss., McGill University, 2006), 225.

Montreal and the Caribbean Cold War: Reading Haitian and Cuban Connections

Amanda Perry

D URING HIS lecture on the Haitian Revolution at the Montreal Congress of Black Writers, Trinidadian intellectual C.L.R. James positions the victorious uprising as a source of pride for Black people in the Caribbean, one that shows "who are the African people in the Caribbean today and what they are capable of."[1] He thus reiterates a sentiment that runs throughout his now canonical history, *The Black Jacobins*, and above all its 1963 Appendix, which ties the Haitian Revolution to the development of political and cultural sovereignty in the Caribbean. The social context of 1960s Montreal would complicate such celebrations of Haiti's past, however, as the question and answer period following his speech demonstrates. A Haitian audience member is the first to respond, and he is less interested in eighteenth and nineteenth century revolutions than in twentieth century dictatorships. He launches into an attack on François Duvalier, describing him as "Black, culturally speaking– a lot of shit about the cultural aspect of Black Power" while also supporting "White American capitalism."[2] James responds by attacking U.S. support for the Duvalier regime, framing it as an attempt to prevent the repetition of another Caribbean revolution: the one in Cuba. Indeed, he begins his talk with a pro-longed discussion of the Cuban Revolution, heralded as the "first of the great revolutions which, after ten years, is stronger than it was in the beginning."[3]

The transnational nature of the events that shook and helped define Montreal's Black activist community in the late 1960s has never been in doubt. Indeed, the predominantly Anglo-Caribbean organization and leadership of the 1968 Congress of Black Writers, the 1969 computer centre occupation at Sir George Williams University and the strong presence of African American militants at the former would lead some contemporary commentators to dismiss these events as the un-Canadian off-shoots of foreign radical movements. Dennis Forsythe begins his 1971 volume on the "Sir George Williams Affair" by criticizing this very move, highlighting the international scope of both imperi-alism and radicalism.[4] More recent scholarship by David Austin and Sean Mills has balanced transnational analysis with asserting the significance of these events to the history of Canada and of Montreal.[5] They each mention a situation that deserves even more attention: Montreal in the 1960s. It was a site of cross-Caribbean encounters, where Anglo-Caribbean students and activists intersected with a growing population of anti-Duvalier Haitian exiles. James' talk furthermore highlights the Cuban Revolution's significance as a major ideological touchstone. At a time when the future of the Anglophone Caribbean was in flux, with some islands still under British control and other states grappling with the transition to postcolonial governance, Haiti and Cuba would seem to represent diverging paths, on opposite sides of the Caribbean Cold War. The U.S.-backed Duvalier dictatorship appeared as a warning that independence was no guarantee of popular empowerment, while Cuba embodied the threat of totalitarian socialism for some and the anti-imperialist dreams of others. For individuals negotiating their position as racialized minorities in Canada, the situations in Haiti and Cuba would also foreground the potentially fraught relationships between race and class-based struggles.

This chapter examines documents surrounding the Congress of Black Writers and the Sir George Williams affair in light of these connections to Haiti and Cuba. At times, the transnational nature of political moments and movements can be read within the trajectory of a single person. As a young Haitian activist, Philippe Fils-Aimé joined the organizing committee for the 1968 Congress of Black Writers and was among those arrested following the 1969 Sir George Williams affair. Drawing on an extended interview, I document Fils-Aimé's participation as a window into the simultaneous convergence and divergence of Anglo-Caribbean and Haitian activism during this time period. Meanwhile, the Cuban Revolution would be at once absent and omnipresent in these events. Though no Cubans appear to have been directly involved, talk of Cuba was everywhere, and many leading figures had close ties to the revolutionary state. These connections to Haiti and Cuba would challenge black activists to think through the potential contradictions of struggles for racial emancipation and against economic subjugation.

Philippe Fils-Aimé in Montréal: Imperial Intersections and Cross-Caribbean Collaboration

"This guy here, me that came here on that winter day, I realized that I was a lost soldier from a banana republic, [a] utopist with big dreams. That's what I was – somehow [I'm] still that."
—*Philippe Fils-Aimé*

Philippe Fils-Aimé's participation in the 1969 computer centre occupation has above all been remembered through one striking episode: during the trial, he presented the chief prosecutor with a vodou doll, unleashing panic in the court room.[6] Behind this headline-grabbing stunt lies a longer story of transnational militancy. Fils-Aimé arrived in Montreal as a young man in early 1967, rapidly becoming enmeshed in both the Anglo-Caribbean and Haitian activist communities. He was a major presence at "Protests and Pedagogy," the commemorative events held at Concordia University in February 2019 for the fiftieth anniversary of the occupation, and in August 2019, I invited him for a formal interview to elaborate on his involvement.

In narrowing my focus to a single life, I adopt one of the methodologies of microhistory, with Fils-Aimé serving as what Lara Putnam might label a "telling example" that demonstrates connections that have hitherto been overlooked or denied.[7] Most accounts of these events provide a collective portrait of the students, with perhaps more attention to the original complainants against Perry Anderson or to Rosie Douglas and Anne Cools as the participants that served prison sentences. This approach tends to highlight either the Canadian setting of the occupation or the Anglo-Caribbean origins of these actors. Tracing the involvement of a single activist paradoxically expands the scope of these events, evoking a transnational context that includes the Duvalier dictatorship, the Vietnam War, and guerilla training camps in the Bahamas. Fils-Aimé's perspective is both valuable in and of itself and a reminder of how little we know about the range of political commitments and personal histories that led people to join the occupation. My main source for the following narrative is Fils-Aimé's own words, as he recounts these events from a distance of fifty years. In this case, concerns about the reliability of memory appeared less compelling to me than the opportunity to enrich the written record and ensure that the details of his participation are preserved.

Fils-Aimé came to Montreal to escape the policies and practices of two governments: François Duvalier's dictatorship in Haiti and the Lyndon Johnson administration in the United States. Growing up in Haiti, he had enjoyed advantages as a result of his social status, coming from a prominent military and intellectual family, and of his appearance as a, "brown kid with greenish eyes." He thus identifies as a beneficiary of a complex form of colorism, outlined by Michel-Rolph Trouillot, within which the Haitian nation is fundamentally conceived of and celebrated as Black, but light skin and European features still carry prestige and can be used to climb the social ladder.[8] Following the election of François Duvalier in 1957 and his rapid consolidation of autocratic power, the position of Fils-Aimé's family would become far more precarious. Duvalier presented himself as a *noiriste*, a champion of Black Haitians, set to retake the country from a light-skinned elite that exercised disproportionate political and economic power. His dictatorship would develop a brutal reputation due to its use of violence, not only against the poor, but also against the upper classes, including women who had typically been spared reprisals.[9] While Fils-Aimé's family had not been specifically targeted, he recalls an atmosphere of generalized terror, generated by the murder of political opponents and the state militia's ability to carry out personal vendettas with impunity.

His family opted for exile, leaving between 1964 and 1965 to join a growing Haitian community in New York. A couple of years later, while briefly based in Texas, Fils-Aimé received a conscription notice to fight in Vietnam. The U.S. government had come to support the Duvalier regime in the name of anti-communism, renewing aid to the country after the Haitian state voted to expel Cuba from the Organization of American States in 1962. Fils-Aimé now faced the consequences of these same anti-communist policies for young men within the United States. He credits his decision not to go to the harrowing accounts of returned soldiers, the desperation of those about to be deployed, and his own developing political consciousness. As he put it, "they were going to Vietnam just like they were in Haiti," referring to the U.S. Occupation of Haiti from 1915 to 1934, and he saw no reason to go fight, "these folks that look much more like [himself] than them." A family meeting in New York determined that he should leave for Montreal as a draft dodger.

Fils-Aimé's fluency in English, reinforced by his time in the United States, would shape his experience in the linguistically divided city that awaited him. Shortly after his arrival in Montreal in early 1967, he fell in with the Anglo-Caribbean intellectual community surrounding the Caribbean Conference Committee. He first met Alfie Roberts, originally from St. Vincent, who then introduced him to Rosie Douglas of Dominica and Anne Cools of Barbados. Through this circle, he would also meet the Trinidadian intellectual C.L.R. James, who he credits with guiding the group's overall ideological development.[10] These meetings would help Fils-Aimé develop a transnational perspective on issues that he had previously seen through a Haitian lens, "I came to understand that hey, we are in an empire… Haiti's not just a special case. There are people in Africa, there are people everywhere who [were] just fighting against this kind of domination." As part of the organizing committee for the Congress of Black Writers, he would furthermore come into contact with key African American militants, and he recalls being especially impressed by James Foreman and arguing about the details of the Haitian Revolution with Stokely Carmichael.[11]

At the same time, he developed contacts within the Haitian community, above all through the conference co-organizer Elder Thébaud, then a graduate student at McGill University, and the Marxist intellectual Max Chancy, who, along with his wife Adeline Magloire Chancy, was a prominent activist and one of the founders of the Maison d'Haiti. Fils-Aimé remembers the Haitian community as a hub for even more radical activism, of which his anglophone collaborators were largely unaware, as Haitian exiles converged in Montreal with the goal of launching an armed offensive against Duvalier. A substantial portion of these exiles were committed communists, and he vividly recalls, "these guys coming from Moscow with some big Russian coats or some furs and some stars, red stars, and a big picture of Lenin." Before leaving the United States for Canada, Fils-Aimé had himself considered going to the Bahamas, where training camps, with murky sources of funding, had been established to plan an invasion of Haiti. As he put it, "the priority in our lives was to go into these camps, was to train to invade Haiti." The 1960s would see numerous unsuccessful attempts to overthrow Duvalier through guerrilla warfare, most involving small groups of militants who were then killed by state forces.[12] Fils-Aimé's repeated references to these efforts are a reminder that revolution was far from just a word for Haitian activists in the 1960s. The armed overthrow of the Haitian state was an active project–even if, as Fils-Aimé joked, many of these militants would ultimately be too seduced by the comfort of their life in Montreal to leave.

Against this backdrop of militancy, Fils-Aimé was initially sceptical of student efforts to protest racist pedagogical practices at Sir George Williams University. Indeed, he had dismissed the matter as, "a bunch of petit-bourgeois students" who "wanted to have better grades" when there was a much more urgent struggle at hand. As he witnessed the psychological effect of this experience of racism among those involved, his perspective shifted. He saw the controversy as an opportunity to raise consciousness among the students and joined the organizing efforts, later participating in the occupation itself. He also describes being, "under certain watch and protection from Alfie and Rosie" due to his status as an anti-Duvalier exile, "All the leadership, they sort of took care of me and made sure that I didn't get in too much trouble because they knew that if they get deported to their country, that's one thing; if I get deported, I'd be killed." When the police stormed the computer centre and Fils-Aimé was among those arrested, he would have the dubious honour of being a foreign national who would not receive the support of his embassy.

Fils-Aimé's account of his arrest, the beating he received from the police officers, and the racism of the guards is harrowing in its own right and largely in line with accounts from other student protestors. He attributes his release above all to international solidarity efforts in the Caribbean and elsewhere, which are well-documented in the press of the time period.[13] He claims, however, that the protestors had an active role in cultivating these connections during the occupation itself. By seizing the computer centre, they also gained access to long-distance calling capabilities, allowing them to contact students on other campuses, as well as figures like C.L.R. James and Stokely Carmichael.

Throughout the interview, Fils-Aimé stressed his fondness for psychological tactics, including his own tendency to adopt an exaggerated, hypermasculine stance as a means of establishing authority. His most famous use of such tactics would occur during the court hearings following the arrests. Inspired by Jerry Rubin, the U.S. activist who had shown up in costume to his hearing before the House Un-American Activities Committee, Fils-Aimé aimed to turn the hearings into a kangaroo court, drawing on and manipulating the cultural stereotypes that he encountered. Some of the security guards were apparently using the search procedures prior to courtroom entry as an excuse to grope women protestors, leading to a skirmish during which he recalls one of them exclaiming, "Ostie de maudite vodou–you fucking vodou boy." Realizing that the concept of vodou had some local resonance, Fils-Aimé decided to take advantage of the situation. He set about making a vodou doll, using a white sheet, adding a black cape to make it resemble a prosecutor, daubing it with red paint, and inserting a needle. When it did not look sufficiently realistic, he added some of his own blood. Fils-Aimé's model was Hollywood rather than Haiti, as these pin-stuck dolls have generally been dismissed as a North American invention. In what he would consider his own miniature version of psychological warfare, he opted for legibility over authenticity.[14] A woman smuggled the doll in for him under her clothes, taking advantage of guards' new caution during the search procedures, and he placed it in a box before delivering it to the prosecutor.

Fils-Aimé's description of the reaction of the courtroom is colourful and incisive. I quote it at length here, with minimal alterations in order to keep his speech patterns intact:

> I... called Mr. Shephard and told him how in Haiti we have a lot of respect for prosecutors and we feel obliged to express our respect by bringing in a special gift. So the guy was very happy to see this very humble young Negro almost begging for mercy, right, so he pat me on the back and he took it. Then he stop and he look at it and he became really white, like pure white, his eyes popping out and he run to the judge and less than two minutes after, five guards jump on me and each took me by one arm

and they transported me in front of the judge, so I think the judge was already ready to give a sentence or something, contempt of court, then I think it was Juanita Westmoreland that said, "well, what is the charge?" So, they spent at least forty minutes or more in some library looking for some charge, but most of these charges had to do with witchcraft that was abolished because that was the beginning of the struggle for laicity. I was there, standing in front of the judge, and enjoying it. Frankly I was just enjoying it because I had never had, in my life, such á feeling of power. Like, I would make a gesture like that, and the lady that was typing, the stenographer, she would almost jump back and the policeman was there. They didn't know if they should touch me or, they looking like, "What's happening? This is serious vodou," because they must have believed in that shit. Like, they were not so civilized after all.

With one gesture, Fils-Aimé had inverted the power dynamics of the court-room, judging the representatives of a supposedly secular society that had placed him on trial for their own superstition. Though the prosecutor would ask for Fils-Aimé's bail to be revoked, he would escape any charges following some manoeuvring by his legal team, which included Westmoreland, the young lawyer from Montreal's Black community that had flown back from Paris to help defend the students.

His move would also make the front page of *La Presse* on March 11, 1970, with the headline, "A Vodou Doll for Mr. Shepherd." The article further demonstrates how the prosecutor's desire to produce an authoritative reading in order to master and control the situation collided with the illegibility of Haitian cultural practices. The description of the prosecutor's reaction is oddly comic, as, "Mr Sheppard said that he had already gone to Haiti (which he called Tahiti) and he knew the symbolic significance of this doll."[15] The joke extends to those doing the reporting, as vodou is spelt inconsistently throughout the piece. Word of the incident would also reach New York, and Fils-Aimé recalls being chastised over the phone by his sister, who worked on Wall Street, for giving the family a bad name and supporting stereotypes about Haitian culture. He received mixed reactions from the other protestors, mentioning that Rosie Douglas and especially Anne Cools disapproved of his tactics. As for himself, while Fils-Aimé is unsure what his doll ultimately accomplished, he remains convinced that it did not hurt their cause. Instead, it made visible a latent fear of foreigners that had already been present in Canadian and Quebecois society, much as the computer centre occupation itself brought anti-Black racism in the country into sharp focus.

Philippe Fils-Aimé's vodou doll would add an undeniably Haitian element to the history of these protests, as well as enshrining his own reputation as a trickster. But the fact that he may have been the only Haitian involved in the occupation, and was almost certainly the only one among the arrested, raises its own questions. How much interaction occurred between Anglo-Caribbean and Haitian radicals in Montreal during the 1960s, and to what extent were the "two solitudes" of francophone and anglophone Montreal reproduced within Montreal's Black community? It is tempting to read into this history a narrative of divergence and missed connections, whereby the Anglo-Caribbean community, so prominent in the 1960s, began to shrink as the Haitian population swelled in the 1970s. In broad strokes, the positions of these groups appear to map onto the exodus of anglophones out of Montreal and the rise of French as the dominant language of public life. In recent decades, few would contest that the core of Canada's Anglo-Caribbean community has been in Toronto, not Montreal.

That said, these two groups intersected in the city historically and continue to do so to this day. David Austin's book on the Congress of Black Writers foregrounds these moments of collaboration. He notes that Adeline Magloire Chancy was among those Haitians who attended the Congress of Black Writers, and much as Fils-Aimé used his meeting with Carmichael to debate the nature of the Haitian Revolution, Chancy would discuss the contemporary situation in Haiti with C.L.R. James.[16] Such moments demonstrate the importance of bilingual activists in bridging political barriers, but they also show how the presence of Haitians challenged approaches to the Haitian Revolution within other Black communities. In the presence of anti-Duvalier exiles, the revolution could not simply function as an inspiring story of anticolonial revolt, but needed to be tied to a complex, evolving social reality.

Other Haitians involved in the Congress of Black Writers include the conference co-organizer Elder Thébaud, who was training as a psychiatrist; he would later set up his practice in New York. According to Adeline Chancy, Thébaud had previously been a member of the *Union national des étudiants haïtiens*, the National Union of Haitian Students, an organization that, at the cost of many lives, mounted an intense struggle against Duvalier.[17] A third Haitian, Josette Pierre-Louise, joined Thébaud and Fils-Aimé on the organizing committee, though it would remain numerically dominated by people from the Anglophone Caribbean, with additional participants from Canada, the United States, and continental Africa.[18] Sean Mills mentions that efforts were made to make the event bilingual and that the name of the conference itself reads as an allusion to the *Congrès des écrivains noirs*, first held in Paris in 1956 and again

Figure 1: Philippe Fils-Aime, Protests and Pedagogy launch, January 29, 2019, Concordia University, Montreal.

in Rome in 1959.[19] In his study of Haitians in Quebec, Mills signals other instances in which these activist communities collaborated, with some Haitians publishing articles in *UHURU*, the newspaper founded in the wake of the computer centre occupation, and anglophone Black activists lending support to the Haitian community when they were threatened by mass deportation in the 1970s.[20] Ultimately, neither the isolation nor the collaboration between the two communities should be exaggerated. Rather, it appears to have been a case where select bilingual activists had an outsized role in making connections possible.

The Cuban Revolution and Montreal's Black Activism
Upon his return from the Congress of Black Writers, Guyanese intellectual and activist Walter Rodney would be barred from entering Jamaica, leading to the famous Rodney Riots that would galvanize the Jamaican left. The incident succinctly links Canadian and Anglo-Caribbean activism, but it also serves as a "telling example" of ties to Cuba and to Haiti. In his Congress presentation, Rodney had praised the Cuban Revolution's successes in fostering Black liberation, and Michel O. West's research reveals that the Jamaican state was as suspicious of his student visits to Cuba and the USSR as they were of his ties to

Rastafarian Black radicals.[21] After his expulsion, Rodney briefly returned to Montreal and then left to spend several months in Cuba. According to Norman Cook, Rodney had fled Montreal after Cuban intelligence officials informed him of a threat to his life. Their messenger was none other than Haitian exile Max Chancy.[22]

In the tableau of Montreal Black activism in the 1960s, Cuba is simultaneously everywhere and nowhere. There appears to have been no direct Cuban involvement in the Congress of Black Writers or the computer centre occupation, but references to the Cuban Revolution are ubiquitous. Like Rodney, many of the individuals connected to these events also had direct ties to the revolutionary state. Within Montreal as elsewhere, the Cuban Revolution was a source of inspiration for a wide swath of left-wing activists. The Canadian government's refusal to join in the U.S. embargo or to cut off diplomatic relations also meant that Canada, alongside Mexico, was one of the few places in the Americas where the Cuban state continued to have an official presence in the 1960s. As a result, Montreal specifically would become a target for terrorist activities by Cuban exiles hostile to the new government. The Cuban pavilion at Montreal's 1967 World Exposition risked violating the event's regulations against politics with its militant exhibit; it would prove popular both for its rum and for the air of danger that accompanied it, with one journalist claiming attendees would joke, "Have they bombed Cuba yet?"[23] The comment was glib but not hyperbolic. A Cuban cargo ship had already been bombed in Montreal's harbour in 1964 by the Miami-based *Asociación Nacionalista Cubana*, as had Cuba's embassy in Ottawa in September 1966. In March of 1967, the same group bombed a Montreal auction house selling goods belonging to Cuban exiles, while April and May of 1967 would witness two abortive attempts to bomb the Expo pavilion.[24] Such attacks would continue throughout the 1970s, the majority of them in Montreal. While most caused more alarm than destruction, the bombings of the Cuban consulate in Montreal in 1971 and 1972 would cause significant damage, with the latter leading to the death of Cuban security guard Sergio Pérez Castillo.[25] In addition to being a rallying cry for the left, Cuba was filling up local headlines.

Many of the activists and intellectuals involved in the Caribbean Conference Committee and the Congress of Black Writers were enthusiastic supporters of the revolution. Alfie Roberts would repeatedly praise Cuban developments and stress their significance to the time period, and Anne Cools had visited Cuba as a representative of the CCC, attempting to secure a Cuban translation of James' *The Black Jacobins*.[26] C.L.R. James himself had attended the January 1968 Congress in Havana, and allusions to the vibrancy of the Cuban

Revolution peppered his speeches at the Congress.[27] Ties between African American radicals and the Cuban Revolution have been the subject of robust scholarship.[28] The Congress' most anticipated speaker, Stokely Carmichael, had declared his solidarity with Cuba in an impassioned speech at Havana's *Organización Latinoamericana de Solidaridad* in 1966 that would be reprinted and distributed in Montreal by the CCC.[29] During his speech at the Congress, Carmichael would repeatedly reference the revolution as a model from which to learn and uphold Che Guevara as a revolutionary authority.[30]

Chancy's role in Rodney's flight from Montreal, meanwhile, underlines the strength of the connections between revolutionary Cuba and anti-Duvalier activists. The Cuban state directly supported efforts to overthrow Duvalier, distributing propaganda in Haitian Creole over its airwaves, acting as a hub for organizing, and at least on one occasion providing military training to Haitian exiles.[31] Cuba's support for armed movements has largely entered the archives through tragic examples. In 1961, Jacques Stephen Alexis, the Haitian novelist and founder of a communist party, would sail from Cuba to Haiti with four men in an attempt to overthrow the Duvalier dictatorship, only to be picked up and murdered shortly after his arrival. In 1968, another Haitian exile, Adrien Sansaricq, who was based in Havana and had accompanied Che Guevara to the Congo, would travel undercover to Haiti as part of a subversive operation. He would be tracked down and killed.[32] While the extent to which these Cuban ties were also filtered through Montreal is hard to evaluate, prominent Haitians who lived in Montreal like Émile Ollivier and Anthony Phelps would visit Havana, and Montreal would also be the site of the official Cuban-Haitian Friendship society, established in 1976 with Ollivier as one of its founding members.[33]

Even when Cuba was not providing material support, the revolution was a powerful source of inspiration and a model for insurrectionary practices. The training camps in the Bahamas that Philippe Fils-Aimé had considered joining envisioned an invasion of the island following the model of "Fidel Castro." Indeed, the very belief that a small group of armed men could overthrow a state seemed sanctioned by Cuba's revolutionary process. Fils-Aimé attributes the failure of these invasions to a lack of preparation and flawed political model, as the, "idea of war was that you go and you take a town and you rouse the population and you march triumphant through the capital." While these conceptions may appear naïve, they also bear traces of Che Guevara's writing on guerilla warfare, which maintained that small groups of (mostly) men, establishing strongholds in the countryside, could incite a social revolution by rallying the masses to their cause. This narrative distorts Cuba's own revolutionary process, downplaying the role of the urban resistance and other organizations in Fulgencio

Batista's overthrow, but it would have material effects by inspiring attacks across the Caribbean and Latin America, with staggeringly low rates of success.[34]

When asked directly about the Cuban Revolution as a source of inspiration during the computer centre occupation, Fils-Aimé situated it as part of a diverse set of influences. Certainly, Guevara was a hero and martyr to many of the students involved, whether Black or white. In this regard, he formed part of a potent cocktail of influences that included the radical wing of the Quebec sovereigntist movement and African American militancy in the United States. David Austin cites student protestor Norman Cook's description of the occupation as having, "at times assumed a circus-like atmosphere as Black Nationalists, Zen masters, Hare Krishnas, Maoists, Trotskyists, anarchists, and Quebec nationalists jockeyed to have their voices heard and to present their solutions to the 'Black problem.'"[35] Amidst this multiplicity of influences and transnational connections, ties to Cuba and to Haiti remain especially revealing, as they encouraged grappling with race as a structural phenomenon.

Reading Race in the Caribbean Cold War

In 1960s Montreal, addressing the Cuban Revolution and the Duvalier dictatorship would require prying apart and examining the tensions between two terms that "imperialism" so effectively bundled together: the struggles against racial discrimination and economic exploitation. In the Anglophone Caribbean, Black radicalism functioned in the 1960s as an oppositional discourse, denouncing ongoing colonial domination and the failures of newly independent states to change the conditions of the dark-skinned majority.[36] In these cases, the continued dominance of a lighter skinned elite and of transnational corporations from the Global North appeared to go hand in hand. Similarly, the repeated insistence by speakers at the Congress of Black Writers that "the system" needed to be destroyed addressed histories of colonialism and enslavement as at once involving racial oppression and economic subordination. The debates about the relative importance of race and class in structuring social relations nevertheless tended to point toward similar enemies. Turning to Cuba and Haiti would complicate this picture, presenting at once an anti-imperialist Caribbean state with a largely white leadership and a brutal dictatorship that claimed to represent Black Power. While the negotiation of these issues is clearest in the speeches and sources surrounding the Congress of Black Writers, these cross-Caribbean comparisons also shed light on the dynamics of the occupation itself.

African American militant James Foreman begins his Congress speech on Martinican intellectual and revolutionary Frantz Fanon by insisting that Fanon "has to be remembered as Che Guevara must be remembered."[37] That Fanon would be compared to Guevara is not surprising; both were revolutionary internationalists who at once theorized and directly participated in armed struggles, with the parallels between their lives extending to their training (Fanon in psychiatry, Guevara in medicine) and their early deaths (Fanon at 37 and Guevara at 39). What is noteworthy is that Foreman then extends this parallel to "Malcolm X, Martin Luther King, and all the other Black martyrs," before asking the audience for a moment of silence for those killed in the struggle for Black liberation.

The inclusion of Guevara, and in other instances Fidel Castro, in lists otherwise reserved for Black leaders would be common in this time period, testifying to the Cuban Revolution's prestige and success in presenting itself as anti-imperialist and anti-racist. After the overthrow of Batista, the new state had ordered the desegregation of beaches and workplaces and reframed racism as an anti-revolutionary attitude. By 1962, the government was declaring that racism had been liquidated on the island. The Cuban state's foreign policy would be explicitly anti-racist, as the government vocally supported and at times granted asylum to Black Power advocates in the United States in addition to encouraging liberation movements on the African continent. Then again, the declaration, attributed to Stokely Carmichael, that Fidel Castro was the Blackest man in the Americas was necessary precisely because Castro was visibly white and had led a largely white and middle-class movement. Organizing along racial lines in Cuba itself would soon be considered illicit and, as early as 1962, criticizing ongoing forms of racism on the island would become taboo in the public sphere.[38]

Incorporating the Cuban Revolution into imaginaries concerning Black liberation would thus involve grappling with the whiteness of its leadership. In his speech in Montreal, C.L.R. James, would write the issue of Cuban race relations out of his narrative about the revolution's fundamental Caribbeanness. He asserts that the radical efforts to transform Cuban society are, "not due to the fact that they are a Black people... [but] due to the fact that they are a West Indian community, closely allied, using a modern language, jammed together, and able to develop themselves with tremendous force."[39] In order to maintain that the Cuban Revolution is both quintessentially Caribbean and the Haitian Revolution's twentieth century heir, he foregrounds an understanding of the region that is grounded in aspects of social structure other than race or African retentions.

Walter Rodney would instead invoke Cuba precisely as he intervened in debates about the presence of white audience members at the Congress. Rodney argues against trying to use African history to prove Black humanity to white people and cites events in Cuba as an example that, "the way of asserting that humanity is by revolutionary struggle."[40] Unlike James, he emphasizes the specific struggles of Afro-Cubans from the nineteenth century onward, but he also highlights that they fought, "alongside white people...who wanted to break the imperialist bonds."[41] Because the Revolution attacked "the system" as a whole, it could lead to genuine Black emancipation. In contrast, his white audience members in Montreal were, "objectively involved in the oppression of Black people so long as they live in a metropolitan centre" that exploits colonial peoples.[42] He thus emphasizes the importance of structural positions in determining the meaning and the limits of solidarity. At the same time, Rodney frames contemporary Cuba as providing more room for Black cultural expression than majority Black Jamaica, as the latter remains bound up in imperial relationships. Here, he suggests that a society's place within imperialist networks is more significant than the bare facts of its racial composition. For both James and Rodney, references to Cuba require negotiating the significance of race in revolutionary struggles to account for the participation of white subjects, and in different ways, they responded by emphasizing the significance of other material conditions, and especially class contradictions.

Turning toward Haiti, meanwhile, would foreground the existence of repressive Black leaders. François Duvalier had adopted a certain pro-Black rhetoric as the language of state, positioning himself as heir to the Haitian revolutionary leader, Jean-Jacques Dessalines and champion of the Black rural masses. As Peter Nicholls documents, the modifications made under the Duvalier regime were largely at the level of the symbolic–installing the *nèg mawon* statue in downtown Port-au-Prince, for example, or adopting Dessalines' imperial flag.[43] The state itself would have as its largest legacy systematic graft and the butchering of its opponents. Nevertheless, Duvalier's rhetorical appropriation of a certain form of "Blackness" changed the conditions for organizing against him. At the Congress, James would insist that the fact that, "Duvalier is black does not matter at all," citing him alongside Moïse Kapenda Tshombe of the Democratic Republic of the Congo as evidence that "Black Power" can itself be oppressive when wielded by a comprador elite.[44] Other critiques went further. In Haitian exile publications like the Montreal journal *Nouvelle Optique*, founded in 1971, one often finds the dissection of race-based politics as a form of mystification that distracts from the more fundamental, economic foundations of power disparities.[45]

During our interview, Philippe Fils-Aimé would echo some of this rhetoric, arguing that, "if it's just a Black and white thing, how do you explain Duvalier?"

He insisted on the Haitian leader's debt to fascist thinkers, and in a similar vein would describe, "narrow Black nationalism" as "very close to fascism." In Montreal, however, Haitians like Fils-Aimé would find themselves as part of a racialized minority, subjected to similar pressures as their anglophone counterparts. Even as the Haitian example made him wary of some approaches to race, Fils-Aimé's time in the city and contact with Black activists from other communities appears to have broadened and reinforced his own understanding of himself as Black. As he declares, "I switched from a Haitian nationalist fighting against neocolonialism to a Black internationalist who should feel at ease in all struggle."

Adeline Chancy's reactions to the Congress of Black Writers demonstrate a similar dynamic. In her notes from October 1968, she celebrates the agreement among African American militants on the necessity of internationalizing the Black struggle and attacking the imperial system itself. She is more cautious, however, in relation to Stokely Carmichael's call for Black solidarity, as she also insists on the need to recognize racism's origins, not in black-white divisions, but in the experience of colonization. To make this argument, she cites René Dépestre's "Adventures of Negritude," "It is colonization that, through steel, fire, and blood, had opened in the very flanks of history the bloody black/white contradiction to conceal and justify relationships of economic exploitation."[46]

Her choice of Depestre is telling, as the Haitian poet and thinker's own views on race were also heavily influenced by his position within Cuba, where he had been living since 1959. Depestre had been invited to speak at the Congress of Black Writers but did not ultimately attend.[47] His scheduled talk on Negritude would instead be given by James, and judging from the fragments that have been cited by David Austin, the Trinidadian appears to have largely praised Negritude's accomplishments as an aesthetic and political movement.[48] In contrast, the article that Chancy cites, first presented by Depestre as a talk at the 1968 Cultural Congress of Havana, is above all an attack on the use and abuse of race-based ideologies by Duvalier among others. During the 1960s, Depestre would also be one of the foremost champions of the Cuban state's claim to have abolished the material foundations of racism, notably through his rebuttal in *Présence Africaine* to Carlos Moore's widely circulating claim that the Cuba Revolution was itself racist.

Like Depestre, Chancy insists in her notes that eliminating racism would require abolishing exploitation, and she identifies *noiriste* ideology, which uses the concept of Negritude to, "mask the formation of a black bourgeoisie playing in turn the role of the dominant class" as a trap that "we Haitians know well."[49] That said, she also stresses the dangers of assuming that changing the economic system would automatically eliminate racism. Her argument that the only true solution is, "revolutionary practice, involving an authentic international solidarity and drawing inspiration from a total humanism"[50] reads similarly to Depestre's characterizations of the Cuban Revolution. Her emphasis on racism as a semi-autonomous ideology, present even among whites who are being exploited, is more reflective of the hard critiques of class-based solidarity movements in the North American context on the basis of their complicity in anti-Blackness. Chancy concludes her notes by underlining that all Black people have, "an account to settle with History," regardless of what country they may inhabit. Like Fils-Aimé, she envisions, and would go on to participate in, a struggle that crossed national boundaries and languages.

These cross-Caribbean conversations about race are furthermore illuminating in evaluating the dynamics of the computer centre occupation itself, particularly regarding the participation of white protestors and disputes over leadership. While the protest directly challenged anti-Black racism, these debates remind us that some of the militants of the 1960s approached racism as part of a broader imperialist structure that was complex and even contradictory in its manifestations. The tendency of Black activists to celebrate the Cuban Revolution provides a model whereby white subjects could become agents of anti-imperialism under appropriate structural conditions. The role of white student activists in the occupation should be recognized, not romanticized, especially given the differential treatment of protestors following their arrests. Nevertheless, their presence is less surprising when the Cuban Revolution, and not only Black Power, is understood as an inspirational antecedent for Black and white protestors alike. Meanwhile, debates about Haiti are a reminder that Black subjects could support and establish oppressive structures in addition to resisting them. Austin's account of the occupation chronicles debates about leadership among the protestors.[51] Viewed with examples like the Duvalier dictatorship in mind, these disputes are more than evidence of ideological differences and personality conflicts; they demonstrate an awareness of the real danger of having the wrong person in charge, even if that person was Black. The fears of agent provocateurs, such as Warren Hart, and suspicions about Black professors being co-opted by the administration likewise show that protesters were wary of being manipulated should they approach racial solidarity too simplistically. Embracing an expanded Caribbean context complicates the relationship between race and anti-imperialism in ways that make these dynamics more legible.

Tracing these transnational ties between the Anglophone Caribbean, Haiti, and Cuba restores to view Montreal's position as a site of exchange within the

Caribbean Cold War. Fils-Aimé's story is, in itself, representative of these transnational contours: arriving in Montreal as a Haitian exile and a Vietnam War draft dodger, he moved between Anglo-Caribbean and Haitian activist communities, each with their differently inflected approaches to revolution and to race. His trajectory is a reminder of instances of collaboration between Haitian and Anglo-Caribbean activist communities, with his infamous vodou doll ensuring that those involved in the computer centre occupation would not forget that there had been a Haitian among them. During the same period, the example of the Cuban Revolution nurtured hopes for radical social trans- formation and the Cuban state actively courted Black activists and intellectuals. Examining these cross-cultural and cross-linguistic exchanges highlights tensions regarding the political significance of race, in light of both the whiteness of the Cuban revolutionary government's leadership and the Duvalier dictatorship's claim to represent Black Power. These ties are yet another reminder that the activism of the period was deeply international in its contours, as those involved sought to articulate local responses to oppressive systems that did not stop at national borders.

NOTES

1   C.L.R James, in David Austin (ed.), *You Don't Play with Revolution: The Montreal Lectures of C.L.R. James* (Oakland: AK Press, 2009), 57.

2   Ibid, 66.

3   Ibid, 52.

4   Dennis Forsythe, *Let the Niggers Burn!* (Toronto: Black Rose Press, 1971), 14-15.

5   David Austin, *Fear of a Black Nation: Race, Sex, and Security in Sixties Montreal* (Toronto: Between the Lines, 2013), Sean Mills, *The Empire Within: Postcolonial Thought and Political Activism in Sixties Montreal* (Montreal: McGill-Queen's University Press, 2010), 95-118, David Austin, *Moving Against the System: The 1968 Congress of Black Writers and the Making of Global Consciousness* (Toronto: Between the Lines, 2018).

6   David Austin, *Fear of a Black Nation*, 136.

7   Lara Putnam. "To Study the Fragments/Whole: Microhistory and the Atlantic World." *Journal of Social History* 39.3 (2006): 619.

8   Michel-Rolph Trouillot, *Haiti: State Against Nation* (New York: New York University Press, 1990), 116-127.

9   Michel-Rolph Trouillot, *Haiti: State Against Nation*, 167; David Nicholls, *From Dessalines to Duvalier: Race, Colour, and National Independence in Haiti* (New Brunswick, NJ: Rutgers University Press, 1996), 214. Sean Mills, *A Place in the Sun: Haiti, Haitians, and the Remaking of Quebec* (Montreal: McGill-Queen's University Press, 2016), 80-1.

10   For more on Alfie Roberts and his analysis of the Caribbean Conference Committee and C.L.R. James, see Alfie Roberts, in David Austin (ed.), *A View for Freedom: Alfie Roberts Speaks on the Caribbean, Cricket, Montreal, and C.L.R. James* (Montreal: Alfie Roberts Institute, 2005).

11   As Fils-Aimé recalls, Carmichael stressed that the revolution was a slave revolt, whereas the Haitian emphasized the leadership of free people of color throughout the revolutionary

process. He would link this understanding of Haitian history to his own convictions that revolutions required a vanguard, which pushed him to take an active role rather than waiting for the masses to rise up.

12   See, for example, Leslie J-R. Péan, ed, *Entre savoir et démocratie: Les luttes de l'Union nationale des étudiants haïtiens sous le gouvernement de François Duvalier.* Montréal: Memoire d'Encrier, 2010.

13   Sean Mills, *The Empire Within*, 105. Multiple articles in *La Presse*, from February to April 1969, mention solidarity efforts in the Caribbean.

14   For some analysis of these attitudes toward vodou, see JM Murphy, "Black Religion and "Black Magic": Prejudice and Projection in Images of African-Derived Religions, *Religion* 20,4 (1990): 323–337; Adam M. McGee, "Haitian Vodou and Voodoo: Imagined Religion and Popular Culture,"*Studies in Religion/Sciences Religieuses* 41, 2 (2012): 231-256. On the use of "dolls," see Suzanne Preston Blier, *African Vodun: Art, Psychology, and Power* (Chicago: University of Chicago Press, 1995), 49-54.

15   "Une poupée vodou pour Me Sheppard." *La Presse*. March 11, 1970. 1. "Me Sheppard a raconté qu'il était déjà allé à Haïti (qu'il a appelée Tahiti) et qu'il connaissait la signification symbolique de cette poupée."

16   David Austin, *Moving Against the* System, 25.

17   Adeline Chancy, private email correspondence. August 20, 2019.

18   David Austin, *Moving Against the System*, 76.

19   Sean Mills, *The Empire Within*, 101, 114.

20   Sean Mills, *A Place in the Sun*, 86.

21   David Austin, *Moving Against the* System, 217, 219, 220, 223, 227. Michael O. West,"Walter Rodney and Black Power: Jamaican Intelligence and US Diplomacy." *African Journal of Criminology and Justice Studies* 1, 2 (2005): 24.

22   David Austin, *Fear of a Black Nation*, 24.

23   Asa McKercher, "Lifting the Sugarcane Curtain: Security, Solidarity, and Cuba's Pavilion at Expo 67." *Other Diplomacies, Other Ties: Cuba and Canada in the Shadow of the US.* (Toronto, Canada: University of Toronto Press, 2018), 97.

24   Ibid, 91.

25   Keith Bolender, "When Cuban-American Terrorism Came to Canada," *Other Diplomacies, Other Ties: Cuba and Canada in the Shadow of the US.* (Toronto, Canada: University of Toronto Press, 2018), 121.

26   David Austin, *Fear of a Black Nation*, 85; Sean Mills, *The Empire Within*, 106; David Austin, *Moving Against the System*, 48.

27   James traveled in the company of another longtime member of the Caribbean Conference Committee, Robert Hill, as well as John La Rose and Andrew Salkey. Andrew Salkey, *Havana Journal* (London: Penguin, 1971).

28   See Ruth Reitan, *The Rise and Decline of an Alliance: Cuba and African American Leaders in the 1960s*, (Lansing: Michigan State University Press, 1999); Mark Q. Sawyer, *Racial Politics in Post-Revolutionary Cuba*, (Cambridge: Cambridge University Press, 2006), 154-174; Besenia Rodriguez, "De la Esclavitud Yanqui a la Libertad Cubana": US Black Radicals, the Cuban Revolution, and the Formation of a Tricontinental Ideology." *Radical History Review* 2005, 92 (2005): 62-87; Cynthia A Young, "Havana Up in Harlem: LeRoi Jones, Harold Cruse and the Making of a Cultural Revolution." *Science & Society* 65,1 (2001): 12-38.

29   Sarah Seidman, "Tricontinental Routes of Solidarity: Stokely Carmichael in Cuba." *Journal of Transnational American Studies* 4, 2 (2012): 1-25; David Austin, *Moving Against the System*, 32.

30   Ibid, 217, 219, 220, 223, 227, 217.

31   Bernard Diederich, *1959: The Year that Inflamed the Caribbean*, (Princeton, NJ: Markus Wiener Publishers, 2009), 52, 54, 85-6, 100.

32   Sansaricq, Lidia, *Traición multiple* (Montréal: Éditions CIDIHCA, 2015).

33   Ollivier, Émile. Documents related to the Institut cubain d'amitié avec le peuple. October 5, 1975 – October 14, 1977. P0349/E2,0004. Fonds Émile Ollivier. Université de Montréal. Montréal, Québec, Canada.

34   Julia Sweig, *Inside the Cuban Revolution*, (Cambridge: Harvard University Press, 2002); Lillian Guerra, *Visions of Power in Cuba: Revolution, Redemption, and Resistance, 1959-1971* (Chapel Hill: University of North Carolina Press, 2012). For Cuban ties to revolts in the Anglophone Caribbean prior to the Grenada Revolution, see Brian Meeks, *Narratives of Resistance: Jamaica, Trinidad, the Caribbean* (Kingston: The University of West Indies Press, 2000). The 1979 revolutions in Grenada and Nicaragua both claimed kinship with the Cuban Revolution, but each followed a substantially different process. See Brian Meeks, *Caribbean Revolutions and Revolutionary Theory: An Assessment of Cuba, Nicaragua and Grenada* (London: MacMillan Caribbean, 1993).

35   David Austin, *Fear of a Black Nation*, 145.

36   Deborah A. Thomas, *Modern Blackness: Nationalism, Globalization, and the Politics of Culture in Jamaica*, (Durham, NC: Duke University Press, 2004); Kate Quinn, ed. *Black Power in the Caribbean*, (Gainesville: University Press of Florida, 2014).

37   David Austin, *Moving Against the System*, 203.

38   Alejandro de la Fuente, *A Nation for All: Race, Inequality, and Politics in Twentieth-century Cuba*, (Chapel Hill: University of North Carolina Press, 2001), 259-316.

39   C.L.R. James, *You Don't Play with Revolution*, 53.

40   David Austin, *Moving Against the System*, 129.

41   Ibid, 129.

42   Ibid, 129.

43   Ibid, 235.

44   Ibid, 26.

45   See, for example, Gil Martinez, "De l'ambiguïté du nationalisme bourgeois en Haïti," *Nouvelle Optique* 9 (1973): 1-32, and Benoit Joachim, "Sur l'esprit de couleur, " *Nouvelle Optique* 9 (1973) : 149-158.

46   "C'est la colonisation qui par le fer, le feu et le sang, avait ouvert dans les flancs mêmes de l'Histoire universelle la sanglante contradiction blanc-noir, pour dissimuler et justifier les rapports d'exploitation économique. " Quoted in Adeline Chancy, Unpublished notes on the Congrès des écrivains noirs (October 1968), 2. Originally in "Jean Price-Mars et le mythe de l'Orphée noir ou les aventures de la négritude." *L'Homme et la société* 7 (1968): 76.

47   David Austin, *Moving Against the System*, 15.

48   Ibid, 22.

49   "nous Haitiens nous connaissons bien" ; "masquer la constitution d'une bourgeoisie noire jouant à son tour le rôle de classe dominante"; Adeline Chancy, unpublished notes, 3.

50   "la pratique révolutionnaire, impliquant une authentique solidarité internationale et s'inspirant d'un humanisme total." Ibid, 3.

51   David Austin, *Fear of a Black Nation*, 145.

On Fire: The Crisis at Sir George Williams University (Montreal) and the Worldwide Revolution of 1968[1]

Michael O. West

I N THE WEE hours of the morning of February 11, 1969, a fire destroyed the computer centre at Sir George Williams University (now Concordia University) in Montreal, Quebec, Canada. It was the culmination of multiple, and related, events that began nearly a year earlier. The Sir George Crisis was part of the worldwide upheaval collectively called the Revolution of 1968, which encompassed not just the calendar year 1968 but also the years on both sides of it. Far from being just another campus uprising, of which there were many during the Revolution of 1968, the Sir George Crisis stood out on several counts. For sheer destruction (more than $2 million), the Sir George Crisis apparently was unrivaled worldwide. As many of the leading actors in the drama were students of African descent, the crisis spoke powerfully to the question of Blackness in Canada. Much of Canadian national identity and collective self-perception, including on issues of race, have been fashioned in opposition to the behemoth to the south (and north), the United States. The Sir George Crisis tested the Canadian color conceit (the notion that Canada, unlike the United States, has no tradition of apartheid and its accompanying racist venom), as it had rarely been tested in the modern era. The outcome offered scant comfort to exponents of the Canadian color conceit. Across a wide spectrum of Canadian society, the barrage of racist behaviors and invectives that accompanied the crisis would not have disgraced white supremacists anywhere, least of all in the United States.

Then there were the international aspects of the Sir George Crisis, which became linked to other developments related to the Revolution of 1968. These include the death of Martin Luther King Jr., the struggle over the Southern African white settler colony of Rhodesia, and the civil war in Nigeria arising from the breakaway Republic of Biafra. The Black students whose protests against racism on campus stood at the foundation of the Sir George Crisis were largely, although not exclusively, from the Caribbean, with all the attendant consequences back in their homelands. Small wonder, therefore, that some of the most notable events in the Caribbean during the Revolution of 1968, from

Jamaica in the northwest to Trinidad in the southeast, were directly linked to the Sir George Crisis. Especially important was the Trinidad Revolution, which the events at Sir George powerfully helped to ignite, and which in turn had an equally powerful impact on developments back in Montreal. Altogether, the Sir George Crisis was not just a Montreal or Canadian affair; it was also an incident with world-historical dimensions and implications.

Opening Context for the Sir George Crisis: The Revolution of 1968, the Death of Martin Luther King, and Black Power

The backdrop to the explosive culmination of the Sir George Crisis in February 1969, if not its ultimate cause, was some ten months in the making, having begun in April 1968. It was a momentous and majestic year, 1968, a year of protest and rebellion worldwide. There are not many historical parallels to the Revolution of 1968.[2] Among the few such parallels is the Revolution of 1848.[3] For worldwide reach, however, the Revolution of 1968 far surpassed the Revolution of 1848. The demographic character of these two global revolutions, 1848 and 1968, also differed. The Revolution of 1848 had a decidedly proletarian character—except few scholars seem to notice that the proletarians in revolt were not just European wage workers, but also enslaved Africans in the French, Dutch and Danish Caribbean, communities whose acts of self-emancipation were among the most profound and long-lasting achievements of 1848. By contrast, the Revolution of 1968 featured, primarily, young people, above all students, such as those involved in the Sir George Crisis.

A seminal event in the Revolution of 1968, including the Sir George Crisis, was the assassination on April 4, 1968 of the King of Love—as Nina Simone instantly christened him. "What will happen/ now that the King is dead?" Simone inquired musically on the passing of Martin Luther King Jr. At his death, King was identified, if not always associated, with three related struggles. These three struggles, which were worldwide in scope, centered on civil rights, Black Power, and Vietnam.

The struggle for civil rights, or the benefits of citizenship, was part of a larger worldwide campaign against colonialism in various forms. The struggle against apartheid, or Jim Crow, as apartheid was called in the United States, was one expression of the global anticolonial campaign—a campaign aimed at turning subjects into citizens.[4] In the post-World War II era, anticolonial nationalist movements in Asia, Africa, the islands of the seas and elsewhere, along with civil rights struggles in the metropolitan centers, largely succeeded in doing just that, turning subjects into citizens, legally speaking.

But then came a rude awakening. The journey from subjecthood to citizenship, it turned out, was more transition than transformation, more reform than revolution. The fundamental structures created by colonialism, including of the apartheid variety, remained in place after colonialism had officially ended. In short, colonialism had given way to neocolonialism, which was citizenship devoid of economic and social content—citizenship that failed to raise the living standards and transform the lives of former subjects.[5]

Which is where Black Power came in. Black Power, which was at once global in scope and integral to the global Revolution of 1968, offered a stinging critique of the emptiness of legal citizenship—citizenship in form alone. Instead, Black Power demanded citizenship with substance, that is, citizenship with socioeconomic content and African-centered cultural affirmation. Vietnam, meaning the United States war of imperialist aggression in Vietnam, represented an affront to Black Power and, more broadly, to the Revolution of 1968. In the particular case of the United States, the Black Power militants were all the more aggrieved because the Vietnam War, which the Vietnamese called the American War, vitiated the quest for substantive citizenship by diverting public funds away from social expenditures at home to military adventures abroad.

Martin Luther King was no Black Power militant. Like the Black Power militants, however, King had become keenly aware of the limitations of civil rights, which, typical of neocolonialism, delivered citizenship in form.[6] Like the Black Power militants, too, King was now demanding substantive citizenship with socioeconomic content, as evidenced by his last great political project, the Poor People's Campaign.[7] King's growing anti-capitalist stance and turn toward the politics of social democracy would earn him unlikely allies. Thus George Jackson, the imprisoned US Black Power militant and self-admitted "Marxist-Leninist-Maoist-Fanonist," claimed King (posthumously) as a fellow traveler, if not an outright comrade. "I'll be easy with it," said Jackson, "slip it in, like it was just common knowledge that King was a Maoist."[8] The King of Love, who was never short on grace (unlike many of those involved in the Sir George Crisis, especially university officials), may well have forgiven Jackson's Maoist imputation. A critic of Marxism and Black Power alike, although an informed one, having taken the time to familiarize himself with the literature on both movements,[9] King objected that the Black Power militants had forsaken the writings of his heroes, Mohandas Gandhi, and Leo Tolstoy. Instead, King groused, the Black Power militants were reading Frantz Fanon's anticolonial *and* anti-neocolonial demarche, *The Wretched of the Earth*. Conceding that it was "a well-written book, incidentally, with many penetrating insights," King all the same lamented that *Wretched* had become the "Bible" of Black Power.[10]

Amid his debate with the Black Power militants, King found himself in the throes of a dilemma. From the purely fiscal standpoint, not to mention the politics and morality of the matter, the war in Vietnam could not be squared with his Poor People's Campaign. Unlike the Black Power militants, though, King averted his gaze, refusing to face the contradiction head on. For a long time, too long, he remained mum on Vietnam, paralyzed by fear—that potent weapon of the powerful. It had not always been like that. In 1966, King had taken part in the historic March Against Fear—the very event that gave popular currency to Black Power as a slogan, if not as a movement.[11] Yet the tongue that had been so loose, and eloquent, in combatting the fear associated with the US anti-apartheid struggle—that very same tongue was tied by fear when it came to the war in Vietnam. On Vietnam, King recoiled at upsetting the US ruling class, major segments of which, politicians, foundations, media, formed an important part of his support network.

Malcolm X, that needle-eye prophet of Black liberation in the United States and icon of Black Power worldwide, had condemned the corrupting clout of the US ruling class on the Civil Rights Movement.[12] Malcolm was now dead but Martin, a sometime target of Malcolm's barbs, which (his grace notwith-standing) he returned, trembled at provoking the fury of those who were waging war in Vietnam. But ultimately Martin, like Malcolm, came from the Black prophetic tradition.[13] King could only bite his tongue for so long. Like the biblical prophet Jeremiah, whom he liked to quote, King had fire shut up in his bones.[14]Fiery jeremiads of a related sort would become part and parcel of the Sir George Crisis, in the course of which fear would also be extinguished by fire.

Pulled by the imperatives of his Poor People's Campaign, and pushed by his Black Power sparring partners, King eventually issued his own public jeremiad against the war in Vietnam.[15] The date of the denunciation was April 4, 1967. Aghast at King's ingratitude, as they called it, to say nothing of his presumption, as a mere civil rights figure, to speak on matters of war and peace, the US ruling class cut him off. The political support, the money, the favorable publicity—all dried up. For good measure the FBI, armed with evidence of King's extramarital dalliances, called to invite him to commit suicide.[16] The King of Love, who indeed had been overly generous with his affections, declined the invitation. No matter: his days were numbered. Back in Memphis, Tennessee, the starting point of the March Against Fear, a white-supremacist assassin laid awaiting. Coincidentally or not, the assassin struck on April 4, 1968—exactly a year to the day of King's denunciation of the Vietnam War, or rather the American War.

Rhodesia Refracted in White and Black, Then and Now

Fleeing the United States, King's assassin was apprehended in London, on the road to Rhodesia, which was then a gathering point for white supremacists worldwide—an operational base for murderers, mercenaries, torturers, and sadists of every variety.[17] Decades after being supplanted by the African-ruled nation-state of Zimbabwe, the ontology of white Rhodesia retains a dazzling, and deadly, hold on the global racist imaginary. Dylann "Storm" Roof, the Nazi-nicknamed assassin who struck in Charleston, South Carolina in 2015, murdering nine congregants in a Black church, styled himself "The Last Rhodesian." Actually Roof, who deliberately targeted a church with origins in the early 1800s, one of whose founders included the martyred anti-slavery conspirator Denmark Vesey, was far from being the last of the breed. There are still many more where he came from, some of whom have operated under the telling hashtag: #MakeZimbabweRhodesiaAgain.[18] For these Rhodesian *bittereinders*, Cecil Rhodes, the eponymous founder of Rhodesia, must not fall, a racist retort to the South African-born, contemporary transatlantic movement called Rhodes Must Fall.[19]

With Black Power in the forefront, the Revolution of 1968 had demanded the fall of Rhodes and his creation, Rhodesia. The first Black Power march in Britain targeted Rhodesia.[20] A Black Power organ in Trinidad condemned Britain for invading its Caribbean colony of "small. Black Anguilla " to suppress Black Power mobilization, while rejecting military action to end settler colonialism in "BIG, WHITE Rhodesia."[21] Still in Trinidad, a Black Power militant condemned the Black prime minister as a neocolonial pawn, "our Afro-Saxon Ian Smith," a reference to the white Rhodesian leader."[22] The Rhodesia refrain could also be heard at the Congress of Black Writers, an event of fundamental importance in the evolution of the Sir George Crisis, and one to which we will have occasion to repeatedly return. Rhodesia remerged as a topic of note during the Sir George Crisis itself. As they battled the university administration over racism on campus, the protesters drew parallels between their struggle and the global campaign to turn Rhodesia into Zimbabwe.[23] For one of those protesters, Stanley Chiwaro, the parallels were personal. A self-described "Brother in struggle," Chiwaro was an African nationalist from Rhodesia, or Zimbabwe-to-be. In a notable nod to Pan-African comity, Chiwaro was also president of Sir George's Caribbean Students' Society, a group whose members were deeply involved in the protests attendant on the crisis.[24]

A March in Montreal and an Accusation of Academic Racism

The murder of Martin Luther King, a critic of Rhodesia, brought out huge throngs worldwide to grieve, to protest, and to remember him. Montreal was no exception. There, as elsewhere, the martyr's blood supplied the paint for a vast multicolor backdrop, with Montreal's King memorial march standing out for its transracial, transnational and, not least, trans-African character. Black people of every description, Canadians, and non-Canadians, Anglophones, and Francophones, domestic servants, and professionals, to say nothing of students at all levels, were prominent among those memorializing the King of Love in Montreal. It was a rare display of combination across national, class, generational, and linguistic lines in Black Montreal.[25] As a mass event, the King memorial march effectively launched the Revolution of 1968 in the city.

The changing wind succeeded in firing up a group of students at Sir George. The students were alleging persistent racial discrimination in a particular class, involving a particular instructor in biology named Perry Anderson. Nor could the complaining students vote with their feet, not if they were biology majors with ambitions of medical careers, as many of them were. They could not avoid Professor Anderson, who taught a required class in their discipline. The students in question were all men of color and foreign. Not all of them, though, were of African descent and from the Caribbean, at least not initially. At the outset, Professor Anderson's accusers included two Asian students, which gave the accusation a Bandung-like quality—the 1955 Afro-Asian Conference, held in the Indonesian city of Bandung, being a touchstone event in the prehistory of the Revolution of 1968, and especially of Black Power.[26]

The Sir George students had been nursing their grievances for some time. Yet, they feared to directly confront power in the form of their instructor—not altogether unlike Martin Luther King facing the quandary of Vietnam. Then came the King memorial march in Montreal, which, for the students, doubled as a march against fear. Newly emboldened, they filed a grievance against Professor Perry Anderson with the university on April 29, 1968, hard on the heels of the King memorial march. The Sir George Crisis had begun. Except it was no longer a Bandung-style undertaking, the Asian students having declined to join their grieving Afro-Caribbean counterparts. For the moment, anyhow, the Black students were on their own.

Since the students filed their grievance near the end of the academic year, the university looked into the matter over the summer. The investigation, if it may be so called, consisted of informal talks, and involved three parties: Professor Anderson, the chair of his department, and the dean of science. The student complainants, who were on summer holiday, had no part in the deliberations.

They were not consulted. This did not prevent the dean from concluding that the allegation of racial discrimination against Professor Anderson was baseless and without merit. The dean did allow that Anderson's teaching needed improvement—the students having accused the professor not just of racism, but also of academic and professional incompetence. Even so, Professor Anderson, then also a graduate student at neighboring McGill University, was promoted, going from the rank of instructor to that of assistant professor.

On returning to school for the new academic year, 1968-69, the students learned, second-hand, of Professor Anderson's vindication. As if to compound the scorn, the university had not even bothered to inform them of the disposition of their grievance. Marvin Gaye, whose music was consistent with the mood of Black Power and formed part of the soundtrack of the Revolution of 1968, may have related to the indignity of it all. Said Gaye in one of his better-known songs: "You could have told me yourself/ that you loved someone else/ instead I heard it through the grapevine." The aggrieved students would not respond to the university in kind, through the grapevine. When again they spoke, theirs would be words of brimstone, aimed directly at academic power. Fire next time.

Significantly, the university had changed the terms, and therefore the target, of the protests. The students' grievance had been specific, aimed at an individual instructor. The university's response transformed the specific into the general. Dispensing with even the pretense of a credible investigation, as even critics of the protesting students admitted, the university resorted to knee-jerk denial, tightly circling the wagon around the accused instructor. Objectively, if not subjectively, Professor Anderson was now embedded in the *laager,* as the white brotherhood (*broederbond*) was called in Afrikaner-ruled apartheid South Africa, which is to say Rhodesia writ large.[27] The students were no longer in contention with an individual instructor. They were now confronting the structures of power in the university—in other language, institutional racism, the organized and coordinated expression of white male supremacy. But that confrontation would have to wait, for the students had more immediate concerns.

The Congress of Black Writers and Black Power at Sir George

The Martin Luther King memorial march earlier in 1968 was merely prelude. The Revolution of 1968 arrived in Montreal full-blown in the latter part of 1968. It came in the form of the antinomian political convention, three of which were held in the city, centering respectively on civil rights, Black Power, and Vietnam. These three issues were transnational in scope. They were the same ones King was grappling with at his death.

In Montreal, Black Power stood athwart the struggle for civil rights in

Canada and the movement against the war in Vietnam, cohering them all. It was therefore appropriate that the Black Power convention was sandwiched between the other two, notably the Conference on Black Involvement in Canada and the Hemispheric Conference to End the War in Vietnam. The Black Power convention, called the Congress of Black Writers, was a momentous event in the evolution of Black Power globally, not just in Montreal and Canada.[28] Contemporary Canadian critics did not see it that way. Summing up the consensus of the critics, journalist Dorothy Eber, author of the first book-length work on the Sir George Crisis, offered with acerbic disapproval that the Congress of Black Writers, "did not waste its time with writing." Eber's generalized "distortion by omission" would elicit a powerful response from Dennis Forsythe, editor of the defining collection on the crisis from the standpoint of the protesters.[29] Contrary to Eber's assertion, the Congress of Black Writers featured numerous writers, of fiction and nonfiction, including some famous names.[30] Unabashedly, the writers and other delegates had gathered with a specific aim in mind. They were at once essaying and assaying toward global Black liberation, on radical and revolutionary lines, which is precisely what raised the hackles of Eber and other critics, in and out of Canada.

The students involved in the Sir George Crisis assuredly were not among those critics. Indeed, many of the students were central players in the Congress of Black Writers, while also engaging with the other two conventions on both sides of it. As they turned their attention back to their campus grievances, the students were on fire, all remaining fears having been drenched in the baptism of the Congress of Black Writers, which the coming uprising at Sir George would mirror in its critique of racism, imperialism, and capitalism. The anti-capitalist *Communist Manifesto*, the key theoretical outcome of the Revolution of 1848, and a document that would powerfully influence antinomian politics worldwide for a century and a half to come, had famously declared that the specter of communism was haunting Europe.[31] At the end of 1968, a specter also began to envelop Sir George Williams University, the specter of Black Power.

Black Power stood for nothing if not for relevance, a word constantly on the lips of its adherents—relevance of all kind, in all matters. Red-hot, the Sir George students rudely and roughly demanded a relevant inquiry into their allegation against Professor Perry Anderson, the veneer of Caribbean courtesy having since vanished. The principal, as the head of the university was then called, agreed, and formed an investigation committee. It was a major reversal. The principal, Robert Rae, had overruled the dean of science who previously exonerated Professor Anderson—and that at the behest of a bunch of Negroes from the tropics, outside agitators all.

The Deans' Coup and the Racist Campaign on Campus; or Thermidor Comes to Sir George

So flagrant an affront to the Canadian white academic patriarchy warranted counterrevolution on campus. Pitchforks at the ready, the aggrieved men of power responded with fire and fury. Neither would stand—Principal Rae nor his ruling, meaning his overruling of the dean of science. Feeling the heat, Rae abruptly resigned, citing "poor health." Physically, Rae was fine—fine enough to soon find alternate employment at York University in Toronto. It was his political health that had declined so dreadfully and rapidly.[32] Rae's removal from office ended all prospects of the investigation of relevance the students had demanded, and he had promised. The Sir George Crisis was now slouching toward the Gomorrah of February 11, 1969.

In 1967, the year before the Sir George Crisis began, a group of military officers, spearheaded by colonels, seized power in Greece. Theirs was called the "colonels' coup." By extrapolation, the putsch against Robert Rae at Sir George may be designated the "deans' coup." The one coup, like the other, was aimed at partisans of the Revolution of 1968. Rae subsequently struck back at those who ousted him, terming them a band of "Pontius Pilates," after the harsh and callous Roman judge who sentenced Jesus Christ to death by crucifixion.[33] Rae had a point. They had something in common with Pontius Pilate, and with the Greek colonels too, the men who assumed power in the deans' coup at Sir George.

At the head of them all stood John O'Brien. Lately dean of the Faculty of Arts, the deans' coup catapulted O'Brien to the top of the university hierarchy, where he remained triumphant for the next decade and a half.[34] The O'Brien regime, as it was quickly dubbed, had been installed. One could say, too, that the Age of O'Brien had begun. Either way, Thermidor, the shorthand for counterrevolution bequeathed by the French Revolution, had descended on Sir George Williams University, although its iron hand had not yet fallen. One need not be a Leninist, which at one historical moment represented the highest stage of resistance to Thermidor, to know what is to be done.[35] John O'Brien and his confederates, a few of whom, though assuredly not O'Brien himself, claimed Leninist credentials, knew exactly what was to be done. It was to put out the firestorm of the student uprising, to which their coup was supplying the fuel. The arsonists were now posing as firefighters—a reinvention so typical of Thermidor.

Disinformation (psychological warfare) was a key part of the reinvention, which was really counterinsurgency on campus, Vietnam-style. The O'Brien regime seized on a trope long deployed by the traducers of Black folk everywhere. The word on campus, quietly circulated in writing by O'Brien himself, was that the protesting students had violent proclivities and potentially posed a danger to the community. Resentful of the racist, and gendered, slur, three Black male students confronted O'Brien in his office. He feigned ignorance, coolly denying the existence of the document they had come to inquire about. Knowing better, the irate students proceeded to rifle through O'Brien's files, privacy and confidentiality be damned. They readily found the smoking gun. Having caught O'Brien in the discursive web of his own lies, the students demanded instant reparation, that is, an apology in writing, which was supplied post-haste.[36]

O'Brien had instant revenge, and what cruel revenge it was. No sooner had the uninvited sable visitors left his office, *mea culpa* triumphantly in hand, than he summoned the police. He had, O'Brien informed the lawmen, been wrongfully imprisoned in his office and "felt compelled to write a letter of apology to the students in order to gain exit."[37] In turn, the police charged two of the three students involved with kidnapping, extortion, and conspiracy, which collectively carried a penalty of up to thirty-three years in prison (O'Brien could not identify the third student, who was wearing a cap with the likeness of Ernesto "Che" Guevara pulled down over his face). Thus was made manifest at Sir George the trope of the dangerous Black man, the violent Black man. It mattered little that affirming the trope also meant ignoring, and erasing, those protesters who were neither Black nor male.

Outside the university, commentators urged the deportation of the agitators—the foreign agitators. Inside the university, the racist and nativist dog-whistling found fertile ground among students. Unlike some of their elders in and out of the university, though, not all students critiquing the protests had mastered the art of racial circumlocution. Or perhaps desired to do so. Several students, unschooled in diplomatic lingo but well acquainted with the idiom of the Ku Klux Klan, and imitating its fashion too, appeared in the Sir George cafeteria, hoods, and all. "Send the niggers back home," their placards bluntly demanded.[38] The specter of Black Power had come face to face with the white-supremacist spectacle. Nor was that the end of it; there was worse to come. Placard-carrying racists would make an even more searing and deadly demand on the dramatic last day of the Sir George Crisis. "Let the niggers burn," they gave out, deploying both the written (placard) and spoken (shouted) word, as the computer centre in which the protesters were holed up erupted in flames— words that were subsequently immortalized in the title of the best-known book on the crisis, *Let the Niggers Burn!*[39] It is worth noting, though, that the demand for deportation preceded the one for immolation, which is to say incitement to racist murder.

The African Canadian Factor: A Tale of Neglect

Demands to punish the protesters, whether by deportation, immolation, or other means, sprang from the assumption that they were all Black and foreign. The conflation of the two, Blackness and foreignness, deepened the erasure surrounding the protests, this time of African Canadians. Yet African Canadians, many of them lacking formal association with Sir George or any other university, were directly involved in the crisis. Some of these individuals came from long-standing and largely working-class Black communities in Montreal, despite a history of social distance between those communities and the city's Black university students, many of them from outside Canada. In and out of Montreal, African Canadians also were made to pay part of the price for the Sir George Crisis, including greater police harassment, increased suspicion by white people, cruder comments in public spaces, even loss of employment.[40]

From the standpoint of loss of personal liberty, it was an African Canadian, Martin Bracey, who paid the highest price of all for the Sir George Crisis. A Sir George student, Bracey was also a member of the International, a Maoist group that provided some of the most militant white supporters of the protests.[41] Politicians and media pundits alike credited (or rather blamed) the International for the popularity of the *Little Red Book,* the famous collection of Mao Zedong's sayings, among the protesters.[42] Actually the *Little Red Book*, then the second best-seller worldwide (after the Bible), was virtually required accessory for partisans of the Revolution of 1968, whether of the Maoist persuasion or not—its popularity aided by its pocket-book size, its sturdy vinyl cover, and its low price, courtesy of Chinese state subsidies.[43]Martin Bracey, no doubt still clutching his copy of the *Little Red Book* (it is unclear if George Jackson ever joined Mao in his political pantheon) was condemned to five years in prison by a vindictive Canadian judiciary, the legitimacy of which he openly and loudly rejected in court.[44]

Bracey's sentence was twice as long as the punishment meted out to any other individual involved the protests, including Rosie Douglas. The single most consequential figure in organizing the Congress of Black Writers, the Caribbean-born Douglas would subsequently, and erroneously, be assigned primary blame for the Sir George Crisis by the managers of Canadian historical memory, which (in this case, anyhow) bears a greater resemblance to the Canadian color conceit than to actual Canadian history.[45] Singling out Caribbean troublemakers (Douglas headed a longer list) and erasing African Canadians, who presumably have no history of making trouble, are merely opposite sides of a single coin designed to underwrite the mythology of the Canadian color conceit.

The Trinidadian Factor and the Myth of Caribbean Exclusivity

Tellingly, it was the critics of the rising on the Sir George campus who emphasized its foreignness, by which they meant its Caribbean-ness. That Caribbean students were in the vanguard of the protests goes without saying. Those who filed the grievance against Professor Perry Anderson, the starting point of the crisis, all hailed from the Caribbean. The occupation of the computer centre, especially, increased the public prominence of certain individuals, a number of them from Trinidad. Notable among these was Kelvin "Rap" Robinson, whose nickname honored the US Black Power personality H. "Rap" Brown (later Jamil Al-Amin), whose legal troubles back home had precluded his solicited participation in the Congress of Black Writers.[46] Also increasing in prominence with the occupation of the computer centre was Leroi Butcher, a subsequent contributor to the collection *Let the Niggers Burn!*, in which he wrote some of the most trenchant lines about the Sir George Crisis as well as the Congress of Black Writers, in which he was also deeply involved.[47] A native of St. Lucia, Butcher was claimed by the Trinidadians, in a good-natured gesture to a "small islander," as spiritually one of their own.[48]

The Trinidadian influence on the occupation of the computer centre was not just political. It was also cultural, as was the case at the Congress of Black Writers, where a Trinidadian-led band, Raymond Watts and His Combo, supplied the music. In the course of the Sir George Crisis, one professorial critic of the protests likened them to a "Caribbean festival," by which he presumably meant carnival.[49] As it happened, the occupation of the computer centre coincided with the run-up to carnival in Trinidad. Imbued with the spirit of the season, aficionados enriched the musical repertoire of the occupation with calypso renditions, some of them created under the inspiration of the protests, consistent with the genre's improvisational nature.[50]

Despite its Trinidadian and wider Caribbean flavor, political and cultural, it is not at all the case that the protests exclusively were a Caribbean undertaking. The narrative of Caribbean exclusivity was not the handiwork of the Caribbean students, who mostly emphasized their Blackness, except (understandably) when responding to attacks on their foreignness.[51] Rather, the Caribbean exclusivist line was the design of nativist Canadian spin-doctors bent on painting the protests as foreign impositions on the Canadian body politic. The amazing diversity of those arrested at the end of the crisis, national, racial, linguistic, and gender diversity, gave the lie to the notion of Caribbean exclusivity. The West Indians were front and center—but they were not alone, not any longer. They had acquired non-Caribbean allies along the way. Ruefully, those allies are largely absent from written accounts of the protests, including accounts by Caribbean participants and writers. With only fleeting exceptions, such omissions are true of even the classic collection, *Let the Niggers Burn!*[52] The self-described "Black manifesto" of the Sir George Crisis,[53] this collection includes prose and poetry by seven male authors who played various roles in the protests, all of them from the Caribbean.

Discordant Caribbean Voices: Indo-West Indians and the Crisis

Pointedly, the Caribbean vanguard role in the Sir George Crisis did not extend to a particular group of students from the Caribbean: those of Indian or South Asian descent. In part, the skepticism of many Indo-West Indians toward the Afro-West Indian-led protests reflected political and ethnic fissures back home, especially in Trinidad and Guyana. The same mindset was evident in the ambivalence of many Indo-West Indians toward Black Power, despite the insistence of its theorists and leaders that Black Power in the Caribbean necessarily encompassed people of South Asian no less than those of African descent.[54]

At Sir George, A. R. Ali voiced what he described as the consensus of South Asian-descended students from the Caribbean toward the protests. Indo-West Indians rejected the militant antiracist stance of Afro-West Indians, Ali offered, because "we knew that, win or lose, any charge of racism brought into the open was bound to do more harm than good." Ali did not deny the reality of Canadian racism. But rather than being embedded in the structures and institutions of society, as the protesters eventually came around to arguing, Ali maintained that racial "prejudice was the child of ignorance and could not be solved by confrontation."[55]

As an antidote to racism, Ali placed his faith in amelioration rather than activism. Accordingly, he went on, he and other Indo-West Indian students, "condemned the methods employed" by the protesters "because we believed that respect could not be demanded but earned." That stance, affirming the existence of racism, albeit characterized as attitudinal, while rejecting confrontational methods to combat it, earned the respect of neither the antiracist activists nor the racist campaigners. Ali summed up the dilemma thusly, "From the Afro West Indian students, we Indo-West Indians are accused of being racists, uncle tomists, opportunists, boot-lickers, stooges of the administration etc. etc. From the Whites, we are dirty niggers, revolutionary pigs who should be deported, ingrates, etc. etc."[56] Ali did not speak for all students of South Asian descent from the Caribbean, including Trinidadian Robert Ranjitsingh, who was among those arrested at the conclusion of the Sir George Crisis. The most conspicuous Indo-West Indian in the protests was Joey Jagan, son of Cheddi

Jagan, a leading figure in Guyanese politics.[57] Joey Jagan, who was also arrested in the end, informally served as his father's Black Power advisor.[58]

Gendering the Crisis: Women in the Protests

At Sir George, women served in much more than an advisory role in the crisis. To be sure, the public leadership of the protests, along with the most visible faces of the rising, were male. In this sense, the Sir George Crisis is comparable to the Congress of Black Writers, which featured an all-male roster of scheduled speakers.[59] In neither case, however, did the androcentric lineup at the podium and the microphone tell the full story of the event. Regarding the Congress of Black Writers, women made up forty percent (twelve out of thirty) of the original organizing committee.[60] Yet if past (and current) practice held, and there is little reason to think it did not, women probably did more of the congress's work than their official representation on its organizing committee suggested. The Sir George Crisis, which was far more wide-ranging in time than the Congress of Black Writers, a months-long series of ever-changing events, as opposed to a four-day happening focused on a set of related themes, likely reproduced related patterns, except more acutely. In human affairs, crises are the greater shatters of social norms and conventions, the real engines of transformation. So, it was also with the Sir George Crisis, which, precisely because of its protracted character, would have opened up new avenues of expression and leadership for women.

One of those women was Valerie Belgrave. A native of Trinidad, like various prominent male actors in the Sir George Crisis, Belgrave was also a veteran of the Congress of Black Writers. At the time of the crisis, she served as secretary of Sir George's West Indian Society, which made her a crucial interlocutor in the group's communications and negotiations with foes and friends alike, the university administration as well as those expressing solidarity with the protests, whether from near or far. A scion of Trinidad's middle class, her father was a medical doctor, the very profession to which those who filed the grievance against Professor Perry Anderson aspired, Belgrave unfailingly was smartly turned out, from head to toe a model of her own unique Black Power sartorial style. Belgrave's then husband (they later divorced), fellow Trinidadian and fellow Sir George student, Teddy Belgrave, complemented her on the cultural terrain. Teddy Belgrave, who went on to a distinguished career in Trinidad's pan music scene as a designer of steel drums, would have been among the foremost calypsonians in the Sir George protests. In the end, the Belgraves were also among those arrested and prosecuted. Having paid her dues to the cause, Valerie Belgrave would make yet another stellar contribution to the Sir George Crisis. In penning one of the finest personal accounts of the crisis, she enriched history and historiography in equal measure, both telling and interpreting the events in which she participated, and for which she (like so many others) was made to pay by the Canadian state.[61]

The Ordinariness of the Protests and Paths Not Taken

The outcome of the crisis was not preordained. It could have turned out differently, but for nativist Negrophobia. Except for the spectacle of Black foreigners in the lead, the Sir George protests were anything but extraordinary. In the Revolution of 1968, the most dramatic form of student protest was the seizure and occupation of campus buildings. Soon, an informal protocol for dealing with such occupations emerged. On taking over a building, the occupiers would issue "nonnegotiable" demands, to which university administrators generally responded with "ultimatums" demanding an end to the occupation. In due course, a peaceful settlement would usually be negotiated, assuming the weary occupiers unilaterally had not already left, having (they said) made their point.

This, roughly, was the formula for ending an occupation by white students in 1967 at Montreal's McGill University—an institution, incidentally, founded by a man who was deeply involved in the business of slavery, James McGill. Just a couple of weeks before the Sir George Crisis came to its inglorious end, Black students at Brandeis University (outside Boston) had seized control of a building that included the university's computer centre, only to abandon their encampment after ten days. Brandeis administrators had learned a valuable lesson from a previous occupation at New York City's Columbia University where involving the police tended to increase support for the protesters. Waiting them out was a better option.[62]

Then there was Sir George strongman John O'Brien and his team of hardliners. They would not play by the rules, not where assumed Black foreigners were concerned, anyhow. It could hardly have been otherwise. The O'Brien regime owed its very existence to a rejection of those rules, which Robert Rae, the defenestrated principal, had vainly sought to respect. Speaking of which, few words were on the lips of the Sir George protesters as often as respect, as the student A. R. Ali disapprovingly observed. "The Black Students," the archival document of the protests announced in aguish, and with total disregard for the women protesters, "are self-respecting men!"[63] It only remained for Aretha Franklin, at once the self-respecting queen of soul and outstanding demander of respect in the Revolution of 1968, "All I'm askin'/ Is for a little respect," to make an appearance at Sir George, as she previously did at a protest at historically Black Howard University in Washington, D. C.[64]However, respect was not something the O'Brien regime would accord the protesters.

Just the opposite. In a final act of disrespect, O'Brien double-crossed the protesters by going back, at the last minute, on an agreement that had been hashed out by negotiators for the two sides to peacefully end the two-week standoff at the computer centre. It was not the first time in the crisis that O'Brien had acted deceitfully: he previously lied about accusing the Black protesters of being prone to violence. When caught in this lie and forced to retract it, O'Brien then turned around and retracted his retraction and, to boot, caused two students to be arrested on charges that potentially carried decades of imprisonment. It followed almost willy-nilly that, in the end, he would reject a negotiated outcome that seemed to offer the protesters a measure of respect, to say nothing of vindication. Instead, O'Brien unleashed the iron hand of Thermidor by calling in the Montreal police riot squad. The protesters, all of them, would be crushed in a military-style operation and hauled off to jail and prosecution, although not before a pair of riotous events ensued.

Of Broken Computers and Bloodied Black Bodies: The Riot Against Property and the Riot Against People

The police operation gave birth to the narrative of the "computer centre riot," the descriptor by which the Sir George Crisis would come to be best known. The general assumption, in the popular usage and imagination, is that the rioters and the protesters were one and the same. In fact, there was not one but two riots in the computer centre on that fateful morning of February 11, 1969, one against property and the other against people. The riot against property, namely the equipment in the occupied computer centre, was the doing of the protesters. It is also this riot against property, that has attracted the bulk of journalistic interest on the subject, along with much of the scholarly inquiry, as befitting a capitalist society with an attention-grabbing media.[65] The second riot was directed against people, meaning the occupiers of the computer centre, and carried out by the aptly named riot squad. Despite a trail of documentary evidence, this other "computer centre riot," perpetrated by the police, has garnered far less attention than the one orchestrated by the protesters.[66]

The riot against property sprang from a sense of betrayal. Throughout the occupation of the computer centre, the computers remained secured and undamaged, the protesters vigilantly guarding the rooms that housed the hulking machines (as computers were then). That is, until the university sent in the riot squad, after going back on its agreement with the protesters. Feeling betrayed, the protesters took out their wrath on the computers, the importance of which they were only too aware: The decision to occupy the computer centre was motivated, in the first place, by reports that the university had designated it a strategic asset worthy of special protection during the protests. Blow after angry blow, the protesters destroyed the computers, using axes they had procured from the emergency fire equipment in the vicinity of the computer center.

The collection of the axes, in advance, invites the question of premeditation—in other words, conspiracy, a charge that would later be brought against the protesters. Had they collected the axes with a specific aim in mind, notably the destruction of the computers? But if the intent all along had been to destroy them, why had the protesters gone through the trouble of taking such meticulous care of the computers for two long weeks? Alternately the protesters, while hoping for the best (a negotiated settlement), could have prepared for the worst (something akin to what actually happened) by collecting the axes. This scenario, too, seems unlikely. In the destruction of the computers, the evidence is more suggestive of spontaneity than premeditation. Confronted with a heavy-handed, military-style police force, the protesters most probably acted on instinct rather than on design in putting the axes to the computers.

The critics would have none of it. Their eyes swilling with crocodile tears, they bloviated about broken computers, all the while thrashing the protesters as so many ferocious luddites and unhinged nihilists.[67] Of the broken accord that drove the protesters into so consequential a blunder, to say nothing of the broken hearts and lives, the critics had nothing to offer—nothing but silence. The critics were equally deafening in their silence about the campaign to criminalize Black men as congenitally violent. Again, the loquaciousness of the critics on the subject of broken computers stood in stark contrast to their speechlessness in the face of demands to deport "niggers," even to burn them. In the event, news of the damage caused by the destruction of the computers, as distinct from the ensuing political and public-relations disaster for the protesters, was (and remains) much exaggerated. In the assessment of one analyst, the damage amounted only to a "major inconvenience."[68] Soon, the computer centre was up and running again, with newer and better equipment—all paid for with insurance money.[69]

The bill for the riot against property settled, no one paid for the other riot, the one against the protesters. And a racist and sexist riot it was, perpetrated by the police. One of the theme songs of the occupation of the computer centre was a tune inspired by the resistance prophecy of Jeremiah,[70] and then set to music in the US African American spirituals, before being delivered to social movements worldwide.[71] The tune defiantly proclaimed: "We shall not/ We shall not be moved/ Just like a tree that's planted by the waters/ We shall not be moved." And yet the Sir George protesters were moved, viciously and violently moved by the Montreal police riot squad. As one policeman, apparently on the way into the computer centre, explained apropos of the protesters: "There won't be any brutality. They'll get what they deserve."[72] Roosevelt Williams, writing in that indispensable text on the Sir George Crisis, *Let the Niggers Burn!* deconstructed the police doublespeak. "Armed with guns and riot sticks and with a racist, capitalist mentality," Williams offered, "the police were prepared to draw blood; and this they did."[73]

As Williams implied, the police had a special animus against those of a darker hue, including the women. Although comprising less than half of the nearly 100 individuals in the computer centre when the police arrived, the Black occupiers were singled out for especially brutal treatment. Black women were prominent among the victims, subjected to bigoted bile as well as sexual violence. Besides deriding them as "Aunt Jemima," the police "in a violent way felt up" black women.[74] "No one was willing to listen to how the black females were taunted verbally and physically," bemoaned Roosevelt Williams, using uncharacteristically cagey language. "The police had their way and were congratulated for it."[75]

The police also had their way with Black men, though differently. Their bodies grounded in broken glass, the men were kicked in the groin and genitalia, the victims of this particular treatment including Leroi Butcher.[76] The story of the longer-term effects of such state terror remains to be told. The police raid on the computer centre, which is to say the police riot, was also an attack on Black sexuality and Black reproduction. The police, on the contrary, were praised for their supposed kid-glove treatment of the protesters in the media, the so-called first draft of history.[77] Not for nothing did the poet of the Black liberation lore, herself an actor in the Revolution of 1968, avow: "You may write me down in history/ With your bitter, twisted lies/ You may trod me in the very dirt/ But still, like dust, I'll rise."[78]

Sir George Ablaze, or Whose Conspiracy?
A Meditation on the Origin of the Fire

Pandemonium arose in the occupied computer centre on that February morning, caused not just by the arrival of the police but also by the eruption of flames. The months-long crisis had included a great many outbursts, some more fiery that others, but all in the form of contretemps. Now, Sir George Williams University was ablaze, literally on fire. It remains a mystery, the origins of that fire. Not so to the powers that were, the university administrators, the politicians, the police, the judiciary, the media, for whom the culprits were self-evident, namely the protesters. Consequently, conspiracy to commit arson, along with the previously mentioned conspiracy to destroy property (computers), would become the two main legal charges against the protesters. The prosecution was reaching. The case in support of conspiracy to destroy the computers faced considerable hurdles, but it could be made with some credibility. The same could not be said for the charge of arson against the protesters, to say nothing of conspiracy to commit arson. In essence, the claim that the protesters deliberately set the computer centre on fire is a claim that they had some sort of collective death pact or exhibited a disposition toward mass suicide. It is an assertion that is flatly contradicted by the actions of the protesters, including their frantic efforts to escape the burning computer centre.

There were three possible ways out of the inferno. One was through the windows, except that route would have entailed jumping from the location of the computer centre: the ninth floor of the fourteen-story building. Braving the frigid temperatures, the protesters did open the windows, but only to get some relief from the choking smoke. No one chose to exit the computer centre through the windows. Seemingly, there was nary a suicidal soul among the protesters. Such, apparently, was the calculation of the police, their *ex-post-facto* claims of conspiracy to commit arson notwithstanding. On the ground, the police strategy was predicated on the protesters behaving the way they actually did; rationally. Accordingly, the police focused on the alternate escape routes, that is, the two doors to the computer centre. At one door, they concentrated their forces, taking care to barricade the other door from the outside, effectively leaving the protesters with only one way out. The protesters, however, were not to be outfoxed. They chopped down the barricaded door, making the axes they had used to destroy the computers do double duty. All the same, the protesters labored in vain, for the police soon rounded them all up. The larger point, though, is that the protesters almost certainly did not conspire to commit arson, if by that it is meant deliberately starting the fire in the computer center.

There are other potential explanations for the origin of the fire. It could have begun accidentally sparked by an electrical malfunction traceable to the destruction of the computers. Perhaps also the culprit was a careless smoker, as undoubtedly there would have been many smokers present, among the occupiers and the police alike, all lighting up indoors, as was the custom in that era. Maybe, just maybe, tobacco, a crop that owed its commodification to the enslavement of Africans and, in the form of the cigarette, reappeared as a nonpartisan adjunct of both the Revolution of 1968 and the Thermidorian reaction to it, was to blame for the fire at Sir George.

But then, again, maybe not. On the origin of the fire, the police, the prosecutors, and the other wielders of power were not the only ones to play the blame game. Some protesters blamed the police, or provocateurs in their pay.[79] Bukka Rennie, who was among those arrested after the door to the computer centre was chopped down, accused the police not only of starting the fire but of doing so with murderous motives. "Their intention," said Rennie, peppering his speech with Caribbean patois, "was to burn we inside a dey, because people were on the streets shouting, burn, niggers, burn."[80] Such an outcome would not have been without precedence. The enslaved African Marie-Joseph Angélique was executed in 1734 for conspiring to burn down Montreal, her body incinerated and scattered to the winds.[81] Yet, while not acting as an execution squad, the police who raided the Sir George computer centre exhibited reckless disregard for Black dignity, Black rights, and Black lives. Even so, the claim that the police set the fire, *for the express purpose of burning its occupants alive*, can be safely discounted—if only because not all the occupants of the computer centre were Black, as the police knew all too well from their informer inside.[82]

While the racial demography of the occupiers fluctuated over the course of the occupation, at the time of the police raid a majority of those inside the computer centre, albeit a bare majority, was white. That many of these individuals came from the Canadian middle class, with a smaller number from the "very rich" Anglophone upper class in Montreal,[83] likely would have acted as a constraint on police behavior, in terms of any action that potentially could have caused serious harm to the protesters as a whole. The police did commit outrages, after taking the occupants of the computer centre into custody, but they were strategic and selective in choosing their victims, reserving the bluntest and most brutal punishment for the Blacks.

To say that the police did not set out to deliberately and maliciously burn up the protesters is not, however, to completely dismiss the hypothesis of police arson. The police were definitely trying to force the occupants of the computer centre to exit through one particular door, which would have made it easier to apprehend them. To that end, the police had barricaded the second of the two doors to the computer centre, a transparent violation of fire regulations. Did this violation serve as a gateway to even more flagrant breaches? That is, did the police also then proceed to start what they conceived as a controlled fire, not to incinerate the occupants of the computer centre, as Bukka Rennie maintained, but rather to smoke them out? Was this the actual conspiracy at the genesis of the fire? Unless the fire began accidentally, as a result of an electrical problem or smoking, the notion of a police-initiated fire that went awry becomes increasingly plausible. Far less plausible, indeed implausible, is the claim that the protesters engaged in a conspiracy to burn down the computer center—in effect, to engage in mass suicide. Whatever may be said about the protesters, and their errors were numerous, chief among them the destruction of the computers, they assuredly were not suicidal.

What is undeniable is that the white mob was openly baying for Black blood. The reaction of the mob, which apparently was well represented among the estimated 2,000-4,000 people who had gathered in the streets below the burning computer centre, would provide the most memorable lines from the Sir George Crisis. Consistent with patterns already charted, the most vicious and vociferous anger was directed at "niggers," never mind that, as noted, most of the occupants in the computer centre at that point were not black. To the police, the whites in the group, especially the women, were "nigger lovers," an invective with connotations of interracial sex, which evidently occurred.[84] Outside the computer centre, meanwhile, the mob kept up the drumbeat. Alongside the signature chant, "Let the niggers burn," were others, like "Burn, nigger, burn," as Bukka Rennie noted and as documented elsewhere.[85] This chant, "Burn, nigger, burn," gave a racist ring to another mantra, "Burn, baby, burn," an oft-repeated maxim in the uprisings in the US African American ghettos during the Revolution of 1968. In addition to being good students and imitators of their American counterparts, Canadian white supremacists apparently were current on the Black struggle in the United States, the better to be able to taunt and mock Black people in Canada.

The Sir George Trial and the "Rodney Riot" as Prologues to the Trinidad Revolution

The bigotry that permeated the Sir George Crisis from beginning to end was reflected in the halls of Canadian justice—where, however, it was veiled in the language of judicial restraint and race neutrality. The mob had proposed to burn "niggers," without the benefit of a trial. The state prosecutors, for their part, sought to lock up the whole lot of those they blamed for the events at the computer centre, the Blacks and the non-Blacks alike, and throw away the key. Prosecutorial wrath was evident in the decision to charge the defendants with conspiracy to commit arson and conspiracy to destroy the computers and other university property, absurd charges that potentially carried equally absurd sentences of up to life in prison. Rawle R. Frederick, the bard of Dennis Forsythe's book on the Sir George Crisis, seemed to paint a poetic picture of the scene, "In obsolete courtrooms the dead/ laugh their lifeless echoes through/ the hollow chambers of time/ while the mouth joustles without music."[86]

The first to face the judicial music in a Montreal court were ten individuals, all of them Trinidadians. This was not accidental. The Trinidad Ten, as they were called, reflected the outsized role of denizens of that island in the Sir George Crisis, especially toward the end. Included among the Trinidad Ten were Kelvin Robinson, Valerie Belgrave, Teddy Belgrave, and Robert Ranjitsingh. After a nine-week trial, the longest jury trial in Montreal up to that point, all ten defendants were found guilty of obstructing the use of property, mainly the computer centre, and fined between $1,000 and $15,000 each.[87] This verdict was a far cry from the original charges (conspiracy to commit arson and conspiracy to damage property), with their possible life-sentence penalty. The verdict also vindicated the value placed on property in a capitalist society. The verdict did not vindicate the prosecution, which effectively lost, the defendants having escaped with little more than the proverbial slap on the wrist, their court-ordered fines paid by the government of Trinidad and Tobago.

Three factors explain the outcome. First, the prosecution, with a weak case but a burning desire for vengeance, had overreached. Second, the accused had an excellent defense team that held the prosecutors to their burden of proof, which proof they patently were unable to produce. Juanita Westmoreland, a Black junior member of the defense team, proved to be especially effective, helping to ensure that the prosecution did not turn the all-white and all-male jurors into a gaggle of meek Pontius Pilates.[88] Third, there was the political factor. Above all, more than a weak case and a good defense, the outcome of the trial of the Trinidad Ten was determined by the Trinidad Revolution, with which it coincided and helped to hasten.

The Trinidad Revolution was the last major event in the Caribbean related to the Revolution of 1968, and the most consequential one. Happenings in Montreal were deeply implicated in the Trinidad Revolution. The starting point of that implication was the Congress of Black Writers, which served as an entree into the arena of Pan-African antinomian activism for various individuals, none more so than Walter Rodney. The Guyanese-born Rodney was then a lecturer in African history at the Mona campus of the University of the West Indies in Jamaica, where he had become entangled with the island's Black Power formations, including Rastafari. Alarmed by Rodney's associations, the neocolonial Jamaican government designated him an outside agitator and targeted him for banishment, a stance very much analogous to that of the Canadian nativists who would soon be calling for the deportation of the Sir George protesters. The difference was that the authorities in Jamaica, home to three of the original six accusers of Professor Perry Anderson, could act quickly on their nativist (if not also racial) prejudice. And acted they did, decisively, Rodney's attendance at the Congress of Black Writers having supplied the opportunity.[89]

On returning from the one island to the other, Montreal to Jamaica, Rodney was denied entry. The Jamaican authorities brusquely sent him back to Montreal, where he had neither job, home, nor family, but where he found solidarity among fellow participants in the Congress of Black Writers. Sir George students were well represented in those expressions of solidarity, including journeying to the Canadian capital, Ottawa, to protest Rodney's expulsion at the Jamaican high commission (embassy). In this way, Rodney's deportation became part of the dress rehearsal for the Sir George Crisis.

They also rehearsed for rebellion in Jamaica, where Rodney first manifested his calling as a "prophet of self-emancipation," to quote from Eusi Kwayana's unjustly little-known mini-biography of his comrade and fellow Guyanese.[90] The Rastafarians, several of whom were among Rodney's most conspicuous Jamaican interlocutors, had a habit of rhetorically summoning fire. "Fire," they often cried out in public, commenting on one social problem or another. Fiery describes well the blowback in Jamaica to Rodney's deportation, which began with rallies and marches by university students and radical intellectuals. The revolt subsequently changed character and turned violently explosive with the entrance of poor urban youths, a social category Eurocentric Marxism historically saw as a potential counterrevolutionary force, the disdained lumpenproletariat, but one viewed more favorably by Marxist-inclined Pan-African theorists like Frantz Fanon and Amilcar Cabral, head of the anticolonial struggle in Portugal's West African colony of Guinea-Bissau.[91] The Jamaican media, also dripping with disdain for the country's poor urban youths, although not from the same perspective as the Eurocentric Marxists, labeled the revolt the "Rodney Riot." The label may have been flattering of Rodney, if not to him, but it was both facile and false. While sparked by Rodney's deportation, ultimately the revolt was directed against Jamaica's neocolonial setup. It was also the most serious sociopolitical disturbances on the island in more than a generation, since the 1930s.[92]

The Trinidad Revolution in the Context of the Sir George Crisis

The events in Jamaica reverberated throughout the Caribbean, most especially in Trinidad. As they had at Mona in Jamaica, students, and teachers at the St. Augustine campus of the University of the West Indies in Trinidad mobilized in opposition to Rodney's deportation, denouncing it as offensive to the very concept of a pan-Caribbean system of higher education. The governing Jamaica Labour Party, which had deported Rodney, and which previously was instrumental in destroying the short-lived political union of the West Indies Federation (1958-1962), was now also seeking to destroy one of the exfederation's two remaining pillars, the University of the West Indies (the other was the West Indies cricket team). So went the cry.[93] In Trinidad, and especially at St. Augustine, the outcry increased during the final phase of the Sir George Crisis and in its aftermath. Students were sufficiently riled up over events in Montreal to physically block Canada's governor general (its ceremonial head of state), who was on an official visit to Trinidad, from entering the university.

What began on campus did not remain on campus. The fuse may have been lit at the university, but the student uprising only turned into a wildfire, the Trinidad Revolution, after it escaped the hallowed halls of the academy and spread into the island's urban centres and heartland. The working class, organized and unorganized, including the all-important union of oil workers, joined the growing rebellion. So also did sections of the middle class. Marching under the banner of Black Power while (literally) beating hard the drums of interethnic harmony, the predominantly (although not exclusively) Afro-Trinidadian-led rebellion advanced deep into central and south Trinidad, the base of the country's sugar industry and home to many Indo-Trinidadians. For some eight action-packed weeks, from February to April 1970, demonstrators seized control of the streets and other public spaces. Even carnival, a veritable civic religion in Trinidad, and a crucible for calypso and calypsonians, came under the spell of Black Power, even if one leading calypsonian, Mighty Sparrow, went out of tune and criticized the Sir George protesters.[94] For breadth, the proportion of the population involved in rallies, demonstrations, and marches, and the sectors of society from which the participants came, the Trinidad Revolution had few, if any, equals in the Revolution of 1968.

The most apt comparison to the events in Trinidad, perhaps, is the May 1968 revolt in Paris against French president Charles de Gaulle. Initiated by students, the rebellion in Paris, like the one in Trinidad, came to encompass large sections of the working class. But then the French student-worker alliance abruptly collapsed, nixing any real prospect of ousting de Gaulle, who previously ignited a firestorm in Canada by veering off script and endorsing independence for predominantly French-speaking Quebec while visiting Montreal. Although angering Canada's Anglophone ruling class, de Gaulle's diplomatic *faux pas* delighted Quebec's Francophone nationalists, numbers of whom would declare solidarity with the Sir George rising on the grounds that they were North America's "white niggers," neglecting only to add that the adjective negated the noun. Anyhow, the French workers, who had more interest in a pay raise than in revolution, downed their banners and left their student allies high and dry after the wily de Gaulle acceded to their wage demands.[95] Seemingly, de Gaulle had found an antidote to the Revolution of

1968, notably in the counterrevolution of 1848, to which some have traced the roots of the Gaullist regime, Karl Marx having provided the discursive foundation in his timeless text, *The Eighteenth Brumaire of Louis Bonaparte.*[96]

The challenges of the Trinidad Revolution were far more intractable than those de Gaulle had faced. The structural problems of neocolonialism, unemployment, underemployment, and the consequent social immiseration, did not readily lend themselves to a state buyoff of mass grievances. Unable to pit workers against students, like de Gaulle had done, the government of Prime Minister Eric Williams descended into crisis. Many of Williams's allies, ministers of state included, began to abandon him. The situation had not always been so dire. A famed historian of slavery and author of one of the best-known books on the subject,[97] Williams had seen better days. As an anticolonial nationalist, he and his People's National Movement enjoyed genuine mass support. A former professor at Howard University, Williams became at once the national tutor and scolder, issuing fierce jeremiads against colonialism, most famously in the peroration "Massa Day Done."[98] The secret to Williams's political success, as an admirer who later became a critic noted, is that "Everything he has ever learnt, and he has learnt a great deal, he is able to stand and say and his popular audience listens for three, four, five hours at a time. This is the West Indies at its best."[99]

Then independence came, and it did not find Williams at his best. Independence begat neocolonialism, and Williams became head of the neo-colonial state. It was an all too familiar tale in the postcolonial world. Even Ghana's leader Kwame Nkrumah, previously a model for the anticolonial Eric Williams,[100] proved unable to evade the neocolonial trap and was ousted in an imperialist-sponsored coup when he protested too much, beginning with the Congo crisis.[101] Nkrumah had also authored the defining text on neocolo-nialism,[102] which became part of the Black Power informal syllabus, cited by the Sir George protesters, among others.[103] Exiled to Guinea after being stripped of power, Nkrumah became a Black Power militant in his own right, with corresponding sympathetic feelings for Biafra.[104] Although representing the same alignment of class forces as the power-holding Nkrumah had done, foremost among them the native petty bourgeoisie, Williams's protestations of neocolonialism were never as loud or earnest as those of the Ghanaian.

As power holders, the differences between Nkrumah and Williams were most striking in foreign affairs, especially Cold War politics. Increasingly, Nkrumah pursued a policy of "positive neutrality" that was highly critical of the Western powers, as on the crucial Congo crisis, while upgrading Ghana's ties with the Soviet Union and China, a difficult diplomatic dance in light of the rivalry between the two communist powers.[105] Concurrently, Williams adopted an anticommunist stance. In typical Cold War fashion, he created a commission on "subversive activities" to identify and root out Reds from various sectors of society, with an emphasis on the labor movement. Externally, Williams was openly hostile to the Cuban Revolution, the litmus test for Cold War allegiance in the region. "To hell with Castro," he thundered from the political platform, referring to Fidel Castro, the foremost Cuban revolution-ary.[106] The single most consequential event in the Caribbean since the Haitian Revolution, the Cuban Revolution would be hailed by many in the Trinidad Revolution.

On Cuba, the contrast between Williams and the power-holding Nkrumah could not have been greater. As president of Ghana, Nkrumah received the visiting Ernesto "Che" Guevara, the second most conspicuous figure in the Cuban Revolution, after Castro. No single individual, barring none, was more *visually* conspicuous in the Revolution of 1968 than Guevara, who died in 1967. Among other places, he was a familiar presence at the Congress of Black Writers and the Sir George protests, his portrait emblazoned on posters, t-shirts, and caps, including the cap worn by the abovementioned student involved in the incident in the office of Sir George strongman John O'Brien. For the Black Power militants, Guevara, an Argentinian-born man of Caucasian descent, came by his iconic status honestly. He had fought alongside pro-Lumumba forces in the Congo, following the assassination of Prime Minister Patrice Lumumba by United States and Belgian forces, acting in concert with their Congolese quislings led by Moise Tshombe, a name that became a Pan-African catchphrase for betrayal.[107] In further appreciation, Guevara's chief discursive legacy, his manual on guerrilla warfare, would find a place of honor on the Black Power syllabus, alongside likeminded revolutionary guidebooks by Mao and Nkrumah. Unlike Nkrumah, Williams would hardly have consorted with a figure like Guevara who, predictably, was on pictorial display in the Trinidad Revolution and who had been hunted down and killed by Bolivia's US-backed army while trying to help make revolution in that country, his fourth such revolutionary undertaking in as many countries, after Guatemala, Cuba, and the Congo. It was only after the danger (the Trinidad Revolution and the Revolution of 1968) had passed that Williams, in conjunction with other Anglophone Caribbean leaders, began to make diplomatic overtures to Cuba, their efforts rendered politically palatable by the previous United States outreach to Mao's China.

Williams's journey from radical anticolonialism to Cold War-style anti-communism may be measured by his relationship with C. L. R. James, another famous Trinidadian and historian. James's life and labor touched on many of the issues under discussion here, including the Congress of Black Writers, where he made several presentations, including on the Haitian Revolution, the subject of his classic work.[108] An intellectual mentor to the young Williams, James also helped to introduce the budding anticolonial Nkrumah to Pan-African circles in London, notably the Trinidadian-born George Padmore.[109] In time, the anticolonial Williams invited James, who by then had been abroad for more than two decades, to return to Trinidad to become editor of *The Nation*, a newspaper established by the People's National Movement as a counterpoint to the pro-colonial press. But things subsequently fell apart.

Two factors, one ideological and the other political, sundered the partnership between Williams and James. One was James's Marxism, which put him at odds ideologically with Williams's anti-communist line. The second factor, which has not received the same attention as the first one, centered on control of the People's National Movement. Apparently dissatisfied with his main role as editor of the party's newspaper, James had greater ambitions. He desired to become chief party organizer, which effectively would have meant supplanting Williams as day-to-day leader of the People's National Movement, James apparently harboring dreams of turning this petty-bourgeois-led nationalist coalition into a force for social revolution. Such an arrangement, James reasoned in a little-cited pamphlet, in which he seemed, superciliously if not entirely unjustifiably, to elevate himself intellectually above Williams, would free the prime minister to concentrate on the affairs of state.[110] Evidently smelling a rat,[111] Williams concentrated on driving James out of the party and, ultimately, out of the country—after delivering a crushing electoral defeat to a rival political movement that James had hastily formed.

Some would seek to undo what Williams had done. Inspired by Darcus Howe, a blood relative of James and a fellow participant in the Congress of Black Writers, a small but vociferous element within the Trinidad Revolution plotted to bring James back to the country and to the political stage.[112] It was not to be. Meanwhile, Williams had become ever more distant from his anti-colonial origins. Assuredly, he never degenerated into a groveling stooge on the order of the Congo's Moise Tshombe. That, however, was cold comfort to the prime minister's opponents in the Black Power and allied revolutionary formations. To them, Williams had morphed into what the *Little Red Book*-quoting Maoists, who were also represented in the Trinidad Revolution, bearing pictures of Mao, colorfully called an "imperialist running dog."

The imperialists, the United States and Britain, with regional satraps like Venezuela in tow, would soon run to Williams's aid. The Trinidad Revolution nearly succeeded in overthrowing him, coming closer than had the Parisian ill-fated student-worker alliance to removing de Gaulle. Having lost control of the streets, Williams sought to claw back his authority by declaring a state of emergency. He then put the army in charge of enforcing the emergency, a decision that backfired, since the army had not escaped the revolutionary fervor. A group of Black Power-aligned soldiers, with junior officers in the forefront, went into rebellion, "fired by the decisive actions of legends like Che Guevara and Patrice Lumumba," as their leading figure explained.[113] With slippery hands, and little of the decisiveness they attributed to their models, Guevara and Lumumba, the rebellious soldiers ambivalently grasped for state power. It was against this backdrop that the imperialist armadas came over the horizon, by air and sea, to foil by intimidation an unlikely, but seemingly possible, outcome to the Trinidad Revolution: the world's first Black Power-controlled state. Another such opportunity would never recur.[114] To riff on Williams's most famous speech, *as a project credibly aspiring to attain state power*, Black Power day was done—in Trinidad and Tobago, in the Caribbean, in the world.

Williams and his colleagues were conscious of the paradox at the heart of their bailout request. In addition to his blasts against the British, the anti-colonial Williams had famously feuded with the United States over its military facility in Trinidad, at Chaguaramas, a struggle that necessarily commanded its own jeremiad from the professor turned politician, this one entitled "From Slavery to Chaguaramas." He would break the impasse over the negotiations to kick the Yankee usurpers out of Chaguaramas, the anti-colonial Williams declared, or the problem would break him politically. Unable to break the Yankees, a less militant Williams bent to their will, accepting a promise that they would eventually vacate their military facility, which promise they kept.[115] Subsequently, Black Power threatened to break Williams. Reluctantly, he swallowed the firewater and summoned his erstwhile imperialist nemeses to break the Black Power siege. "'Look at you sons of bitches, you always cursing the goddam Yankees and the first time your arse is in fire, it is the Americans you've turned to,'" one of Williams's ministers reportedly told his cabinet colleagues in the prime minister's absence.[116] It was, however, a false dichotomy. Hypocrisy has never really been a foe of self-interest, which coexistence enabled the Williams regime to survive the Trinidad Revolution, much praise to the imperialist bailout.

Canada in the Trinidad Revolution and the Precedence of the Trinidad Ten

The case against the Trinidad Ten did not survive, much praise to the Trinidad Revolution. Although militarily defeated, like the Sir George protesters, the

Trinidad Revolution exerted a powerful influence on the kangaroo proceedings against Trinidadian nationals in a distant Montreal court. Perhaps the Trinidad Revolution would have happened with or without the Sir George Crisis, but not the way it did. As it actually unfolded, Canada occupied a unique, and catalytic, role in the Trinidad Revolution, all because of the Sir George Crisis. The events that culminated in the revolution were launched at the beginning of the previous year, 1969, in solidarity with the Sir George protests. In its halcyon days, February to April 1970, Canada remained in the bull's-eye of the Trinidad Revolution, a target singled out for special derision.

The Trinidad Revolution was a political potpourri of multiple, inconsistent, and contradictory forces. On the imperative of opposing what they termed Canadian imperialism in the Caribbean however, the revolutionaries were of one accord. No nation, barring none, was as prominently, and negatively, featured in the Trinidad Revolution as Canada. Ahead of Britain, the old slave-holding power, former colonial master and still a major player in Trinidad's sugar industry, the commodity on which Eric Williams's scholarship was founded; ahead of the United States, which effectively (if unofficially) supplanted Britain as Trinidad's overlord during World War II, including taking control of the oil business, destined to become even more lucrative than sugar; ahead of all foreign actors, Canada was singled out in the Trinidad Revolution. The most conspicuous targets of the demonstrations were Canadian-owned enterprises, foremost among them banks. A key organizer of those demonstrations explained the logic in a letter to Walter Rodney, who was then at the University of Dar-es-Salaam in Tanzania, having been unofficially debarred from Anglophone Caribbean universities. Writing during the decisive phase of the Trinidad Revolution, the male narrator noted that the demonstrators wanted to "dramatize the plight of our Black brothers facing trial in Canada," oblivious to the fact that two of the Trinidad Ten were women. Two major targets of the demonstrations, the narrator went on, were the Canadian High Commission and the Royal Bank of Canada, that behemoth of Canadian finance capital.[117]

The Canadians should not have been taken unawares, for they had been given fair warning. In January 1970, on the eve of the trial of the Trinidad Ten, Geddes Granger had visited Canada. The single most conspicuous figure in the Trinidad Revolution, Granger launched his political career from the University of the West Indies at St. Augustine, as student leader of the campus agitation in support of the Sir George protests. Speaking in Montreal, Granger condemned Canadian racism and the prosecution of the Trinidad Ten, intimating that Canadian economic interests in the Caribbean could also be placed in the dock and subjected to trial by fire in the streets of Trinidad.[118] He was as good as his word.

As a leading personality in the Trinidad Revolution, Granger, who later changed his name to Makandal Daaga,[119] became legendary for his marching. Of the modalities of seizing state power, what was to be done, he seemed blissfully unaware, presiding over endless dawdling, one of the major weaknesses internal to the Trinidad Revolution.[120] No more a Maoist than he was a Leninist, Granger nevertheless was the consummate long marcher, albeit toward no particular strategic end. In all his marching, though, Canadian imperialism and the treatment of Trinidadians and other West Indians in Canada remained central issues.

So toxic was Canada that even Eric Williams, in his most vulnerable and desperate moment during the revolution, shunned potential Canadian assistance. He scoured the Caribbean in search of support, from Jamaica to Barbados to Guyana, where Prime Minister Forbes Burnham, who a decade later would order the assassination of Walter Rodney, lamented his inability to offer concrete help. Having come up empty-handed in his own backyard, Williams looked longingly across the Atlantic to Nigeria, where the recent defeat of Biafra and the end of the civil war had left many soldiers with little to do.[121] No praetorian guard would be forthcoming from Nigeria. Even so, the Nigerian army officer Lieutenant Colonel Theophilus Danjuma, who earned his spurs battling Biafra, would be appointed president of the international military tribunal that tried the soldiers involved in the attempted overthrow of Williams, perhaps a sort of payback for the Black Power romance with Biafra, including in the Trinidad Revolution and among the Sir George protesters.[122] After exhausting all other options, Williams turned to the United States and Britain. There was, however, one nation from which he pointedly ruled out accepting aid: Canada. Williams, the US ambassador to Trinidad and Tobago explained, feared "adverse reaction" locally to any approach to Canada.[123] In Trinidad, Canada had the dubious distinction of being rejected by the revolution and the counterrevolution alike. Never before, apparently, had Canada occupied such a prominently negative place in a major Caribbean event. It was a rude shock to the national self-perception, Canada being portrayed as an imperialist bully, ruder perhaps than the questioning of the Canadian color conceit by the Sir George protesters.

These were the circumstances in which the verdict of the Trinidad Ten was rendered in Montreal. The defendants had not burned, as the mob desired, but they also had not been condemned to rot in prison, as their other tormentors, the state prosecutors, demanded. For the prosecution, the trial of the Trinidad Ten was a test case that would determine the fate of the remaining accused persons, who numbered more than eighty. Consequently, the relatively light punishment of the Trinidad Ten became a template. Reeling from a severe setback in its test case, the prosecution threw in the towel and offered plea deals to all the other accused, who would be allowed to go free by paying a fine and pledging to refrain from political agitation for a period of time. All but a handful of those who were offered this deal accepted it.

The holdouts included Rosie Douglas. In a surrender to the Canadian color conceit, and an assault on historical verity, Douglas would end up being demonized in the national historical memory as the main protagonist in the Sir George Crisis and the evil genius behind the protests, including the destruction of the computer centre. Also turning down the prosecution's plea deal was Anne Cools. An activist with deep roots in Montreal's Black radical circles, the Barbadian-born Cools was an important voice in the Sir George protests, known for her strong support of women's rights, then and later.[124] A third accused person to reject the plea deal was Martin Bracey. The aforementioned African Canadian Maoist, Bracey would be confused with Rosie Douglas by one prominent white critic of the protests, apparently unable to tell one Black man from another—that is, Eugene Genovese, then a member of the Sir George faculty, advisor to the university administration during the crisis, Marxist scholar (he subsequently renounced Marxism) and, not least, prominent historian of slavery in the United States.[125]

All three holdouts, Douglas, Cools and Bracey, would be tried, convicted, and imprisoned. Of the three, Bracey received the longest sentence, largely for acrimoniously renouncing the authority of the court, unlike Douglas and Cools. Two of Bracey's Maoist white Canadian comrades, Gail August and Leo Barker, who also refused the plea deal and contested the right of the Canadian judiciary to try them, were convicted and sent to prison. The common denominator among these defendants, especially Douglas and Cools, who faced the same charges as the Trinidad Ten, was an absence of sustained external political support during their trials. It was not so much that none of them were Trinidadian nationals, but that all of them were tried after the Trinidad Revolution had been defeated. The avenging hand of victor's justice was no longer being stayed by the politics of the street in faraway Trinidad, or anywhere else, the quest for vengeance having been especially transparent in the case of Martin Bracey, an uppity Negro militantly espousing a third-world Marxist ideology and daring to question the legitimacy of the Canadian judicial system. It was not only in Canada, however. The state of Trinidad and Tobago also went after participants in the Trinidad Revolution, not just the soldiers involved in the failed putsch but also civilian protest leaders like Geddes Granger.

Conclusion: The Sir George Crisis and the Crisis of Historical Memory

The state, whether in Canada or Trinidad, had no monopoly on the pursuit of victor's justice. The academic winners at Sir George also trumpeted their triumph. Five months after the military-style suppression of the occupation of the computer centre, a committee appointed by the university to inquire into the origins of the crisis issued its report. In the period leading up to the end of the crisis, the composition of the committee had been the subject of bitter disputes between the university administration and the protesters. The suppression of the occupation ended those fraught discussions, freeing the university to proceed with a committee of its own choosing, devoid of any input from the protesters. The outcome was predictable. In its final report, the committee roundly rejected the allegation of racism against Professor Perry Anderson and recommended that the university "express its confidence in his impartiality."[126] The university duly accepted the recommendation,[127] unsurprisingly, since the committee's report doubled as validation of the deans' coup against Principal Robert Rae, who had essentially repudiated a previous report by the dean of science exonerating Professor Anderson. The committee's report was also the latest installment in an ongoing struggle, which continues to this day, around how to remember the Sir George Crisis, or whether to remember it at all.

The issue of historical memory came into sharp relief on the tenth anniversary of the crisis, in 1979. To mark the occasion, the Sir George alumni magazine interviewed Rosie Douglas. Himself a Sir George alumnus, Douglas had graduated before the onset of the crisis, by which point he was a graduate student at McGill. At the time of the interview with the alumni magazine, Douglas had completed his prison sentence and had been deported from Canada, the lone protester to be sent "home" in that fashion, albeit long after the event had passed. Douglas had not suffered the further punishment of being burned, like the enslaved Angélique of yore, but his interview would be, metaphorically if not literally.

Dramatically John O'Brien, the chief beneficiary of the deans' coup and still very much Sir George's maximum leader, rejoined the debate over historical memory. With characteristic wrath and vengefulness, O'Brien overruled the editors of his school's alumni magazine and ordered the destruction of the entire run containing the Douglas interview, all 31,000 copies, presumably by pulping rather than committing them to a bon fire. By his own admission, O'Brien acted without even reading the offending interview.[128] The prophet Jeremiah, usually burning with righteous indignation, had temporarily tempered his fire, and demanded to know: "Is there no balm in Gilead; is there no physician there?"[129]

The songwriter would eventually answer affirmatively, declaring: "There is a balm in Gilead/ To make the wounded whole." But there was no balm at the top of the Sir George hierarchy to bind up the wound from the crisis, now festering for a decade, at least in O'Brien's mind. Utterly devoid of the physician's healing touch, he was yet playing the role of the hanging judge, still the unpenitent Pontius Pilate.

Destroying the magazine was not the first time that O'Brien had sought to manage memory of the Sir George Crisis. Five years earlier, in 1974, he had overseen a merger between Sir George and a nearby Catholic institution, Loyola College, to form Concordia University. That, anyhow, is the official creation story. It is also probably not the full story. The crisis had tainted the Sir George brand, which, especially in the wake of the blowup of February 11, 1969, had become (on this reasoning) associated with unpleasant activities, to say nothing of un-Canadian ones. Accordingly, the nomenclatorial transition from Sir George to Concordia may be seen as another act of erasure engineered by O'Brien. It was best to whitewash memory of events best forgotten, but which some, like the garrulous Rosie Douglas, seemed determined to keep alive. In a manner of speaking, Sir George was made to die a sacrificial death, crucified on the calumniating cross of the Canadian color conceit, so that the myth of national racial innocence could live. Concordia, a name rhyming with Canada and redolent with notions of harmony, represented the resurrection and the new life.

It followed that, in the Age of O'Brien as well as in the post-O'Brien era, the harmonic narrative ruled out official university reckoning with the Sir George Crisis. Even colonial regimes had a habit of ordering investigations into rebellions and disturbances. More recently, governments worldwide, from South Africa to Brazil to the Solomon Islands, have created commissions to ferret out the truth of crimes and misdeeds committed by previous regimes.[130] The Canadian state has made attempts to admit, if not exactly to redress, its long train of criminal conduct vis-a-vis the indigenous peoples.[131] In the United States, universities (although not the state) have sought to come to terms with their involvement in slavery, apartheid and related crimes against humanity.[132] But not at Concordia, where "conjuring up the dead of ... history," as Karl Marx phased it in his *Eighteenth Brumaire*, has been debarred in favor of silence and silencing, evasion, and erasure.[133]

Yet, there is no statute of limitation in the search for truth. Concordia, perhaps prodded by student protests of the Sir George variety, may yet venture where John O'Brien and his successors, following his lead, feared to tread. The writ of the resulting investigation would necessarily include the mysterious fire that accompanied the suppression of the occupation of the computer centre, the event that gave birth to one of the most diabolical lines, and the most persistent one, to emerge from the Sir George Crisis—the extrajudicial *auto-da-fé*, "Let the Niggers Burn." Perhaps the burning light of truth will yet shine on those developments. If that should come to pass, it may not just be Cecil Rhodes whose fall will be demanded. Heads could also roll in Montreal and elsewhere in Canada, allegorically speaking. The final acts of the Sir George Crisis may not yet have been performed; its concluding scripts still unwritten.

The actual history is a tale of an event that has had profound, if yet to be acknowledged, consequences for the late Sir George Williams University, reconstituted as Concordia. The Sir George Crisis was also a significant event in the series of momentous events that comprised the Revolution of 1968. The Sir George protesters took courage from the mobilization in Montreal occasioned by the death of Martin Luther King and were encouraged in their campus campaigns by the struggle to make Rhodesia fall and give life to Zimbabwe. Biafra, described in its national anthem as the "Land of the Rising Sun,"[134] a description affirmed by many in the global Black Power movement, became a weapon in the arsenal of detractors of the Sir George protests.[135] Walter Rodney, expelled from Jamaica for the offense of Black Power agitation, which expulsion sparked an uprising locally, would find succor in Montreal, including among the budding Sir George protesters. Sequentially, Montreal-based mobilization against Rodney's expulsion would be a harbinger of things to come at Sir George, where no matter how compressed and circumscribed their sphere of operation, or how tortured and clumsy some of their actions, the protesters were endeavoring to respond to the prophetic call to self-emancipation, in the manner of Rodney. The Trinidad Revolution, surely one of the most fascinating and tantalizing events connected to the Revolution of 1968, was organically linked to the Sir George protests. As if in gratitude, the Trinidad Revolution would exercise a powerfully salvific effect in the case of the protesters turned criminal defendants in Montreal. Through much of it all could be detected the aftereffects of the Montreal-convened, sprawling smorgasbord called the Congress of Black Writers, which served variously as a sounding board and fountainhead for subsequent happenings. Such was the world in which the Sir George protests unfolded, a world in which the protesters and what they wrought had a hand in helping to make. 'Twas a flicker in the flame of '68, the Sir George Crisis."

NOTES

1   I am to thank the editors of this collection for inviting me to address the conference where the initial draft of this chapter was presented. My appreciation to Laura Hill for her input on several points. I owe a substantial debt to David Johnson for reasoning with me, most notably on questions surrounding the Trinidad Revolution. Special thanks and a big shout out also to David Austin for his comments on this work.

2   George Katsiaficas, *The Imagination of the New Left: A Global Analysis of 1968* (Boston: South End Press, 1987); Mark Kurlansky, *1968: The Year That Rocked the World* (New York: Ballantine Books, 2004).

3   Mike Rapport, *1848: Year of Revolution* (New York: Basic Books 2009); Douglas Moggach and Gareth Stedman Jones, eds., *The 1848 Revolutions and European Political Thought* (Cambridge: Cambridge University Press, 2018).

4   Mahmood Mamdani, *Citizen and Subject: Contemporary Africa and the Legacy of Late Colonialism* (Princeton: Princeton University Press, 1996).

5   Kwame Nkrumah, *Neo-Colonialism: The Last Stage of Imperialism* (London: Nelson, 1965); Frantz Fanon, *The Wretched of the Earth*, trans. by Constance Farrington (New York: Grove Press, 1965).

6   Following a longer tradition dating back to the period of enslavement, the exponents of Black Power in the United States adopted a colonial model that viewed African Americans as an oppressed nation, similar to colonized peoples elsewhere in the world. The first major US Black Power text set the tone. See Stokely Carmichael and Charles V. Hamilton, *Black Power: The Politics of Liberation in America* (New York: Vintage Book, 1967).

7   Charles Fager, *Uncertain Resurrection: The Poor People's Campaign* (Grand Rapids: Eerdmans, 1969).

8   George Jackson, *Soledad Brothers: The Prison Letters of George Jackson* (New York: Bantam Book, 1970), 235.

9   Cornel West, ed., *The Radical King: Martin Luther King Jr.* (Boston: Beacon Books, 2015); Adam Fairclough, "Was Martin Luther King a Marxist?", *History Worshop*, 15, no. 1(1983), 117-125.

10   Martin Luther King, Jr., "Black Power," in Clayborne Carson, ed., *The Autobiography of Martin Luther King, Jr.*, (New York: Grand Central Publishing, 1998), 329).

11   Aram Goudsouzian, *Down to the Crossroads: Civil Rights, Black Power, and the Meredith March Against Fear* (New York: Farrar, Straus, and Giroux, 2014).

12   See, for example, George Breitman, ed., *Malcolm X Speaks: Selected Speeches and Statements* (New York Pathfinder Press, 1989).

13   James H. Cone, *Martin & Malcom & America: A Dream or Nightmare* (Maryknoll, NY: Orbis Books, 1991); Peniel E. Joseph, *The Sword and the Shield: The Revolutionary Lives of Malcolm X and Martin Luther King Jr* (New York: Basic Books, 2020).

14   Jeremiah 20:9 (King James Version).

15   Clayborne Carson and Kris Shepard, eds., *A Call to Conscience: The Landmark Speeches of Dr. Martin Luther King, Jr.* (New York: Grand Central Publishing, 2001), 139-164.

16   David J. Garrow, *The FBI and Martin Luther King, Jr.* (New York: Penguin Books, 1983).

17   Gerald Horne, *From the Barrel of a Gun: The United States and the War Against Zimbabwe, 1965-1980* (Chapel Hill: University of North Carolina Press, 2001).

18   John Ismay, "Rhodesia's Dead—but White Supremacist Have Given It New Life Online," *New York Times Magazine* (April 10, 2018).

19   Roseanne Chantiluke, Brian Kwoba, and Athinangamso Nkopo, eds., *Rhodes Must Fall: The Struggle to Decolonise the Racist Heart of Empire* (London: Zed Books, 2018). Rhodes Must Fall refers to the student protests in South Africa to decolonize universities by removing

statues to imperialist Cecil Rhodes and advocating free tuition. The movement spread to Oxford University in the UK.

20   Edward Scobie, *Black Britannia: A History of Blacks in Britain* (Chicago: Johnson Pub. Co., 1972), 277.

21   *Moko*, April 11, 1969 (bold in original).

22   Raffique Shah, "Reflections on the Mutiny," in Selwyn Ryan and Taimoon Stewart, eds., *The Black Power Revolution, 1970: A Retrospective* (Port of Spain: University of the West Indies, St. Augustine, 1995),507).

23   Dorothy Eber, *The Computer Centre Party* (Montreal: Tundra Book, 1969), 115-116, 138.

24   *Georgian*, January 28, 1969. This organ was the Sir George student newspaper.

25   Pat Pajonas, "'All the World Knows the Score...'", *Direction One*, March 1969.

26   For a fuller account of the Sir George Crisis and its antecedents and impact, see Michael O. West, "History vs. Historical Memory: Rosie Douglas, Black Power on Campus, and the Canadian Color Conceit," Part I, *Palimpsest*, 6, no. 1(2017):, 84-100; Michael O. West, "History vs. Historical Memory: Rosie Douglas, Black Power on Campus, and the Canadian Color Conceit," Part II, *Palimpsest*, 6, no. 2 (2017):178-224.

27   Ivor Wilkins and Hans Strydom, *The Broederbond* (New York: Paddington Press, 1979).

28   David Austin, "All Roads Led to Montreal: Black Power, the Caribbean, and the Black Radical Tradition," *Journal of African American History*, 92, no. 4 (2007):516-539; David Austin, *Fear of a Black Nation: Race, Sex, and Security in Sixties Montreal* (Toronto: Between the Lines, 2013), 94-128; West, "History vs. Historical Memory," Part I.

29   Dennis Forsythe, ed., *Let the Niggers Burn!: The Sir George Williams University Affair and Its Caribbean Aftermath* (Montreal: Black Rose Books, 1971) 3.

30   David Austin, ed., *Moving Against the System: The 1968 Congress of Black Writers and the Making of Global Consciousness* (London: Pluto Press, 2018).

31   Karl Marx and Friedrich Engels, *The Communist Manifesto* (London. Verso, 1998; first pub. 1848).

32   West, "History vs. Historical Memory," Part II, 180-181.

33   Robert Rae, "In Defense of Student Activism: A Reply," in Tim and Julyan Reid, eds., *Student Power and the Canadian Campus* (Toronto: Peter Martin Associates Limited, 1969), 64-71.

34   Officially, Douglass Clarke, previously vice-principal, became acting principal when Robert Rae resigned. But Clarke, who only remained in the position for some months, was just a placeholder keeping the principal's seat warm for O'Brien, who actually was in charge all along.

35   Vladimir Il'ich Lenin, *What Is To Be Done?: The Burning Questions of Our Movement* (New York: International Publishers, 1929; first pub. 1902); Vladimir Il'ich Lenin, *Imperialism: The Highest Stage of Capitalism* (Moscow: Foreign Language Pub. House, 1951; first pub. 1917).

36   *Georgian*, February 3, 1969.

37   Eber, *Computer Centre Party*, 85.

38   *Georgian*, February 4, 1969.

39   Forsythe, ed., *Let the Niggers Burn!*

40   Some of these stories were told at the conference that formed the basis of this collection, most notably a remarkable session featuring participants in the Sir George Crisis. See also Bertram Boldon, "Black Immigrants in a Foreign Land," in Forsythe, ed., *Let the Niggers Burn!*, 22-39.

41   Dorothy Eber offered a rather salacious account of the Maoists in *Computer Centre Party*, 101-107.

42   Forsythe, ed., *Let the Niggers Burn!*, 9, 14, 115, 132-133.

43   Alexander C. Cook, ed., *Mao's Little Red Book: A Global History* (New York: Cambridge University Press, 2014).

44   *Georgian*, October 22, 1971.

45   West, "History vs. Historical Memory," Parts I and II.

46   West, "History vs. Historical Memory," Part II, 186-193.

47   Leroi Butcher, "The Anderson Affair," in Forsythe, ed., *Let the Niggers Burn!*,76-109; L. R. Butcher, "The Congress of Black Writers," in ibid., 69-74.

48   Bukka Rennie, who was in the thick of the Sir George protests, whose Trinidadian-ness is not in doubt, and who had definite ideas of what it meant to be Trinidadian, said the following of Butcher some four decades after the fact: "That is my closest friend.... He is a St. Lucian, but if you hear him talk and behave you wouldn't believe he is St. Lucian, you would believe he is Trinidadian because of his whole approach, and he was the real bulldog." See Bukka Rennie, Interview in *Trinidad & Tobago Review*, January 31, 2010

49   Eber, *Computer Centre Party*, 84.

50   Ibid,. 27.

51   *Georgian*, January 28, 1969. This was a special issue of the Sir George student newspaper. Christened the "Black Georgian" and edited by the protesters, it was their key archival takeaway from the crisis, one in which they outlined their case against the university administration and showcased their support on and off campus.

52   Rocky Jones, the outstanding African Canadian activist from Nova Scotia, earned only a couple of passing references in the collection. The most prominent African Canadian exponent of Black Power and a key player in the Congress of Black Writers, Jones appeared at Sir George at a crucial moment in the crisis to offer support to the protesters. Alas, Jones's posthumously published autobiography contains a number of factual errors about both the Congress of Black Writers and the Sir George Crisis. See Forsythe, ed., *Let the Niggers Burn!*, 59, 64; Burnley "Rocky" Jones and James W. St. G. Walker, *Burnley "Rocky" Jones, Revolutionary: An Autobiography* (Halifax: Roseway Publishing 2016), 115-149.

53   Forsythe, ed., *Let the Niggers Burn!*, 5.

54   Walter Rodney, *The Groundings With My Brothers* (London: Bogle-L'Ouverture Publications Ltd, 1969); David G. Nicholls, "East Indians and Black Power in Trinidad," *Race* 12, no. 4 (1971),. 443-459; John Gaffar La Guerre, "The Indian Response to Black Power: A Continuing Dilemma," in Ryan and Stewart, eds., *Black Power Revolution*, pp. 273-307; Ken Parmasad, "Ancestral Impulse, Community Formation and 1970: Bridging the Afro-Indian Divide," in Ryan and Stewart, eds., *Black Power Revolution*, 309-317.

55   *Georgian*, February 19, 1969.

56   Ibid.

57   Cheddi Jagan, *The West on Trial: My Fight for Guyana's Freedom* (New York: International Publishers, 1966).

58   Michael O. West, "Seeing Darkly: Guyana, Black Power, and Walter Rodney's Expulsion from Jamaica," *Small Axe*, 25 (2008),. 93-104.

59   David Austin, ed., *Moving Against the System: The 1968 Congress of Black Writers and the Making of Global Consciousness* (London: Pluto Press, 2018).

60   West, "History vs. Historical Memory," Part I, p. 88.

61   Valerie Belgrave, "The Sir George Williams Affair," in Ryan and Stewart, eds., *Black Power Revolution*, 119-131.

62   Michael Rosenthal, with Pamela Ritterman and Bob Sherman, "Blacks at Brandeis," in Patrick Gleeson, ed., *Essays on the Student Movement* (Columbus: Charles E. Merrill

Publishing Company, 1970), 101-107; Stefan M. Bradley, *Harlem vs. Columbia University: Black Student Power in the Late 1960s* (Urbana: University of Illinois Press, 2009). The critics of the Brandeis occupiers included Brandeis professor Pauli Murray. A notable legal scholar, theologian, Black feminist, and lesbian, Murray was generally ill-disposed toward Black Power. See Pauli Murray, *Song in a Weary Throat: An American Pilgrimage* (New York: Harper & Row, Publishers, 1987), 386-414.

63 *Georgian*, January 28, 1969.

64 Ibram Henry Rogers, "The Black Campus Movement: An Afrocentric Narrative History of the Struggle to Diversify Higher Education, 1965-1972" (PhD dissertation, Temple University, 2009),96.

65 See, for example, Dorothy W. Williams, *The Road to Now: A History of Blacks in Montreal* (Montreal: Véhicule Press, 1997) 118-138; Fred Kaufman, *Searching for Justice: An Autobiography* (Toronto: University of Toronto Press, 2005), 157-164; Marcel Martel, "'Riot' at Sir George Williams: Giving Meaning to Student Dissent," in Lara Campbell, Dominique Clément, and Gregory S. Kealey, eds., *Debating Dissent: Canada and the Sixties* (Toronto: University of Toronto Press, 2012). 97-114.

66 Butcher, "The Anderson Affair," in Forsythe, ed., *Let the Niggers Burn!;* Bryan D. Palmer, *Canada's 1960s: The Ironies of Identity in a Rebellious Era* (Toronto: University of Toronto Press, 2009), 284-287; Sean Mills, *The Empire Within: Postcolonial Thought and Political Activism in Sixties Montreal* (Montreal: McGill-Queen's University Press, 2010), 104-108; Samah Affan, "Ethical Gestures: Articulations of Black Life in Montreal's 1960s" (MA thesis, Concordia University, 2013); Paul C. Hébert, "'A Microcosm of the General Struggle': Black Thought and Activism in Montreal, 1960-1969" (PhD dissertation, University of Michigan, 2015); West, "History vs. Historical Memory," Part II.

67 G. David Sheps, "The Apocalyptic Fires," in Tim and Julyan Reid, eds., *Student Power* 36-42; Eugene D. Genovese, *In Red and Black: Marxian Explorations in Southern and Afro-American History* (Knoxville: University of Tennessee Press, 1984; first pub. 1971), lviii; *Time*, February 21, 1969.

68 Alexander Ross," You Can't Really Kill a Computer With An Axe," in Tim and Julyan Reid, eds., *Student Power*, 42.

69 Eber, *Computer Centre Party* 245.

70 "For he shall be as a tree planted by the waters, and that spreadeth out her roots by the rivers…." Jeremiah 17:8 (King James Version).

71 David Spener, *We Shall Not Be Moved: Biography of a Song of Struggle* (Philadelphia: Temple University Press, 2016).

72 *The Paper*, February 11, 1969.

73 Roosevelt Williams, "Réactions: The Myth of the White 'Backlash," in Forsythe, ed., *Let the Niggers Burn!*, 122.

74 *Loyola News*, February 28, 1969; *Georgian*, March 7, 1975. The latter is an interview with Don McKay, an editor of the *Georgian* who covered the occupation of the computer centre.

75 Williams, "Réactions: The Myth of the White 'Backlash," 122.

76 Ibid, 116-117

77 *Time*, the US-based international magazine, got into the act, praising the Montreal police for their "exemplary restraint." See *Time*, February 21, 1969.

78 Maya Angelou, "Still I Rise," in Henry Louis Gates Jr. and Nellie Y. McKay, eds., *The Norton Anthology of African American Literature*, 2nd ed. (New York: W. W. Norton & Company, 2004),. 2156-2157.

79 Eber, *Computer Centre Party*, 251, 294; Eric Siblin, "Rosie the Red Stops Smashing the State," *Saturday Night* (May 27, 2000):,27-34.

80   Rennie, in *Trinidad & Tobago Review*, January 31, 2010.

81   Afua Cooper, *The Hanging of Angélique: The Untold Story of Canadian Slavery and the Burning of Old Montreal* (Athens: University of Georgia Press, 2007).

82   Steve Hewitt, *Spying 101: The RCMP's Secret Activities at Canadian Universities, 1917-1997* (Toronto: University of Toronto Press, 2001) 150-155; Martel, "'Riot' at Sir George Williams," 105-109.

83   Eber, *Computer Centre Party*, 10.

84   Norman Cook, a Sir George student who played a key role in organizing support for the protesters turned criminal defendants at the end of the crisis, had the following to say: "There were upward of 500-600 people on a regular basis inside the computer centre during the occupation. I mean babies were conceived there. It was an occupation with all the racial confusion of the time. There were sisters screaming at white women taking down their panties in the night." An African Canadian who went on to a distinguished career as statesman and man of letters, Cook did not implicate himself in any of the "confusion"! Author's telephone interview with Norman Cook, August 22, 2009. On the question of interracial sex, see also Austin, *Fear of a Black Nation*.

85   *Loyola News* (Loyola College) February 28, 1969.

86   Rawle R. Frederick, "Words Not Music," in Forsythe, ed., *Let the Niggers Burn!*,143.

87   Dorothy Eber, "Notes on the Trial of the 'Trinidad Ten,'" *Canadian Forum*, October 1974, 21-25; Kaufman, *Searching for Justice*, 157-164.

88   Eber, "Notes on the Trial."

89   Norman Girvan, "After Rodney: The Politics of Student Protest in Jamaica," *New World Quarterly* 4, no. 3 (1968):59-68; Anthony Payne, "The Rodney Riots in Jamaica: The Background and Significance of the Events of October 1968," *Journal of Commonwealth and Comparative Politics* 21, no. 2 (1983):158-74; Rupert Charles Lewis, *Walter Rodney's Intellectual and Political Thought* (Detroit: Wayne State University Press, 1998), 85-123; Michael O. West, "Walter Rodney and Black Power: Jamaican Intelligence and US Diplomacy," *African Journal of Criminology and Justice Studies* 1, no. 2 (2006):1-50.

90   Eusi Kwayana, *Walter Rodney* (Georgetown: The Catholic Standard Ltd, 1986) 3.

91   Fanon, *Wretched of the Earth*; Richard Handyside, ed., *Revolution in Guinea: Selected Texts by Amilcar Cabral* (New York: Monthly Review Press, 1969); Africa Information Service, ed., *Return to the Source: Selected Speeches of Amilcar Cabral* (New York: Monthly Review Press, 1973). The idea, in Black Power circles, of the lumpen-proletariat as a revolutionary vanguard is best associated with Eldridge Cleaver, whose 1968 primer was widely read, including by the Sir George protesters. See Eldridge Cleaver, *Soul on Ice* (New York: A Delta Book, 1968).

92   Ken Post, *Arise Ye Starvelings: The Jamaican Labour Rebellion of 1938 and Its Aftermath* (Boston: Nijhoff, 1978).

93   See, for example, *Moko*, October 28, 1968. The inaugural issue of this magazine, based at St. Augustine, was devoted to the Rodney affair, which sparked its founding.

94   Ivar Oxaal, *Race and Revolutionary Consciousness: A Documentary Interpretation of the 1970 Black Power Revolt in Trinidad* (Cambridge, MA: Schenkman Publishing Company, Inc., 1971); Raoul Pantin, *Black Power Day: The February 1970 Revolution* (Santa Cruz, Trinidad and Tobago: Hatuey, 1990); Ryan and Stewart, eds., *Black Power Revolution*.

95   Andrew Feenberg and Jim Freedman, *When Poetry Ruled the Streets: The French May Events of 1968* (Albany: State University of New York Press, 2001).

96   Karl Marx, *The Eighteenth Brumaire of Louis Bonaparte: With Explanatory Notes* (New York: International Publishers, 1963; first pub. 1852). This text also appears as *The Eighteenth Brumaire of Louis Napoleon*.

97   Eric Williams, *Capitalism & Slavery* (Chapel Hill: University of North Carolina Press, 1944).

98   Selwyn R. Cudjoe, ed., *Eric E. Williams Speaks: Essays on Colonialism and Independence* (Wellesley, MA: Calaloux Publications, 1993); Eric Williams, *Inward Hunger: The Education of a Prime Minister* (London: Deutsch, 1969); Colin A. Palmer, *Eric Williams & the Making of the Modern Caribbean* (Chapel Hill: University of North Carolina Press, 2006).

99   C. L. R. James, *Dr. Eric Williams: A Biographical Sketch* (Port of Spain: P.N.M. Publishing Co., 1960), 15.

100 Williams claimed that, in origin, his People's National Movement had two models: Nkrumah's Convention People's Party, the first mass anticolonial nationalist movement in Africa, and Mohandas Gandhi's Indian National Congress. The point, clearly, was to appeal across Trinidad's ethnic lines to people of African and South Asian descent. In the event, the People's National Movement only had limited support among Indo-Trinidadians.

101 For Nkrumah's view of the coup against him and his critique of imperialist intrigues in the Congo, see Kwame Nkrumah, *Dark Days in Ghana* (New York: International Publishers, 1968); Kwame Nkrumah, *Challenge of the Congo* (London: Panaf Books Ltd, 1967).

102 Nkrumah, *Neo-Colonialism*.

103 This point was made by veterans of the Sir George Crisis at the conference that formed the basis of this collection.

104 June Milne, ed., *Kwame Nkrumah, the Conakry Years: His Life and Letters* (London: PANAF, 1990), *passim*

105 W. Scott Thompson, *Ghana's Foreign Policy, 1957-1966: Diplomacy, Ideology, and the New State* (Princeton: Princeton University Press, 1969).

106 Williams, *Inward Hunger*, 335. Although distancing himself from Castro and the Cuban Revolution politically, as a historian Williams was keenly aware of their importance. His synthetic history of the Caribbean, which came out the year of the Trinidad Revolution, used Castro as a bookend. See Eric Williams, *From Columbus to Castro: The History of the Caribbean, 1492-1969* (London: Deutsch, 1970).

107 Che Guevara, *The African Dream: The Diaries of the Revolutionary War in the Congo* (London: Harvill, 2000).

108 C. L. R. James, *The Black Jacobins: Toussaint L'Ouverture and the San Domingo Revolution*, 2nd ed. (New York: Vintage Books, 1963; first pub. 1938); David Austin, ed., *You Don't Play With Revolution: The Montreal Lectures of C.L.R. James* (Oakland, CA: AK Press, 2009); Austin, ed, *Moving Against the System*.

109 C. L. R. James, *Nkrumah, and the Ghana Revolution* (London: Allison and Busby, 1977); George Padmore, *The Gold Coast Revolution: The Struggle of an African People from Slavery to Freedom* (London: Dennis Dobson Ltd, 1953).

110 James, *Dr. Eric Williams*, 14-15. James praised Williams in this pamphlet as someone of considerable political acumen whose chief deficit was a lack of experience in party political organizing. After breaking with Williams, however, James drastically changed his assessment of the prime minister. Prior to his book on the Haitian Revolution, James now asserted, he had not engaged in psychobiography, "but after a number of years I thought I could attempt it with Toussaint. And maybe in my autobiography I will attempt it with a much more insignificant person. I will write an analysis of Eric Williams which will astonish everybody. I know that *petit-maitre* very well." Alas, James never published the promised autobiography. See C. L. R. James, "Lectures on the Black Jacobins," *Small Axe* 8 (2000): 112). This article was first given as a talk in 1971. In his own memoirs, Williams attacked James for abusing his role as editor of *The Nation* to "build up himself and his family, and his personal articles on George Padmore and the James family were widely resented." See Williams, *Inward Hunger*, 268.

111 Nkrumah, whom James mentioned or evoked several times in his little-cited pamphlet, began his political career in the Gold Coast (colonial Ghana) as chief organizer of an established nationalist movement, before defecting to form a rival and ultimately more successful one, the fabled Convention People's Party, in which Williams (as noted) found a model.

112 Deryck R. Brown, "The Coup That Failed: The Jamesian Connection," in Ryan and Stewart, eds., *Black Power Revolution*, 543-78; Robin Bunce and Paul Field, *Darcus Howe: A Political Biography* (London: Bloomsbury, 2014).

113 Shah, "Reflections on the Mutiny,"514.

114 Although involving individuals who came out of the Black Power movement, the Grenada Revolution was not a Black Power event. By the time of the Grenada Revolution in 1979, Black Power had long ceased to be a viable political force in the Caribbean, although it retained some cultural resonance. See Brian Meeks, *Radical Caribbean: From Black Power to Abu Bakr* (Barbados: University Press of the West Indies, 1996).

115 Williams, *Inward Hunger*, 204-246.

116 "'Mr. Q': A Politician Recalls 1970," in Ryan and Stewart, eds., *Black Power Revolution*, 597.

117 Ralston Granger to Rodney, March 31, 1970: Atlanta University Center Archives, Rodney Papers, Box 2, NJAC file. See also Peter James Hudson, "Imperial Designs: The Royal Bank of Canada in the Caribbean," *Race & Class* 52, no. 1(2010): 33-48

118 *La Presse* (Montreal), January 13, 1970; *Montreal Gazette*, January 16, 1970. The Caribbean protesters themselves previously made a similar point, asserting, in response to demands for their deportation, that "Canadians and Canadian exploitative capital can also 'be sent back'" from the Caribbean. See *Georgian*, January 28, 1969.

119 His new name honored two figures associated with antislavery, a tradition Black Power claimed as an integral part of its inheritance. The first figure, Makandal, was a maroon in prerevolutionary Haiti who sought to overthrow slavery through mass poisoning of slaveholders. The second figure, Daaga, was a survivor of the Atlantic slave trade who was forcibly conscripted into the West India Regiment garrisoned in Trinidad, the island's praetorian guard of slavery and colonialism, and who led a mutiny in the regiment.

120 Roy Mitchell, "The Making of Makandal Daaga," in Ryan and Stewart, eds., *Black Power Revolution,*, 97.

121 "'Mr. Q': A Politician Recalls 1970," 594-595.

122 Militarily defeated but politically unbroken, Trinidad's Black Power activists would strike back at Danjuma, accusing him to war crimes in the campaign against Biafra. See *Black Sound* 1, no 2 (1970).

123 US Embassy to State Department, April 22, 1970: US National Archives, RG59, Box 2630, file Pol 15.

124 David Austin, "Anne Cools: Radical Feminist and Trailblazer," *MaComere* 12, no. 2 (2010): 68-76; Belgrave, "The Sir George Williams Affair, 130; Kaufman, *Searching for Justice*, 163-164.

125 West, "History vs. Historical Memory," Part II.

126 Eber, *Computer Centre Party*, 314.

127 In due course, Professor Anderson was granted leave to complete his PhD in the United States (at the University of Oregon), subsequently returning to his job at Sir George, which had been held for him during his absence and which he kept until retiring from the university some three decades later.

128 *Georgian*, February 23, 1979.

129 Jeremiah 8:22 (King James Version).

130 Onur Bakiner, *Truth Commissions: Memory, Power, and Legitimacy* (Philadelphia: University of Pennsylvania Press, 2016).

131 Truth and Reconciliation Commission of Canada, *Honouring the Truth, Reconciling for the Future: Summary of the Final Report of the Truth and Reconciliation Commission of Canada* (2015).

132 *Slavery and Justice: Report of the Brown University Steering Committee on Slavery and Justice* (Providence, 2003); *Report of the Working Group on Slavery, Memory, and Reconciliation to the President of Georgetown University* (Washington, D. C., 2016); *President's Commission on Slavery in the University* (Charlottesville: The Rector and Visitors of the University of Virginia, 2018).

133 Marx, *Eighteenth Brumaire*, 16.

134 The novelist Chimamanda Ngozi Adichie would turn this into "half of a yellow sun." See Chimamanda Ngozi Adichie, *Half of a Yellow Sun* (New York: Anchor Books, 2006).

135 Michael O. West, "'Send the Niggers Back Home': The Image of Biafra in the Sir George Crisis," in Christiana Abraham, Nalini Mohabir, Ronald Cummings, eds., *Visualities of a Protest* (forthcoming).

Musings on Walter Rodney, the Black Power Movement and Race and Class in Guyana

Nigel Westmaas

Widely recognized for his celebrated works *How Europe Underdeveloped Africa, Groundings with My Brothers,* and *A History of the Guyanese Working People,* Walter Rodney was at the forefront, either in print or in person, of the protest movements in the United States, Canada, and the Caribbean in the 1960s and 1970s. But as this paper argues, his position on the Black Power movement in the USA, and his own comparative position on the Black Power movement in the Caribbean, was very consistent with and sensitive to the multiracial makeup of countries in the Anglophone Caribbean like Guyana, Trinidad and Tobago and to a lesser extent Jamaica. This sensitivity may have emerged from his family background. Rodney's parents were early members of Guyana's Peoples Progressive Party (PPP) and after the split of that party in 1955-57, his parents remained with the faction of Cheddi Jagan, a leader of Indian origin, that retained the party's name. Secondly, Rodney's multiracial awareness would have also been enhanced when he returned to the Caribbean and re-engaged with local political and social developments. It is also possible that Rodney's scholarly years in London at SOAS (School of Oriental and African Studies), would have been an environment where he met and worked with students from across racial backgrounds, and ideological, and social perspectives from the 'colonial' world. We also witness through his writings (some published from speeches), his consistency in his attention to multiracial intimacies. To put it another way, Rodney's Marxism offered an explicit engagement with "intersectionality," to borrow a more recent theoretical framework, which foregrounded social class and race.[1] To be sure, a significant component of intersectionality that Rodney would have failed to have consistently engaged was that of gender. This is not to say that Rodney never engages gender. In the last chapter of *History of the Guyanese Working People,* he does discuss women in the urban areas, and in one of his pamphlets he talks about women withdrawing from the labour force in the post-emancipation period, although he does not necessarily pursue the implications of these historical details. The question of Rodney and gender is one that requires its own separate analysis. I recall several conversations with the late Andaiye about various aspects of this weakness or absence in Rodney's holistic political and social outlook. Yet, interestingly enough, it was the same Rodney, and I again cite Andaiye, "who put in a line in the WPA' party programme of 1979" that "included housewives in working class households as part of the working class or working people." In pursuing this material and argument, it should be noted that this chapter's focus is restricted to the Anglophone Caribbean and not the Dutch, Hispanic or Francophone Caribbean.

The Setting

One of the stark realities, as represented by Guyana, is that the state and society which emerged after independence with the peculiar blend of nationalism and relatively secure economies, collapsed simultaneously, albeit with differing outcomes, under the combined force of inter-ethnic rivalry and its dialectical twin, the general crisis instanced by the dominant global ethos of capital. But to assume that there was a fundamental and swift change after independence is largely an exaggeration. As Gordon Lewis has established, independence, "unlike emancipation, is merely a redefinition of the legal status of the society not necessarily bringing in its wake a profound social metamorphosis such as characterized post-emancipation society, inherits those problems created by the slave and Creole societies."[2] Moreover, the race issue, always central in a racially heterogeneous society, was complicated by the imperatives of independence, and 'nation-building', and modernization among other popular labels. Prior to independence in 1966, the International Commission of Jurists, established to study racial imbalance in the Guyana Public Service, stated the following on the importance of race relations in the colony:

> The present racial disharmony in British Guiana is due in no small degree to the uncertainties and tensions of a community passing from colonial tutelage to full independence. While the grant of independence will not in itself provide a solution to the country's racial problems, and may even create fresh problems, we believe that until it is achieved, the community will not find self-reliance, the common purpose and cohesion of nationhood that are necessary for the successful pursuit of a racially integrated society.[3]

After independence, the struggle for succession in Guyana took essentially a two party, two-race course, even amounting to some extent the separation of 'class' and ideological boundaries from race. In practical terms, this entailed that a given political party would be supported exclusively on the basis of ethnic considerations, and the electoral data supports this conclusion, then and since. This may have accounted for the enduring electoral strength of the Marxist Cheddi Jagan over an extended period despite the hostility and indifference to Marxism, even from among his supporters. The end product of this organizationally for the PPP was a curious amalgam of a labor and business base drawn from the Indian population. Similarly, the Forbes Burnham government found large-scale support across class in the Black population. In any event, the successful regime that emerged under the British Westminster electoral system continued to rely on imperial sponsorship and recognition for their holding of the line against communism. To paraphrase Martin Carter, Guyana was both "victim and vehicle" of imperial machinations.[4] Correspondingly, the respected Guyanese economist Clive Thomas, arguing from a social science framework, suggested that the leaders of the independence movements, some of whom became heads of state after independence, "sought to demobilize and de-politicize the masses to prevent any further entrenchment of mass politics in the society at large."[5]

Enter Rodney

By the 1960s, the challenges to the reading and writing of African history had become more pronounced. The strains between the old and the new were to become dramatically apparent with the contribution of a young Guyanese historian, Walter Rodney. The late historian is widely recognized for two major academic contributions to African historiography.[6] Following in the tradition of scholarship forged in the midst of Pan-Africanism which spanned the previous half-century, he succeeded in the footsteps of Pan-African academic titans such as W.E.B Du Bois, George Padmore and Henry Sylvester Williams.

Rodney's scholarship nonetheless had a unique ingredient. It appeared to embrace both the epistemological and political trends in academia. Indeed, Rodney's embryonic development and work as a scholar were sustained at every turn by his political and social activism. While this was not surprising given his background of political activism in the various public spheres he encountered, it was galling to many adversaries that Rodney's academic activism was informed by a radical Marxist approach. By the early 1960s, the philosophy of Marxism had retained a strong influence in various countries in the colonial and "post-colonial" world. This would dramatically lead to a political explosion in Jamaica in 1968, a direct consequence of this fusion of politics and professional history as embodied in Rodney's activism.

Rodney's arrival in Jamaica as a lecturer in 1968 came in the context of his professed respect for the Jamaican people (first as an undergraduate in the early sixties, and later during student life at London University). The Jamaica in which Rodney now lectured was a rigidly stratified society. The Jamaica Labour Party government of Hugh Shearer was in power, having won the 1967 elections and the country was characterized at the time by police brutality, strikes against social oppression, and stagnation in town and country. Rodney's now infamous trip to Canada in 1968 appears to have set in motion an opportunity for the Jamaican government, which reviled his activism, to settle once and for all the Rodney issue by preventing his return. He had left Kingston, Jamaica to attend the Congress of Black Writers in Montreal. His participating in the Congress, of course, enhanced his internationalist credentials and Marxist connections. However, the subsequent ban on the historian (along with Clive Thomas and Joey Jagan), came as a shock to the academic community, to his friends and supporters, students all over the Caribbean but, more importantly, to the Jamaican masses and the Rastafari. It also exemplified the lengths to which neo-colonial governments in the region would go to prevent radical activity, extending of course to Black Power activism.

The Sir George Williams University protest in 1969 also brings into focus cross-racial solidarity involving another Guyanese, the Indo-Guyanese son of Dr. Cheddi Jagan whose reputation as a "communist" is well established. To recall, during the Montreal protest, Joey Jagan was arrested during the uprising and even wrote about the protest.[7] Joey's involvement in the event would have made news, especially following his banning from Jamaica along with two other prominent Guyanese Walter Rodney and Clive Thomas. The symbolism for Guyana of Joey Jagan's public activities would not be lost. But did it fundamentally have an effect on cross-racial unity in Guyana the way Rodney entered the Indo-Guyanese community? Not likely, except in symbolic terms. As Michael West reports, citing the American embassy, the banning of Joey Jagan only "excited mild interest among most Guyanese."[8] Did it actually place the multi-racial question in Guyana into focus? One can argue that it would have had little comparative effect, because (a) Joey Jagan was not as active on the ground as Rodney was and would have been subsumed in the peculiar Guyanese racial context under his father's shadow. In fact, Joey Jagan was reported as representing his father by a Jamaican based US diplomat.[9]

In 1969 when Rodney published *Groundings*, he had already developed a more embracing position on his conception of Black Power. He observes in the same volume: "Black Power in the West Indies means three closely related things: (1) the break with imperialism which is historically white racist; (2) the assumption of power by the black masses in the islands; (3) the cultural reconstruction of the society in the image of the blacks."[10] In the same vein he articulates, perhaps earlier than anyone else, his sensitivity to the Asian question:

> I maintain that it is the white world which has defined who are blacks, if you are not white then you are black. However, it is obvious that the West Indian situation is complicated by factors such as the variety of racial types and racial mixtures and by the process of class formation. We have, therefore, to note not simply what the white world says but also how individuals perceive each other. Nevertheless, we can talk of the mass of the West Indian population as being black, either African or Indian. There seems to have been some doubts on the last point, and some fear that Black Power is aimed against the Indian. This would be a flagrant denial of both the historical experience of the West Indies and the reality of the contemporary scene.[11]

As Perry Mars notes about the burning issue behind Rodney's interaction with Black Power, "it is often asserted that whereas conditions within the United States favour adherence to the more race or nationalist approaches, those in the Caribbean are more receptive of the class-based paradigm."[12]

In 1971, Walter Rodney wrote a short, relatively unknown piece on the African American revolutionary George Jackson who was killed in prison that same year. But again, this work exemplifies Rodney's interest not only in the global Pan African struggle, but the intersectionality of race and class struggle in the USA. In the piece, Rodney connects the Jackson repression and conditions in the USA for Black people to the global solidarity struggle stressing that, "international solidarity grows out of struggle in different localities."[13] But, Rodney is also aware of the limitations of comparisons and the difference in context between the USA and other areas of the world, and certainly the Caribbean from whence he came. He writes of the US: "the phenomenon of a race encrusted within a class in the particular way that the black working class is situated, and functions is definitely not found anywhere else."[14] Similarly, Rodney expands on his experience in teaching in two geographic locations:

> I have taught in Africa and I have taught in the Caribbean, and I have met a large number of black students in this country (i.e., in the US). There just isn't that same degree of commitment. In my opinion, the African student is highest in his or her motivation, and then comes the Caribbean student, and then the black American."[15]

The words of the editors in a new book on Rodney's previously unpublished study of the Russian Revolution are instructive of Rodney's evolution on the Black Power issue:

> Some interpret Rodney as having begun his life with Black Power and racial politics, before progressing toward a more orthodox Marxist analysis as he matured and became a scholar. Rodney was indeed a strong proponent of Black consciousness, pride, and power. However, such false dichotomous race/class readings of Rodney ignore his praxis, where theory was always historically grounded and attentive to the complexity of lived experience. Rodney deepened his early exposure to socialism through engaged study of Marxism and the Russian, Cuban, Tanzanian, and other socialist revolutions, always using a critical dialectical approach.[16]

Rodney's writings (in contrast to more popular texts), emphasize the differences not only in his own views on Black Power, but also the general disconnect between Black Power in the Caribbean and North America. Among these writings (one arising from a speech) are *Marx in the Liberation of Africa* and *In Defence of Arnold Rampersaud*. Both booklets affirm Rodney's ideological praxis. In pursuing the argument via these booklets, I am thereby assessing Rodney's implicit and explicit critique of US Black Power from the prism of (1) ideological and class perspectives, and (2) the multiracial peculiarity of Guyana and, by extension, other Anglophone Caribbean societies in relation to North America.

Enter Carmichael

Before Rodney returned formally to the region, another Black Power icon visited the region in 1970 in a moment that "Black Power activity" was humming. He was Stokely Carmichael, the American Black Power activist who later changed his name to Kwame Ture. Carmichael was born in Trinidad but left for the United States at the age of eleven, settling first in New York. He was invited to Guyana by Ratoon, a radical grouping mainly composed of members of the University of Guyana community and whose leaders included noted Guyanese academics Clive Thomas, Josh Ramsammy, and Omawale, among others. Although Ratoon was not in itself a Black Power group, it did advocate for multiracial unity but, "by accident and error"[17] invited Carmichael to Guyana, as one critic surmised.

Rodney was not in Guyana during the period of Carmichael's visit but the regional influence cast by the Guyanese revolutionary was evident. Newly declassified confidential documents demonstrate palpable concern on the part of the British and Commonwealth foreign office (and no doubt their US counterparts), over the activities of Stokeley Carmichael. The documents reveal the disconnect between Carmichael in relation to the local ethnic and racial makeup in Guyana and Trinidad and Tobago. Carmichael, who had been banned in Trinidad and Tobago for allegedly calling for the violent overthrow of the Eric Williams regime, found a better, though reluctant, host in Guyana. The difference in reception for Carmichael in Trinidad and Guyana can be traced to developments in Guyana, when the Forbes Burnham regime, after cozying up to the Western powers in late pre-independence and post-independence, was now beginning to assume a new political and diplomatic mantle that later eventuated in many African American Black Power activists finding in Guyana a safe haven from US racism. Indeed, the anvil of Burnham's foreign policy was beginning to turn towards 'third world' and leftist identifications. It was in this context that Guyana proved a more favorable setting for the controversial Black Power leader. And the thesis is confirmed by the worried diplomatic corps (and presumably intelligence agencies), prior to and in the wake of Carmichael's Caribbean sojourn. In February 1970, ASCRIA (African Society for Cultural Relations with Independent Africa), with the support of the Guyana state, had hosted the "Pan-Africanist and Black Revolutionary Nationalists Seminar" in Georgetown and invited Prime Minister Burnham to open the session. During his address, Burnham invited African freedom fighters everywhere to see Guyana as a place of refuge. And this invitation was extended to North American Pan-Africanists and Black Power activists.[18]

The US Black Power icon made inflammatory comments toward another race group at a public forum in Georgetown in the presence of a fairly diverse audience of Indo-Guyanese. The group, mainly students who went to the activity with political activist Paul Tennassee,[19] ostensibly there to offer solidarity to the Black Power leader, were reportedly turned off by statements made by Carmichael to wit that, "Indo-Guyanese should find an appropriate and corresponding slogan and ideology."[20] Since Ratoon, a multiracial organization, had invited Carmichael, it was probably in this environment that Indian students turned up to hear the Black Power leader. One Guyanese newspaper put his intrusion in even more graphic language:

The Black Power leader, who arrived in Guyana on Sunday, has made a series of vitriolic speeches calling for armed revolution in the fight against imperialism, capitalism, and the white power structure. He has also aroused the animosity of many people in the multi-racial republic because of his concept of Black Power, which he says is for Negroes only and excludes Indians and other non-whites.[21]

More importantly, Carmichael also alarmed Guyanese progressives, including the host organisation Ratoon who saw his 'Black Power' advocacy cross the lines with respect of the fragile multiracial unity that emerged in the post-independence period. It has to be borne in mind that Burnham, to whose government Ratoon was opposed, had seized upon Carmichael's presence and he even, "hosted a luncheon for Carmichael and his party,"[22] capitalizing on the visit.

One of the confidential diplomatic notes stated:

> Stokeley Carmichael left Guyana on 10 May. His performance in this country was publicly criticised, even condemned, by a number of people although the motives of the people concerned differed widely. His definition of Black Power as African Power provoked a blast from the President of the Maha Sabha, the largest Hindu organisation in Guyana. He castigated Carmichael for undoing the efforts of the Government and organisations such as his own in rebuilding the fabric of national unity.[23]

Rodney's colleague, celebrated economist, and academic Clive Thomas, was also cited as opposing Carmichael's' views at a symposium at the University of Guyana on "Ideology and the Black Revolution."[24] Thomas reportedly made it "clear that he strongly disagreed with Carmichael's views" and "pointed out that Pan-Africanism is an eminent ideology for Africa and that on its own it had a definite revolutionary potential everywhere except three societies, those of Surinam, Trinidad, and Guyana." [25]While this confidential memo used the words of Thomas and was self-serving in motive and interpretation, these were in line with those of the Ratoon group and Rodney, which stuck generally to the principles of multiracial unity in Guyana.

The developments in Trinidad and Tobago in 1970-71 are well chronicled. Brinsley Samaroo of more recent vintage suggests a narrative that begins with the February 1970 protest by the National Joint Action Committee in front of the Royal Bank of Canada in Port of Spain in solidarity with the Caribbean students on trial for the George Williams University uprising in Montreal, Canada (1969). According to Samaroo, "public anger deepened on May 15 as the state ordered that no airlines should carry Stokeley Carmichael (who was due to visit neigbouring Guyana) to his Trinidad homeland."[26] This substantial tension in Trinidad and Tobago forced an apprehensive diplomatic corps representing the British and Americans to take note of the Black Power leader's visit to Guyana.

The situation in Trinidad also shows that Guyanese politics was no quirk. Allowing for local agency and constitutional particularity, Trinidad was essentially beset with the same ethnic problems. In the Trinidad case, if we are to step aside for a moment, the 'Black Power' revolt presumed national, all-embracing multi-ethnic support. One of the leading players in the military events of 1970, a young Indian army lieutenant at the moment of the uprising, Raffique Shah, claimed the Trinidad revolt as a bid to "eradicate racial divisions in the society, to mold one nation, one people."[27]

But this confidence was not universally shared and spokespersons of both ethnic groups were skeptical of the positive interpretation. According to eyewitnesses, the reception accorded the marchers then was at best polite. Spokespersons of NJAC, and the movement in general, tended to exaggerate its significance, even deeming it the 'birth' of Afro-Indian unity. Several subsequent decades of disunity between the two racial groups in both Trinidad and Guyana nevertheless support empirical evidence to the contrary. The debate about race is still contentious and illustrates the deep-seated divide between Africans and Indians in the Caribbean. One Trinidadian scholar, Kumar Mahabir, even denounced the significance of Indian participation in the Black Power revolt of 1970 insinuating they were "token symbols" used by advocates of the Black Power movement for strategic, symbolic, and political reasons. He asked rhetorically, "How would blacks respond if Indians now raised their clenched fists in the air and shouted, 'Indian Power?'"[28] In a practical sense, very few ethnic-based organisations in the region have managed to resolve the problem of ethnic division, even if their spirit was inclined differently.

In some sense, Carmichael's views on the Indians in Guyana and Trinidad and Tobago in the 1970 imbroglio was seemingly at odds with his own recall of his early years in Port of Spain, Trinidad. He talks in his autobiography about, "reasonably civil and tolerant" relations between Africans and Indians in his country of birth.[29] Yet, in this expansive autobiography he devotes very little attention to his ban from his country of birth in 1970. Carmichael finally returned to Trinidad and Tobago in 1996 to an impressive welcome where he noted, "the reception was really most extraordinary, especially for someone who had officially been banned from the country for most of his adult life."[30]

Rodney Redux

Rodney's arrival in Guyana from his Tanzania sojourn brought the apparatus of his thinking into the Guyanese political praxis in several iterations. The first of these was evident in his alertness to the multiracial imperatives of the Guyanese political situation after decades of division. And his speeches (published afterwards) were distinctive in their approach and clearly identified his concerns with class and race. The taut voice of Black Power, as even handed as it was originally in Rodney's *Groundings,* virtually shifted now that he became more engrossed in addressing the multiracial imperatives of Guyanese society. This was not a surprise to Eusi Kwayana, the political figure, author, educator, teacher, playwright, and founder member of the Working People's Alliance, who wrote, "methodical by nature, Walter Rodney on his return began systematically to inform himself about where the country had reached, how organisations, cases and individuals stood in respect of one another... He told the only press conference he had ever addressed as an individual: 'I aspire to be a Marxist-Leninist'.[31]"

In his lifetime, Walter Rodney defied all sorts of conventions. Although a committed Pan-Africanist Rodney, unlike others in his field, broke practically with some of the approaches to Black Power. Part of this defying of convention was derived from his Marxist outlook. Another was an active sense of the multiracial nature of Guyana society and his concurrent sensitivity to the issue of race relations. When he gave active solidarity to an Indian taxi driver, Arnold Rampersaud (and member of the opposition PPP) who was charged with murder of a Black policeman, James Henry, Rodney had entered an environment and community that traditionally did not witness multiracial solidarity from a Black politician with this level of activism in multiracial solidarity. And this was the case with Forbes Burnham's PNC, a historically Black supported political party in a country riven with ethnic or racial insecurity. One that Guyanese poet Martin Carter had memorably described as having, "not leaders, but people who follow in front,"[32] alluding here of course to the herd mentality of race. In 1977, Walter Rodney gave a speech in defence of Rampersaud who was on trial for the murder of Henry. Rampersaud was an activist of the Peoples Progressive Party led by Cheddi Jagan and the racial significance of the context and setting of the trial was not lost on the Guyanese. During his three trials (a consequence of hung juries), Rampersaud's case had acquired international attention and an "Arnold Rampersaud Defence Committee" had been established. The case made a positive impact on multiracial unity and contributed organically in the subsequent development of a broad anti-dictatorial alliance in the country. After alerting the public to what he deemed the manipulation of race in the case, Rodney highlighted the "the overwhelmingly black jury... being called upon to decide the innocence or guilt of this Indian from the Corentyne."[33] But immediately after he explains the racial dynamic of the case,

Rodney prods the audience to come to terms with the underlying class analysis of the context in which Rampersaud was on trial, "Because as I said before, you start with one thing, you end with another. The system doesn't stop at racial discrimination. Because it is a system of class oppression, it only camouflages its class nature under a racial cover. And in the end, it will move against anyone, irrespective of colour."[34]

I contend that Rodney was influential in the case and its outcome not only by virtue of his active politics, his scholarly reputation and activism, but by his method of public disassembling of a much-known Guyanese problem. This was unsurprising, as Rodney was renowned, whether in Kingston, Jamaica, London or Georgetown, Guyana for his conflation of academic and socio-political problems. While out of work in Guyana for the period 1974-1980, Rodney held bottom house classes at several locations including his home. Students drawn from the University of Guyana students, some of whom were activists of other parties, including the PPP and PNC, would partake in these sessions. In one course offering advertised in December 1977 to be taught at his home titled *Marxist Ideology and Guyanese History*, Rodney stated it was, "intended to deepen an appreciation of Marxist historical method and its application to Guyana. It is open to anyone with or without previous familiarity with Marxist ideology."[35] I do recall that I attended about three of the sessions in 1977-1978, and my recollection is that they were usually about 30-40 people in attendance from across social class. In other terms, there were middle class and working-class citizens in attendance at these classes, and the classes served as my own introduction to Guyanese (and global) history like it has never been taught before. It was yet another iteration of 'groundings' writ large.

Attending the Rodney class was actually a seminal moment of political change for me. My father was associated with the PPP from its inception and in Guyana, families usually follow their family's political choices, sometimes for life. But this class and the meetings with individuals in attendance attracted me to Walter Rodney and subsequently to the WPA, a party in which I became an activist and to which I still belong, if membership can be conceptualized in diasporic terms. As far as the content of the class is concerned, it was structured quite informally to allow for differences in education level and social class disposition. Here was Rodney at the apogee of his own Marxist outlook, weaving it in dialectically with a Guyanese audience and material pulled directly out of the Guyanese experience without conceding the importance of understanding the contradictions in the global capitalist system as it related to Guyanese history, economy, and environment. This act of public education is not to be underestimated. Rodney, to Guyanese or people in different parts of the world in which he lived and worked, was no conceited, self-referential intellectual. It is a little-known fact that in the late seventies, at the height of the mobilization against the Burnham regime, Rodney had no problem, as "Dr. Rodney," in taking karate self-defence classes under the tutelage of fellow WPA activist Tacuma Ogunseye, a black belt instructor in his own right.

In Guyana, Rodney's practical intervention was almost identical with his sojourn elsewhere if you add the race-class dialectic. Whether with bauxite or sugar worker, the urban or rural unemployed and "lumpen," he was active unto death. He shared his substantial scholarship while fighting for critical causes in which the working people and the oppressed were involved.

Another lesser-known speech titled "Marxism as a Third World Ideology" defends Marxism as an ideology of use value for the 'third world' societies and demonstrates Rodney's core ideological concerns with the application of Marxism to the region.[36] In it, he refers to a hypothetical argument about a society having its own ideology and counterposes it with the use of material from colonial Europe. In so many words, his defense of Marxism rested upon his worldview that class analysis was a global feature of human society and should not be rejected solely on account of its assumed origins in Europe:

> If one were to enquire of an individual who says: I'm a Ghanaian and I'm concerned that Ghana should have its own ideology, and I do not believe that ideology should be imported (that would normally be the terminology), I feel that we must come up with something authentically Ghanaian, that same individual will have no problem using a telephone, a motor car, electricity, and so on. He does not ask you for a specific Ghanaian mode of locomotion, and he doesn't not reject, a priori, a motor car as having originated in Europe or Japan as the case might be. He does not reject, a priori, electricity and ask for some peculiar Ghanaian mode of illumi-nation when he's indoor. And when he therefore says that he will reject Marxism as an alien ideology, he's making a distinction between the scientific mode of society and social relations...and that distinction is essentially a bourgeois distinction.[37]

In *Marx in the Liberation of Africa*, addressed to a mainly African-American audience wary of Marxism, Rodney rued the tendency among a few African academics to eschew the works of Europe in the name of establishing a veritable purity of analysis. In reference to the rejection of Marxism as 'European' by some Africanists, Rodney noted that those who had a problem with Marx and

MARXIST IDEOLOGY AND GUYANESE HISTORY - Course

This course is intended to deepen an appreciation of Marxist historical method and its application to Guyana.   It is open to anyone with or without previous familiarity with Marxist ideology.

COURSE OUTLINE

I   MARXISM AND THE ENVIRONMENT
     The Guyana Coast and Hinterland

II   TECHNOLOGY - THE HISTORICAL ROLE
     Application to Guyana

III HISTORICAL PERIODISATION
     Europe, the Caribbean, and Guyana

IV   CONTRADICTIONS IN CAPITALISM
     The Business Cycle - Europe and Guyana

V   CLASS AND CLASS RELATIONSHIPS
     Developed Capitalist Societies and Colonial Societies
     The Guyanese Working Class

The Course is designed provisionally to last for ten weeks meeting Wednesdays from 5.30 to 7.30 p.m. at 186 Aubrey Barker Street, South Ruimveldt Gardens. The first session will be Wednesday, December 14th.,1977.   Course tutor is Walter Rodney.

Recommended Basic Texts on Marxist Ideology:

The Communist Manifesto
Historical Materialism, Maurice Cornforth
The German Ideology

Any text which provides a chronological outline and descriptive information on Guyanese history may be used.

Further reading material will be suggested at discussion sessions.

Figure 1. Handout, Walter Rodney "bottom house" classes, 1977.

Engels appeared to have had no difficulty with electricity. "Was Edison a racist"? he inquired.[38]

In both these documents, he paused to critique the notion that Marxism was a foreign ideology in showing how the very same audience that sought to reject Marxism as foreign potentially violated their logic about 'foreign' when they accepted objects of use-value like light, hence his rhetorical question. Charles Dickens' ability to provide agency to the working class in England and yet still be one of the fiercest racists from England (just recall Dickens' support of Governor Eyre in Jamaica in the aftermath of the 1865 Morant Bay rebellion) is a case in point. Perhaps Rodney could have been more cautious with his

example, but language is psychological, and we are in no position to compre-
hend the tactical impact of Rodney's comparison at the moment.

In sum, it is evident from the varied nature of the unrest in Guyana, that
Rodney's influence was naturally more direct and present in Guyana in the five
years between 1975 and his death. Yet, his sway as scholar-activist was continuous after his assassination, both in the form of student and youth protest and
political protest on and off campus.

Finally, certain broad principles emerge when one assesses Rodney's
political and social activity. First, Rodney's commitment to public and open
critiques of the society in which he "currently" lived. Second, the promotion of
scholarship that is qualitative, and 'relevant' to active life. Third, the practice of
Rodney's scholar-activism with a tendency to be polemical, resulting in a
fascinating dance between the polemical and the academic without either
suffering. And finally, and most relevant for this essay, Rodney's consistent
Marxist outlook over time. In the final analysis, it appears that scholarship that
is enmeshed in activism has been historically beneficial and inspirational. In
another little-known piece by the historian published in the Guyanese journal
Transition in 1978, Rodney re-established that consistent ability to update his
Marxist framework and analysis and his acute awareness of the changing world
situation and the need to adapt. He acknowledges, for instance, in the article
that, "imperialism has proven itself more powerful and resilient in the periphery
than had been suggested in interpretations of 'moribund capitalism.'"[39] What
better or more accurate premonition for the current situation we face in the 21st
century? As one author mused, "we entered the twenty-first century without
revolutions, without Bastilles or Winter Palace assaults."[40] Or we might well add
in an era of apparent global cynicism, where are the 'Walter Rodneys', embody-
ing the spirit of the times? And what can be learned, if anything, from that
collective memory of a period when this revolutionary scholar blazed a trail of
fight and optimism?

NOTES

1   Kimberle Crenshaw, "Mapping the Margins: Intersectionality, Identity Politics, and Violence
     against Women of Color," *Stanford Law Review* 43, no. 6 (July 1991):1241-1299.

2   Gordon Lewis, "The Challenge of Independence in the Caribbean", in Beckles, Hilary &
     Shepherd, Verene, *Caribbean Freedom* (Princeton: Markus Wiener Publishers, 1996), 511.
     Lewis does not address what he means by problems of slave and creole society. He does
     however refer to 'problems' such as excess population and low wage economies and poor
     living standards. The arrival of indentureship he implies, also gave rise to a multiracial
     society. His reference to 'creole' is thus historically located in the pre-indentureship period
     (i.e., before emancipation in the Anglo-Caribbean in 1838). The reference 'creole' should
     therefore be taken in its original meaning, that is, locally born descendants of Africans
     enslaved in the new world.

3   International Commission of Jurists, 1965.

4   Martin Carter, "Man and Making-Victim and Vehicle," Edgar Mittelholzer Memorial Lectures, Fourth Series, Ministry of Information and Culture, October 1971.

5   Clive Thomas, *The Poor and the Powerless*, (New York: Monthly Review Press, 1988), 70.

6   See Walter Rodney's How Europe Underdeveloped Africa (1972), as well as History of the Upper Guinea Coast 1545-1800 (1970).

7   As noted by Paul C. Hebert in his PhD dissertation "A Microcosm of the General Struggle" (University of Michigan 2015), 269.

8   Michael West, "Seeing Darkly: Guyana, Black Power and Walter Rodney's Expulsion from Jamaica" *Small Axe*, 25 (February 2008), 97.

9   Ibid, 96.

10   Walter Rodney, *Groundings with my Brothers*. (London: Bogle-L'Ouverture Publications, 1969), 28.

11   Ibid, 28.

12   Perry Mars, "Caribbean Influences in African-America Political Struggles," *Ethnic and Racial Studies* 27, no. 4 (July 2004),568-569.

13   Walter Rodney, "George Jackson," November 1971.

14   Robert Hill, *Walter Rodney Speaks: The Making of an African Intellectual* (Trenton: Africa World Press, 1990), 105.

15   Ibid, 4.

16   Jesse Benjamin and Robin Kelley. "'An African Perspective'" on the Russian Revolution in Walter Rodney's *The Russian Revolution: A View from the Third World* (New York: Verso, 2018), xxxv The text of *A Russian Revolution: A View from the Third World* is drawn from the lectures he gave while teaching in Tanzania.

17   Paul Nehru Tennassee, *Guyana: A Nation in Ruins* (Toronto: Clarion Typesetting, 1982), 22.

18   Prior to the Pan Africanist declaration, Guyana had welcomed refugees from Biafra (Nigeria) and Malawi beginning in 1967.

19   Paul Tennassee at the time of the incident was an Indo-Guyanese teacher who held some association with the Ratoon grouping, the same group that had invited Carmichael. Tennassee later returned fully to Guyana in the late 1970s and was active in the Right to Work Association, which he had established. He subsequently established and became leader of the Democratic Labour Movement (DLM).

20   Paul Nehru Tennassee, *Guyana: A Nation in Ruins*, 22.

21   *Guyana Chronicle*, May 7, 1970

22   Tyrone Ferguson, *To Survive Sensibly, or to Court Heroic Death* (Georgetown: Guyana National Printers, 1999).138.

23   Confidential memo: KG Ritchie, to Caribbean Department, Foreign and Commonwealth Office, 15th May 1979.

24   A Guyanese CID (Criminal Investigation Report) of 1982 alleges that Rodney had met Carmichael before in the 1960s.

25   Confidential memo: KG Ritchie, to Caribbean Department, Foreign and Commonwealth Office, 9th May 1970.

26   Samaroo Brinsley, "The February Revolution (1970) as a Catalyst for Change in Trinidad and Tobago" in *Black Power in the Caribbean*, ed. Kate Quinn (Gainesville: University Press of Florida, 2014).

27   *Caribbean Daylight*, May 12, 2000.

28   *Caribbean Daylight*, May 12, 2000.

29 Stokely Carmichael, *Ready for Revolution. The Life and Struggles of Stokely, Carmichael* (New York: Scribner, 2003).37.

30 Ibid, 31.

31 Eusi Kwayana, *Walter Rodney* (Georgetown: Catholic Standard, 1988), 8.

32 Martin Carter, "The Race Crisis –British Guiana:" Speech at the Inter-American University of Puerto Rico, 1964. See p.92 *Kyk-Over –Al* 49/50, June 2000.

33 Walter Rodney, "In Defence of Arnold Rampersaud," 5. The significance of the location "Corentyne" is very Guyana specific. The Corentyne is an area where historically Indian Guyanese reside in more numbers than African Guyanese.

34 Ibid, .9.

35 Handout, Walter Rodney "bottom house" classes, 1977 (see Fig. 1). Source: author's personal archives.

36 I myself attended several of Rodney's classes in 1977 at his bottom house in South Ruimveldt as a very young and unprepared student. At the well-attended classes Marx's *German Ideology* and Lenin and other Soviet texts were used extensively and creatively along with assessments of Guyana's own political, social, and environmental development.

37 Walter Rodney, "Marxism as a Third World Ideology," 10-11.

38 Walter Rodney, "Marx in the Liberation of Africa" (Georgetown: WPA, 1981), 14.

39 Walter Rodney, "Transition" in *Transition* 1, no.1 (1978).

40 Enzo Traverso, *Left-Wing Melancholia-Marxism, History and Memory* (New York: Columbia University Press, 2016),.9.

Rumblings of a Revolution: Trinidad, 1970 and the Sir George Affair[1]

Raffique Shah

Introductory Note

One year after the occupation of the Sir George Williams University computer centre, Trinidad erupted in Black Power protests led by the National Joint Action Committee (NJAC) and others. NJAC was an organization formed by Makandal Daaga (Geddes Granger) and Dave Darbeau in 1969 on the St. Augustine Campus of the University of the West Indies, in part to rally support for their compatriots on trial in Montreal. By 1970, students in Montreal were facing grave charges and the possibilities of deportation or prison for their role in the Sir George Williams occupation. In solidarity, protesters in Trinidad marched from the Canadian High Commission to the Royal Bank of Canada on February 26, 1970, where Daaga proclaimed: "Our students in Canada felt that their dignity was affected. They protested. They were hounded and chained".[2] The protests, sparked by racist attitudes towards, and brutal treatment of, the students at Sir George, soon transformed into Trinidad's Black Power movement. Young students, radicals, working class people, oilfield workers, sugar workers, and others joined together "under slogans of black solidarity, African-Indian unity, and an end to white and foreign domination of the country's economy".[3] Mass demonstrations continued unabated; in an effort to suppress the protests, Prime Minister Eric Williams declared a state of emergency in April and ordered military defense to quell unrest. However, Lieutenants Raffique Shah and Rex Lasalle, did the unimaginable and disobeyed orders, leading troops into mutiny and shielding protesters from state violence until Venezuelan and US warships appeared off the coast of Trinidad to restore William's authority.[4]

Raffique Shah, educated at Sandhurst, the Royal Military College in the UK, is highly respected for his courageous role in Black Power. He also went on to contribute to Trinidadian society through his role as a union leader and newspaper columnist. Here, Shah offers us a personal account of Black Power from his memoir in progress. In this telling excerpt, he maps the intricacies of transnational conversations across the Caribbean and its diaspora (Trinidad, Cuba, Canada, the USA and Britain), shaped by friendships of those who identified with Black Power across race, and mobilized by the spirit of independence into liberatory action. The radical actions taking place from Montreal to Port of Spain to London and elsewhere were all shaped by anti-colonial struggle bound in the fight against anti-Black racism. Thus, it is not coincidental that Darcus Howe, the nephew of C.L.R. James, a member of the British Black Panthers and a renown anti-racist activist in the UK, was part of a group of intellectuals who dialogued with the young lieutenants, as Shah recalls.

Shah, an Indo-Trinidadian son of a sugar worker, might seem an unlikely person to be supported by a British Black Panther and eventually become a leader in Black Power; however, the politics of resistance in the Caribbean and its diaspora is filled with such examples. For instance, among those arrested during the Sir George protests was Joey Jagan, son of Guyanese political leader Cheddi Jagan, himself a child of indentured labourers. Historically, there are earlier precedents: in the late 1920s, the secretary of the United Negro Improvement Association (UNIA) office in Montreal was Indo-Caribbean (Felix Mahomed), and in the 1930s, Hucheshwar G. Mudgal (of Indo-Trinidadian background) was the editor of Marcus Garvey's *Negro World*.[5] Thus, at different historical crossroads, we witness Indo-Caribbean involvement in Black Power movements, suggesting a personal relationality to the cause.[6] Perhaps, as Shah illustrates, to talk about Black Power in the Caribbean is also to talk at the intersections of race; note Shah's friend, "a burly, bearded Indian," Krishna Gowandan, or Wally Look Lai, "a small-framed Chinese" from Couva, both engaged in their own ways in acts of Black liberation. In considering the role of Asian-Caribbeans within Black Power, we need to remember the historically expansive conversations of transnational Black radicalism that held both resistance and relationality.

❖ ❖ ❖

Budding Revolutionaries

Mass uprisings that sometimes lead to revolutions do not come like the proverbial thief in the night, as some political theoreticians postulate. They are invariably preceded by widespread acts of defiance by diverse sections of the population. When those in authority fail to heed the signs of a gathering storm, they sometimes pay the ultimate price.

By early 1968, as the junior officers pursued our campaign for change, Rex Lasalle and I increasingly saw ourselves as budding revolutionaries.[7] Besides voracious reading of radical literature, some crucial coincidences would influence our politicisation. A month or so after I had taken up duty as a platoon commander in January 1967, I was in Port of Spain one afternoon waiting for a route taxi to Chaguanas. I was on my way home. I stayed at my parents' Boccaro Village home most weekends when I was not on duty. While milling around the taxi stand, I heard someone shout, "Raffique Shah!" I looked around and saw a burly, bearded Indian grinning at me, it was Krishna Gowandan.[8] We had both spent our childhood (and in his case, his boyhood) on the Brechin Castle sugar estate where our fathers worked at the factory. After my family left the district when I was about age four, I lost contact with him, but from my father I learned that he had successfully completed his Cambridge exams and had gone into teaching.

"Krishna!" I responded warmly. "How are you, man?" I had not seen him in many years—in fact, since we were boys (he was a few years older than I). "So you are one of the crack-shot soldiers they have trained to kill leftists like me, eh?" he said, grinning as we shook hands. I was somewhat taken aback by this remark. I had read that he was among the militant trade unionists, and his name and photograph were often in the newspapers. "Me?" I asked, remaining warm towards him. "Why would I want to kill you, Krishna?" The conversation that followed was of little consequence. But that chance meeting would prove to be propitious—at least for Rex and me. We discussed mundane matters and exchanged telephone contacts. I did not let him know what my political views were…I didn't dare; it would have been too risky. And he said nothing about his plans to go off to Cuba with George Weekes and others to attend the OLAS conference in August, mere months after that chance encounter.[9]

In the ensuing months, I would rekindle my relationship with Gowandan and introduce him to Rex. Rex and I often hung out in Central Trinidad where most of my boyhood friends lived. By then we had acquired cars, and outside of our military interaction and political development, we behaved the way most young men did. Neither of us drank much alcohol (in fact, none of the junior officers did), but we enjoyed bar hopping with our friends, chasing girls (hell, we were around age 22, fit, eligible bachelors, lacking only money, since our salaries were paltry and our parents not rich!), doing wild things young men are wont to. I had linked back with boyhood friends like Raffick 'Bobby' Garib, Edmund 'Hique' Roberts, Kazim 'Rick' Alibaksh, all from the Freeport district, and Randolph 'Fobs' Chandrakate, a classmate of mine from Presentation College, who lived in Chaguanas. Then I met Paul 'Leslie' Harrison, another ex-Presentation boy who now worked with the national airline, BWIA. He, in turn, was part of a small 'posse' that was not averse to violence and confrontation, having engaged the country's most notorious criminals at the time—the Poolool brothers of Caroni—in conflict.

We enjoyed hanging out with this circle of friends. It allowed us to 'ground with the grassroots', much the way Walter Rodney was doing in Jamaica. Given our thinking and the state of politics in the country, we could not help but try to educate them politically. Besides healthy discussions, we also lent them books to read. Soon, many of these hitherto apolitical young men developed a political awareness that many might have been deemed beyond their mental capacity. Indeed, without consciously setting out to do so, we had begun forming revolutionary 'cells'.

Gowandan, once he sensed our political inclination, introduced us to other leftists, initially Clive Nunez and Joe Young. When Rex and I learned that Gowandan was the main link with Cuba, our adventurism got the better of us. We first requested, and later demanded, that he arrange a trip to Cuba for us. That was a very dangerous proposition. Cuba was a communist country and Fidel Castro was seen as fomenting revolution in Latin America and the Caribbean. As army officers, we were not expected even to think outside the conservative, neo-colonial box, far less entertain revolutionary thoughts. Gowandan was petrified by our insistence on making a trip to Cuba. For him, that could mean facing charges of subversion and possibly jail. Gowandan was not daring; a Marxist, yes; defiant towards the establishment, yes; but courting serious repercussions by conspiring to get two army officers to Cuba? He was shit-scared. He made every attempt to dissuade us from even considering it, coming as our demand did in the wake of Ché's assassination in Bolivia, and the CIA stepping up its 'communist watch' in Latin America.

But we could not, in our romantic minds, pass up on an opportunity to visit Cuba. We hoped we would meet with Fidel and other heroes of the Cuban revolution. We saw ourselves engaging them in discussions and garnering a sense of what revolution was all about. We wanted to see how socialism was faring in Cuba. This seemingly crazy idea would come to fruition much later. But once the seed was planted in our psyche, we never let up.

Parts of the 'Revo': Local and Transnational Circles

In the meantime, international resistance to imperialism and the unleashing of the capitalist dogs-of-war in the Third World built up to a virtual crescendo. In direct response, revolutionary movements multiplied many-fold across the world. Locally, it was little different. As had happened in previous epochs of revolutionary upheavals, groups of one strain of Marxism or other—orthodox Leninists, extreme Maoists, Trotskyites and many more, cropped up every-where. Learned attorney and devoted Marxist, Lennox Pierre would later sum it up thus: during the Russian revolution in the second decade of the 20th century, multiple socialist groups were not uncommon—and one-man 'groups' very common!

As the spirit of revolution swept through rural districts and urban centres, the university and even secondary schools, many foreign-tutored radicals returned home. Among them were some men Rex had known from Belmont who had earlier migrated, either seeking employment or higher education, mainly in Britain, but also in the USA and Canada. Raymond Watts was one such person. He was not a scholar, merely a worker who was schooled in struggle as he coped with eking out an existence in London. He soon fell in with others, mainly intellectuals, who had mastered Marxism by reading the very books Rex and I had found difficult to digest while we attended Sandhurst.[10]

Through our contact with Raymond, Rex and I met Wally Look Lai, an Oxford graduate and columnist with the *Express*. On the eve of the 1970 upheaval, he would become editor of the OWTU's *Vanguard* newspaper, which soon became a powerful propaganda tool for the mass movement. Wally, a small-framed Chinese who had grown up in Balmain, Couva, the son of a shop-keeper, was very bright and had gained entry to Oxford University. Wally and Raymond were friends of Radford 'Darcus' Howe, who had also migrated to Britain after graduating from Queens Royal College. Darcus was a nephew of C.L.R. James.[11] He, like the others, had engaged in political activism in Britain, and had attended the Black Writers Conference in 1968 in Montreal. Darcus was also a member of the Renegades steel band at a time when pan and violence mixed easily. In fact, even before Renegades came into being, Darcus had belonged to an East Dry River 'gang' known as 'Lawbreakers'. So Darcus and Raymond had a feel of life and living among the grassroots of the society, more so in urban Port of Spain. They, in turn, introduced us to Franklin Harvey, a Grenadian radical who lectured at UWI, and later, Lloyd Best, another intellectual, also from UWI. Best and Dr. James Millette were co-founders of the New World Group, about which we knew little, except that it comprised intellectuals who had seen the futility of neo-colonialism that was imposed on all newly-independent Caribbean countries.

In time, we formed a loose group that comprised Raymond, Darcus, Wally, Franklin, Rex and myself. Serious political discussions would ensue, but in spite of our close relations, Rex and I were unaware that 'CLR' (or 'Nello', as James was fondly called) had mentored these men politically when they studied and worked in Britain. They never brought his name up during our discussions. As far as we knew, CLR, who lived in England, was unaware of this very important connection between his acolytes and two young army lieutenants.[12]

By the latter half of 1968, Rex and I had moved deeper into the realm of revolution even as we remained at one with our brother officers regarding the state of the army. We still agreed with them that there was need to change the high command in order to forge the kind of military that was suitable to the country's needs. But for their own safety, we did not tell the other officers of our contacts with radical elements on the outside, of our discussions on the state of the country and the state of the army. We used the 'need to know' principle that was standard in covert operations. We realised we were entering uncharted, dangerous political waters. We did not intend to take our brother officers into that orbit of uncertainty, to endanger their careers and lives.

Between 1967 and the end of 1969, the revolutionary spirit that haunted the country emerged from underground, spilling openly onto the streets and workplaces and schools and ghettoes, Increasingly, Rex and I felt very much part of the 'revo' even though we could not openly attend meetings or marches. What was remarkable about our transformation was that even though we interacted with men who were far superior to us intellectually, radicals who were mostly older and more experienced, we were the ones with the daring and zeal to take the discussions to higher levels, from theory to praxis. In this regard, the few soldiers who attended these meetings were of similar mind.

If anything, the civilians—Look Lai, Watts, Howe, Harvey, Harrison and others—were in awe of our insistence on radically transforming both the army and the country. Maybe our youthful exuberance combined with our military training gave us a feeling of invincibility. While the intellectuals were all talk and theory, we were action-oriented. That may have been a fundamental flaw in our development. But at age 24, we threw caution to the winds of revolutionary change that had started gaining gale-force strength on the ground. Rex and I, and our fellow radical soldiers, felt we needed to initiate action that would take the movement from the ground into confrontation with those who wielded political power, those who were wedded to neo-colonialism, who saw this part-free, part-slave existence as the only option for the people of this richly endowed country.

We could not accept that as our fate, as the future of our nation. And what we could not accept, we were convinced we could change. It was against this very complex background that we committed ourselves to one daring initiative. Whatever it took on our part, we would not allow the increasingly unpopular government to use the army against the restless masses. We would revolt, put our lives and our careers on the line, rather than stain our patriotic hands with the blood of our people.

Rumblings of Revolution

The events of 1970 did not steal upon the country silently, suddenly. More like a volcanic eruption than an earthquake, the social and political explosion had given many warning signals. For several years earlier, but more intensely from 1967, workers across the country had resorted to wildcat or sustained strikes to protest against poor wages and working conditions, and backward leadership in their unions. The unemployed, better educated and increasing in numbers after independence, rallied against a kind of hopelessness that seemed to be their lot in life. Communities, urban and rural, found dramatic ways to bring attention to their plights, from poor infrastructure to absolute neglect. Even secondary school students got into the act for the first time in the country's history. The street marches grabbed national attention in February 1970 through their sheer size and rapid escalation, and NJAC emerged as the flagship of the armada of discontent. But NJAC was not a monolith, nor was it solely responsible for mobilising the masses. It did, however, provide a rallying point for scores of radical groups as well as thousands who belonged to no organisation. Its magnetism came from the oratorical and organisational skills of its passionate and charismatic leaders.

Most young people who joined the mass movement had their groundings in radical organisations that had mushroomed across the country, pre-dating NJAC. They had acquired identity consciousness and absorbed revolutionary thinking from a phalanx of bright young radicals who had come from diverse social and educational backgrounds. Influenced by images emanating from the Black Power struggle in the USA, they grew their hair in the then fashionable 'Afro' style. Men wore beards with pride. For the first time, people donned dashikis, a traditional African robe fashioned from colourful printed cotton that became a symbol of black identity. Colonialism had systematically stripped its victims, more so enslaved African than Indian indentures, of their cultures, religions and identities. European and Western values—clothing, hairstyles, foods, names, customs—had been drilled into their descendants' psyche, so much so that they had lost their roots.

Earlier, in January-February 1969, in far-off Canada, an event occurred that would impact the struggle in Trinidad and Tobago in a way no one could envisage at the time. A group of students and worker-activists numbering around a hundred staged a 'sit-in' at the Computer Centre of the Sir George Williams University (now Concordia) in Montreal, Canada. Among them were 10 students from Trinidad and Tobago. They were protesting the administration's refusal to deal with allegations of racism against a biology lecturer. They occupied the Centre for 14 days. On February 11, a mysterious fire broke out, trapping those engaged in the protest. The students, who were asleep when someone smelt something burning, used a fire-axe to escape the inferno—only to run into armed police who beat and 'arrested scores of them. As they were rounded up, handcuffed, and taken away in police vehicles, some whites gathered on the street outside shouted, "Let the Niggers burn!" Interestingly, of the 97 persons arrested, 55 were whites. All were charged with a number of offences, including arson, which carried a penalty of life imprisonment. Many spent weeks in jail before being released on bail.

The repercussions of the 'George Williams Affair' as it came to be known, reverberated not only in Canada, but also in Caribbean countries, most of all in Trinidad and Tobago. Here, as political and race consciousness heightened, the incident galvanised students and trade unionists, among others, into protest action. Weeks after the students' arrests, Canada's Governor-General, Sir Roland Michener, made a state visit to this country. He could not have chosen a worse time. On February 26, he and an official entourage attempted to enter the St Augustine campus of the UWI, where he was scheduled to formally open Michener Hall, a new student residence built with money donated by the Canadian government.

To the consternation of many on the university campus, and the shock and embarrassment of the Williams government, militant students blocked the main entrance and successfully prevented Michener from entering the campus. The Government and UWI's administration did not understand just how much the 'George Williams Affair' had incensed the increasingly politically conscious students. That incident was relatively insignificant in the global scheme of revolutionary struggles. Yet, it emerged as one catalyst for the events that would shake the foundations of Trinidad and Tobago in 1970.

The 'George Williams Affair' had its roots in the Civil Rights and Black Power uprisings in neighbouring USA, and the generational upheaval that gripped the world during that turbulent period. The students involved had marched in Canada when Martin Luther King was assassinated in April 1968. They had participated in the historic Second Black Writers Conference at the nearby McGill University in October that year. They were witnesses to the anti-Vietnam War demonstrations that spread across North America. They knew, too, that many young Americans fled across the border to Canada to escape conscription into the military. Many of the George Williams students had gone to Canada merely to pursue higher education, with little or no political awareness. But as the battle for Black identity and the war against racism erupted in the USA, they could hardly escape the tide of discontent.

So, when Professor Perry Anderson brazenly discriminated against Black students in his Physiology class (a pre-requisite to pursuing medicine) by persistently failing them, those affected, acting through the vibrant West Indian Society on the campus, filed charges of racism against him. The university's administration frustrated their attempts to have the issue resolved through dialogue, which was when the students decided to stage a 'sit in'. This was a popular mode of protest at the time: protestors would occupy the premises linked to the oppressors, make their demands, and 'sit in' in the buildings until they got justice. In this instance, their peaceful occupation of the Computer Centre failed to have the desired effect—that is, force the administration to discipline the racist lecturer. Instead, the authorities promoted Anderson and later called in Montreal's riot police to clear the students from the Centre. Then came the mysterious fire, which occurred as they slept. The students claimed they did not set it. They asked, with reason, "Why should we endanger their own lives?" Yet they were charged with arson, among a number of felonies.

That incident, and the subsequent indictment and trial of the 10 nationals of Trinidad and Tobago, galvanised already agitated university students in Trinidad.[13] It was why Canada's Governor-General Roland Michener faced such a hostile reception when he visited. Prior to that, West Indians seeking higher education or a better life, saw Canada as a relatively safe haven. The 'Affair' tarnished Canada's image, although the country continued to be the preferred destination for both students and migrants from the Caribbean.

What was noteworthy about the 'Affair' is that among the large group that occupied the Centre, the majority were whites, some of them French Canadians.[14] Their active presence in the protest, as happened elsewhere in the world, showed that the fight against racism and injustice knew no colour boundaries. Because of the way the university evolved—it was run by the YMCA and catered for workers to access tertiary education through night classes—the student body comprised large numbers of working-class whites.[15]

As the Black Power struggle intensified in Trinidad, the 'Affair' gave a fillip to militant groups here. Besides the Michener incident, local students forged links with their comrades in Montreal. Shortly after the arrests in Canada and the Michener protest in Trinidad, two of the principal activists in the embryonic NJAC, Geddes Granger and Dave Darbeau, journeyed to New York where they met with representatives of the George Williams student body. The latter drove with them to Montreal, where they held meetings that would lead to mutual support for their respective struggles.

The 'George Williams Affair' might have faded had the Canadian authorities not bungled the matter. They held many of the students for weeks before granting them bail, and later pursued their trial on criminal charges.

Radical lawyers from French-speaking Quebec, who had their own issues with
the Ottawa Government, defended them. The authorities decided to try the 10
Trinidadians, the largest block from any foreign country, first. Among the more
prominent were Ian 'Teddy' Belgrave and his wife Valerie, Bukka Rennie,
Glenda Edwards, Hugo Forde, and Edmund Michael. A Grenadian, Kennedy
Frederick, was considered part of this group. From elsewhere in the Caribbean,
Dominica's Rosie Douglas, who would later become Prime Minister of his
country, and Barbados-born Ann Cools, later a senator in Canada's Parliament,
were also among the students arrested.

It would take a year before the 'Trinidad 10' came before the courts. But
the 'Affair' had generated such interest among activists in this country, the
Michener protest paled by comparison. On the anniversary date of the arrests,
February 26, 1970, the first Black Power march was staged in Port of Spain in
solidarity with the students on trial in Montreal. It targeted Canada's High
Commission and the main branch of the Royal Bank of Canada. It was that
demonstration that triggered the almost daily series of meetings and marches
that would culminate in the declaration of a state of emergency.

In Canada, the students and activists who supported them, did not sit idly
and await their fate in a court that was stacked against them. Besides securing
bail by mobilising support from the community, in January they travelled to
Ottawa and protested at Trinidad's High Commission in that city, demanding
to speak with Prime Minister Williams regarding their plight. The envoy,
Matthew Ramcharan, contacted Williams, who was at the time visiting Jamaica.
The usually arrogant Prime Minister actually spoke with one student and agreed
that his government would pay their legal fees and any fine imposed on them
at their trial. He would honour this commitment when, in February 1970, the
Trinidad students pleaded guilty to a lesser count of occupying the Computer
Centre and were fined $1000 Canadian each.

According to Teddy Belgrave, the judge, who had adopted an almost hostile
stance in the early part of the trial, did an about-face after demonstrations
against Canadian interests erupted in Trinidad. Canadian journalists had
travelled to Trinidad to cover the protests. Television reporters interviewed
Darbeau, Nunez and Kelshall Bodie, three senior NJAC leaders. The trio vowed
'fire and brimstone' against Canadian interests in Trinidad should their 'brothers
and sisters' on trial in Montreal be dealt with harshly:

The interview with Dabreau and others featured prominently on
Canadian television news, Belgrave said. That, and the intensification of
the struggle in Trinidad, seemed to have influenced both the

Government in Ottawa and the judge in Montreal. The court accepted the guilty pleas on the lesser count of occupation of the Centre, first entered by Frederick. The other charges, the most serious being arson, were never pursued. So, the events in Trinidad did have an impact on the outcome of the 'George Williams Affair'.

In Montreal, Douglas and Cools had opted for individual trials, which would take long to be heard. When they finally faced the court, Cools was sentenced to eight months imprisonment, and Douglas two years—the heaviest penalty imposed on any participant in the 'Affair'.

As a sequel, some of the students returned to Trinidad on March 22 to a tumultuous welcome from hundreds of demonstrators NJAC had massed at the Piarco Airport.[16] Several of the students would join with the umbrella organisation, taking part in, among other protest actions, the historic 'March to Caroni'. None were arrested and detained when the State of Emergency was declared in late April.

NOTES

1   We are grateful to share this edited excerpt from Raffique Shah's forthcoming memoir. A big thank you to Gabrielle Jamela Hosein for her help in facilitating this process.

2   Robin Bunce and Paul Field. *Darcus Howe: A Political Biography*. (London: Bloomsbury, 2013), 77.

3   Brian Meeks. *Narratives of Resistance: Jamaica, Trinidad, The Caribbean*. (Kingston: University of the West Indies Press, 2000), 49.

4   As Andre Bagoo points out, Eric Williams had requested help from the former imperial power, Britain, as well as from Venezuela, Guyana, Jamaica, and at one point, from Nigeria, and Tanzania. Raffique Shah and other resisters were facing violent suppression not just from the state, but internationally as well (see *The Undiscovered Country*. Leeds, UK: Peepal Tree 2020, 161).

5   Tony Martin. "African and Indian Consciousness." Chapter 6. *General History of the Caribbean* Vol 5 UNESCO, 2003.

6   See David Theo Goldberg. "Transcript: [Paul Gilroy] in conversation with David Theo Goldberg," University College London. July 8, 2020. https://www.ucl.ac.uk/racism-racialisation/transcript-conversation-david-theo-goldberg.

7   Like Shah, Rex Lassalle was a lieutenant in the Trinidad and Tobago Regiment and was one of the leaders of an army mutiny in April 1970 as part of Black Power Revolution.

8   By the mid 1960s, Krishna Gowandan was already a political figure in Trinidad and Tobago. He was a key figure in the labour unrest in March 1965 when 15,000 sugar workers went on strike. When Eric Williams responded to the strike by suspending civil rights and declaring a State of Emergency, this brought the Afro-Trinidadian-dominated Trade Union Congress into alliance with the Indo-Trinidadian sugar workers. Gowandan was part of the leadership of the All Trinidad Sugar Estates and Factory Workers Union.

9   George Weekes and Joe Young (also mentioned in this chapter), are often discussed as being among the leading post-independence trade unionists in Trinidad. Weekes led the struggle to democratize the Oilfield Workers Trade Union (OWTU). Both Weekes and Gowandan

attended the First Conference of the Organization of Latin American Solidarity in Havana, Cuba from July 31 to August 19, 1967.

10   Shah trained at the elite Royal Military Academy Sandhurst in England. For a brief discussion of Shah's time at Sandhurst see Egbert Gaye's article, "Revolution at the Doorstep of Trinidad and Tobago in the Montreal newspaper *Community Contact,* April 17, 2015. Gaye talks of that experience as being politically formative; "Shah says their convictions leading up to 1970 were shaped by the writings and speeches of leaders involved in civil rights and human rights battles around the world. At Sandhurst, where the library brimmed with books and other sources of information, they read voraciously."

11   Darcus Howe's role in the Mangrove Nine trial is recounted in director Steve McQueen's epic film of Black British history *Small Axe* (2020). For a fuller account of his political life, see: Robin Bunce and Paul Field. *Darcus Howe: A Political Biography.* (London: Bloomsbury, 2013).

12   The formation of the CLR James study circle, where young activists and intellectuals read and discussed the works of James was important to unfolding events in Montreal.

13   See Interview with Juanita Westmoreland-Traoré in this volume for an account of the trial.

14   For a discussion of the composition of the legal team see the Interview with Westmoreland-Traore in this volume.

15   Sir George Williams University started with evening classes that were offered by the YMCA. This Educational Program began in 1851 and continued in various facilities of the YMCA in downtown Montreal. For more on the history of the institution, see the Concordia archives: https://www.concordia.ca/offices/archives.html.

16   For a vivid account of the 'Trinidad 10's' return, see Interview with Juanita Westmoreland-Traoré in this volume.

the secret name: diasporic disremembering

Alexis Pauline Gumbs

MY GRANDFATHER said the word "school" like it was the secret name of the true God. The very word had power. But what kind of power? Black power?

It is very unlikely that my grandfather Jeremiah Gumbs, representative for Anguilla to the United Nations during the 1967-1969 Anguillan Revolution, never heard about the Sir George Williams Occupation in Montreal in 1968. But he never mentioned it to me. Or if he did, it does not appear anywhere in our years of recorded conversations and I do not remember him ever bringing it up. If you decide to continue reading this, you will not gain any new information about the occupation of what is now Concordia University. You will not learn how the participants of the Anguillan revolution at the time thought about the occupation. I do not have that information. Four years ago, when I spoke at Concordia University upon the publication of my first book, I did not even know that occupation had taken place. What I have is an archive of unknowing, an intimate wonder about how an important historical event was not only suppressed in the narrative of the history of Quebec, but also in the intergenerational silence that surrounds education, aspiration, and progress in Caribbean diaspora. These are my theories on why no one told me.

blackout

There was one room. The school my grandfather went to was one room full of children who would not be quiet. I guess that depends on your definition of quiet. The tall white teacher, resentful of being sent to the smallest, insignificant outpost of the British empire, to teach these Black children thought they could never be quiet enough. So, he beat them. If they coughed. If they sneezed. If they wheezed. For the sound of their breathing, he beat them. My grandfather was there, wearing a flour-sack sewn into pants by his mother. The abuse was so total, so extreme, and unwarranted, my grandfather cannot finish describing it. His young memory barricaded the doors. "Most of my childhood," he said, "I don't remember." The quiet in him, the intended product of colonial schooling. He learned it was not safe to breathe.

Theory #1: Class Difference

My grandfather was not of the class of people who could go away to school. Not even a little bit. As an Anguillan, going away to school would have meant first going to St. Kitts because Anguilla did not have a complete secondary education on the island at that time. But my grandfather was the youngest of nine outside children. There was not money for food. There was not money for shoes. Let alone money for books. So, despite the fact that he aced his exams and was at the top of his class, scoring so high on tests they had to be sent for external review because no one thought he could possibly be that smart, he could not continue his education. His mother needed his hands at home. It took me a long time, listening back over tapes of my grandfather speaking to my father to really understand this. Maybe because in school I studied a tradition of Caribbean literature written only by the people who went away to school. The scholarship kids. My grandfather spoke the unpublished reality of the irrelevance of educational scholarships for starving children.

When I hear about the racist biology professor who failed all-his Black students to keep them from taking medical school spots he thought should rightfully go to white Canadians, I think of my grandfather's teacher. When I think of the students at Sir George Williams breathing smoke and running for their lives, I think about how my grandfather could not breathe in the class-room, without physical punishment. How the educational colonial authority treated the students like encroaching disease, like germs to be beaten back with disciplinary immunity. Wouldn't my grandfather have identified with those students who defied that racist white teacher and demanded recognition? Theory #1 says maybe he would have, but class got in the way. He did not identify with the scholarship children, the representative geniuses, the people with enough resources to go to school in Canada. Was that it?

Out

If someone were looking at it from the outside (it is as if I am always looking from the outside, although I know no one can ever get outside of it), it could look like we love school more than we love each other. Look how often we leave each other for school and never come back. Look how school teaches us out of the language of being together. Look what happens to our time.

The narrative says, no, school is a means to an end. School is how we make each other proud, and train to fetch the money we need to keep each other alive. It is how we show each other our worthiness. School is not avoidance. It is just more crucial than our time together. Because time with each other is our most expensive (did someone say wasteful?) expenditure. Everybody knows, especially in the Caribbean, you only make money from time away.

Theory #2 Effective Tokenization

Eventually, my grandfather did go away. In the 1940s, he left Anguilla and lived in the house of one of his older sisters. He went to high school as an adult in New York City. His sister gave him bus fare but he walked every day to school in the snow and the rain and uphill (both ways) so he could send the bus fare home to Anguilla for his mother. And in his senior seminar, the last class he needed to get his high school diploma, he encountered a white woman teacher who told him proudly, "No Black student has ever passed my class." According to the legend of this story which he told me year after year, he responded "Well, I will be the first." I will not pause to write a whole book on the narrative of being first and how it severs, how it separates, how it punches holes in communities. I will simply say "I will be the first" stood in for determination and dignity for my grandfather. He fulfilled his prophecy.

Lest you think my grandfather had bought into the idea of exceptionalism, he was not an individualist. He told me about how he worked together with his fellow students. How he tutored one classmate in math so well that the student's father gifted my grandfather his first nice pair of shoes, which he was able to wear to his graduation. According to this Jewish student's father, his son never would have completed high school without my grandfather's help. My grandfather also told me that he took responsibility for teaching his whole class a math sequence that their teacher could not make clear to them. My grandfather the student, the youngest of nine, the small island dreamer, the future revolutionary, was community minded. And the fact remained, he was the only Black student in the class.

His final paper for his senior seminar was about Gandhi and non-violence. He did secondary research, reading every book he could find about Gandhi and in a booming voice he ended his final presentation with, "And that is the impact of the life of the non-violent leader Mohandas Gandhi." The teacher applauded him and smirked. "Your presentation was almost perfect," she told him when he had finished. "Only one thing. You said 'Mohandas,' but his name is 'Mahatma Gandhi.'" He knew from his research that Gandhi's first given name was Mohandas, and that Mahatma was an honorific given to him as a leader, so he corrected his teacher. He passed the class, and the teacher told him she was very proud. He had really taught her something. The liberal imaginary might applaud the individual commitment and dedication of my grandfather, his exceptional overcoming. What a learning experience for a woman who up to that moment did not realize she could learn anything from a Black person. But that is not what my grandfather told me. He said to me, and this is on tape too, "That woman was a racist. Think about all the Black students she failed, probably for no reason. Not one had passed her class in all those years? I should be proud? Think about how she stood in their way."

The moral of the story as my grandfather told it to me had two layers. First was the lesson he instilled in almost every story he told me growing up, "Don't let someone else tell you what you can't do." Underneath it was the grief for the collective, the harm that teacher had caused for so many years, the shadow story of the other students who walked uphill both ways, and because this teacher taught the final course needed for graduation, they had an even steeper journey, leaving school empty-handed because the teacher believed at best, that Black students were not equipped to pass her class, and at worst that the perceived rigor of her class *depended on* it being out of the reach of Black students. And she worked in a system that would never force her to consider that maybe that pattern of so-called failure was *her* failure as a teacher. And where were those Black students who had also faced her racism? My grandfather had no access to them. He was there alone.

I think of my grandfather's teacher and how she made herself into a barrier to access for everything that her Black students would have been able to access with their high school diplomas. How she saw herself as faithful to an institution designed to exclude. Wouldn't my grandfather have identified with those students in Montreal who defied that white racist teacher and demanded recognition? Theory #2 says maybe he would have, but he was so effectively tokenized that he had no concept of Black collective resistance to education. School was something you survived alone. Or didn't. Was that it?

only

I'm still dealing with the myth of my incomprehensibility. All this time as the 'only one' in educational settings can corrupt the idea of understanding. Maybe I am incapable of understanding. Maybe this system is incapable of understanding me. Maybe it was me. Already incomprehensible when I got here. It took me a long time to understand that the function of educational systems is not understandability, it is compliance. So now I am working on the legend. The dangerous story of what happens now, with all this beautiful generative failure. And the miracle that you completely understand. You completely understand why I cannot comply.

Theory #3: An Honest Affinity for Machines

After high school graduation, my grandfather enrolled at City College, but never started classes. The War Powers Act passed, and he joined the U.S. military as a path to citizenship. He said that he took the officer's exam and scored well but racist superiors said there was no way he could become an officer. He was stationed in North Carolina at NC A&T for training, and he remembers that the women at Bennett College were beautiful, but the racism he experienced while wearing his uniform, especially on the bus, was so ugly that he never returned to the U.S. South, to the state of North Carolina where I live now. His favorite story to tell about being in the army is the story of the visiting general. The general-in-charge of the training operation was hosting a visiting general who was to observe their training set-up and report back, but there was no one there who could lead the troops in drills. He called out to ask who would lead the drills and my grandfather stepped forward. He led these drills, right in the middle of the football stadium and the soldiers moved together like a well-oiled machine that the visiting general gave a favorable report and the general-in-charge felt in my grandfather's debt. "You did that for me," he asked my grandfather, "What can I do for you?" My grandfather said, "You can get me out of this damn army."

To this day, I do not know what the exact paperwork shuffle was, but I know that my grandfather was honorably discharged without serving active duty and that he therefore gained U.S. citizenship under the War Powers Act. Simply because he could get people to move together like a well-oiled machine.

My grandfather took a course in radio. Putting them together, taking them apart, wiring technology. He said he was great at it. He said he had job offers from NBC and CBS. But he turned them down. "Alexis, I work too damn hard to work for somebody else," he told me over and over again.

But, for a while, he did work for someone else. My great grandfather. My grandfather married my grandmother and took on her father's coal and ice company. One day, it would be his own business that he would update to heating and air-conditioning. But before all that, one winter out on the truck, he said, a 2000-pound block of ice slid off into the street. And to save the ice and prove his worth to his father-in-law, he jumped off the truck and picked it up and put it back on. "How could I lift that Alexis?" he would ask me every time he told the story. I was wondering the same thing.

When I think of winter in Montreal, and a computer the size of a room, when I think of cold and heavy and a student occupation strategy that says our safest bet is to be as close as possible to valuable machines, I think of my grandfather. How I always wonder if strength for him meant to become in some parts machine. I could hear him letting go of some of that wiring in our conversations. But he never spoke of the Sir George Williams occupation. Theory #4 says maybe he would have if he did not identify with the machines. Is it because of the fire, the police beatings, the blame, the many arrests, the death of Coralee Hutchison? In the end, being that close to the machine did not keep them safe. Is that why he did not tell me?

close

Even as I write this, type it into a machine, I am struggling not to pick up and engage the other two machines on my desk, a phone, and a tablet. Are there too many ways to be plugged in to the wireless network that tells me it is my best chance at connection, at recognition at sense, if not sensory than conceptual? The software programmers say the designs of the apps in my phones are like slot machines. And that we are all gambling addicts. They are right. I keep refreshing my phone hoping someone will tell me something better than the story I am living. My grandfather would pronounce my name "E-Lexis" like he knew I was an electronic child. Future mother of countless emails. Granddaughter of machine.

Theory #4: There was too much going on

To be fair, whenever I talked to my grandfather about the 1960s, we were not talking about Canada. We were not talking about students. We were always talking about the referendum and Governor Bradshaw and the situation with St. Kitts and the United Nations and the revolution. By the time my grandfather returned to Anguilla in the mid-1950s, at the insistence of my grandmother who suspected he was hiding something (evidence points to the high probability that he was, but that's a different essay), he had been away for 18 years. All that time he had been sending school supplies and money for a school building he had never seen. And so, they asked him to speak at the graduation. The graduation of a group of students who were not even born when he left. My grandmother said they should build a hotel on the beach (there were none), and they started their second business. Sent the children to religious and private boarding schools in the United States and went back and forth running the heating and air-conditioning business in New Jersey and the hotel in Anguilla. "Never again," he said at the graduation, "will I abandon my people."

So, in 1967 the Anguillan people were fed up with so many decades of being the neglected third island in the St. Kitts, Nevis and Anguilla trio. With being far away from all the other British holdings and yet forbidden to trade with the close island neighbors colonized by the French and Dutch. With all requests for investment in education and infrastructure being roundly ignored. With the threats of Governor Bradshaw in St. Kitts who said he would, "starve the Anguillan people and put pepper in their soup." My grandfather was with them. In 1967, in the weeks leading up to the vote where the 6000 people of Anguilla decided by almost unanimous referendum that they wanted to secede from the British Empire, my grandfather was excited. The hotel became a place for meetings and planning. On the local scale, St. Kitts was seen as the primary enemy. But in the global public relations discourse, this tiny island was facing off against the entire British Empire, the idea of empire, colonization, and subordination. When the British Army landed in Anguilla there was hardly anyone to meet them except for mosquitoes. The soldiers themselves were confused. Most of the Anguillan men were on surrounding islands working, as usual, and so they were greeted mostly by women and children and goats. The *New York Times* printed a drawing of a lion roaring full force at a tiny mouse.

Meanwhile, my grandfather had a friend who had a friend in the United Nations, and so he went to go speak on behalf of Anguilla. Some say there was a scheduling issue. Some say they never went through protocol. What my grandfather said is that when he got off the elevator to leave the UN, he just looked down at the floor and acted dejected. The next day, the *New York Times* printed that the UN had refused to acknowledge Anguilla. "I never said that" my grandfather said smiling. But that is how he got in to actually speak at the UN with a whole lot of press in the days following. What was I supposed to learn? There is power in smallness. There is power in silence. There is power in the gap.

Ultimately, the Anguillan revolution was a gap in time. Two years later, the colonized elite would renegotiate for Anguilla to be under the *direct* dominion of the British Empire instead of via St. Kitts. The ten families of the Valley who had held cultural and social power continued to wield it, consenting to juris-dictional colonization from Britain and eventually to economic colonization by the United States and a number of other players. Anguilla is part of the British West Indies to this day. As his own act of protest, my grandfather would not step out of his house during visits by the royal family to the island of Anguilla, lest anyone mis-interpret his presence in the street as celebration. He taught me that, "there is no greater sin than colonialism."

But, for those two years so much was possible. According to my grand-parents, those revolutionary years were the only time in Anguilla's history when water was freely available to the public. My grandmother, Lydia Gumbs, one of the first Black designers trained at Pratt Institute, designed the revolutionary Anguillan flag and honorary passports and stamps that they sold to help fund the island in those gap years. They also applied for and received a grant from the Ford Foundation (which, as Noliwe Rooks and others have taught us, had their fingers in all kinds of Black liberation efforts, projects and experiments including my dissertation 40 years later). The possibility of Anguilla was interesting to everyone. My grandfather mentioned Black Power activists from the U.S. eyeing Anguilla as a potential Black Utopia. He also mentioned members of the mafia eyeing the island as a place to hide money. For my grandparents, the time of the revolution was a time of practice. What did direct, self-determination look like for a place as small as Anguilla? How do you fund the basic needs of a population with an economy that is mostly conceptual, banking on the brief publicity of the New York Times coverage of the revolution and the guarantee that Anguillan stamps would be rare collectors' items almost instantly? Maybe, most importantly to my grandfather, though this was not what he said, it was an opportunity for an outside child, a person whose parentage and class background put him far outside the traditional Anguillan story about power, to play a role in shaping the identity of his country. The revolutionary period in Anguilla was a period of movements all over the world and Black student uprisings and takeovers on several college campuses. It was a time characterized by the grand possibilities of the brave actions of the global majority of people who were told they were small by the thousand indignities of colonialism and slavery.

I think about the students at Sir George Williams and the striking image of their direct action, the fact that they threw the punch cards out of the window, interrupting wage value and labor documentation in ways that went beyond their school. When I think about what it took to live, to feed each other, to sleep in a space that was not made for life. When I think about the negotiations and coalitions that emerged in that barricaded space. The first thing I think of is free water for the people on a desert island and how that referendum may have been the last time such a critical mass of Anguillans agreed on one thing. But my grandfather didn't mention the occupation of Sir George Williams. Theory #4 says maybe he would have if he was not reliving his own experience of big possibility in a small place, for a small time. Maybe he would have if he was not talking to a wild granddaughter prone to student protest since first grade. Maybe he knew and did not say. Or maybe he did not know at all.

reason

If I could, I would ask my grandfather what he thought, what he knew about the student occupation in Montreal. I would ask him many other questions too. The last time I spoke to my grandfather, I was on the phone in my college dorm room at Columbia. I was part of a group of students engaged in direct action and alternative education for Black studies, Latino Studies, Asian American Studies and Native American Studies. I had already broken many rules and been called to task by many administrators for the tactics we used which were voicemails of love poems to all the campus phones, mirror installations in the bathrooms used by the undergraduate college presidents and their guests, well placed short speeches at alumni gatherings, leaked information to the campus newspapers, and public festivals of decolonization on Christopher Columbus Day. During our last conversation, on my grandfather's 91st birthday, he did not tell me to be careful. He did not say, "Did you ever hear what happened to those Black students in Montreal. He did not tell me much of anything. He asked. Specifically, he asked me, "Do you know what you are doing?" I said one word, "Yes." Not one for goodbyes, my grandfather simply grunted, to let me know that he had heard me. And then he hung up the phone.

Black Power in Twentieth Century St. Vincent and the Grenadines

Kirland Ayanna Bobb

G ROWING UP in Georgetown, St. Vincent and the Grenadines, one might hear in reference to someone, "Oh he was a Black Power man, darn scamp." As a child, it always puzzled me as to why Black Power men were often referred to in that way. It was not until I was a student at the University of the West Indies that I learned about Black Power as a movement and its presence in the United States, Jamaica, Trinidad and Tobago, and Britain. Despite the movement's presence in the recent memory of Vincentians, the literature remains silent on this history. Black Power has been a subject extensively researched and discussed especially within the context of the United States and to a lesser extent, Canada, Europe and the larger Caribbean territories. However, there has been a glaring absence in the literature with regards to the history of St. Vincent and the Grenadines and its twentieth century Black Power movement. This chapter draws on oral sources as well as private and public archives to situate St. Vincent and the Grenadines in the networks and histories of Black Power activism, by first examining how Black Power was mobilized and organized, and then examining the circulations of Black Power discourse.

The 1960s and 1970s was an era of change due to the global Black radical protests, cultural change and political activism which also swept the shores of St. Vincent and the Grenadines. The various trappings which constituted the movement for Black Power was manifested in 1968 and 1970s St. Vincent and the Grenadines. As Stokely Carmichael pointed out in a book co-authored with Charles Hamilton, we might understand Black Power as, "a call for Black people to unite, to recognize their heritage, to build a sense of community. It is a call for Black people to begin to define their goals, to lead their own organizations. It is a call to reject the racist institutions and values for this society."[12] Black Power was fundamentally a matter of value, in respect to black peoples' social positioning and psychology.

Black Power was one aspect of Vincentian history that created profound changes in the lives of many locals. Its absence from the extensive discussions about

Black Power globally should in no way imply that the movement was not present on the island. In fact, its presence is a recent memory among those who lived through it. This discussion both sheds light on that significant period of Vincentian history while also attempting to add to the global conversation surrounding the twentieth century Black Power movement. The various experiences recounted by witnesses and participants of the movement reveal new and critical insights into an important part of the Vincentian most recent past.

Black Power in the Vincentian Context

1968 was when the first wave of the movement struck the island. St. Vincent and the Grenadines was still a colony of Britain, dominated by white people. The economy was heavily dependent on agriculture; nearly two-thirds of the arable lands were in white possession. Besides the meagre constitutional changes that came with emancipation, the early colonial system remained intact. Major commercial business houses, such as gas stations and supermarkets, in Kingstown, were still owned by mainly white proprietors. Banks were owned and operated by foreign whites and tended to employ workers who were either of white or light-skinned complexions. Job promotions, particularly in banks were dependent not on academic achievements or work experience but rather primarily based on one's skin colour. In the political sphere, where economics and politics worked hand in hand, the holders of economic power dictated who held political power. This meant that in St. Vincent and the Grenadines, like other West Indian islands, political decisions were made by those with economic powers. These decisions served to benefit them only and marginalized another section of Vincentian society, occupied by the Black peoples, who during this time were mainly oppressed fieldworkers with very small wages and without any form of economic or political power. Beyond that, society was conditioned to believe that anything associated with white was good while 'Blackness" was a curse. Being black-skinned, under colonial domination, was associated with a life of poverty.

Against this backdrop, a number of youths across the island became politically and racially conscious. This era of the country's history saw youths questioning their identity and the position in which the colour of their skin had placed them within the Vincentian societal structure and the world by extension. This simple act of questioning was an act of Black Power. This curiosity and thirst for new knowledge became instrumental for the eventual emergence of the Black Progressive Movement in the late 1960s and early 1970s on the island. Answers to these questions led to new knowledge that, in turn, led to the eventual rise of local Black Power activism. The movement did have a space in the colony in the late 1960s and 1970s since progressive minds were better aware of their reality, which challenged an oppressive racial and class system, inherited from years of colonization. Regionally and internationally, white privilege and Black inequality was visible, and it was at the time openly proclaimed. The support system that came with the Black Power movement inspired communities to resist colonial oppression. Black Power was a call for Black people to get themselves together and proclaim that Black is not inferior. It was an attempt to change the rhetoric about Black people.

Influences: Student Protests and Transnational Networks

External Black radical activities paired with a disgruntled local population facilitated the space for islanders to become receptive to the Black Power movement. In the case of the St. Vincent and the Grenadines, the idea was not only imported from the United States but was heavily influenced by the Rodney Riots in Jamaica 1968, the 1969 Sir George Williams University Affair in Canada and the 1970 Upsurge in Trinidad. Interestingly enough, each event was linked in some way to Canada's Black radical twentieth century movement and the involvement of Vincentians in some way or the other, even if Canadian narration of this period overlooks or criminalizes Black involvement in radical activism. The Rodney Riots saw the intimate involvement of Vincentian student, Ralph Gonsalves, who at the time served as the president of the Guild of Undergraduates at Jamaica's Mona campus of the University of the West Indies. These-so-called riots were triggered by Walter Rodney's visit to Canada to attend the 1968 Black Writers Conference. According to reports, Gonsalves was part of this massive protest of students and working-class Jamaicans in the streets of Kingston which challenged the government's decision to ban historian, revolutionary intellectual, Caribbean nationalist, Black Power advocate, activist and lecturer, Walter Rodney.[3] The involvement of Gonsalves, a son of the soil, would have made the coverage of the event a priority since Vincentians would have seen themselves as connected to the Rodney event.

Another event that influenced the twentieth century Black Power movement inside St. Vincent and the Grenadines was the Sir George Williams University Affair in Montreal. In 1968, six West Indian students accused a professor of racial discrimination based on unfair grading. The frivolous treatment the authorities gave to the complaints of Black Caribbean students sparked a sit-in and peaceful protests. Vincentian students, Arnhim Eustace, Kerwyn Morris, Rodney John and Alfie Roberts were involved. Having completed their studies at the Canadian University, Eustace and Morris returned home and became heavily involved in the upstart of this radical activism that was seen in the island in the early 1970s. Morris was one of the leading founding members of the Education Forum of the People (EFP), while Eustace was a prominent activist of the movement. John and Roberts both remained in Canada. Roberts in his continued support of the local movement sent articles, books, and other information to the island, spreading Black radical rhetoric across the island.

The Sir George Williams University Affair did not just impact the lives of the students involved in the event. It was influential to youths across St. Vincent and the Grenadines. According to Parnel Campbell, who was a student in Canada at the time, the involvement of Caribbean students in the Affair triggered the need for a Caribbean island tour, which was spearheaded by a student delegation out of Montreal, Canada. The aim of the tour was to bring clarity within the region about the Sir George Williams University Affair in an effort to respond to the propaganda that was circulating at the time. According to Campbell, the students explained what actually transpired. Terrence Ballantyne, medical student from Trinidad, came to St. Vincent and the Grenadines and upon his visit he spoke at a public meeting held at the Market Square, Kingstown on 4th March 1969, organized by a few members of the staff of the Boys' Grammar school. It was from this outreach that the very first structured Black Power group was formed. According to Campbell, the Education Forum of the People (EFP), was directly influenced by the Sir George Williams University Affair.[4]

While the University of the West Indies and the Sir George Williams University sparked the regional movement for Black Power, it fully manifested in Trinidad and Tobago in what has been dubbed the 1970 Black Power Revolution. This February Revolution was an attempt to force socio-political changes in the twin island republic, but beyond that, it too was influenced heavily by the Sir George Williams University Affair in Canada. This 1970 event saw a number of students from the St. Augustine campus of the University of the West Indies, protesting against the Canadian government's arrests of Caribbean students, specifically the Trinidadian students, charged for the Sir George Williams University Affair. Information about the protests in Trinidad was distributed to St. Vincent and the Grenadines along the vibrant trading lines between both territories. Renwick Rose, founding member of BLAC, in an interview indicated that St. Vincent and the Grenadines was in the practice of trading ground provisions, goat, fowls etc. with Trinidad, which resulted in contacts between both spaces. Trading was not limited to goods but extended to information. In fact, a number of Vincentians learnt about the Black Power movement and its ideologies, through this same trade whether it was via casual conversations or newspapers. According to Rose, the Trinidadian newspaper, *Trinidad Express*, which frequented the shores of the colony, was influential.[5]

Connections to anti-colonial struggles across the African continent, activities in the USA and Europe as well as the local remnants of the Garvey Movement of 1919, were also present. However, they were not the immediate triggers that caused Vincentians to organize themselves. It took instead three different campuses of young intellectuals, both regional and international, to actively protest an oppressive system which then led to the formation local Black Power groups.

A Local History of Black Power Groups

The movement inside St. Vincent and the Grenadines emerged as early as December 1968, months after the Rodney Riots in Jamaica. It was felt that Black people needed to unite, rediscover their roots, take stock of themselves and fight the exploiter. There emerged on the island more than five Black Power organizations during the twentieth century which came from both intellectual and grassroots organizing. Different groups felt that Black Vincentians needed to be taught the truth about their history and understand where they came from, develop their own value system, uplift the masses, and own the power to control their own affairs.

The Education Forum of the People, EFP

The intellectual wing of the movement was the Education Forum of the People (EFP), organized in December 1968 and officially launched on April 11, 1969. The EFP was formed by University graduates, some of whom were either involved in or supported both the Rodney Riots in Jamaica of 1968 and the Sir George Williams University Affair in Canada in early 1969. Parnel Campbell has noted that the EFP's founding membership included Kenneth John, Eddie Griffith, Parnel Campbell, Winty Roberts, and Kerwyn Morris.[6] These men, according to Junior "Spirit" Cottle, were students who had returned home from Canadian universities with a much broader understanding and perspective relative to Black empowerment and its relevance to the Vincentian's Black community, having encountered racism in the unfolding of the Sir George Williams University Affair.[7] EFP membership was mainly teachers from the urban secondary schools-the Boys' Grammar School, Girls High School and Bishop College (Kingstown). Two of these teachers were Michael 'Mike' Browne and Arnhim Eustace. Overtime, active membership was increased with people like Burns Bonadie, Ken Ballantyne and John Cato joining the EFP.

The organization's mandate and objective were to undertake the planning

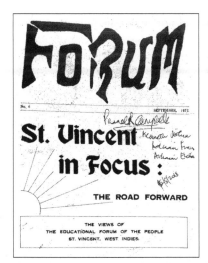

Figure 1: "Forum" issued September 1972; Flambeau September 1967. Views expressed are those of the EFP, St. Vincent W.I.[9]

and arranging of forums, seminars, panels, and discussions throughout the islands addressing the education system, labour problems, economic development, African and West Indian History, sanitation, human rights, principles of good governance, legalization of marijuana just to name a few. It was reported that by the end of September 1969, the EFP held public meetings throughout the island in the main towns and villages.[8] Every Friday night, according to Rose, the EFP met at the Market Square, Kingstown and educated listeners about the struggles of Blacks both locally and internationally. These meetings helped to inform the masses about daily injustices, whether these were based on their skin colour or their limited access to economic wealth. This helped in awakening the consciousness of the Vincentian Black community. Amongst other speakers at these meetings were Rosie Douglas (Dominica), Father Hayden (USA) and Masinini (South Africa).

In an effort to further educate Vincentians about the movement and current issues and injustices, the EFP issued two quarterly publications called the *Forum* and the *Flambeau* (see figure 1). They served to change the slave master's rhetoric about the history of St. Vincent and the Grenadines. Both magazines attempted to reinterpret Vincentian history from a national point of view to awaken the society out of its slumber of indifference. This process of social awakening was useful in nation building. The Education Forum of the People, according to Rose, was the first organization on the island to have raised conversations surrounding Black Empowerment in an open and structured manner.[10]

Young Socialist Group – YSG

The Young Socialist Group (YSG) also emerged alongside the EFP as another early radical progressive organisation. Formed in 1969, it was considered grassroots in nature because of its ideologies, leadership, membership, and issues which were all community oriented. According to Jomo Thomas, former member of Yulimo, the YSG dabbled in some elements of Black Nationalism but saw Marxism as the answer.[11] The founders of this movement included Caspar London, Hugh Ragguette, and Delroy Browne. YSG saw the need for a revolutionary dialogue and expanded their reach by publishing pamphlets and magazines in stenciled form.

In 1971, the YSG registered a monthly paper called the *Revue,* which circulated in areas outside the city, Kingstown. In keeping with their grassroots approach, the YSG made every effort to educate the masses and the *Revue* made an impact on the society, becoming the bitter enemy of exploiting classes who tried to stop the publication by spreading negative propaganda about YSG. In April of 1973, the *Revue* successfully made its first appearance as a full-fledged newspaper.[12] In an interview, Hugh Raguette notes that the YSG aimed to eradicate widespread illiteracy, class discrimination and exploitation of workers by education gained from their monthly paper, public meetings, seminars, and workshops.[13] This early organization provided not only a grassroots approach to Black powerlessness but provided a space for Vincentians, particularly the poor laboring classes, who didn't necessarily relate to the members of the Educational Forum of the People, which was comprised of mainly teachers and university graduates.

The Organisation of Black Cultural Awareness – OBCA

Two years after the YSG, another grassroots movement, named the Organisation of Black Cultural Awareness (OBCA), was formed. This was the brain child of Jim Maloney and Robert 'Patches' Knights. According to Cottle, one of the founding members of OBCA, Maloney came with a radicalised perspective after his exposure to the ghetto in Trinidad, mixing with ordinary people.[14] Robert 'Patches' Knights, on the other hand was oriented into the Black Power movement in Trinidad and Tobago.[15] Following its formation, recruiting people for OBCA was critical. Maloney's recruitment process was geared towards the ordinary Vincentian and was done on a one-on-one basis. Similar to Walter Rodney's approach, Maloney brought an awareness and consciousness by engaging discussions that concerned Black History and social injustice with persons who occupied the slums/ghettos. Now while it has been widely accepted that the EFP brought the Black empowerment ideology to the island, one can also argue that OBCA took the Black Power ideology to the ordinary and average Vincentian. This urban-based movement was known for spreading the idea of Black Nationalism and Black empowerment throughout the island through various means. A bulletin was published and distributed across the island free of cost. The members of OBCA were encouraged to read and many became engaged in the habit of reading Black literature specifically those written by Walter Rodney, *Groundings with my Brothers* and C.L.R. James, *The Black Jacobins*.[16] This was mainly because both Rodney and James, at the time, were the most highly respected regional Black Power advocates.

An interesting and unique element relative to this organisation within the Vincentian Black Power narrative was its affiliation with marijuana. According to Junior 'Spirit' Cottle, founding member of OBCA, Maloney introduced the smoking of marijuana as part of the social and political practice of the group. Marijuana smoking went against the grain of society's colonial and middle-class norms but was in line with Rastafari thought, religious and political identity and thus represented a radicalised practice. The practice was a challenge to the system and an expression of freedom. Marijuana use became so noticeably affiliated with OBCA that it was popularly referred to as the 'Black Power Cigarette' by locals. This 'Black Power Cigarette' was an addition to OBCA's recruitment process that pulled youths towards the movement and assisted in its lack of finance. The majority of the membership were unemployed and selling marijuana, according to Cottle, and this helped in the provision of funds for OBCA.[17]

The Black Liberation Action Committee (BLAC)

A year later in 1972, some of the members left the organization and formed another Black Power group, the Black Liberation Action Committee (BLAC) located in the lower part of Kingstown. Renwick Rose, one of the founders, in an interview mentioned that BLAC, at its inception, laid out a ten point agenda. Included in the action plan were matters relating to National Independence, Pan Africanism, Land Reforms, Caribbean Integration, and a call for a radical change in the education system. Education was understood to be a powerful tool related to national goals and the type of society intended to be built. It was used as the main instrument in the conditioning of the minds of Black people. It reinforced class distinctions and beauty standards. According to Rose, it was the same education that was needed to be used to help Vincentians unlearn the myths relative to Blackness and by extension the Black Power movement. This was a critical part of the radical change needed. For instance, Robert "Patches" Knights, founding member of OBCA, in an interview stated that Sir Rupert

John, Governor General, allegedly referred to the persons who were in support or sympathetic to the Black Power movement as, "people on the lunatic fringe who should be picked up and put in the mental asylum."[18] These were some of the notions and beliefs which BLAC clarified for the public. In an effort to educate the masses, the movement held public rallies, educational sessions/ classes, and cultural sessions. Poetry and drumming were used as instruments for explaining and clarifying misconceptions. Scholarships were granted by the organisation to assist students at secondary schools, along with the purchase of uniforms and other school essentials to enable children to attend schools. This was BLAC's way of contributing to the education of the masses. In BLAC's continued effort at broadening its reach across the island, a copy of an underground publication called *BLAC*, was first issued during 1974. Rose in an interview mentioned that, like OBCA, BLAC's popularity grew because of an association with marijuana. Members affiliated with BLAC were labeled marijuana users in general. According to Rose, the older and more conservative Vincentians interpreted anyone affiliated with Black Power Movement as being marijuana users.[19] This outlook brought with it a host of issues within "respectable" society.

ARWEE

The movement began finding ground in the rural spaces. In the early parts of the 1970s the ARWEE, movement arose in Diamonds Village on the northern end of the colony. 'ARWEE' is Vincentian vernacular for 'All of Us.' ARWEE, the movement, was founded by Oscar Allen, Earlene Horne, Solomon Butler, and Simeon Greene. As its name suggests, it was a community based movement with an agenda built on Black empowerment, nationalism and socialism. Simeon Greene notes that while the group focused on Black empowerment, its main focus was also on education. Adult literacy at the time was paramount, hence the group offered evening classes to adults. The classes offered by ARWEE became so popular that Greene boasted of teaching 150 students on just one evening.[20]

Initially, the organisation started out doing community work while functioning also as a pressure group to the government. ARWEE started a shop business named "People's Supply," along with working farmland to generate monies for the group. The majority of the membership was local. ARWEE was rooted in the community with a very loose leadership but there were also associates from as far as Georgetown, including a teacher, Ferdinand 'Ferdie' Toney. It also engaged in its own cultural activities, with strong African cultural practices, including play writing, and performances in drumming and poetry.[21]

The organization produced a quarterly publication called *ARWEE* that aided in pushing of the group's agenda. ARWEE featured articles that discussed political, social, cultural, and economic issues that plagued the colony at the time. According to the *Justice* newspaper, on January 19, 1984, ARWEE opened a building, named the Walter Rodney Centre in Diamonds Village. It housed a community library and classrooms. The main purpose of the centre was, "to help form the skills, the consciousness and social practice of Caribbean people who are gripped by the hunger for real emancipation."[22] The decision to name the centre after Walter Rodney is worth mentioning. Almost a year after Rodney's assassination, it was felt that it was only fitting to dedicate the building, geared towards educational progress, after him.[23] Oscar Allen and Walter Rodney were very good friends, having met in Jamaica. Allen had left St. Vincent and the Grenadines to study Theology in Jamaica. This was where he met Walter Rodney. Allen was expelled from his course of study then later returned as a radical champion for the poor. Many adults from Georgetown, who were youths then, identify Allen as the person responsible for their involvement in Black Power. One can argue that Allen's exposure to and his friendship with Rodney helped to broaden his knowledge about Black people's oppression, radicalised his view, and helped to push the local movement for radical change.

Youlou United Liberation Movement – Yulimo

As Black power continued to grow in the colony, the leaders of the different organisations felt that the State was not taking the movement seriously. The government did not consider the different movements a threat so they mostly ignored them before the formation of Yulimo. Advocates soon realised that challenging the system as a united front was far more impactful than challenges from three or four different small groups. This reasoning led to the formation of the Youlou United Liberation Movement (Yulimo) on February 2, 1974. Its official launch came on August 1, 1974, framed by a Marxist-Leninist stance with a Black power orientation. Yulimo was the product of the fusion of three organizations, the YSG, OBCA, and BLAC and was considered the working-class party designed to fight for the cause of working people. In 1975, Yulimo launched its labour arm called the National Union of Progressive Workers (NUPW), which was short lived. Yulimo's popularity among the youths warranted the formation of a student arm of the movement called Organisation for Unity and Rights of Students, (OURS). Overall, this amalgamated urban based group was able to draw its membership from across St. Vincent and the Grenadines.

Jomo Thomas described Yulimo as 'fierce', 'militant', and 'uncompromising.' Thomas joined in 1976, while a student at the St. Martin's Secondary School. He recounts how public protests against police brutality and foreign domination were a regular part of the group's activities, with picketing almost every day from 7:30am to 5pm with about 5 or 10 persons while others joined in after working hours.[24] In 1974, Yulimo's publication *Freedom* was launched and was later changed to *Justice* in 1979. Both *Freedom* and *Justice* were used as tools to mobilise mass support from the public. *Freedom* was known for attacking government policies and revealing information about the activities of the government and the private sector in St. Vincent and the Grenadines. Renwick Rose, editor at the time, mentioned that Yulimo took a socialist position with a Black Nationalist leaning. For Rose, this was socialism within the context of State run education, land reforms, health, and amenities (Vinlec at the time was owned by a British company.[25]

The New Rescuers Movement (NRM)

Other organisations across the island included, the New Rescuers Movement (NRM), located on the Leeward side of the island in Chateaubelair, which had Black power ideologies in its origin and is known to have actively rejected colonialism. Members of the NRM were mainly workers, peasants, or the unemployed who sought a means to challenge an unjust system. On September 12, 1975, the NRM engaged in a demonstration during the visit of the Premier to the government-owned Richmond Vale Estate. According to the report in *Freedom,* people were demonstrating against social conditions, including the constant oppression of the poor, misrepresentation of a false representative, hunger, dread conditions on the estate, and other hardships. Their protests used placards stating demands: "WE WANT JOBS, SUGAR, LANDS, LARD OIL, IMPROVE ESTATE CONDITIONS, and others." [26] This protest action taken on by the NRM was a direct response to a colonial system designed to serve Whites.

Black Power Discourse and the Public Sphere: Newspapers and Public debate

Black power can be viewed as a confrontation between the forces of power demanding change and the (white colonial) forces of power dedicated to preserving the status quo. As a result, the period of the late 1960s and early 1970s can be seen as one of the most repressive periods of the island's recent history. While Black Power was simply geared towards uplifting Black people, this did not shield it from attacks. Responses to Black political organizing were in no small way bolstered by colonial ideals. The movement emerged at a time when Black politicians were perhaps the "whitest men" in the Caribbean. Moreover, there were in circulation preconceived negative notions about Black Power activities stemming from newspaper and television reports and images. Sons and daughters were punished, if seen with pamphlets or any materials relating to Black Power. In essence, the Black Power movement was portrayed as something destructive. Those in authority capitalised on this portrayal to play on the fears and prejudices of the people.

As early as 1969, based on articles logged in the Vincentian newspapers, there were two binary narratives circulating in the colony. There was an anti-Black Power narrative and the pro Black Power narrative. For those who opposed the movement, the main argument was that Black Power was not relevant to the Vincentian society because 90% of the Vincentian population was Black. They also argued that unlike the United States, the region's political offices were now held by Black men. For them, Black leadership equaled Black Power which in reality was not the case. Black Power advocates, on the other hand, argued that the movement was much needed because while it was true that most islands at the time had black-skinned men as Premiers or Prime Ministers, these leaders were in no real position to represent the interests of the Black masses. Leaders at the time simply sat in a position of authority but lacked the power which was necessary to create major changes to the aged, oppressive colonial system that the Black Power movement was seeking to transform.

The general misrepresentation of the Black Power movement inside St. Vincent and the Grenadines by the public was reason for concern. Suspicion of Black progressive groups were shaped by associations with socialism which circulated in the global context of the Cold War.[27] Many believed that a socialist society would take away the bit of freedom that they already had. Emerging groups as well as individuals made a concerted effort, at the onset, to educate people by explaining the Black power ideology. These efforts were shown in newspaper articles. One article by Frederick X in the *Vincentian* newspaper entitled 'Black Power, what is it?' elucidated, "Black power is the consolidation of political and economic resources by Black people to achieve power through group unity, determination and endeavor. Its aim is to build racial pride and refute the notions that Black is ugly, evil and worthless."[28]

The public newspapers at the time illustrate the social anxieties as well as the rich debates. Ralph Gonsalves for example challenged the notion that Black Power was an American import by positing that Vincentian society, though it had Black leadership, was dominated in all areas by whites. Gonsalves expanded his argument by stating that whites in St. Vincent possessed two-thirds of the arable lands, business houses, banks, and economic decisions were made by whites and white people dominated social life.[29] Gonsalves, though light skinned, was accepted by the majority of the movements' followers in the fight against colonialism not only because of his involvement in the Rodney Riots but because many understood that Black power went beyond skin color. It also involved fundamental questions of sovereignty and solidarity.

During the same period, The EFP issued an article in the *Forum* on 10th April 1970, which explored the difference between Black power and Black authority. According to the article, Black power had more to do with the transformation of Black thinking relative to white culture and its standards of beauty and value while Black authority, on the other hand, was more about the Black faces that were heads of government at the time.[30] As the movement grew, supporters were seen setting their own standards of beauty, with elements of African culture. African dress, the Afro hairstyle, and African names becoming a trend. An interesting letter by Franko to the *Vincentian* newspaper noted that young intelligent men were wearing full face beards and bushy heads. The writer considered these individuals as a savage tribe of people in a civilized community.[31] These different expressions of the Black Power movement resulted in attacks on style. For instance, a local qualified barber condemned the Afro Style. In his letter to the *Vincentian* newspaper, he stated that the style was not suited for young people because in his opinion it made the look, "sick, dotish, lazy, savage, and grimy." The style, according to him, suited folks over age 70.[32]

While the printed word was instrumental in the spreading of Black Power ideologies and contestations, there were others who spread the movement through graffiti prints on public walls. A letter from Franko in the *Vincentian* newspaper on March 28, 1970, mentioned that "observing on walls the word 'BLACK POWER' written up in 'crab foot' writing."[33] The placement of the words 'Black Power' graffitied on walls made the concept, idea, and movement something visible daily for a number of Vincentians.

Alongside the growth of the Black Power movement was the growth in repressive state activities. The governments of Guyana, Antigua, St. Kitts and Dominica had passed various acts which were designed to stifle criticism and infringe on the freedom of expression. The experiences of the Black Power movement inside St. Vincent continued with the erosion of the freedom of the press and the banning of books, magazines, or newspapers which even faintly spoke to or supported the idea of Black power or socialism. Based on the enforcement of a Prohibition Publication Act stemming from 1939, a series of seizures and court cases where individuals were charged with possession of undesirable and seditious publications followed. For example, in June 1975, the

Vincentian reported that, at the Arnos Vale airport, Caspar London was accosted by the Police and Customs officials.[34] Later the same year, London was made to answer charges of, "possession of prohibited Publication to wit: a copy of Ho Chi Minh on Revolution selected writings 1920-1966 sec.8(2) of the sedition and Undesirable Publications Ordinance No.2 1939 as amended No.17 of 1941."[35]

In response to the ban placed on literature, in July of 1975, Yulimo wrote a letter to the Minister of Home Affairs inquiring about the literatures prohibited from entering the State and the reasons for the prohibition but to no avail.[36] The attacks on literature continued. An article titled, "Police Officers raided ARWEE" reported that on, "February 17th ,1977 at 6am a party of seven police officers entered the office of ARWEE. They claimed to be looking for marijuana. In the end, they carried away some of our literatures."[37] According to Rose, up until 2001, St. Vincent and the Grenadines had a list of prohibited literatures. As late as 1984, Rose was arrested for having in his possession the Cuban *Granma* newspapers along with literature from the Soviet Union.[38] The banning of literature was so rampant to the point where authorities ended up illegally seizing books based on just their names, as is illustrated by the seizing of such books as the *Industrial Revolution*, just because police officers saw the word 'revolution' and became frightened.[39] The keepers of the colonial system were aware of the power of print, therefore it became important that the spread of the printed word that spoke to Black empowerment and other radical ideologies be contained.

Arrests and detentions during the 1970s by police became the norm for many of the advocates of the movement. On the morning of May 20, 1970, armed police carried out a raid on the homes of members of the EFP, John Cato, Kerwyn Morris, and Parnel Campbell. According to the *Forum*, the police indicated that they were in search of firearms, ammunitions, and prohibited literatures. Upon leaving, the police are said to have taken a quantity of books which included many of those used as students at University.[40] On May 27, 1973, Cottle wrote in a letter that in 'Bottom Town' (Kingstown), poor people were being brutalized and tear-gassed without even warning to get out of their houses. [41] Although not illegal, it was forbidden by authorities, for more than two people to congregate in the streets. This resulted in scores of Kingstown youths being interrogated, imprisoned and charged for loitering.[42]

By 1975, the radicalizing climate over the colony, meant that locals were aware of the injustices Blacks were facing outside of St. Vincent and the Grenadines and wanted change. The numerous local Black progressive organizations and newspaper debates that emerged were a direct spill off from the global wave of the Black Power protests and activism. In a space where the majority of the population lived in impoverished conditions, and within circumstances of powerlessness, the oppressed found it easy to identify with groups fighting for the causes of the poor and against social injustice.

The movement for Black Power helped shaped the twentieth century history of St. Vincent and the Grenadines, despite its absence from the historical record. Additionally, the events occurring in Canada, United Kingdom and the United States had an impact on the emergence of the local movement. Canada, specifically the Sir George Williams Affair, brought awareness to Vincentian students exposed to the harsh reality of racial inequality. It created a springboard from which people from the region were able to recognize their own every day. This included women also. Though the local narrative is quite silent about women's involvement, it was understood that women provided a support system for the movement and many of the forerunners' female partners stood in support of the Black Power movement. Their acts of resistance are said not only to have been shown in their dress, Afro hairstyles, protests, and rallies but Earlene Horne, a member of ARWEE, made a number of appearances at public rallies as a speaker.

The Rodney Riots and the 1970 Trinidad Revolution, rooted in events in Canada, became two of the greatest influences that saw the emergence of the Vincentian Black Power movement. It can be argued that the cause for the movement may have been similar to other spaces, however, the St. Vincent's chapter had its own unique twist because of the conditions that the Vincentian population had been exposed to. With a tradition of radicalism, tracing all the way back to the Garifuna peoples, the fight for sovereignty continued during the twentieth century but under different conditions. The aim, similar to those of the local chapter of the Garvey movement of 1919, remained consistent during the mid-twentieth century. That thirst for total economic, social, cultural, and political freedom while challenging the system continuously to gain some form of genuine liberty had always been a deeply rooted Vincentian practice.

NOTES

1   Walter Rodney, *Groundings with my Brothers* (London: Bogle- L'Ouverture Press Ltd., 1969), 25.

2   Tony Thomas and John Riddell, *Black Power in the Caribbean; The 1970 Upsurge in Trinidad* (New York: Pathfinder Press, 1971), 3.

3   Ralph E. Gonsalves, *The Making of 'The Comrade': The political journey of Ralph Gonsalves* (Kingstown: Strategy Forum Inc., 2010), 19.

4   Parnel Campbell, personal interview, September, 4 2018.

5   Renwick Rose, personal interview, September 4, 2017.

6   Campbell, interview.

7   Junior "Spirit" Cottle, personal interview, August 30, 2017.

8   *The Vincentian,* July 19, 1969: 1.

9   The sixth publication of *Forum* was issued in print form rather than the usual stenciled form. This publication educated its audience about the EFP. Discussed in this issue are matters that concerned the Vincentian society's politics, economics, culture, and Caribbean integration. Articles included topics such as Education, Religion, Black Power, Law, and Justice, and Trade Unionism just to name a few, written by members of the EFP. Information for prospective members were also included as part of their recruitment drive.

10   Rose, interview.

11   Jomo Thomas, personal interview, August 21, 2017.

12   *The Freedom,* August 1, 1974: 1.

13   Hugh Raguette, personal interview, April 13, 2018.

14   Cottle, interview.

15   Robert "Patches" Knights, personal interview, January 22, 2018.

16   Cottle, interview.

17   Ibid.

18   Knights, interview.

19   Rose, interview.

20   Simeon Greene, personal interview, August 24, 2017.

21   Greene, interview.

22   *Justice* January 19.1981: 3.

23   Greene, interview.

24   Thomas, interview.

25   Rose, interview.

26   *The Freedom,* September 26,.1975: 9.

27   *The Vincentian,* August 23, 1969: 5.

28   *The Vincentian,* May 3, 1969:2.

29   *The Vincentian,* August 23, 1969: 5.

30   *The Forum,* April 10, 1970: 13.

31   *The Vincentian,* March 28, 1970: 4.

32   *The Vincentian,* May 20, 1972: 8.

33   *The Vincentian,* March 28, 1970: 4.

34   *The Vincentian,* July 11, 1975: 1.

35   *The Freedom,* November 21,.1975: 4.

36   *The Vincentian,* July 11, 1975: 1.

37   ARWEE. "The Working Class Speaks." 1977:7.

38   Rose, interview.

39   *The Freedom,* July 11, 1975:3.

40   *The Forum,* March 31,.1972: 19-20.

41   *The Freedom,* October 11,1974: 3-4.

42   *The Forum,* March 31, 1972: 19-20.

Transnational Marronage: The *Abeng* Archives

Ronald Cummings

THE NEWSPAPER *Abeng* was published between the months of February and September 1969.[1] Although the life-span of the publication was relatively short, it was an important intervention in the critical public discourse of the time and still offers keen historical insights into the counter-cultural formations that were taking shape, as well as allows us to read some important articulations of the ideological underpinnings of Black Power in the Caribbean region at the end of the 1960s. The historian Robert A. Hill locates the newspaper within a tradition of soundings of anti-colonial resistance, particularly in his reference to *Abeng* (along with the *New World Quarterly*, which preceded *Abeng* and which lasted between 1963 and 1968) as blowing the "horn of Black Power in Jamaica".[2] Hill's reflections echo the articulations of *Abeng*'s own editorial collective. In the first issue of the newspaper, the editors locate their work in a lineage of Maroon practice through their explicit discussion of the publication's name:

> The paper is to be an instrument for Jamaicans to communicate with one another. The Abeng was used by the Maroons and other Jamaicans in bygone days to communicate with one another in a very precise and special way in much the same way that this paper would like to do.[3]

Recalling the Abeng "of bygone days" into their present, the editors position the publication as both an inheritance and as an instrument to continue a call for the unfinished work of freedom. Hill's discussion restates this vision. Locating the paper (as well as Black Power) in a tradition of marronage, he notes that the:

> Abeng was the name of the steer's horn used by the Jamaican Maroons to communicate in battle. The choice of Abeng as the name for the newspaper was intended to be a reaffirmation of the culture of resistance as well as a clear identification with the Afro-slave roots of Jamaican culture…the symbolic valence of the horn was apt.[4]

However, Hill also importantly locates the newspaper within the circuits of transnational Black radicalism not only by linking it with *New World* (primarily through his examination of the figure of the Caribbean intellectual George Beckford who was a key contributor to both publications) but also by noting that it "issued from the effort to sustain and extend the movement associated with Walter Rodney and the events surrounding what came to be referred to as 'The Rodney Affair'" in Jamaica.[5] In 1968, when the Caribbean historian and activist Walter Rodney was prevented from re-entering Jamaica following his travels to Montreal to participate in the Congress of Black Writers, students at the University of the West Indies (UWI), where Rodney had been teaching, took to the streets in protest of the Jamaican government's ban. "The Rodney Affair", as it came to be known, gathered such support and momentum that it has become a landmark moment in the history of Caribbean student activism. While situating *Abeng*'s interventions within that historical moment through key considerations of Beckford and Rodney and their periodizing and period-defining narratives, Hill also points to Abeng's significance as extending beyond the immediate context of its emergence both by looking back to the history of Maroon resistance but also by arguing that its "arrival ushered in a new cultural and social energy that would be felt throughout the entire Caribbean region".[6]

Indeed, we can mark *Abeng*'s significance as a space of energetic public thought and debate in a number of ways including through an attention to its impressive list of contributors, collaborators and co-conspirators. Rupert Lewis notes that "Abeng in 1969 was the coming together of a variety of trends—Rastafarians, Garveyites, businessmen, …lawyers, UWI academics and disillusioned PNP activists".[7] Even more impressive and useful to consider are the number of recognizable names that Lewis lists among the newspaper's contributors and editorial team who were all, in their own regard, key figures in the Jamaican intellectual and political scene, particularly the political left: "Abeng involved Norman Girvan, Robert Hill, George Beckford, Rupert Lewis, Dennis Daley, Peter Figueroa, Tony Bogues, Robin Small, Ras Negus, Richard Small, Ronnie Thwaites, Arnold Bertram, D.K. Duncan, Trevor Munroe, Paul Miller, Ken Post and Wilmot Perkins".[8]

Lewis' essay, "Learning to Blow the Abeng", outlines the foremost context for the emergence of *Abeng* as the turbulent Jamaican 1960s, referencing specific events such as "the Henry protest of 1960; the activities of Millard Johnson's Garveyite People's Political Party; the Coral Gardens disturbance of 1963; the return of Garvey's body from London in 1964;…the visit of Emperor Haile Selassie in 1966; the anti-Chinese riots of 1965 and the national state of emergency of 1966-1967".[9] In this regard, we might read his work as offering

one historiographical approach to the examination of the formation of *Abeng*
highlighting the contemporary, practical and intellectual currents that shaped
the newspaper's formation.[10] We might also usefully consider this approach
alongside Rex Nettleford's work in *Mirror Mirror: Race, Identity and Protest in
Jamaica*, which emphasizes the question of genealogies and transitions as a way
of understanding *Abeng* as a formation.[11] Foregrounding issues of transitions
and change, Nettleford situates Black Power in Jamaica at the end of the 1960s
by thinking about its relationship to previous moments and movements such
as the emergence of Rastafari, in the context of the previous decade, as well as
engages with the question of its capacity for facilitating change. He argues that
"the end of the decade of the sixties will partly be remembered in Jamaica for
the country's involvement with the phenomenon of Black Power just as the
beginning of the decade brought Rastafarianism face to face with the society".[12]

In revisiting discussions in the pages of *Abeng* in this chapter, I want to
seize on some of the transnational connections glimpsed in the work of Hill,
Lewis and Nettleford to argue for an understanding of *Abeng* within a framework of transnational marronage. In particular, I examine the coverage of the
Sir George Williams University (SGWU) protests in *Abeng* as one site where
we might see the interweaving of struggles, agendas and even personages. For
example, Robert Hill who also participated in *Abeng,* and who Lewis discusses
in his work, was one of the figures connected with the C.L.R James Study Group
(CLRJSG) and with the 1968 Congress of Black Writers and thus with student
activism in Montreal.[13] I use the concept of transnational marronage here to reflect on Black radicalism as marked by interconnected moments, strategies and
spaces of resistance. Transnational marronage as a critical framework calls
attention to interlinked sites of struggle dedicated to undoing the legacies of
plantation life and its logics and structures of power and relation. We see explicit
attention to this question in Robert Hill's discussion of the work of George
Beckford (and his involvement in both *New World* and *Abeng*) as part of what
he termed "a revolutionary intellectual tradition of dread thought in the
Caribbean".[14] In particular, Hill allows us to note the inteconnections but also
the distinctions between these groups, while also mapping the trajectory and
impact of Beckford's work "as an 'intellectual dread' of the Caribbean plantation complex".[15] We also see attention to dismantling the legacies of and a critical
concern with "the wake of the plantation"[16] in Rupert Lewis' essay where he begins
by locating *Abeng* within a wider geography and history of struggle. As Lewis
puts it: "[t]he anti-establishments movements of the 1960s and 1970s were
essentially movements concerned with eliminating the legacies of racial,
economic, class oppression from the colonial experience".[17]

My own discussion situates both the formation of *Abeng* and the Sir George Williams University occupation as acts of transnational marronage. In the case of *Abeng*, the framework for understanding their intervention *as* marronage lay in the fact that, as the editors repeatedly noted and critiqued, the "colonial experience... continued after political independence".[18] The region continued to be structured by the plantation as a mode of relation and power. Although the decade of the 1960s was marked by political independence in Jamaica in 1962, struggles for decolonization remained ongoing as the stories in *Abeng* testify. In the first issue of *Abeng*, alongside the column in which they address the naming of the paper was also another article that stridently critiqued the then Jamaican Prime Minister, Hugh Shearer, for "speaking strongly against British Honours in the Jamaican Parliament", then only a few months later accepting a title and appointment to the Privy Council from the Queen. In their commentary, the editors move beyond simply noting how this perpetuated a defined colonial relationship (plantation distributions of power)—they also explicitly highlight the transnational context of the struggle for decolonization in their discussion of and attention to the Anguilla Revolution. In the months of March and April further articles would also appear in *Abeng* on the subject of Anguilla and the people's struggle for decolonization there.

In the February 1 article, the query is raised whether Hugh Shearer, in his newly appointed role on the Privy Council, would be able to consult on the issue of Anguilla. The column attends to the fraught and fragile politics of sovereignty of the time in regional and relational terms rather than in bounded national terms. While Jamaica had attained political independence by that time, its fellow Commonwealth territory was, in 1969, embroiled in sovereignty struggles which would, only a few days after the publication of the first issue of *Abeng*, result in Anguilla voting to declare itself an independent republic (on February 6) and a month later (on March 11) also result in a British envoy, William Whitlock, being dispatched from the metropole to calm the revolutionary waters, only to be expelled from the island at gunpoint, a few days later, for his proposal to install a new interim British administration as a way of ending the political uprising and impasse.

In attending to this transnational network of revolution and solidarity, we should also note how Caribbean political and sovereignty struggles also inform an understanding of events in Montreal. However, the primary framework for understanding the Sir George Williams University occupation as marronage and as a challenge to the persistence of plantation politics might be seen in the explicit articulations of what the students at Sir George, along with their supporters and allies, discussed as Canadian imperialism. Their protests consistently offered an ideological reframing of Canada, not as a space of freedom journeys (or as distinct from the U.S. to the south) but instead as implicated in, and as part of, structures of white domination.

We see one of the most cogent articulations and analysis of this Canadian imperial structure of relations (racial, military and economic) in Dennis Forsythe's edited volume *Let the Niggers Burn!: The Sir George Williams University Affair and Its Caribbean Aftermath*, published in the immediate wake of the occupation in 1971.[19] In this collection, the articles and discussions focus not only on documenting the events at Sir George, but also seek to situate them in a wider historical framework. In Forsythe's introduction, for instance, he challenges an understanding of the Sir George Williams University protests in isolated terms. Rather, he argues that we should see "the Sir George Affair, and other incidents of this type, as part of a 400-year old story".[20] He circles back to this idea of its transnational interconnectivity in the closing chapter titled "The Unfinished Revolution" where he locates Sir George within a still unfolding (post 1699) story of "Black resistance to white domination".[21]

A close attention to Canadian imperial power is also seen in Delisle Worrell's chapter in that book.[22] In his essay "Canadian Economic Involvement in the West Indies" Worrell challenges notions of Canadian "goodwill"[23] in order to examine, what we might rephrase (using Walter Rodney's critical vocabulary) as processes of underdevelopment.[24] Worrell situates these unequal relations of power and resources as a key feature of the economic relationship between the Caribbean and Canada and examines histories of banking, insurance, mining, manufacturing and tourism as "whoreism,"[25] to think about economic vulner-abilities and colonial inequalities as central to Caribbean-Canadian histories.

The concept of transnational marronage that I use in this chapter might thus be seen as explicitly extending insights offered by Forsythe and by Worrell and reminds us that the uprising and protest in Montreal had its roots in practices and experiences of white structures of power, which resulted in the instances of Canadian racism and discrimination experienced by the students at Sir George Williams University. In reading the Sir George Williams University occupation as marronage, my discussion here is also in dialogue with more recent writings including the work of the Black feminist-historian Kelann Currie-Williams where she argues we should read events at Sir George, as she puts it, "in the legacy of marronage."[26] According to Currie-Williams, "Without question, the events of the Sir George Williams Affair were acts of resistance, of refusal, and of dissent towards careless treatment and anti-blackness within the university".[27] Against this backdrop of the colonial racial logics, which underpin the event and which are made explicit in the analysis of writers like

Forsythe, Currie-Williams reads a radical practice of community in the act of occupying space with each other. She reads this *as* marronage. She also situates the occupation in the context of 1960s racial and political struggle: "This legacy of marronage and its preoccupation with care, sees itself throughout the 1960s in the form of sit-ins and protests, articulating the creation of another kind of community of support for Black life and a perpetuation of acts of radical fugitivity".[28]

Currie-Williams additionally argues that the establishment of the C.L.R. James Study Group (CLRJSG) was one key instantiation of this *practice of marronage* as "a mode of relation".[29] But as David Austin reminds us in his work, the students in Montreal were *studying marronage*[30] through their reading of the history of the Haitian Revolution in *The Black Jacobins*: "Members of the CLRJSC read the *The Black Jacobins* with the Caribbean in mind . . . as they attempted to chart a course towards Caribbean liberation in the 1960s and 1970s" (272).[31] Thus, while *Abeng* in Jamaica drew on the memory of Maroon resistance in the stories of the Jamaican Maroon Wars, protestors in Montreal were inspired and informed by the legacies and stories of the Haitian Revolution remembered in C.L.R. James' writing. In thinking about the work of *Abeng* in relation to the Sir George Williams University occupation, we might trace a transnational geography of consciousness not only connecting different historical moments but also connecting Kingston, Montreal, London, Port-au-Prince, Port of Spain to name a few spaces. Both *Abeng* and the protests in Montreal were part of a wider interconnected transnational call for Black freedom and dignity. Considering these transnational echoes, resonances and uprisings allows us to appreciate and begin to understand the complex interconnectedness of these geographies and temporalities of struggle.

As noted above, the first issue of the newspaper, *Abeng*, appeared on February 1, 1969, two days after students at Sir George Williams University began occupying the computer centre. We might thus read the soundings of *Abeng* as concurrent with but also as helping to amplify events taking place at Sir George. The first of the articles on the occupation to appear in *Abeng* was published on February 22 (Vol. 1, No. 4) under the title "Students Fight Racism in Canada." The article offered an account of the students' actions by outlining a chronology that started with the filing of the complaint against Professor Perry Anderson in April 1968 and traced events to February 18, 1969 when the students were charged with mischief and conspiracy to commit arson. In addition to this attention to a longer unfolding of events, beyond the dramatic happenings of February 11, 1969, when the police raided the computer centre and arrested the students, what is notable about the framing of the account, in this instance, is the specific attention to a transnational framework, to transnational movement and to collaboration. The article, for example, includes a photograph with a reporter from *Abeng* and two students from Sir George Williams University, Terrence Ballantyne and Patrick Townsend, at the airport in Jamaica and announces that Ballantyne and Townsend "are travelling through the Caribbean on a fund-raising tour."[32] As Kirland Ayanna Bobb notes in her essay in this volume, this tour that was undertaken by the students was not just about raising funds. They also engaged face-to-face meetings throughout the region as part of the task of combatting and clarifying stories about the protests that were being circulated through the North American and mainstream media.[33] The article closes by inviting support for the students' cause by calling for readers to make contributions to the February 11 Defence Fund organized by community members in Montreal or by sending contributions to the Guild of Under-graduate Students' Union at the University of the West Indies, Mona campus.

This strategy of mobility and collaboration, that is narrated here, is part of what I also read as a tradition of transnationalism and marronage. We see glimpses of this in Antonio Benítez-Rojo's work, *The Repeating Islands,* where he writes of historical practices of flight and movement as central to maroon practice and a narrative of resistance in the region in the age of colonial conquest. According to Benítez-Rojo:

> One day, when global investigations of this theme are undertaken, the Caribbean will astonish everyone by how close it came to being a confed-eration of fugitives, of outlaws. I am not exaggerating; in the last decade of the eighteenth century there were slave rebellions and massive escapes in literally all of the region's islands of which the Haitian Revolution was only a part, the part that triumphed visibly. Furthermore there seemed to have been mysterious personages travelling here and there carrying secret words and letters.[34]

For Benítez-Rojo, slave rebellions, though radically important, only constituted one part of a repeating Maroon narrative. The practice of carrying stories and messages —"secret words and letters"— throughout the archipelago constituted still another part. We see this strategy replayed in the journeys of Ballantyne and Anderson as reported in *Abeng*.[35] Benítez-Rojo's mapping of these strategies within and through the framework of the meta-archipelago and of the repeating island allows us to connect these moments and histories across time as different parts of what he terms "an enormous branching narration that will serve as an alternative to the 'planter histories.'"[36] His reference to the Haitian Revolution also allows us to recall the specific *study* of the Haitian Revolution in which the students in Montreal engaged. We might thus read these students as complexly participating in the tradition of resistance, this maroon practice, that they were studying.

Abeng's attention to these transnational connections might also be further understood within a specific history of student activism. The solidarity of the students at the University of the West Indies with students in Montreal, which is demonstrated here, is undoubtedly linked to the UWI's Guild of Students' own role in mobilizing the protests a year before, in 1968, in support of Walter Rodney. *Abeng* also importantly allows us to think of these narratives of student struggles in intertwined, relational terms (much like the framework Antonio Benítez-Rojo offers). The February 15 issue of the *Abeng* (Vol. 1, No. 3), includes a story about student protests taking place at the Jamaica School of Agriculture (JSA) in February 1969.[37] Much as with the story of the students at Sir George, the JSA protests have fallen from widespread critical attention. However there are several noteworthy echoes in the coverage of these events which *Abeng* allows us to see. As with events in Montreal, the violent role of the police in supressing student protests is patently evident. The February 15 article details the beatings and injuries of a number of students protesting on the grounds of the JSA campus as well as documents the repressive actions of the school's administration. The article closes by outlining the students' grievances as well as noting the solidarity and support received "from UWI students, certain teacher training colleges and other student bodies."[38] It also includes a list of demands including a call for the resignation of the principal, the suspension of the inspector who "led the police attack" and a demand for a "full public inquiry."

Several of these points of focus recur in the subsequent coverage of the Sir George Williams University protest and its aftermath in *Abeng*. The front page of the March 8 issue (Vol.1, No. 6) includes the headlines "Immoral, white racist Canadian Police Beat, Terrorise, Insult our Black Brothers and Sisters" and details the brutality of the Canadian police. The account echoes some of language used almost a month before in *Abeng* in describing "the police attack" on the JSA campus. In considering both articles, we also note a forthright structural critique that makes visible the coloniality of systems of state policing both in Canada and the Caribbean.[39] The front-page article on March 8 is also noteworthy not just for its detailed, focused yet succinct recounting of police violence, but also its notable attention to gender in that it highlights the specific ways in which women were targeted and handled as part of the Montreal February arrests.

The March 14 issue of *Abeng* (Vol. 1, No. 7) was the final issue to carry coverage about the Sir George Williams University Protests and includes two articles on the subject. The first of these, "Black Students Acted in Defense of Rights and Property," examined questions surrounding who started the fire and who destroyed the computers in the computer centre. The article highlighted the conduct of respect by the students who had been occupying the computer centre over the two weeks prior to the invasion by the police and the subsequent destruction of property. In focusing on these questions *Abeng* makes relevant the call for a commission of inquiry advanced in the context of the case of JSA protests and arguably foreshadows several of the questions and concerns that have come to mark the historiography of the Sir George Williams University protests. However, while a number of the articles in *Abeng* were concerned with understanding and outlining what happened in Montreal, it is also true that the *Abeng* coverage made explicit the transnational context and stakes of this history through an attention to the debates and events that were happening in the Caribbean region. This can be seen particularly in another article which appeared in the March 14 issue and which focused specifically on the examining and contextualizing the details surrounding the Canadian Governor-General, Roland Michener's trip to the Caribbean in February-March 1969.[40]

The editorial, titled "Canada's White Lies" situates Michener's visit within the wider context of regional geo-politics, history and Caribbean-Canadian relations in two key ways. First it reminds readers of Michener's twin role as Canadian representative and the representative of the Queen, in his position as Governor-General. In this way it takes up the immediate context of the happenings of February 1969 to ask why Michener was being granted particular state formalities in the wake of the stark mistreatment of Caribbean students in Canada but it also attends to longer histories and questions of sovereignty and freedom in the Caribbean by recalling the context of empire. In the second instance the article foregrounds questions of hospitality as part of its reflections on relations between the Caribbean and Canada both historically and in the moment of 1969. The article opens in the following way:

> West Indian students in Montréal have been discriminated against, brutalized, arrested and are now on trial. The Canadian Governor General has come and was showered with hospitality. The largest Canadian warship-The Provider-called here last week on a Caribbean cruise. And 850 Canadian troops are "exercising" in the John Crow Mountains and in the Cockpit country so as to "get accustomed to tropical conditions".[41]

This opening connects a number of interrelated concerns. The examination of all of these together raises meaningful queries about narratives of Canadian civility. This opening also importantly calls attention to the militarization of Canadian nation-state politics through the referencing of the Canadian warship in the Caribbean and of Canadian troops in the interior of Jamaica. Through an attention to these moments and spaces, the article additionally provides another way of understanding the militarized and legalistic responses by the Canadian state to the events of February 1969 as part of a wider exercise of Canadian state militarized praxis. In other words, the transnational framing here allows for a more rigourous critique of Canadian nationalism narrating it not in benign but militarized terms.

In addition to the comments about hospitality and the critique of the militarization of the Canadian state, in reading this account, one can hardly miss the sly references to Canadian border politics. Prior to the period of the 1960s, Canada excluded Black and Caribbean peoples on the premise that they were not suited to the climate of Canada. In asking whether the Canadians troops in Jamaica were there "to get accustomed to tropical conditions", the editorial ironically recalls this history of racial exclusion from Canada situating Canada within global geographies of white supremacy, while also raising real questions about the Canadian state's purpose and role in Jamaica. The queries are extended through a number of other questions which follow:

> Did they send their biggest warship at this time to intimidate black people in the West Indies? Are the troops in Portland and the Cockpit studying the terrain to prepare to move in if Canadian bauxite, banks etc. were to come under attack? No part of Canada is tropical. So what are they preparing for?[42]

The imperialist and neo-colonial histories of Canadian involvement in the Caribbean that one can trace through institutions of banking and bauxite are explicitly referenced here. This intervention is framed as provocation for further thought. Beyond the mere content of the questions here, it is also worth noting the rhetorical turn to questioning as a particular mode of intervention. This is not a simple, foreclosed indictment of Canadian imperialism but an opening up of multiple lines of inquiry for further exploration and discovery.

The critique, which is offered here, is also made more poignant because of the specific evocation of the Maroon territories of the John Crow Mountains and the Cockpit country. These areas were Maroon lands in the east and west of the island respectively that had been successfully defended against British army invasions during both Maroon wars in the eighteenth century and decreed by treaties signed with the British Crown as lands the Maroons "shall enjoy and possess, for themselves and posterity for ever."[43] The creation of these treaties designated these spaces as sites of Maroon territorial sovereignty within colonial geographies. By specifically referencing this geographical and historical terrain, the writers in *Abeng* position the Canadian presence on this land as an act of occupation of Maroon territory by a foreign force and as a threat not only to Jamaican sovereignty but also a well-fought-for history of Maroon sovereignty. In so doing, they recall Maroon presence and significance as not just linked to "bygone days" and to the past but also as part of the question of freedom and sovereignty in the post-independence present. These questions of Black sovereignty were also central to the story of the uprisings in Montreal. We might thus read this as another part of this complexly transnational narrative.

Conclusion

Abeng's coverage of the SGWU protests in many ways served to link that event to longer histories of Black freedom struggles. However, at the same time, the discussions that unfolded on the pages of the newspaper also called these longer histories into the present as important texts and contexts for understanding the pivotal moment of the late 1960s and its freedom struggles. In particular, they connected contemporary events, including those in Montreal, to geographies and histories of marronage in ways that identified the New World plantation as a consistent backdrop to the unfolding present. This allowed for an articulation and analysis of Canadian imperialism, the examination of the persistence of plantation logics and a recontextualization of the many ways in which the histories of the Caribbean and Canada are intertwined. While discussions about the Sir George protests, in the context of the region, have tended to focus on connections with Trinidad (because of the presence of a number of Trinidadians among the group of students who raised complaints at Sir George as well as the number of Trinidadians who were made to stand trial), *Abeng*'s registering of the Jamaican context offers a useful and important extension of this discussion and considers implications and lessons for the wider region. The *Abeng* archives also complicate and expand contested questions of sovereignty, in post-independence Jamaica through an attentive look at the multiple dimensions of Canadian imperialisms. Ultimately, what emerges in *Abeng* is also a revisioning of marronage, one which approaches that history and practice as not just linked with the past but also with the present and as the work of Antonio Benítez-Rojo shows, as one that repeats within the meta-archipelago.

NOTES

1   The entire archive of *Abeng* has been digitized and can be found at the digital Library of the Caribbean (dLOC). https://dloc.com/UF00100338/00003/allvolumes?search=abeng.

2   Robert A. Hill, "From *New World to Abeng*: George Beckford and the Horn of Black Power in Jamaica, 1968–1970." *Small Axe*, 24 (2007): 1-15.

3   "Why Abeng?", *Abeng* 1, no. 1 (February 1969).

4   Robert A. Hill, "From *New World to Abeng*", 3.

5   Ibid., 5.

6   Ibid., 5.

7   Rupert Lewis, "Learning to Blow the Abeng: A Critical Look at Anti-Establishment Movements of the 1960s and 1970s." *Small Axe*, 1 (February 1997): 6.

8   Ibid., 6.

9   Ibid., 7.

10   We might further mark a critical genealogy through noting the fact that Lewis' essay appears in the very first issue of the Caribbean journal *Small Axe*.

11   Rex Nettleford. *Mirror Mirror: Race, Identity and Protest in Jamaica*. (Kingston: W. Collins and Sangster, 1970).

12   Ibid., 115.

13   See David Austin. *Fear of a Black Nation: Race, sex, and security in sixties Montreal*. (Toronto: Between the Lines, 2013) and David Austin, ed., *Moving Against the System: The 1968 Congress of Black Writers and the Making of Global Consciousness*. (London: Pluto, 2018).

14   Robert A. Hill, "From *New World to Abeng*", 2.

15   Ibid., 2.

16   I take this concept from Deborah A. Thomas. *Political Life in the Wake of the Plantation: Sovereignty, Witnessing, Repair*. (Durham; London: Duke University Press, 2019).

17   Rupert Lewis, "Learning to Blow the Abeng", 5.

18   Ibid., 5.

19   Dennis Forsythe (ed.). *Let the Niggers Burn!: The Sir George Williams University Affair and Its Caribbean Aftermath*. (Montreal: Black Rose Books, 1971).

20   Ibid., 4.

21   Ibid., 193. Forsythe's timeline doesn't begin with European colonial arrival and conquest (1492) but rather with a series of revolutions and mutinies. What is also noteworthy is that Forsythe does not only recall or focus on landed or land-locked revolutions but he also includes the mutinies that happened aboard ships during the transatlantic trade of Africans.

22   Delisle Worrell, "Canadian Economic Involvement in the West Indies" in Dennis Forsythe (ed.), *Let the Niggers Burn!: The Sir George Williams University Affair and Its Aftermath*. (Montreal: Black Rose Books, 1971), 41-56.

23   Ibid., 41.

24   Walter Rodney. *How Europe Underdeveloped Africa*. (London: Bogle-L'Ouverture Publications, 1972).

25   Delisle Worrell, "Canadian Economic Involvement in the West Indies", 49.

26   Kelann Currie-Williams, "In the Legacy of Marronage: The Sir George Williams Affair and Acts of Refusal, Protest, and Care." Special issue on Protests and Pedagogy: Black Studies and the Legacies of the 1969 Sir George Williams Student Protests in *Topia: Canadian Journal of Cultural Studies*, Eds. Ronald Cummings and Nalini Mohabir. (Forthcoming, Fall, 2021).

27   Ibid., np.

28   Ibid., np.

29   Here she references and builds on Ronald Cummings, "Maroon In/Securities". *Small Axe* 57 (2018): 47–55.

30   I use the notion of study here to also echo Fred Moten and Stephano Harney's work in *The Undercommons: Fugitive Planning & Black Study*. (New York: Minor Compositions, 2013)

31   David Austin, "The Black Jacobins: A Revolutionary Study of Revolution, and of a Caribbean Revolution," in Charles Forsdick and Christian Hogsbjerg (eds.), *The Black Jacobins Reader*. (Durham, NC: Duke University Press, 2017), 256-277.

32   *Abeng* 1, no. 4 (February 22, 1969). Further details of this tour are recounted in the chapter "Black Power in Twentieth Century St. Vincent and the Grenadines" by Kirland Ayanna Bobb in this volume.

33   Dorothy Williams' chapter also allows us to see these student and community papers as sharing this goal.

34   Antonio Benítez-Rojo. *The Repeating Island*. (Durham: Duke University Press, 1996).

35   It is useful to note that *Abeng* was not simply narrating these movements and networks. We might argue that it was also part of this process of circulation. In his chapter in this volume, Rupert Lewis recounts sending copies of the newspaper to his sister in Montreal who shared it with other students at Sir George Williams University.

36   Ibid., 254.

37   The site of these protests at the Jamaica School of Agriculture allows us to think specifically about the connections to plantation politics and of the afterlife of the plantation.

38   *Abeng* 1, no. 3 (February 15, 1969).

39   We might also consider how this critique is echoed in contemporary calls for police and prison abolition that have garnered more widespread public attention in recent years.

40   Michener was the first Canadian Governor General to visit the Caribbean. The timing of his trip was no doubt man to smooth diplomatic relations between the Caribbean and Canada in the wake of the Sir George protests. His tour of the Caribbean also forms a counter archive and a counter itinerary to the student's tour reported in the February 22, issue of *Abeng*.

41   *Abeng* 1, no. 7 (March 14, 1969).

42   Ibid.

43   Beverly Carey. *The Maroon Story*. (Gordon Town: Agouti Press, 1997), 356.

Black Power in Montreal and Kingston

Rupert Lewis

L ETTERS WRITTEN to me by my sister when she went to study at Sir George Williams University in 1968 and my replies from the University of the West Indies (UWI), Jamaica campus, have enabled me to capture a sense of how we were living as students and responding to the Black Power movement and student unrest in Kingston and Montreal in the 1968-1969 period. Parallel anti-racist protests were taking place in the two localities and there were interactions between people involved at Sir George and activists in different Caribbean islands. But there was little cause-and-effect with respect to what happened in Montreal and what transpired in the Caribbean. These interactions are not straight lines but zigzags between young Caribbean students studying in Montreal and their families and friends back home, some of whom gave them solidarity. Large numbers of young people, mostly in their teens, throughout the English-speaking Caribbean were ready to show solidarity and to respond collectively against injustice.

The Jamaican vote in 1961 to leave the West Indian Federation meant that the regional dream of a federal state had collapsed. But with the attainment of political independence by Trinidad and Tobago and Jamaica in 1962, there emerged a post-colonial sensibility expressed in Black awareness among emerging musicians, singers, novelists, journalists, educators, and aspiring entrepreneurs who were not prepared to continue with the racial, economic, and political legacies of the plantation system. In the case of Jamaica, some of this Black awareness had to do with the growing influence of Ras Tafari among the youth. Moreover, there arose, particularly in 1968, global political movements, Black Power activism in the United States and student activism in Europe, China and countries in Latin America and Africa.

After half a century, it is impossible to re-imagine what it felt like to be a young man in his early twenties in the culturally and politically explosive environment of Kingston, moving from community to community in search of cheap and secure lodgings in the wake of police surveillance after the October 16, 1968 demonstrations. These demonstrations were a response to the government's banning of Dr. Walter Rodney from re-entry to Jamaica. In those tumultuous times, the risk of arrest for being an activist who had helped organize the demonstration by the University of the West Indies (UWI) students was high, and Jamaican Special Branch police monitored the activities of Black Power activists on the UWI campus.

But the correspondence between my sister and I provides some concrete evidence of who we were and what we talked about. I had forgotten the kind of emotional, psychological, and material pressures that we were both sharing. We were uncertain about what the future held but in our respective ways, we were trying to shape our future.

Rose Lewis, my sister, had gone to study at Sir George Williams University in 1968 and in her first year had registered for a mix of Arts and Science subjects. After a tour of the university, she wrote:

> It is fourteen floors and has many thousands of students in attendance. I think I am going to like it there. The atmosphere is very relaxing and informal, and it really will be something for me to wear pants to my lectures.[1]

Fifty-one years later, reflecting on not being able to wear pants at high school, Rose has said:

> I guess Westwood High School endeavoured to instill lady-like characteristics so wearing pants was not allowed. We wore straw jippy jappa hats to church which I didn't like! Regulation socks and shoes were enforced I guess all the typical things for boarding schools based on British culture. Faculty was made up of about 30% expatriates.[2]

Lady-like grooming was part of a process of defining how women should dress, the way they should speak in the English language, how they should walk, eat, and eventually become good wives and homemakers. Grooming in 'good' manners reinforced patriarchal values in a neo-colonial context where conceptions of 'Britishness' were desired, coupled with the inculcation of a deep, internalized racism against Africa and its practices in religion, foods, and language. The latter were tagged in a very negative way. Girls' high schools, particularly boarding schools, had this tradition of grooming throughout the Anglophone Caribbean. The creation of a middle-class Christian Black was the outcome of missionary education. Britain was referred to by many as the 'mother-country' and through religion, language, a strong inculcation of English history, literature, and the cultural influence of British teachers, the psychological grooming was reinforced. Princess Alice (1883-1981) of the British Royal Family[3] and last grandchild of Queen Victoria was a patron of Westwood's Board of Trustees and when she visited the girls were drilled to curtsey and say, "Yes Ma'am, No Ma'am" when they were introduced to her.[4] Stuart Hall points out that this schooling was, "designed to cultivate and conscript a British-oriented, subordinate 'native' elite."[5]

It was against this background that Rose, then 19, was enjoying the freedom from boarding rules at Westwood High School[6] in Trelawny Parish and from family constraints arising from living with her aunt and uncle in Montego Bay. She was relaxed and said she slept a lot. She fell in love with the flowers and houses in Montreal and wrote, "It still seems like something out of the story books to me."[7] But she was anxious about becoming a landed immigrant and how she would live on $20 per week as her savings went down. She was lonely and, though glad to get away from Montego Bay, she at times got homesick for familiar faces. Rose lived with a family in walking distance of Sir George while she looked after their eight-month-old child. She had three evenings per week for school and a day off each week. As such, she had embarked on the life of a migrant, pursuing a degree but not yet sure what her career choice would be.

Rose did not find "outright colour prejudice" in Montreal, but making friends was challenging:

It's pretty tough making male friends in a big place as Montreal because you don't know who is who. Furthermore, just a few of the dark guys are really (sic) seen with dark girls. Most of them stick to white girls who sometimes support them. Mark you I see nothing wrong with that. It is their life.[8]

After this matter-of-fact response to Black males with white girls she went on to inform me:

A Biology professor at Sir George was asked to stop teaching because the students said he was a racist. The black students had a sit-in which proved most successful. At Sir George there isn't much problem where racial unrest is concerned. Being over here makes me realise that I am indeed proud of being black. This revolution if handled properly could be most effective.[9]

She did not elaborate on the kind of revolution she was thinking about, neither did I interrogate her.

Early in 1969, Rose wrote that the charge against the biology professor had been made in May 1968 by West Indian students:

...but it was kept within the Science Faculty for the past ten months. When the guys realized that nothing was being brought up about the issue, the Administration was informed in December....the past two weeks have been a series of meetings and confrontations which up to now has ended in deadlock... The atmosphere at the University is charged with tension...because so many things have been brought to light... Yesterday three black students were to go to court for breaking into the Principal's office...[10]

Rose noted that the computer centre had been taken over and that two of the demands the students made were that "all criminal charges against the black students be removed and that the hearing goes on by a committee which is acceptable to both sides."[11]

Rose was becoming more involved with the events and her self-awareness as a minority person was developing, "all this black consciousness was bound to break out..."[12] A month later, she followed up:

The situation at Sir George is quiet on the surface but we blacks are receiving suspicious and dark looks. I couldn't care less as I am becoming quite adept at outstaring anybody. I have nothing to be ashamed of... You hear talk about the shame of burning the computer, of taxpayers' money, of sending the niggers home etc ... the computer centre was burned but I wonder whether the black students could have done otherwise. They were being deliberately ignored and apart from those ninety odd students, the rest of the student body was completely unaware of the issue at hand.[13]

When job-hunting, she noted that when employers heard that she was at Sir George they became suspicious. A number of Jamaican students had been charged for offences related to the burning of the computer centre and some had been imprisoned. One of them was Douglas Mossop, the boyfriend of someone who was a close friend of our family.

Over time Rose became more involved and was to travel to Toronto to attend a fund-raising fete to help finance the legal defense of the students charged. The fete was raided by the police. Having been on the sidelines, she was now engaged and had become emboldened:

Lo and behold at about 12 p.m. or so about thirty or more policemen came into the building. Some came into the room in which the party was, others took up positions at entrances and exits of the building. The word went out that no one could leave until he or she produced an ID card. A few left but the majority remained, demanding to know why this was necessary. We were told that we were serving liquor without having a license and that some of us were underage..."

Rose and two girlfriends decided to stay. She continued:

the funny thing was that none of us wanted to leave, we were not even scared. Then a real cool thing happened. Someone put on the James Brown record, 'I'm black & I am proud' and Jugo B (Rupert's pet name), everyone just went mad. Whether you had a partner or not you dancing & singing, 'I'm black & I am proud.[14]

Then, on October 13, 1968 she wrote of an event which was to have major repercussions in Jamaica and the rest of the Anglophone Caribbean:

In Montreal this weekend the Negro community has just put on a conference on Black Power with all the main people present. Of course, Stokely Carmichael will be chief. It started today and really is going to be a success. This conference is at McGill University. If I can find $5, I might go but at the moment I have to be watching my expenditure until I have bought my textbooks and required articles of clothing for the imminent cold weather.[15]

This was the fateful 'Black Writers Conference'[16] that Walter Rodney had attended and on his return from which he was confronted with the Jamaican government's ban on his re-entry.

Walter Rodney was a brilliant speaker and knowledgeable about African history having done his PhD. at the University of London on the Upper Guinea Coast during the period of the Trans-Atlantic trade. Rodney had come to the UWI after teaching at the University of Dar es Salaam in Tanzania and had been part of important discussions about agrarian reform and the role of the university in developing countries. He also knew and spoke a lot to community groups about African Civilizations. But his links with Rastafarians in Jamaica was viewed with suspicion by the authorities, who feared a link between radical socialists and Black nationalists.[17]

In a fragment of a letter, I outlined the consequences of the October 16 demonstrations and the violence that ensued by police and citizens:

1. Two persons were killed by gun shot, 1 electrocuted, 2. Ninety buildings were damaged, some of them by fire. 3. Thirteen buses were completely burnt out, seventeen buses were badly damaged, a civilian wounded by gunshot, eleven policemen injured. The University was cordoned by police and military.[18]

UWI students were not responsible for the loss of life and destruction, but our demonstration had stimulated and tapped into pent-up anger among off-campus young people.

Even before the pro-Rodney demonstrations, I had been involved in Black Power activism. At age 21, I had just completed a B.Sc. (Economics) degree majoring in Government, was doing graduate work in Political Science at UWI and was a teaching assistant. I was active in the Black Power group at the university and was the editor and publisher of *Bongo-Man* which featured articles by Walter Rodney (Guyana), Amy Jacques Garvey, Garth White, Peter Phillips, Trevor Munroe, Marcus Garvey Jr., (Jamaica) Timothy Callendar (Barbados), and Wayne Brown (Trinidad). In the months after the Rodney demonstrations, a group of people drawn from academics, professionals, inner-city youth, and women decided to form the Abeng group and to publish a weekly newspaper called *Abeng*. The 'abeng' was the cow horn used by Maroons (runaway slaves), during slavery to communicate in the mountainous territory where they had built their communities. In 1969, I was one of the founding editors of the *Abeng* newspaper along with Robert Hill, historian and Garvey scholar, who had both participated in the "groundings" with Walter Rodney in Jamaica and was a speaker during the Congress of Black Writers in Montreal,[19] economist George Beckford, and philosophy lecturer Horace Levy, who had abandoned the Jesuits. I wrote Rose telling her how the *Abeng* group organized to sell the newspaper:

> Every weekend, we go into places like Port Antonio, Morant Bay, Mandeville, Browns Town and elsewhere selling the paper. Would you believe that four plain clothes policemen held me and a friend at gun-point in Port Antonio because we were taken for strangers in town. Anyway, my friend had his ID card and someone identified me. We are being very careful now and paying special attention to security. We are experiencing a social revolution now and it has affected me in very personal ways.[20]

Moko, a radical newspaper founded by the historian James Millette, was the counterpart to *Abeng* in Trinidad and *Moko* reported on the events at Sir George Williams. I sent copies of these publications to Rose, which she read and helped to circulate among students at her university. Of *Abeng* and *Bongo-Man* Rose wrote, "The *Abeng* really is good and the *Bongo-Man* is tremendous."[21] It was the support of Amy Jacques Garvey (1896-1973) that really made publishing *Bongo-Man* worthwhile. She contributed to it and posted nearly forty copies to contacts abroad.[22] My scholarship was withdrawn in 1969 for an article in *Bongo-Man* titled "Who You Gonna Turn To" written by Bongo Peter (Phillips), in which he referred to a top policeman as a "sadistic hook-nosed fucker." There was an investigation by UWI but the letters to Rose indicate that the suspension of my scholarship was temporary. Towards the end of 1968, I wrote to Rose:

> Now I'm defending Black Power, but you must understand that this is not a hate white people campaign I'm embarking on. If this were so I would not have spent so much time in putting out a magazine in which attempts are made to understand our position and define it clearly. In Jamaica now, to be outspoken is dangerous. Shearer (the Prime Minister), has even warned Church leaders about preaching sermons against him. Some of my friends are in prison while six await trial next week. Black Power for me is a clarion call to black people to understand themselves historically and move off from that position to an understanding of their present relations in society. This may sound vague now and I'm not going to elaborate but I hope you'll examine the magazine and that I may be able to find words to express this very important concept.[23]

So, this was a time of social upheaval. In Jamaica, there were those who were vehemently opposed to the demonstrations, but many were shocked by the assaults of the Jamaican state on students and young people. The confluence of Black Power sentiments and the student demonstrations led to regional mobilization on the three residential UWI campuses in Jamaica, Trinidad, and Barbados. There was a network of students and sympathetic academics, some of whom were connected to grassroots community initiatives in their respective territories which included the non-campus territories in the Windward and Leeward islands. There was a strong sense that we had to take things into our own hands. This meant forming trade unions and political groups, publishing mimeographed magazines and agitational sheets, forming study groups, researching the region's history, economics, political systems, and in some cases re-examining Garvey's *Philosophy and Opinions*, Fanon's *Wretched of the Earth*, Marx's *Capital*, and some of Lenin's writings. The New World Group, which had been formed in British Guiana in the early 1960s by the economist Lloyd Best, was a regional aggregation of academics on the three UWI campuses in Trinidad and Tobago, Jamaica, and Barbados. James Millette (Trinidad and Tobago), the economists George Beckford, Norman Girvan (Jamaica), Sylvia Wynter, Jamaican cultural critic and thinker, and the Barbadian novelist, George Lamming, were among the contributors. There were New World groups in Puerto Rico, St. Kitts, and St. Lucia, while the Caribbean diaspora was served by a group at McGill University, Montreal, in which the Canadian economist Kari Levitt was actively working alongside Lloyd Best and Allister McCyntyre, among others.[24] In addition, there were fledgling New World groups in New York and Washington D.C. They all felt compelled to think seriously about the meaning of sovereignty, imperialism, culture, racism, class, inequality, and ideology. [25] The cultural and political climate was therefore receptive to delegations of students seeking financial support in defense of the students on trial for the destruction of the computer system at Sir George Williams University. On February 18, 1969 Rose wrote:

> Ninety-seven students have been arrested among which there are twenty-three W.I. (West Indian) students. The hearing is today... I, however, have to go to classes tonight ...a section of the building has been closed for a week to clear up the debris... Everybody is tense and of course most are completely against the arrested students. It was unfair to burn the computer centre but that was the only way to make the administration and other students wake up and take some active part in what happens around them. The administration is to be blamed for staying behind closed doors throughout all this. It is so hard to write about it and I am so sad about the whole affair.

There is a sense of ambivalence in Rose's letter as she seems to be doing her best to hold the line in support of the students given negative public response to media portrayals of their actions.

At the time Rose was writing her letter, the Guild of Undergraduates at the UWI, Kingston campus, was preparing to meet a delegation of two students from Sir George Williams. In Jamaica, the Guild of Undergraduates President was Ralph Gonsalves of St. Vincent. He, Arnold Bertram and Glenville Hinds, Jamaican members of the Guild Council, had all taken part in the demonstration against the ban.

On February 20, 1969, these students addressed a meeting organized by the Guild in the Arts Lecture Theatre at the Jamaica campus. My recollection is that the talk was well attended and from the transcript of the talk and Q&A session afterwards, there was considerable interest in what had taken place and how students should respond. However, it should be remembered that the general view popular in Jamaica's newspapers was that these students were blowing the opportunity they enjoyed for higher education and that they should not have gotten themselves into this mess. Some of these students came from families which had never had a member with a university degree. These were the young people who would make their families proud and provide a better life for themselves. Moreover, for most Jamaicans, Canada was the land of opportunity not racism, and even if there was racism, the students needed to steer clear of trouble and pursue an education.

The two Sir George Williams students were Terrence Ballantyne and Pat Townsend. Ballantyne was the main speaker, and the anger against the racism of the lecturer and the failure of the university to remedy the complaints of the students was palpable in his speech. He narrated how the lecturer in question behaved towards the West Indian students who were Black and discussed the failure of the university administration's mechanisms to deal with the complaints, and the tactics of protest.

Their first tactic was to take over all the administrative buildings but the problem was that the administrative buildings were in several locations in downtown Montreal. So, they decided on occupying the computer centre:

We held the computer room for twelve days and during the twelve days, the University administration issued a statement to the press, that these students are quite orderly, they are keeping the place in a clean fashion and they are checking the room to see that the temperature of the room where the computers were remained constant so that the computers would not be spoiled. Now what happened is that we never intended to get this damn thing blowing up as it really blew up. We were just hoping that by keeping the computer room and preventing the university to do business in Montreal, because we should mention that they pay some of the hospitals and some of the banks in the computer room, and we felt that if we held on to this for a while we would apply enough pressure to the business places outside, they in turn would apply to the university and of course we would get our four or five demands.[26]

Another shift in tactics took place when the Black students decided to enlist the support of the white students:

> We decided to put on a little more pressure, and this was by trying to get some of the white students involved. These fellows have a habit that they love nigger people and they like to come down to be with us and all that sort of crap. Now, we were not approaching them on the question of black and white, we were approaching you (sic) on the question of justice and injustice. If you are on the side of justice come with us. If you are not on the side of justice, get to hell out.[27]

Ballantyne went on to describe the difficult physical circumstances of the occupation:

> After staying in this place for twelve days, 300 people crammed in a room that can hold 75...we decided to take over from the 7th floor up. Now, from the 7th floor up you have the labs, you have the cafeteria, you have one or two administration offices and of course you have the library.[28]

But the University had police:

> Sleeping in the building; they were on the 13th floor. So, from the time the boys started to work, the police were in the building about ten minutes after. I understand that there was a fight between the police and the students, and the boys ran into the computer room and barricaded themselves... Now what happened henceforth I am not at liberty to say because this is before the Court and we expect that the boys are going to use a hell of a lot of this in their defence.[29]

Ninety-seven students were arrested and were charged, 49 were from the West Indies but there were also non-Caribbean students from Canada, Australia, Iran, and Poland. The objective of Ballantyne and Townsend's visit was to raise money for their defence.

The meeting was chaired by Trevor Munroe, a young lecturer in the Department of Government, UWI. The transcript does not include the questions asked by the students, only the answers by Ballantyne and the comments by Munroe. The role of violence was a main theme in the discussion. Ballantyne reported that in Montreal in recent times there had been three bombing incidents in which 26 people were injured. In his comments, Trevor Munroe tried to link the occupation and trial to an ongoing student protest in Jamaica in response to the closure of the Jamaica School of Agriculture by the Jamaican government. He tried to draw tactical lessons from the Sir George Williams experience for the students at the Jamaica School of Agriculture: "The students who were mobilized and because of their mobilization managed to get these committees set up, then go back to the class-room and it is then university administration which appears to be flexible, clamps down."[30] One of the central themes in this period of the late 1960s and the 1970s was the tactical options open to protest movements. Munroe posed the issue in the following way:

> ...the most important thing is how to get across, not only to the Canadian government, but to persons who are minded to behave in racial discrim-inatory ways and then call in the police to defend them, that is going to cost them... It is going to cost them in places where it hurts most. And that is in economic terms.[31]

At a different meeting, the mother of Douglas Mossop (the Sir George Williams' Jamaican student who had been arrested), briefed students at UWI on the case and after she spoke some 70 of us went down to the Canadian High Commission and handed in a petition which called for the postponement of the trial and establishment of a Commission of Enquiry to investigate what had happened at Sir George Williams University.[32]

In Barbados, students at the UWI campus burnt effigies of Professor Anderson, the lecturer who had discriminated against the Black students. The Sir George Williams incident was also a trigger particularly in Trinidad where students in late 1969 prevented the Canadian Governor-General Michener and Prime Minister Eric Williams from entering the campus and in February and March 1970 students with mass support from the public embarked on a march against Canadian businesses in downtown Port of Spain.[33] The demonstrations eventually led to violent clashes with the government of Prime Minister Eric Williams, a near military coup and a guerrilla movement in which UWI students were involved.

The Sir George Williams University occupation and fire in the computer centre together with the trial of the students all had important repercussions in radicalising groups throughout the English-speaking Caribbean. These incidents formed a trigger for heightened Black Power thinking, personal transformation, and socialist conceptions of post-colonial development, and in the context of the times, transnational solidarity became part of Black Power thinking. The mining of these letters shows that there is a rich, hidden, and scattered archive of Caribbean radicalism from the 1960s to the 1980s. These histories are concealed in memories, letters, little magazines, many of them mimeographed or cyclostyled, and also in radio broadcasts. These all need to be digitized. This represents a huge task for young scholars: to help unearth these materials, interview aging participants, and analyse these materials before they are lost.[34]

NOTES

1   Rose Lewis to Rupert Lewis, September 8, 1968, personal archive, Rupert Lewis, Kingston, Jamaica.

2   Rose Lewis, personal communication to Rupert Lewis, November 24, 2019.

3   Princess Alice, an aunt to Queen Elizabeth II, was also Chancellor of the University College of the West Indies.

4   Interview with Nora Lewis (Rose Lewis's younger sister who also went to Westwood), November 24, 2019.

5   Stuart Hall and Bill Schwarz, *Familiar Stranger: A Life Between Two Islands*, (Durham: Duke University Press, 2017), 117.

6   Westwood High School was started in 1882 by a Baptist pastor, Rev. W.M. Webb and was part of British imperial schooling to prepare Black women from the peasantry, agricultural working class and the emergent middle class for subordinate positions in teaching, nursing, administrative and clerical functions in the colonial system. Rose's mother, Lettice Monteith Lewis, had attended Westwood, went to Shortwood Teacher's College and had married Fergus Lewis, a Baptist minister. Fergus Lewis had attended Calabar Theological College that had been started by the Baptists in the 1840s.

7   Rose Lewis to Rupert Lewis, December 21, 1968.

8   Ibid.

9   Ibid.

10   Rose Lewis, February 1, 1969.

11   Ibid.

12   Ibid.

13   Rose Lewis to Rupert Lewis, February 28, 1969. Walter Rodney's PhD. was eventually published as *A History of Upper Guinea Coast, 1545-1800* (New York: Monthly Review Press, 1970).

14   Rose Lewis to Rupert Lewis, May 6, 1969.

15   Rose Lewis to Rupert Lewis, October 13, 1968.

16   For discussion of the Congress of Black Writers see David Austin, "Introduction to Walter Rodney." *Small Axe*, September 2001: 60-65. Also, David Austin, *Fear of a Black Nation*, chapters 6 and 7, Kindle version.

17   For an overall analysis of Walter Rodney's life and work, including the period he spent in Jamaica as a professor and his expulsion from Jamaica see Rupert Charles Lewis, *Walter Rodney's Intellectual and Political Thought* (Kingston: The Press University of the West Indies and Detroit: Wayne State University Press, 1998), and especially chapter 5, pages 85-123; Robert A. Hill in Clairmont Chung (ed.), *Walter A. Rodney: A Promise of Revolution* (New York: Monthly Review Press, 2012), 65-67.

18   Rupert Lewis to Rose Lewis, undated letter, first page missing, circa October 1968.

19   For more on *Abeng* see David Scott, "The Dialectic of Defeat: An Interview with Rupert Lewis," *Small Axe*, 5(2), 2001, 98-113 and David Scott, "The Archaeology of Black Memory: An Interview with Robert A. Hill, *Small Axe*, 3(1), 1999, 100-102.

20   Rupert Lewis to Rose Lewis, April 1, 1969.

21   Rose Lewis to Rupert Lewis, February 18, 1968.

22   Rupert Lewis to Rose Lewis, fragment of letter, January 25, 1969.

23   Rupert Lewis to Rose Lewis, December 9, 1968.

24   For more on New World, and especially in Montreal, see Kari Levitt, "The Montreal New World Group," in Brian Meeks and Norman Girvan (eds.), *The Thought of New World: The Quest for Decolonisation* (Kingston and Miami: Ian and Randle Publishers), 71-80.

25   See *The Thought of New World: The Quest for Decolonisation,* eds. Brian Meeks and Norman Girvan, Kingston: Ian Randle Publishers, 2010.

26   Terence Ballantyne, "Sir George Williams University Incident", February 20, 1969, transcript of speech made at the UWI, Jamaica, In Rupert Lewis archive, Kingston, Jamaica. 4.

27   Ibid., pp. 4-5.

28   Ibid.

29   Ibid.

30   Munroe in Ballantyne, ibid., p. 11.

31   Ibid., p. 13.

32   Rupert Lewis to Rose Lewis, March 10, 1969.

33   See *The Black Power Revolution 1970 – a Retrospective,* eds. Selwyn Ryan & Taimoon Stewart with the assistance of Roy McCree, (Port of Spain, Institute of Social and Economic Research, 1995). Also, *Black Power in the Caribbean,* ed. Kate Quinn, (Gainesville: University Press of Florida, 2014), for documentation and authoritative analyses.

34   The Digital Library of the Caribbean – dLoc – located in Miami has already embarked on the collection of several of these ephemeral publications in addition to more substantial works.

Black Radical Thought and Caribbean Feminism: Reconceptualizing Black Transnational Protest

Océane Jasor

I N FEBRUARY 2019, a group of faculty and students at Concordia University organized *Protest and Pedagogy: The legacies of Caribbean student resistance and the Sir George Williams Affair, Montreal 1969*, a ten-day program of public workshops, roundtables, and an archival/art exhibition, culminating in an academic conference to commemorate the 50th anniversary of the "Sir George Williams Affair." I co-facilitated a roundtable, *Gender and Protest*, whose aim was to highlight the gendered experiences of some of the female protestors during the Sir George Williams Computer Centre Occupation in 1969. As the discussants shared their stories and memories, it became obvious that easy conceptualizations of "gender" were not going to be applicable. At first, I was unsettled by the discussants' scant focus on their experiences *as women*. However, as I endeavored to write this piece, reflecting on the participants' oral stories and problematizing their lessons, I started to appreciate what they meant in relation to the Caribbean's legacy of radical protest narratives, past and present.

On February 4th, 2019, Brenda Dash, Yvonne Greer, and Michelle Serano were invited to Concordia University to discuss the series of events that came to be known as the "Sir George Williams Affair." They were meeting again, fifty years after the student protest that changed the conversation about racism in Canada. It was an emotional reunion, as some of them had vowed never to step foot inside the institution again. After nearly two hours of reminiscing and analyzing the turmoil around the "Computer Centre Occupation," and answering the audience's questions, the women, teary-eyed, hugged each other for a long time. That emotion suffused the entire room, and many of the young Black female students in the audience thanked Dash, Greer, and Serano for the selfless, if poorly acknowledged, role they played in what they described as a critical Black liberation struggle. As I facilitated the discussion between the women who partook in the Computer Centre Occupation, I was mindful of its connections with the emerging Caribbean Black Power movement and became interested in situating the Sir George Williams protest within a wider reflection on gender and feminist theorizing in relation to Caribbean postcolonial and radical praxis.

The Black Power movement framed the Black liberation struggle in a specific and holistic way. Unlike the more liberal and "gradualist" process of social justice of the Civil Rights movement,[1] Black radical thought is generally characterized by its uncompromising stance on political transformation, cultural decolonization, internationalism, pan-African solidarity, and anti-colonialism. Despite the negative connotation that the term 'radicalism' carries, which may explain the relatively poor scholarly attention that Black Power radicalism has received until recently, this era, led by critical and tireless Black scholar-activists, opened up a new ideological and discursive prism through which to apprehend other liberation efforts, including Black feminism.[2] In this discussion, I treat 'radicalism,' 'protest,' and 'feminism' as discrete terms even though the activities they describe frequently overlap. I do so to highlight the influential role that Black radicalism has had on Black protest in general, and Black feminist organizations in particular.

Peniel Joseph suggests that a renewed scholarly interest in Black Power radicalism "represents a new phase of Black protest history that might best be described as 'Black Power Studies.'"[3] As scholars continue to uncover archival material of this era, it becomes clear that the history and legacy of Black Power radicalism can extend and complicate studies of contemporary protest and social movements. By highlighting some of the period's understudied subjects, spaces, and traditions (radical Black youth and students, women and feminism, Afro-Caribbean intellectuals and activism, internationalism), this chapter seeks to contribute to historical studies of Black political thought and to explore the implications of Black Power for feminist praxis. A main objective is to flesh out the link between the legacy of radicalism and protest and Caribbean feminism. In what follows, I reflect on the lessons of *Protest and Pedagogy,* and the Gender and Protest roundtable, before exploring the question that feminist theorizing poses to a Caribbean intellectual and radical tradition, both home-bound and diasporic.

For all intents and purposes, the Sir George Williams Affair, described as, "the single-most important manifestation of Black power in Canada," underlines the Caribbean connection to Black Canadian politics.[4] West Indians who had migrated to Canada in the 1950s and 1960s to get an education became, in many ways, key actors in shaping the Black Canadian radical tradition. In his compelling account of Black Power in Canada, David Austin relates the leading role that Caribbean women and men played in Montreal-based political organizations such as the 1965 Caribbean Conference Committee (CCC)[5] the 1969 Congress of Black Writers[6], and eventually the Sir George Williams Affair. In this sense, West Indians' efforts to organize against racism and systemic oppression have had foundational significance for the emergence of a Black consciousness in Montreal and the Black radical movement in the Caribbean.

While Austin has demonstrated the profound impact that the student protests at the Sir George Williams University had on the development of Black Power in both Canada and the Caribbean, others have explored the inter-relationships between Black Power in the Caribbean and Black Power in other geographic and often diasporic locations. Broadening the spectrum of inter-actions and ramifications of the movement provides the background against which Black Power radicalism was taking hold in the Caribbean. If Caribbean Black Power was truly, as Meeks suggests, "a movement for radical change of the social and economic system in the Caribbean" one can reasonably wonder about the kind of gendered transformation that occurred as part of the move-ment and in its aftermath.[7] Scholars agree that the Caribbean Black Power movement and its radical liberation rhetoric offered a discourse of race that neglected gender.[8] Indeed, there is little comprehensive gendered analysis of those revolutionary times. Several authors have recognized its implicit mascu-linist nature. Meeks asserts that "women were everywhere present in the 'struggle,' but they were almost everywhere subordinate to male leadership."[9] Westmaas, considering Guyanese Eusi Kwayana's unsung contribution to Black Power, writes, "gender is an acknowledged area of some weakness historically for the Pan-Africanist movement, and Kwayana has been a frequent critic of this shortcoming.[10] Similarly, depicting the Congress of Black Writers that took place at McGill University in 1968, Austin eloquently comments:

> In many ways, the event was a product of its time, full of machismo and male bravado. Tellingly, women activists and writers were conspicuously absent from the roster of speakers, despite the fact that, behind the scenes, women played a crucial role in organizing the congress. In fact, the celebrated singer and South African exile Miriam Makena was the only woman with a high public profile in attendance, and she did not speak, but was present in the shadow of her new husband, Stokely Carmichael. And almost as if to emphasize the subordinate place of women, the bulk of the speakers directed their comments to the 'brothers' in the audience, seemingly oblivious to the presence of women in the room."[11]

Caribbean feminist theorists and global pan-Africanist scholars have interrogated the erasure of women from "Black internationalism."[12] Black and Brown women's contributions to early movements of Black liberation, made both in formal and informal spaces, have remained largely excluded from narratives of radical protests. However, bringing forth the role of Amy Ashwood Garvey, Marcus Garvey's first wife, within UNIA, Rhoda Reddock tells a cautionary tale about widespread assumptions of the dissolution of feminist subjectivities within race-centered narratives. Instead, she argues that in the African diaspora, a distinct women's consciousness was emerging as early feminist activists invested themselves in nationalist and identity struggles. She argues that from its onset, Caribbean feminism was grounded in the specific socio-economic realities of women in the region at that time.[13] This argument challenges critiques of feminism as an idea external to the Caribbean *and* complicates assumptions about the non-existence of feminist demands within nationalist and protest movements.[14]

Women and Black Protest

In 1968, six Caribbean students filed an official complaint of racial discrimination and inappropriate conduct against Professor Perry Anderson, a biology teacher at Sir George Williams University. It was reported that Anderson had been intentionally giving Caribbean students lower grades, regardless of the quality of their work. The initial student complaint eventually culminated in the 'student occupation' of the Computer Centre on February 11th, 1969. Imara Ajani's documentary *An(other) Antilles*, screened as part of *Protest and Pedagogy* event series, explores the experiences of Black Caribbean peoples who immigrated to Montreal in the 1960s and became involved in the Black Power Movement and the Sir George Williams Affair. Dr. Dorothy Wills, one of the several West Indian women who took part in the Computer Centre "sitting," recollects:

> We spent a lot of time just talking about being Black in Montreal, quite aside from the marks of the students. We would laugh and say that people take the computer centre and make it into a community centre...and we would joke, and we would laugh, we'd tell stories about back home and what would happen back home if this happened and stuff like that. It was like a big family, and all the family members would participate in the discussion. It was all of us together that made the sitting and there was not any one person that was in charge. We all rallied around the students

and many of us cooked at home and we brought food down to the students for them to eat. So, every night they had supper. I would come home from work and feed my family, and many times I brought my kids with me to the computer centre to join the sitting.

By the time I got down there, I just saw computer cards raining down on MacKay Street, and I started running up and down to the building because I could not get into the building. So I stayed there with my two kids and then all of the sudden I said 'oh my God, we're going to need money for legal defense…so I started walking up and down and asking people 'you have donations for legal defense of those boys?' and they would give me money, and when I turned out my pocket empty, I had collected over $600 to give a deposit to the lawyer. Some people gave me money, other people were telling us off and swearing at us and saying we came to their country to break up their university, to destroy their computers, and that they should send all of us back to where we came from.

And there were people who were working in the houses as domestics; some of them lost their jobs. They said 'after what you people did at Sir George, we don't want to see you here.' And it was a very hard time, but we survived, and the community rallied.

It is telling that Dr. Wills referred to the detained as 'boys,' when in fact women were also arrested by the police that day. It points to the greater visibility of the male students, and perhaps to the fact that radical protests for social justice are still largely represented as a masculine affair. Similarly, Michelle Serano's, one of the roundtable's speaker, disclosure of her experiences as a student protestor is not gender-specific:

I can tell you about all the arrests; the fact that we were denied bail, stayed in jail for close to 14 days, were expelled from the school… I was in my fourth year on a scholarship… which you know, disrupted the plans that a lot of us had for higher education.

In fact, when asked by one of the moderators if they thought they had a different experience than the male students involved, all three women agreed that they did not think there was any difference. Yvonne Greer stated:

We were quite a few women... I think I just read that there were forty-something women, of the arrested, and we were all very active, so I cannot say that the women were doing something different from what the men were doing. I was not treated any differently.

Brenda Dash added:

This is an interesting question because I am probably one of the least gender-conscious people that I know. So, wherever I am, I am, and I don't think 'oh it's all women or it's all men.' I didn't see where gender played a role...not in terms of our work.

Dr. Wills' recollections also expose another important aspect of the Sir George Williams Affair, the strong comradeship between the protestors, both women and men. She speaks of a movement charged with ideals of justice, goodwill, respect, and even cheerfulness. Although these characteristics might appear trivial, they bear valuable consequences for social movements. I have quoted at length from Dorothy Wills' comments in *An(other) Antilles* to illustrate some of the informal activities, oftentimes "un-visible" as David Austin puts it in the documentary, undertaken by women. Here, I use the term "un-visible" to refer to the presence, actions, and subjectivities that are made to be unseen, or rather that can only be seen through a distinct frame of reference. In the absence of any theorization of this almost magical erasure of women's experiences and forms of leadership, women such as Valerie Belgrave, who was arrested during the protest, and Coralee Hutchison who lost her life because of police brutality during the Computer Centre occupation,[15] as well as the number of others who were arrested because of their involvement in the movement, disappear.

Furthermore, while Caribbean women have invested all aspects of everyday life with their activism, Black radical moments of the past are still widely thought of as male-centric activism and intellectualism. For example, Valerie Belgrave, the only female student protester to have written about the occupation, notes the interest in her fashion choices, not the reasons for her involvement at the time.[16] Omitting an analysis of women's collective action creates fundamental shortcomings in the way we theorize social movements. Feminist theories of social movements, which attend to articulations of race and gender within protest groups, yield lessons for theorizing about collective action and feminist organizing. The body of work on social protest by feminist writers, both in and outside of the region, diverges significantly from that of mainstream scholars of social movements whose work still poorly reflects key feminist ideas.[17] In what follows, I examine Caribbean feminist theorizing and organizing from the 1970s to the present and discuss the women's movement, its challenges, negotiations, and possibilities.

Caribbean Feminist Thought in the Caribbean Radical Tradition

The "un-visibility" of Caribbean feminist ideas within the Caribbean intellectual tradition is a common trope.[18] However, several Caribbean feminist scholars have challenged the idea of radicalism being located outside of feminist circles and have effectively placed feminist thought on a continuum of radical discourses and practices in the region.[19] Haynes, while recognizing that the contributions of Caribbean feminist thought may have been overlooked, nonetheless affirms that Caribbean feminist thought, "has emerged as one of the Caribbean's most original and critical strands of thought."[20] Similarly, Mohammed writes:

> the decade of the seventies ushered in new levels of consciousness among Caribbean peoples, as evidenced by the Black Power movement and an emergent socialism and class consciousness which would take root in different forms in several societies in the region… It seems to me that the baton has been passed on to the women's movement in the decade of the 80s and now the 90s.[21]

Haynes concludes that, "the so-called decline of radical scholarship in the Caribbean is only justifiable if one discounts Caribbean feminist scholarship as part of the Caribbean intellectual tradition."[22]

Analyzing Caribbean feminist thought demands that we grapple with the state of feminist consciousness in the Caribbean. Feminist scholarship has made one thing clear: Caribbean women do not constitute a unified, homogeneous group. Instead, their perceptions of gender consciousness and/or feminist consciousness are multiple, fragmented, and often clash with each other as women inhabit different social locations and pursue conflicting strategies to achieve their goals.[23] While some women unapologetically brand themselves 'feminist', others vehemently reject the term. Many are on an uncertain journey, carefully threading and negotiating how feminism may apply to their lives and help them make sense of their lived experiences of discrimination, but also gauging the misogynous repercussions they are sure to face. Yet, while feminist consciousness may still be a hazy concept in the Caribbean, the scholarly work and activism of feminists in the region have ensured that 'gender consciousness' has permeated the fabric of Caribbean societies.[24] If feminism is, in many respects, still 'becoming,' feminist epistemologies have certainly exposed the scope of gendered Caribbean realities, from love and intimate relationships to economic and political policies.[25]

I, along with others, propose that another significant contribution of feminist scholarship and activism to Caribbean radicalism has been its attention to its own plurality and exclusions. Caribbean feminists have daringly confronted 'difference' in contexts outside of Western feminism. They have sought to deepen understandings of feminist theorizing about women and gender, particularly as these relate to multiple axes of difference and oppression, including race, class, culture, geography, and sexuality. Moving beyond the Black/white binary that characterizes European and North American theorizing on difference, as well as the early Pan-Africanist movement, Caribbean feminist thought is fundamentally rooted in the fabric of postcolonial Caribbean societies. Feminist scholarship has denounced manifestations of power in the specific contexts in which they occur. It has extensively theorized on race/ethnic inequalities, or any other social marker fraught with unequal power relations, in the region; these issues taking, at times, dominance over gender.[26] Yet, part of the problem for the lack of recognition that Caribbean feminist ideas have received among Caribbean male thinkers may be that feminism has been reduced to "women's issues." In other words, to many, feminist theory is nothing but the addition of 'gender' to socio-economic theories formulated by men.

The Possibilities of Caribbean Feminism

At the end of the *Gender and Protest* Roundtable, both the students and the wider public were intent on interrogating the ways in which young women today can continue to challenge oppression and injustice in their communities and beyond. Recognizing that the spirit of militant resistance that characterized the 1960s and early 1970s had become more diffuse, and although Greer, Serano, and Dash, had not articulated their activism in gendered ways, they longed to identify specific issues they could rally around and articulate ideas that speak of their particular experiences of oppression as young racialized *and* gendered subjects living (and/or born) in Montreal. It is this intergenerational, interracial, and transnational exchange between women who protest racial and gender injustice when and where they see it that I wish to highlight. Witnessing and facilitating the exchange prompted me to reflect on the promises and possibilities of contemporary women's struggles and new social movements in the Caribbean and its diaspora. What can young people contribute to feminist activism; and perhaps more importantly, how can feminist activism serve their ideals of social justice at a time when so many claim that we live in a "post-feminist era?" Is Caribbean feminism relevant to Caribbean women (and men) in the diaspora and beyond? If so, how do we engage with lived experiences of systemic oppression from different geographical locations and socio-political contexts? I do not claim to answer these difficult questions here. However, the Roundtable certainly created a space where transformative *and* gendered possibilities for social change could be imagined.

The discussion between the veteran Sir George Williams protestors and the younger audience exposed how fluid, contextual, and socially-located feminist consciousness proves to be. While the protestors did not identify with 'feminism', some of the young women who looked up to their activism, unapologetically espoused and promoted feminist ideas. Such contradictions then beg the question, how can Caribbean feminism's lessons about collaborating and organizing across 'difference' be applied to women's activism at the transnational level, and in Canada in particular? One important deterrent to solidarity and organizing that Caribbean feminists have flagged is the tendency to hierarchize knowledge and practice across "global" spaces.[27]

Taking a transnational feminist approach to social movements is useful to point out the power relationships between relevant actors within distinct nation-states. In this sense, it can be a subversive notion when opposed to the amorphous, disembodied, ubiquitous 'global'. Transnationalism, with its variety of traditions, discourses, embodiments and family arrangements, allows for new understandings of forms of governmentality and outcomes that can create, "the conditions of possibility of new subjects."[28] If anything, transnational feminism teaches us that the series of intersections leading to marginalization (gender, race, ethnicity, sexuality, class) have spurious borders, and therefore, should be linked to processes across borders.[29] Alissa Trotz , highlighting the link between diasporic realities and local processes, suggests that :

> if we start with the lives and survival strategies of Caribbean women and men, their uneven circulation and mobility map a transnational social field that stitches Canada and the Caribbean together and makes it impossible to insist on the separability of the two if an adequate accounting of this complexity is to be rendered.[30]

Importantly, one of the ways in which this connection is most visible is through Caribbean women's activism for gender and racial justice in Canadian communities.[31]

Caribbean epistemologies, grounded in socio-economic structures of power, in histories of enslavement, colonialism, but also revolution and resistance, have been essential to the formulation of counter-hegemonic discourses and alternative modes of living and thinking. Caribbean radicalism, in light of its post-independence disillusions, is often discussed in the past tense, which tends to deny its critical and decolonizing present and an array of possible futures. In my mind, what was most striking, and this is admittedly impressionistic, about *Protest and Pedagogy* was the resonance that actors, near and far, in the Caribbean Renaissance moment, a moment *and* movement in which the political discourse, renewed through the imperatives of decolonization and Third World independence movements, centered justice, dignity, and self-determination, still had among students and community members in Montreal. In particular, the audience was most interested in the kind of militancy that characterized the Caribbean movement of the 1970s, and interrogated the place that Caribbean pedagogies still had in and beyond the diaspora. The yearning for more knowledge about these early feminists that contributed relentlessly to the conversation about gender and race in the region was also striking. This is not new. Others have reported similar inquiries.[32] The conversations that emerged at the *Gender and Protest* roundtable indicate that Caribbean feminist pedagogies and activism have not ceased to be relevant, despite recognition of the need for feminist scholarship to attend to current issues and grounded in young people's realities.[33]

The renewed transnationality of Black resistance is a phenomenon to which Caribbean feminist thought has much to contribute. One young African woman in particular, spoke of the need for Black women living in Canada to forge wider diasporic networks. Inspired by the anti-racist struggle of the women that took part in the Sir George Williams Affair, she yearned for spaces and practices of resistance that could transcend both ethnic boundaries and territorial borders. Young Black Montrealers' longing for a contemporary place and voice that will reflect their gendered, raced, and diasporic politics is not insignificant for Caribbean Feminism. It offers a way to bridge the spurious division between academia and activism, which continues to plague women's movements in the Caribbean and elsewhere.[34] The young people in the audience looked for ways to turn academic knowledge into tangible actions, and to ground the latter in feminist research and analysis. Patricia Mohammed suggests that the forms this budding activism will take are precisely what will be at the center of Caribbean Feminist Thought in the future.[35] Most importantly, young diasporic feminists' renewed enthusiasm for activism in Montreal could help shift the inaccurate portrayal of women as 'helpers' or 'supporters' of Black protest to leaders in contemporary social justice movements. This could mean new objectives, new strategies, and importantly, new outcomes in women-conscious organizing beyond Montreal.

NOTES

1   Christopher M. Tinson, "'The Voice of the Black Protest Movement:' Notes on the *Liberator Magazine* and Black Radicalism in the Early 1960s," *The Black Scholar* 37, no. 4(2008): 5.

2   Perniel E. Joseph, "Black Liberation without Apology: Reconceptualizing the Black Power Movement," *The Black Scholar* 31, no. 3-4(2001).

3   Ibid, 2.

4   David Austin, "All Roads Led to Montreal: Black Power, the Caribbean, and the Black Radical Tradition in Canada," *The Journal of African American History* 92, no. 4(2007): 529.

5   Austin specifies Robert Hill, Anthony Hill, Rosie Douglas, Anne Cools, Alvin Johnson, Hugh O'Neile, Franklin Harvey, and Alfie Roberts as the group of West Indians who formed the CCC. He also identifies C.L.R. James as central to the work of CCC (Ibid, 518-19).

6   The Congress of Black Writers counted Rosie Douglas as one of its key organizers.

7   Brian Meeks, "Black Power Forty Years On," In *Critical Interventions in Caribbean Politics and Theory* (Jackson: University Press of Mississippi, 2014), 83.

8   See Meeks, 2014; Quinn, 2014; Westmaas, 2014.

9   Meeks, "Black Power Forty Years On," 84.

10 Nigel Westmaas, "An Organic Activist: Eusi Kwayana, Guyana, and Global Pan-Africanism." In *Black Power in the Caribbean*, edited by Kate Quinn (Gainesville: University Press of Florida, 2014): 172.

11 Austin, "All Roads Lead to Montreal," 523.

12 See also Ford-Smith, 1988; Bair, 1992; Campbell, 1994; Taylor, 2000; McPherson, 2003; Reddock, 2007; Stephens, 2005; Reddock, 2014.

13 Rhoda Reddock, "Contestations over National Culture in Trinidad and Tobago: Considerations of Ethnicity, Class and Gender." In *Caribbean Portraits: Essays on Gender Ideologies and Identities*, edited by Christine Barrow, 414-435. (Kingston: Ian Randle Publishers, 1998).

14 See also Jayawardena, 1986; Bair, 1994.

15 Austin, "All Roads Lead to Montreal."

16 Valerie Belgrave, "The Sir George Williams Affair." *The Black Power Revolution 1970: A Retrospective*. Eds. Selwyn Ryan and Taimoon Stewart. (St. Augustine, Trinidad and Tobago: The University of the West Indies, 1995); "Memories of a Hot Winter," *The Caribbean Review.* August 3, 2017. https://www.caribbeanreview.org/2017/08/memories-hot-winter/.

17 See also Reddock, 1998; Taylor, 1999; Haynes, 2017.

18 Carole Boyce Davies, *Black Women, Writing and Identity: Migrations of the Subject.* (New York and London: Routledge, 1994); "Sisters Outside: Tracing the Caribbean/Black Radical Intellectual Tradition," *Small Axe 28*, no.13.1 (2009): 217-229.

19 See also Mohammed, 1991; Haynes, 2017.

20 (Haynes 2017: 30).

21 Patricia Mohammed, "Towards a Caribbean Feminist Philosophy," *CAFRA News* 5, no. 2-3(1991):21.

22   (Haynes 2017 48).

23   Lizabeth Paravisini-Gebert, "Decolonizing Feminism: The Home-Grown Roots of
     Caribbean Women's Movements." In *Daughters of Caliban: Caribbean Women in the
     Twentieth Century*, edited by Consuelo López Springfield, 3-17. (Bloomington Indiana
     University Press, 1997).

24   Patricia Mohammed, "Like sugar in coffee: Third Wave feminism and the Caribbean, "*Social
     and Economic Studies* (2003): 5-30

25   Eudine V. Barriteau, "Issues and Challenges of Caribbean Feminisms, Keynote Address at
     Inaugural Workshop on Recentering Caribbean Feminisms," Centre for Gender and
     Development Studies (UWI, Cave Hill, Barbados, 2002).

26   See also Baksh-Sooden, 1998; Barriteau, 2003, 2017; Reddock, 2007; Rowley, 2010; Haynes,
     2017).

27   Paravisini-Gerbert, "Decolonizing Feminism"; Alissa D. Trotz, "Going Global?
     Transnationality, Women/Gender Studies and Lessons from the Caribbean," *Caribbean
     Review of Gender Studies* 1(2007): 1-18.

28   Inderpal Grewal and Caren Kaplan, "Global Identities: Theorizing Transnational Studies of
     Sexuality," *GLQ: A Journal of Lesbian and Gay Studies* 7, no. 4(2001): 671.

29   Vrushali Patil, "From Patriarchy to Intersectionality: A Transnational Feminist Assessment
     of How Far We've Really Come," *Signs* 38, no. 4(2013): 847-867.

30   (Alissa Trotz, "Going Global?", 10.

31   Yvonne Bobb-Smith, *I Know Who I Am: A Caribbean Woman's Identity in Canada.*
     (Toronto: Women's Press, 2003).

32   See also Andaiye, 2002; Hosein, 2002; McKenzie, 2004; Massiah, 2004; Castello, 2006.

33   See also Andaiye 2002; Barriteau 2002.

34   Linda Peake et. al, "Feminist Academic and Activist Praxis in Service of the Transnational."
     In *Critical Transnational Feminist Praxis*, edited by Amanda L. Swarr and Richa Nagar, 105-
     123. (Albany, NY: State University of New York Press, 2010).

35   Patricia Mohammed, "The Future of Feminism in the Caribbean, "*Feminist Review*
     64(2000): 116-119.

On Reparations: Canada and the case of the Sir George Williams University Computer Affair

Afua Cooper

> *There is a unique and preceded moral debt owed to African peoples that has yet to be paid—the debt of compensation to Africans as the most humiliated and exploited people in the last four hundred years.*[1]

The Case for Reparations

The National Coalition of Blacks for Reparations in America (N'COBRA) offers the following components in its definition of reparations:

> Payment of a debt owed; the act of repairing a wrong or injury; to atone for wrongdoings; to make amends; to make one whole again; the payment of damages; to repair a nation; compensation in money, land, or materials for damages.[2]

Reparations is a core principle of any truth and reconciliation project. Before reconciliation can occur, the truth of what happened between the offended and the offender must be articulated, and made public. The offender has to show remorse by making a public apology, and at the same time, provide restitution often in the form of financial compensation to those who have been wronged. For reconciliation to be meaningful, reparations must be made.

The case for reparations for African-descended people in the Americas whose ancestors were stolen from Africa and enslaved in the Americas by Europeans, has been in the public consciousness for a long time now. African-descended people, since the end of slavery whether in the British Caribbean (1833-1838), or the United States (1863-1865), have pressed their former slaveholders for reparations for the centuries of free labour and wealth they and their progeny provided for these slaveholders.

In the 1890s, Callie House, an African American washerwoman, began seeking reparations for former slaves. She persevered in her struggles right up to the 1920s.[3] House's struggle has been taken up by several groups and individuals within the United States context. N'COBRA is one such group that keeps the issue of reparations for African American descendants on the Black liberation agenda.[4] Rastafarians in Jamaica, since the 1950s, have been demanding that the queen of England pay Jamaicans £20 million for the theft and stolen labour of their ancestors. In 1833, the British abolished slavery in their empire. Instead of giving some compensation to the freed slaves, the British, recognizing the property principle as sacrosanct, paid £20 million in compensation (in today's money, £11.6 billion) to slaveowners including individuals, families, corporations, and institutions.[5] Rastas thus made an inverse claim—the compensation rightly belonged to the enslaved people, and because they did not receive it, it belonged to their descendants. Rastas to this day are still pressing for that £20 million. Their demand has been taken up by the Caribbean Community and Common Market (CARICOM) Reparations Committee in recent times. In the CARICOM model, reparations are pursued as a development strategy for the entire Caribbean region. It is framed as not only reparations for African enslavement, and European colonization, but also for the genocide of the Indigenous people of the region.[6]

Since 2013, the CARICOM Reparations Committee, led by Hilary Beckles, has successfully worked to shine the spotlight on reparations as an issue of Black development. Mention must also be made of the untiring work of United States Congressman, John Conyers, who since 1989 (to 2019) introduced a bill every year in the House of Representatives to study the effects of slavery on African Americans and propose reparations for this population. In the US presidential campaign of 2020, candidates, especially Democrats, have discussed reparations for the African American community, as part of their debate items. And as of today, the debate around reparations has been ignited across North America, since the 2020 police killing of George Floyd in Minneapolis.

But how does Canada fit into this? Oftentimes, Canada does not appear on the radar in discussions about the African Diaspora, international Black studies, and in the reparations debate. However, in recent times, there has been an incipient reparations movement in Canada, most exemplified by the Global African Congress (GAC). In 2018, the theme for the Black Canadian Studies Association's (BCSA) Conference held in Regina, Saskatchewan, was "Reparations Start with a Formal Apology for Slavery and Anti-Black Racism." The BCSA felt that given the mood of the time, the topic of reparations was pertinent. In 2019, the BCSA once again took up the theme of reparations at its annual conference held in Vancouver. The conference theme had the subtitle "Demanding Reparations and State/Institutional Accountability." As these two conferences suggest, reparations for Black people has become an item of discussion within Black studies circles and in the Canadian Black community at large.

In 2017, the United Nations Working Group of Experts on People of African Descent, completed its investigations into Black life in Canada. The report painted a grim picture of the historical and contemporary experiences of Black life in Canada under such rubrics as criminal justice, education, health, and employment. Among its many recommendations for the amelioration of life for Black Canadians, the experts called on the federal government to apologize for slavery and consider reparations for historical injustice.[7] Though the federal government to date has not responded to the report, it is important for the cause of reparations in Canada, that an international body has recognized the fact of Black enslavement in Canada, the sufferings Black people endured as a result, and that reparations at least be considered.

What is clear is that Black folks within the Americas are asking for reparations for slavery, racism, colonialism, and the underdevelopment of societies with predominantly Black populations, and where Black people also live as minorities. In all the cases mentioned above, what would potential claimants ask for? A cash payment? A development package for communities in which Black people live? What might this restitution look like? During slavery, Blacks had their labour stolen to enrich their white owners, the cost of the robbed labour cannot be estimated. The enslaved were brutalized, maimed, killed, and violently oppressed in diverse ways. They had their lineages fractured, their cultures broken, and their heritage decimated. Under slavery, to justify the enslavement of Africans, white owners and their allies developed an anti-Black ideology that rendered Blacks as subhuman and articulated a theory of Black inferiority and white superiority that is still a cornerstone of racist thought to this day.

Historical Claims for Canadian Reparations to the Black community

The foundation for and insertion of the economies of the Canadian Atlantic colonies (Newfoundland, Nova Scotia, Prince Edward Island, and New Brunswick) into world commerce was through the endeavour of the Triangular trade. A corollary of this branch of commerce, was what came to be known as the West India trade. This centred on the principal economic arrangement between the Caribbean slave colonies and the Canadian provinces.

David Eltis and Stephen Behrendt, scholars of the slave trade, in their massive research project on ships used in the Transatlantic slave trade discovered that at least sixty ships used in the British slave trade were built in Canada—in the shipyards of Nova Scotia, Quebec, New Brunswick, and Newfoundland.[8] This is not surprising because shipbuilding was an important facet of the overall trade endeavour of Maritime businessmen. These men reinvested capital earned from the West India trade in shipbuilding and banking.

One of these slave ships, the *Sarah*, was built in Newfoundland. Notes from the Slave Trade Database about this ship, states that, "The *Sarah*, a 154-ton brig… was built in Newfoundland in 1788. She left Bristol, England on September 21, 1789 on her maiden voyage in the slave trade…. On the 3rd voyage she was shipwrecked on the way back to England, after disembarking her cargo in Kingston, Jamaica. In total, an estimated 626 slaves left Africa, on her, 458 of whom survived to disembark in Jamaica."[9] The *Sarah* engaged in at least three slaving expeditions. These facts clearly show the slavery nexus between West Africa, Newfoundland, England, and the Caribbean and reveals that the eastern colonies were part of the Atlantic slavery system.

Additionally, these Atlantic provinces sold salted fish (herring, cod, mackerel), salted beef and pork, lumber, horses, wheat, and other wood products to Caribbean slave plantations in exchange for sugar, molasses, rum, cocoa, and coffee grown by enslaved Africans. The dried protein from Canada fed the slaves, and the wood products built what Eric Kimball calls, "Caribbean plantation infrastructure": houses and shelters, mills, barrels, casks, pails, and buckets used to store the sugar products for export.[10] Moreover this arrangement also facilitated a coastal slave trade as enslaved Africans were shipped from the Caribbean by Canadian merchants and businessmen and sold in Canada as various advertisements in the archives attest.[11]

If salted cod was the dominant Canadian produce exported to the slave colonies, sugar was the main product that the latter colonies traded with Canada. Canadian colonists from all walks of life—from the yeoman farmer to the wealthy shipping magnate—used sugar or molasses as sweetener probably without giving a thought to the brutality and hardships its production meant for the Caribbean slaves that produced it. Sugar work was harsh and murderous, and Canadians from all walks of life, knowingly or unknowingly helped to fuel a system of exploitation that doomed hundreds of thousands of Africans and their descendants to a life of misery and early death.

A symbiotic relationship existed between Canadian merchants and their Caribbean slaveholding counterpart. In Nova Scotia for example, many of the leading mercantile families built and consolidated their wealth through the West India trade. Monies derived from West Indian slavery was invested into other branches of commerce such as shipping, banking, and shipbuilding. Mather Byles Almon, for example, was a Canadian merchant with interests in the Caribbean. He used his wealth to help establish the Bank of Nova Scotia in 1832.

Fifty-seven years after its founding, the Bank of Nova Scotia expanded internationally into the Caribbean, followed by the Royal Bank of Canada and the Canadian Imperial Bank of Commerce (CIBC). Canadian banking interests became the largest foreign network of banks across the region. Following political independence of Caribbean countries, expatriates continued to control banks (and the wider economy) and held discriminatory practices towards hiring local Black and Brown employees. The 1970 Black Power movement in Trinidad was galvanized by the arrests of students protesting racism at Sir George Williams in Montreal, as well as the racism practiced by Canadian banks in the Caribbean.[12]

The long arm of slavery also touched educational institutions. The founder of McGill University, James McGill was a slave owner.[13] Dalhousie University, founded in 1818, received its original endowment from the Castine Fund, monies earned from the slave-based Caribbean trade.[14] Marguerite d'Youville, the founder of the Grey Nuns, bought and sold slaves. One of Concordia University's libraries is named after this order of nuns. Historical evidence of Canada's involvement in the slave trade surrounds us.

Montreal, Black Canada, and the Historical Struggle for Black Dignity

Slavery began in New France in the early 17th century. Nearly a hundred years later, in 1734, a fire ripped through the city of Montreal. Marie-Joseph Angélique, born in Madeira, Portugal and sold into slavery in New England and New France, was accused of setting fire to her enslaver's home and to much of the city. Angélique was tried, found guilty by the colonial court, tortured, and executed. However, this is only one side of the story, as narrated through the colonial documents. As I state in *The Hanging of Angelique*, "let us remember that arson was a tool of resistance commonly used by enslaved Africans throughout the length and breadth of the Americas."[15] We know that six weeks before the fire of which Angelique was accused of setting, she had fled slavery. She was eventually caught and returned to her mistress. Back in her owner's household, Angelique spoke openly about her desire to run away from slavery again, and to find freedom. This enslaved woman was one of the tens of thousands of enslaved Blacks throughout the Americas who resisted their servile condition and engaged the struggle for Black liberation and dignity. We need tools beyond the court document to understand the struggle for Black dignity in the face of slavery, racism, and oppression.

While slavery was abolished in the British colonial world, including, the Canadian provinces in 1833, emancipation did not abolish racism nor did it usher in full equality for the newly freed Black population. Though, Blacks were now legally free, whites still retained control of society in the most fundamental ways. In the post-slavery era, whites reinscribed a social, political, and economic order which had them placed firmly at the top, with Blacks were still pushed to the bottom. This racial hierarchy manifested itself in racial segregation and the colour bar.

Historically, the issue of Black marginalization, and the treatment of Black people as second-class citizens has been fully evident in the area of education for Black children. During the 19th century as the education state expanded across the Canadian provinces, segregated education for Black children became the norm. This was because white school officials and white parents, particularly in Ontario and Nova Scotia, the two provinces with the largest Black populations, refused to allow Black children to attend the local common (public) schools with white students. The fact that Black parents paid the school tax which in theory should have ensured the education of their children, made this denial even more extraordinary.

As white school supporters continued to bar Black children from attending the common schools, provincial legislatures responded by enacting legislation that created segregated schools for Black students. These Acts were legislated in 1844 and 1850 in Ontario, and in 1836 for Nova Scotia. The schools they created often lacked adequate resources (blackboards, chalk, textbooks, benches, and desks), the teachers—majority Black—were poorly paid, and the buildings often compromised—leaky roofs, insufficient insulation, and cramped. The vast majority of Black children received inadequate schooling or none at all, as sometimes, the nearest separate school was far from the residence of the children. It was not until 1965 and 1983 in Ontario and Nova Scotia respectively that these segregation acts were repealed. The curtailment and denial of education of Black children had a devastating impact of the life opportunities of Black children and on the economic and social advancement of the Black community. [16] Today, the education of Black children or lack thereof remains one of the most serious structural problems affecting the national Black community.

For most of the nineteenth century, Black people experienced segregation in other areas of life. Churches, hotels, inns, lodges, cemeteries, theatres, restaurants, and ferries enforced a colour bar. There were lack of employment opportunities for Blacks, and most were confined to specific jobs like housemaids, domestics, butlering, labourers, and farm hands. Later in the century, Black men were specifically hired to be sleeping car porters.[17] The lack of employment opportunities meant that Black people were confined to specific low-paying jobs, which translated into limited financial advancement for Black communities. In other words, there is a direct correlation between Black life chances in Canada today and the history of slavery and racial discrimination in this country.

Discrimination by whites against Blacks also manifested itself geographically. Africville and Preston in Nova Scotia, Hogan's Alley in Vancouver, Buxton in Ontario, Little Africa in Fredericton in New Brunswick, The Bog in Charlottetown PEI, and Amber Valley in Alberta are examples of residential segregation that resulted from anti-Black racism. At the same time, Black communities were often destroyed by white settler colonial caprice for land. Hogan's Alley and Africville are salient examples of this. Africville was razed in 1967, and thus forms a key part of the historical narrative of the late 1960s in which the events of 1969 at Sir George Williams University unfolded. These events are often discussed separately and thus narratively rendered as exceptional. However, when considered in the same context, these events all reveal the pervasive anti-Black racism that has characterized Canadian life and histories, and which were met with Black resistance and protest in the 1960s.[18]

Another key part of the story of Black life in Canada pertains to the history of immigration restrictions. Many of the legal restrictions around Black immigration were only relaxed in the late 1960s. As the nineteenth century closed, and the 20th century opened, immigration became an instrument of white control of the Black body. At Confederation in 1867, Canada pursued an immigration policy that rested on the concept of a "white man's country." People of colour living in other countries were not desired as immigrants. Coloured folks, especially Black people, were thought of as dirty, lazy, and polluting. The new prime minister, John A. Macdonald publicly declared that Blacks were not desired as immigrants and singled out Black men as dangerous to the safety and purity of white women. [19] As a result of these specific sentiments against people of colour, the government embraced policies and passed laws to stop Black people migrating to Canada. Despite the prohibitions against Black migration, a few thousand Blacks managed to slip in from 1867 to 1910. However, rising hysteria against Black people coming into the country led the Canadian government, headed by Wilfrid Laurier, to pass an order-in-council banning Black migration in 1911. The relevant part of this order reads: "For a period of one year from and after the date here of the landing in Canada shall be and the same is prohibited of any immigrants belonging to the Negro race, which is deemed unsuitable to the climate and requirements of Canada." The work of Ruth Harris, Linda Carty and Makeda Silvera significantly challenge the myth of a Canadian liberal ethics of inclusion.[20] Centering the question of gender, they each show how Black women in particular represented a source of labour from which the Canadian state thought work could be extracted without the granting of the full rights and recognition of citizenship. As Linda Carty puts it, under the West Indian domestic workers scheme (1955-1967), "thousands, of women came to Canada annually to do the work that white women now refused." Situating this in a broader context, Carty additionally notes that, "prospective employers repeatedly argued their need for Caribbean immigrants as seasonal farm labourers and domestics." An overt colour bar was integral to Canadian immigration policy and was not removed until 1967, with the institution of a points system that values "highly skilled" immigrants (and codes race).

It took an entire century for race and colour to be removed as impediments to immigration, yet migration laws were wielded as a weapon against the student protesters at Sir George who were threatened with deportation. This country has always refused to tolerate criticism from Black migrants. In 1967, Ted Watkins, a Black Canadian Football League (CFL) player and American immigrant, told a CBC audience that he often felt Canada was like Mississippi (he said this in the midst of the Black Civil Rights Movement in the US, and its harsh repression by police). The Toronto Star, in a follow-up report, did not investigate Canadian racism but rather asked whether Watkins would be fired for having the audacity to call out racism.[21]

The Canadian Black population has been treated like a squatter population, not deserving of full rights as Canadian citizens and British subjects. Similarly, the treatment of Black migrants by the Canadian state has mirrored that of the treatment of internal Blacks.[22]

In the last 40 years of the 20th century, the Black community has been subjected to racial profiling, and over-representation in police arrests, prisons, and jails. Tragically, Black people, especially men, have been the principal victims of fatal police shootings. It has been noted that in the Greater Toronto Area, Black people are 20 times more likely to die at the hands of police violence.[23] Additionally, there has been a chronic drop-out rate in high schools for Black youths, which translates into a denial of economic opportunities for Black people across generations.

As we learn, reparations can be framed not only as an issue between a specific individual or nation, but also between groups, individuals, and particular institutions. I will now address the issue of reparations for a single incident that took place at a Canadian institution of higher learning.

Sir George William University/Concordia University and the Question of Reparations

> The year was 1969 and winds of change, social
> and political, were blowing around the world. Montreal
> became central in the many struggles for liberation
> in North America, the Caribbean and Africa.
> What happened at Sir George Williams University
> on February 11, 1969 was part of that momentum.[24]

The 1969 Sir George Williams University Computer Affair, also called the "computer riot" has the distinction of being one of the largest student protests against racism in Canada.[25] It was sparked by the complaint of six Black Caribbean biology students, who, alleging racism, noted that their professor, Perry Anderson marked their assignments unfairly. The protest made headlines nationally and internationally. In Canada, the mainstream media did not frame the incident as one which arose from students with a rightful complaint, but rather narrated the students as "foreign agitators." [26] In the Caribbean, reports called attention to Canadian racism and imperialism. The incident also had diplomatic repercussions. In fact, the government of Trinidad and Tobago, paid the bail money for the Trinidadian students who were arrested and jailed on February 11, 1969. In total, the sum of money the newly independent government of Trinidad and Tobago gave to students to pay bail money and legal costs, amounted to more than $111,000 (TT dollars).[27]

The aftermath of the Computer Affair meant shattered lives and curtailed futures for many Black students and families. The original students whose activism sparked the protests did not collectively achieve their goals of becoming doctors. Kennedy Fredericks had a warrant of arrest out for him and fled Canada to parts unknown. The career of Fredericks and his future prospects vanished. Meanwhile, the Black community was put under surveillance by the Canadian state.[28] For the university, it involved a deep soul-searching but also strategic administrative manouvers. One result of this was the setting up of an ombudsman office (one of the first in Canadian universities). In 1974, Sir George Williams University merged with Loyola College, changed its name, and whitewashed its history, becoming Concordia University.[29]

At the 50th anniversary of the Computer Affair in 2019, a two-week schedule of events titled "Protests and Pedagogy" was held at Concordia University.[30] It was accompanied by an extensive archival and art exhibit on the computer affair curated by Christiana Abraham, which was meant to excavate and share the archives and this history with the community. At the conference, which concluded this program of activities, several persons, in particular the historian Michael West, called for: a recognition of the history of the 1969 protest at Sir George through various means, and for the University to take steps to address this history including a remembrance that centres the students themselves, and the sacrifices they made.

How might we remember this incident, from the point of view of the students and their supporters? Phrasing the issue in this way is also a call for the university to shift its terms of accounting for this event, which has often been marked by a recourse to the stocktaking of the damage caused to property rather than the impact on lives. Such a register of events (which focuses on computers and infrastructure over lives), reenacts the colonial scene of the burning of Old Montreal and the telling of that story in ways which have centered the burning of property rather than the liberatory strivings that we might see in the life and narrative of Angelique. How might we help to repair the trauma suffered by the students, especially the Black students, at the hands of the university administration, and of the Montreal governmental authorities, and the police? Therefore, one asks, what would reparations for the Sir George Williams University students and the Montreal Black community look like? How would Concordia University make reparations? How might the City of Montreal also address this history in an ethical way? How do we link calls for Concordia to pay reparations to discussions around demands for Canada to make reparative amends to the Black community for the long legacy of racism and oppression?

Dalhousie University's *Report on Slavery and Race* provides some inspiration and lessons for reparative measures in the case of Concordia.[31] Between 2016 and 2019, I chaired a panel which investigated Dalhousie University's history on slavery and race, and its imbrication with anti-Blackness. We conducted a two-continent, multi-country research on the university itself and on its founder George Ramsay, the 9th Earl Dalhousie. In 2019, I wrote the accompanying report and delivered it to Dalhousie University and the larger community. Our recommendations were not declarations for reparations per se; however, they provided a reparatory framework and a model for how the university might, "atone and make amends." We thought the university might do this under the following rubrics: regret and responsibility, recognition, and repair. Under these categories, 12 recommendations (including additional sub-recommendations) were articulated.

The computer incident that took place at Sir George was a unique affair. It galvanized the student population on campus, and it mobilized the local, national, and international Black communities. This incident was shaped by and contributed to the Black power and anti-racist movements of the 1960s and 1970s. And while it underscored resistance on the part of Black Canadians as political actors, it led to the unleashing of the force of the Canadian state on a vulnerable and margnalized Black community as Black people, students, and non-students, were placed under heavy police surveillance. Black organizations were infiltrated by state agents. The Computer Affair was also the tipping point for Canadian police surveillance, because out of this the Canadian Security Intelligence Services, or CSIS, was born.[32] The computer affair also put under the spotlight fraught political and economic relations between the Caribbean and Canada.[33]

Neither Montreal nor Concordia University has fully acknowledged the event, or the harm done to the students and to the Black community at large. How might this be accomplished?

1. Reparations for the Black community vis-à-vis Concordia would begin with an apology from Concordia University to the African Canadian community in Montreal, and to the students who were penalized by the affair, and to their families who continue to suffer trauma from it. This apology would contain the following phrasing:

    > "We are sorry for the university's handling of the Sir George
    > Williams Computer Affair and the devastating impact this has had
    > on the Black community. We were wrong in calling the police on the
    > students. We are sorry for the ruinous impact this has had on the
    > lives, careers, and futures of the students and their families. We are
    > particularly sorrowful at the death of student Coralee Hutchinson
    > who was beaten on the head by the police on 11 Feb. 1969, and whose
    > death shortly after was likely caused by the head wound. However,
    > to say that we are sorry means very little if this apology is not
    > followed by positive action. Therefore, in the name of reconciliation,
    > we propose the following in order to make some amends."

2. The university's list of actions should include the launching of a commission of inquiry into the cause of the fire which destroyed the computer room, and the cause of which was blamed on the students who occupied it. However, the students remarked that they did not set the fire. Thus, to date, the cause of the fire is unknown. The inquiry could delve into such questions as to the origins of the fire. Did the students set the fire? Or

was it the police? Could the fire have been the work of agent saboteurs? Having an inquiry would bring some closure to the trauma experienced by some of the participants and their families.

3. The creation of a plaque or public sculpture or memorial to commemorate what was Canada's largest student protest would express the significance of this event. The plaque would honour the students involved, those who were arrested, jailed, deported, and killed. This plaque would be placed on the side of the Henry Hall building which housed the computer lab, or on the sidewalk in front of the building. The plaque could be commissioned by the university, the municipality, the province, or the federal government.

    A piece of public art, such as a sculpture should be erected in the vicinity of location where the protest took place. Recently, the mayor of Montreal, Valerie Plante, acknowledged that there is systemic racism in Montreal, and promised to address it.[34] One way for the city to do so, is to create public art that would memorialize the computer affair, and honour the 400-year history of Black people in Montreal. A black artist should be commissioned to create this public art.

4. The Exhibit on the 1969 Affair, which was curated by Christiana Abrahams, a professor at Concordia, should be on permanent display at the school, and embark on a travelling tour across Canada to teach students about one of Canada's founding civil rights moments.

5. The money paid by the government of Trinidad and Tobago, should be calculated into today's money, and this could be used to establish scholarships for Trinidadian students, or students from the wider Caribbean. Additional monies could be garnered to establish scholarships, bursaries, and fellowships for Black Canadian students and those from the African diaspora. A resource and support centre dedicated to Black students would also form part of these reparatory actions.

6. Fifty years after the demands were made, Concordia should finally commit to the establishment of a Black Studies program which would be housed in a dedicated Black Studies Centre. Concomitant with this would be a cluster hire of Black faculty and staff.

7. As part of Concordia's anti-racist strategy, the university would work to ensure that all first-year students take classes, lectures, and courses on anti-

Black racism at Concordia, have a thorough teach-in on the Computer Affair, and learn the 400-year Black history of Montreal and Quebec, and of the long-standing connection between Montreal and the Caribbean.

These reparative gestures might function as one way of grappling with these complex, fraught, and painful histories and serve as concrete moves towards a public and social discourse that takes the value of Black lives and freedoms in Canada seriously.

NOTES

1   Organization of African Unity Eminent Panel of Experts studying reparations, in V.P. Franklin, "Commentary-Reparations as a Development Strategy: The Caricom Reparations Commission," *Journal of African American History* 98, 3 (2013): 363.

2   Raymond Winbush. *Should America Pay? Slavery and the Raging Debate on Reparations.* (New York: Amistad Press, 2003), xxi.

3   Mary Frances Berry. *My Face is Black is True: Callie House and the Struggle for Ex-Slave Reparations.* (New York: Random House, 2006).

4   For a discussion on the evolution of the Reparations movement in the US see Winbush, *Should American Pay?* On N'COBRA, see the chapter by Adjoa A. Aiyetoro, "The National Coalition of Blacks for Reparations in America (N'COBRA): Its creation and Contribution to the Reparations Movement," 209-225.

5   Nicholas Draper. *The Price of Emancipation: Slave-Ownership, Compensation and British Society at the End of Slavery.* (Cambridge University Press, 2013).

6   Professor Hilary Beckles has laid out the case for Anglo-Caribbean reparations in *Britain's Black Debt: Reparations for Caribbean Slavery and Native Genocide* (Kingston, Jamaica: University of the West Indies Press, 2013).

7   Report of the Working Group of Experts on People of African Descent on its mission to Canada. United Nations, 11-29 September 2017.

8   David Eltis, Stephen D. Behrendt, David Richardson, and Herbert S. Klein. *The Trans-Atlantic Slave Trade: A Database on CD-ROM* (Cambridge and New York: Cambridge University Press, 1999).

9   David Eltis. https://www.slavevoyages.org/voyage/database. See also, *Bristol, Africa, and the Eighteenth-Century Slave Trade to America* Vol. 4. 1770-1807. Bristol Record Society's Publications, Vol. 47. See page 157 for info on the slave ship *Sarah*. The quote is from the Jamaican-based factor, John Fowler to ship owner James Rogers of Bristol. The quote is from a letter from factor John Fowler to ship owner James Rogers, taken from Jamaicanfamilysearch.com.

10   Eric Kimball, "What have we to do with slavery? New Englanders and the Slave Economies of the West Indies," in Sven Beckert & Seth Rockman (eds.), *Slavery's Capitalism: A New History of American Economic Development.* (Philadelphia: University of Pennsylvania Press, 2016), 182.

11   See for example the *Halifax Gazette*, 30 May 1752 (Nova Scotia Archives).

12   See Peter James Hudson, "Imperial Designs: The Royal Bank of Canada in the Caribbean," *Race and Class* 52, 1(2010): 33-35. For a personal account of the Sir George protest and its reverberations in the Caribbean see Valerie Belgrave, "The Sir George Williams Affair," in Selwyn Ryan and Taimoon Stewart (eds.), with assistance of Roy McCree, *The Black Power Revolution: A Retrospective.* (St. Augustine: ISER, University of the West Indies, 1995), 119-131.

13   See Rosaline Hampton. *Black Racialization and Resistance at an Elite University*. (Montreal: McGill University Press, 2020).

14   Afua Cooper, *Dalhousie's History (op cit)*, 60-65.

15   Afua Cooper. *The Hanging of Angelique: the untold story of Canadian slavery and the burning of Old Montreal*. (Athens: The University of Georgia Press, 2007), 9.

16   On the Ontario Separate School Acts, see Kristin McLaren, "We had no desire to be set apart': Forced Segregation of Black Students in Canada West Public Schools and the Myth of British Egalitarianism." *Socal History/Histoire Sociale* 37, 73 (2004): 1-24. On the eduction of Black Canadian children across time and space, see Awad Ibrahim & Ali A. Abdi. *The Education of African Canadian Children: Critical Perspectives*. (Montreal: McGill-Queen's University Press, 2016). On segregated schooling in Nova Scotia see Sylvia Hamilton's *Little Black Schoolhouse* (Maroon Films, 2007).

17   See for instance, Cecil Foster. *They Call Me George: The Untold Story of Black Train Porters and the Birth of Modern Canada*. (Windsor, Ontario: Biblioasis, 2019).

18   For discussion of Sir George and Africville in relation to each other see Rinaldo Walcott and Idil Abdillahi's *Black Life: Post-BLM and the Struggle for Freedom*. (Winnipeg: ARP Books, 2019).

19   Constance Backhouse. *Petticoats and Prejudce: Women and the Law in Nineteenth-Century Canada*. (Toronto: Women's Press, 1991), 53.

20   Ruth L. Harris. *The Transformation of Canadian policies and programs to recruit foreign labour: The case of Canadian Female Domestic Workers 1950s-1980s*. (Michigan State University (diss.), 1988); Linda Carty, "African Canadian Women and the State: "Labour Only, Please" in Peggy Bristow, Dionne Brand, Linda Carty, Afua Cooper, Sylvia Hamilton, Adrienne Shadd (eds.), *We're Rooted and They Can't Pull Us Up: Essays in African Canadian Women's Histories*. (Toronto: University of Toronto Press, 1994), 193-229*)*; Makeda Silvera. *Silenced*. (Toronto: Williams Wallace, 1983).

21   Peter Graham and Ian McKay. *Radical Ambition: The New Left in Toronto*. (Toronto: Between the Lines, 2019),133.

22   R. Bruce Shepard and Sarah-Jane Mathieu have dealt with the issue of anti-Black racism in Canadian immigration policies in their respective tomes. See Shepard, *Deemed Unsuitable: Black from Oklahoma Move to the Canadian Prairies in Search of Equality in the Early 20th Century Only to Find Racism in their New Home*. (Toronto: Umbrella Press, 1997); Mathieu, *North of the Color Line: Migration and Black Resistance in Canada, 1870-1955*. (Chapel Hill: University of North Carolina Press, 2010).

23   Leyland Cececco, "Black Toronto residents 20 times more likely to be shot dead by police, study says," *The Guardian*. December 10, 2018.

24   Egbert Gaye, "Something Happened…50 Years Ago," *Montreal Community Contact*. January 24, 2019).

25   I prefer the term "Affair" as opposed to "riot." A riot occurred only after the police arrived at the computer lab on 11 February, attacked the students and broke up the occupation. For two weeks before that time, the students carried out a peaceful occupation of the lab, and their allies and supporters held meetings across the campus and at other places in Montreal.

26   Marcel Martel, "'Riot' at Sir George Williams: Giving Meaning to Student Dissent," in Lara Campbell et. al (eds), *Debating Dissent: Canada and the Sixties*. (Toronto: University of Toronto Press, 2012), 98. For a full reading of this chapter, see pages 97-114. David Austin's *Fear of a Black Nation* has also made a significant contribution to our understanding of the Sir George Affair. *Fear of a Black Nation: Race, Sex and Security in Sixties Montreal* (Toronto: Between the Lines, 2013), 129-156.

27   For more on the circumstances that led to the government of Trinidad paying the Trinidadian students' legal fees and fines see Belgrave, "The Sir George Williams Affair," 130-131.

28   David Austin. *Fear of a Black Nation: Race, Sex, and Security in Sixties Montreal.* (Toronto: Between the Lines, 2013).

29   Professor Michael West has also done an important excavation and analysis on the Sir George University Computer Affair. See his article, "The Art of Engagement Forum, Part I, History vs. Historical Memory, Rosie Douglas, Black Power on Campus, and the Canadian Color Conceit," in *Palimpsest*, 6, 1 (2017):84-100; and "The Art of Engagement Forum, Part I, History vs. Historical Memory, Rosie Douglas, Black Power on Campus, and the Canadian Color Conceit," in *Palimpsest*, 6, 2 (2017):179-224.

30   For details of this event see https://protestsandpedagogy.ca

31   *Report on Lord Dalhousie's History on Slavery and Race.* Dalhousie University. September 2019.

32   For a detailed and intriguing account of state surveillance of Black people see: The "Police #3-Dirty Tricks," *Canadaland Podcast* (November 11, 2020).

33   Austin, *Fear of a Black Nation*, 129-176.

34   John Macfarlane and Benjamin Shingler, "Valerie Plante promises change after report finds Montreal has 'neglected' fight against racism, *CBC* (June 15, 2020).

Looking Backward, Looking Forward: The Sir George Protest at 50 and Beyond

David Austin

VERY FEW members of my generation knew about the Sir George protest in the late eighties and early 1990s. I learned about it in 1989, when I discovered Dennis Forsythe's anthology, *Let the Niggers Burn! The Sir George Williams University Affair and Its Caribbean Aftermath* (1971). At about the same time, I also discovered Walter Rodney's *The Grounding with My Brothers* (1969), a small collection of speeches, three of which he delivered in Montreal in 1968 during the Congress of Black Writers and in the immediate aftermath of his expulsion from Jamaica. I was in high school at the time, but in retrospect, both books contributed to my decision to move from Toronto to Montreal.

By 1990, I had begun to feel stifled by the freewheeling but often limited discussions that we routinely had at Third World Books and Crafts on Toronto's Bathurst Street. The bookstore was a place to explore the world through the exchange of ideas. At that time, many of the conversations centered on Afro-centricity and the ideas of scholars such as Molefi Asante, Dr. Yosef Ben-Jochannan, and Cheikh Anta Diop, among others, but there was often a refusal to appreciate that kingdoms generally consist of monarchs and masters on the one hand, and subjects and slaves on the other. We also debated the virtues of Malcolm X versus Martin Luther King Jr. and discussed Apartheid and the civil war in Angola, to name only a few of the issues. Some of us protested the Royal Ontario Museum's *Into the Heart of Africa* exhibition, but more often than not, our political conversations were less grounded in local historical, social, and political experiences and when they were, they frequently uncritically veered towards the politics of representation that is perhaps best summed up as the demand for "more Black faces in high places" with little or no consideration of how class shaped intra-racial politics.[1]

There was the notable exception of the classes on dialectics that were conducted in the basement of the bookstore by Norman 'Otis' Richmond and

Raymond Watts. Richmond was born in Arcadia, Louisiana but he grew up in Los Angeles where he was member of the sixties doowop soul group, The M-M's & the Peanuts. He later became a member of the Detroit-based League of Revolutionary Black Workers before moving to Toronto where he co-founded the Afro-American Progressive Association (AAPA) in the late sixties. Norman also hosted two popular radio programs on CKLN – "Diasporic African Music" and "Saturday Morning Live"—that many of us tuned into on a weekly basis. The late Raymond Watts was born in Trinidad. He was a musician and a former member of the Caribbean Conference Committee based in Montreal in the mid 1960s. I later discovered that he was the person who had first proposed the idea to organize the 1968 Congress of Black Writers in Montreal, and that he had played a significant role, as a civilian, in the aborted 1970 military attempt to remove the government of Eric Williams from power.[2] I was not directly involved in the dialectics study group, but I would often listen in on conversations between Norman, Raymond, Robin Battle, and Richard Sutherland. Robin and Richard were regulars at the bookstore and the three of us engaged in incessant cultural and political discussions. They participated in the dialectics study group and our conversations were often an extension of those meetings. Along with Mesfin Aman, they were also members, or at least had been, of the Toronto chapter of the All-African People's Revolutionary Party (AAPRP) that was guided from Guinea by Kwame Touré (formerly Stokely Carmichael), and we often discussed books that were on the AAPRP's reading list.

In their own ways, the bookstore's proprietors, Gwendolyn and Leonard Johnston, attempted to inject a sense of sobriety into our youthful penchant to both learn and to prematurely proselytize. Gwendolyn was soft-spoken, understated, and unassuming in her approach with us. Lenny, as we affectionately called him, had been a train porter and a member of the Brotherhood of Sleeping Car Porters, the Communist Party of Canada (CPC), and later the AAPA. He did not mince words and he would let you have it, both explicitly and often expletively, if he felt you were wasting time on nonsensical ideas. This encouraged us to think before speaking, or sometimes not speak at all.

It was in the bookstore that we discovered the work of, among many others, Walter Rodney, Frantz Fanon, bell hooks, Patricia Hill Collins, and C.L.R. James along with the work of people whom I would later meet, get to know and in some instances collaborate with, including Robert Hill, Horace Campbell, and Rupert Lewis. Lennie also kept a copious stash of communist material by Lenin, Stalin, Marx, Engels, and Mao from his days in the CPC. The bookstore was like a second home for me, for many of us, but as one prominent academic once confided in a private conversation, as a gay Black male, it was not a welcoming environment for him and, as I can attest, views that were routinely expressed on gender, and especially sexuality, in the bookstore were often primitively patriarchal and horrendously homophobic.

After eight years in Toronto (Scarborough), it was time for me to leave. I had completed two years of primary school in Montreal between 1980 and 1982 and visited the city on occasion, including for basketball tournaments, and so the city was very familiar to me. As a cosmopolitan centre with a strong political history that both Forsythe and Rodney's books capture, Montreal was the logical option when I considered where to attend university. I do not recall discussing Sir George in any great detail at the bookstore, but in Montreal I found myself in the curious position of being among the few of my generation to demonstrate a keen interest in Montreal's Black and Caribbean radical political history (in other cases, most of the attention was devoted to U.S. historical examples). My curiosity endeared me to people who had been politically active in the sixties and seventies, and I became absorbed by that generation's stories. Through them and others who were now living abroad—people such as Viola Daniel, Celia Daniel, Bridget Joseph, Alfie Roberts, Franklyn Harvey, Gene Depradine, Robert Hill, Laurette Solomon, to name some of them—I learned about the extent to which Montreal had been a diasporic center of Caribbean and Black Power politics, and I eventually began to record and write about the politics and history of that time. I felt a sense of responsibility to share what this political history represented in public fora, events, and conferences whenever the opportunity presented itself in Canada, and then increasingly in the U.S., the Caribbean, and the U.K.

Despite the positive responses to what was "new history" for those of us who were a generation or more removed from the events, I soon began to feel a sense of unease. Many were attracted to the romance of the story–a protest, student occupation, the speaking of truth to power, smashed computers, a building up in flames, and the corresponding state violence courtesy of the Montreal police.[3] But what about the current implications of the protest in terms of the politics of our moment? How could Sir George inform our understanding of contemporary political dynamics? It was as if I had been meditating on the same song, and there was now a need for to take distance from the narrative, to rethink it. As this volume attests, the reflection and rethinking on the significance of Sir George is being carried out by a new generation of activists and academics, alongside their predecessors.

The success of the *Protest and Pedagogy* conference in February 2019 is an indication of how far our appreciation of Sir George has come. And while we cannot say that Sir George is now a popular part of Caribbean and Canadian lore, there is no doubt that a great deal many more people in the Caribbean, Canada, the U.S., and the U.K. are now aware of it than before. But in reflecting on how far our appreciation of this history has come, we are left with a pressing question, one whose response is perhaps so obvious that it is generally assumed, even when the question itself is not posed: What is the significance of the Sir George Williams protest and its related events? And related to this: now that more intellectual labour on the protest is in motion, what does this work do, and for whom does it do what it does? And to whom does this history belong to or, put another way, who has the right to claim it as their own, and why, and in what ways and contexts?

During a relatively recent roundtable at Concordia University, a French Quebecois professor recalled the history of the Quiet Revolution, a moment of intense French nationalism that ultimately contributed to the *francisation* of the province's institutions and the dismantling of English Canadian dominance in the province. As is customary in conventional accounts of that historical moment, the political part played by people of African and Caribbean descent was soundly minimized. And yet, it was in Quebec, in the city of Montreal, that the Sir George protest unfurled; and, despite what a prominent Quebec academic refuses to fully appreciate, Black politics and Sir George attracted and inspired members of the Quebec and English Canadian left, including prominent figures within the Quebec Liberation Front (FLQ), and was part of a sustained history of Black struggle and internationalism in Quebec, North America, and the Caribbean.[4]

Of course, Black Montreal's tradition of self-organization begins long before Sir George. The Colored Women's Club (1902) was one of many organizations established at the dawn of the twentieth century to humanize the existence of people of African descent in Montreal. So too was the Union United Church (1907), and the Negro Community Centre (1927). There was the Order of Sleeping Car Porters that was founded in 1917 in Winnipeg and which counted many Black Montrealers among its members. Marcus Garvey's Universal Negro Improvement Association (UNIA) also officially established a chapter in Montreal in 1919.

Louise Langdon Norton arrived in Montreal from Grenada in 1917 and she worked with her uncle, Egerton Langdon, to establish the Montreal chapter of the UNIA. She married Earl Little in Montreal's Union United Church in May 1919 and the two were active within the UNIA before moving to Philadelphia by 1920.[5] The Guyanese writer Jan Carew suggests that she, along with her husband and her uncle, "laid the foundation on which all the succeeding Black Power movements in Canada and the United States were built."[6] This might sound like a touch of hyperbole, but only if we ignore the fact that Louise Langdon Norton's son, Malcom Little, was literally a child of the Garvey movement. We know him as the Malcolm X, who would later blaze a trail *en route* to becoming one of most influential popular political figures of the post-Second World War period.

In the last years of his life, Malcolm shifted towards a more explicit Black internationalism and what we might describe as a more socialistic outlook.[7] This perspective was influenced by his travel on the African continent, including Ghana and Tanzania, both of which were engaged in a political experiment with their own brand of socialism. It is also quite possible, even likely, that he read C.L.R. James's conversations with Leon Trotsky in Coyocan Mexico in 1938 on the "Negro Question," published by the socialist group in which James was once an active member and which would publish many of Malcolm's most important speeches in the aftermath of his assassination. Like Martin Luther King Jr., he perhaps read James's seminal revolutionary study of politics through the prism of the Haitian Revolution, *The Black Jacobins: Toussaint L'Ouverture and the Haitian Revolution*. And according to James' friend, the lawyer Conrad Lynn, who was closely associated with Malcolm X, Malcolm memorized James' document, "The Revolutionary Answer to the Negro Problem in the United States" while in prison in the early 1950s.[8] In that essay, James argues that Black struggles both possessed an independent vitality of their own and, equally important, had the capacity to significantly impact American social and political life and to exert influence on the American working-class as a constituent part of the struggle for socialism.[9] When we consider the local and international impact of Malcolm, King, the Civil Rights and Black Power movements, James' argument anticipated the significance of Black struggles in the 1960s and 1970s, including the protest at Sir George.

While the tradition of Black and Caribbean struggle in Canada and internationally is proudly "owned" by the people that made it, it is also both constitutive and a constituent part of the currents of international Black and Caribbean radical politics, the broader left, and politics in general. This point is not about the need, flawed desire, or yearning to feel included within some vague conception of the mainstream or "universal history," but about recognizing that history, once made, often reverberates, and extends beyond the boundaries of those who made it.

The Caribbean students involved in Sir George were part of the migration circuits that brought them to Canada in search of education and employment possibilities that alienation and underdevelopment spawned by African enslavement, Indian indentureship, and colonialism did not afford them at home. The protest was a response to the Du Boisian "problem" of unfreedom in the post-emancipation period. This is a phenomenon tied to the enslavement of Africans in the Americas, including in Canada–slaves whose labour was once valued for producing surplus-value that resulted in the profits that fueled capitalism and an unparalleled accumulation of wealth in Europe and North America. Once emancipated, the formerly enslaved found themselves in the dubious Du Boisian position of being a surplus population whose labour, once essential, was now precarious and superfluous. The response of people of African and Caribbean descent to the problem in the post-plantation period was migration in search of opportunities and what Sylvia Wynter refers to as "nativization," that is to say the ongoing cultural adaptation as a form of resistance to what is, taking its cue from Cedric Robinson, commonly referred to as racial capitalism.[10] But as I have suggested elsewhere, rooted in a fear of the political potential of a restive Black population, the state's response "has been the confinement of blacks to housing projects; the profiling and policing of Black lives, which frequently results in extrajudicial death; and perhaps the penultimate penalty—the penitentiary. This is all part of what might be described as the plantation-to- plant-to prison pipeline—the state's response to the Du Boisian 'problem.'"[11] This, or course, is true in Canada too, where people of African descent, along with Indigenous peoples, are disproportionately incarcerated and the recipients of state violence propagated by the police. And, to state an obvious but disrespected truth, this is one reason why we need to resist the wholesale adaptation of dubious ideas (i.e., Afropessimism) that misdirect us away from the very specific and concrete experiences that, rooted in particular places and times, but possessing their unique historical realities and characteristics, are nonetheless part of a larger canvas of particular experiences that make up what might be described as the transnational "Black experience".

Dissent and protest in the face of oppression and injustice is not only natural and normal, but necessary, and its absence cedes even greater space to authoritarian tendencies. Sir George, as a moment of Black self-organization and dissent created a space, albeit momentary and at times fleeting, for genuine allyship between people of African and Caribbean descent (both Asian and African) and Indigenous peoples, French Quebeckers, and Anglo Canadians. In response, the Canadian state, in collaboration with its U.S. counterpart, deployed legal and extra-legal measures–Warren Hart is the best-known example–to disrupt and destroy Black dissident groups in Canada which, it feared, would serve as a catalyst for revolutionary fervor in Canada and internationally.[12]

Sir George largely remains a footnote in Caribbean and Canadian history, even though it was arguably the most sustained and far-reaching North American university protest in terms of its national and international scope and implications. Its relative absence in sixties' political lore reflects the intellectual and political apartheid that pervades in the consciousness of those academics and activists who are determined to cling to Eurocentric and elitist conceptions of history and progress in favor of an incomplete, but albeit inflated and privileged perception of themselves and their place in the world.

In an article about the Jamaican economist George Beckford's transition from the New World Group to Abeng and his concept of "Black dispossession," the Jamaican historian and theorist Robert Hill, who himself was a central part of the Caribbean political community in Canada whose work precipitated the protest at Sir George, argues that theory and practice is mediated by organization.[13] To slightly invert this syllogism in the form of a question in relation to the circumstances that converged to make the protest a reality, we might ask: what theories and ideas can we draw today from the political practice that Sir George embodies? And if the point is to not simply dissect and analyze the world, but to change it, then how might the political moment that Sir George encompassed inform our capacity for political organizing today, organizing that will, in turn, produce its own set of ideas on political organizing and social change? This is perhaps where the ongoing reflection on Sir George, and the surrounding events and movements that both precipitated and ensued from it, will continue to take us in the coming years.

NOTES

1   The *Into the Heart of Africa* exhibition was mounted in 1989. Its curator appears to have intended for it to be an ironic and critical take on colonialism in Africa, but for many, it presented Africa from a colonial and missionary perspective, depicting the continent as a place of darkness and Africans as primitive and backward. This incensed members of Toronto's Black community and led to months of weekly protests and altercations with the police before the exhibition was closed in August 1990. For more on the exhibition and reactions to it see Shelley Ruth Butler, *Contested Representations: Revisiting Into the Heart of Africa* (Peterborough: Broadview Press, 2008).

2   For more on Raymond Watts, see Raffique Shah's chapter in this volume on the 1970 Mutiny in support of the Black Power movement in Trinidad and Tobago.

3   For an insightful analysis of the romance, along with the tragedy and mystery associated with the Sir George narrative see Ronald Cummings and Nalini Mohabir, "On the Poetics of a Protest: Literature and the Sir George Williams Protest," *sx salon* 33, February 2020. http://smallaxe.net/sxsalon/discussions/poetics-protest.

4   I am referring here to Jean Phillipe Warren, professor of sociology at Concordia University. In a review essay of *Fear of a Black Nation: Race, Sex, and Security in Sixties Montreal*, he

suggests that the book's ideological views negatively color the book. His misrepresentations are many, but what he ultimately fails to appreciate is that the book is a political meditation that draws from and is largely written within the Caribbean and Black radical intellectual and political traditions, of which Black Montreal was a constituent part, in order to think about contemporary politics; and that, while Black radical politics do not characterize the totality of Black politics of the time, it had an impact well out of proportion to the number of people who involved in Sir George, the Congress of Black Writers, and Black radical politics in general. See Jean-Philippe Warren, «Le défi d'une histoire objective et inclusive. *Fear of a Black Nation: Race, Sex and Security in Sixties Montreal* by David Austin» in *Bulletin d'histoire politique*, 23(1), 2014, 264-291.

5   For more on Louise Langdon Norton see Merle Collins' assiduous reconstruction of her life in "Louise Langdon Norton Little, Mother of Malcom X," *Caribbean Quarterly*, 66(43), 2020, 346-369. According to Collins, Malcolm's Grenadian great grandparents were originally from Nigeria, and were Muslims. See also Jan Carew, *Ghosts in Our Blood: With Malcolm X in Africa, England, and the Caribbean* (Chicago: Lawrence Hill Books, 1994), 112-133. Henry Langdon was Louise Langdon Norton's cousin. For more on him and the UNIA in Montreal see David Austin, "Regarding Henry: Lessons on Autonomy from one of Montreal's Oldest Black Activists," *Hour*, July 22-29, 1993.

6   Carew, *Ghosts in Our Blood*, 131.

7   The term "socialistic" was a term that Malcolm X used about African nations on the path to socialism. He also referred to them as socialist. See Manning Marable, *Malcolm X; A Life or Reinvention* (New York: Viking, 2011), 336-337, 399-400.

8   See Paul Buhle and Lawrence Ware, "Afterword: Reviewing — and Renewing — the C.L.R. James Legacy for the Twenty-First Century," in Paul Buhle, *C.L.R. James: The Artist as Revolutionary* (London: Verso, 2017), 203.

9   C. L. R. James, "Revolutionary Answer to the Negro Problem in the USA," in Anna Grimshaw, ed., *The C. L. R. James Reader* (Oxford: Blackwell, 1992), 182-183.

10   Sylvia Wynter, "Black Metamorphosis: New Natives in a New World" (unpublished ms., n.d. [1970s]), 571, 43. For an insightful and concise analysis of racial capitalism in our current moment see Zophia Edwards, "Racial Capitalism & COVID-19," *Monthly Review* 72(10), March 2021, 21-32.

11   David Austin, "Dread Dialectics," Small Axe 24(3), 2020, 234. See also "The Plantation-to-Plant-to Prison Pipeline: David Austin interviewed by Aziz Choudry" in Choudry (ed.), *Activists and the Surveillance State: Learning from Repression* (London: Pluto Press, 2019), 117-128.

12   Warren Hart was an FBI agent who, in that capacity, became captain of the Baltimore chapter of the Black Panther Party. He was later loaned to Canadian state security (the Royal Canadian Mounted Police), in the early 1970s to infiltrate, disrupt, and destroy Black groups. As an *agent provocateur,* he trained young Black men in the use arms and explosives and attempted to embroil figures such as Rosie Douglas and other Black political leaders in Canada to engage in acts of subversion. For more on the RCMP's fear of Black politics, its response and on Warren Hart's role as an agent see the Canadaland podcast: https://www.canadaland.com/podcast/the-police-3-dirty-tricks/ and David Austin, *Fear of a Black Nation: Race, Sex, and Security in Sixties Montreal* (Toronto: Between the Lines, 2013), 155-156, 157-176.

13   Robert A. Hill, "From *New World* to *Abeng*: George Beckford and the Horn of Black Power in Jamaica, 1968-1970," *Small Axe*, 11(3), October 2007, 13-14.

BIBLIOGRAPHY

"A Breakdown." *The Paper.* February 17, 1969

"A Chronicle of Events." In *Statement*, January 28, 1969: 2.

Abraham, Christiana. Forthcoming. "Critical Curating as Decolonial Practice: Protests and Pedagogy: Representations, Memories and Meaning. Anatomy of an exhibition." *TOPIA* (2021).

Adichie, Chimamanda Ngozi. *Half of a Yellow Sun.* New York: Anchor Books, 2006.

Affan, Samah. "Ethical Gestures: Articulations of Black Life in Montreal's 1960s" MA thesis, Concordia University, 2013.

Africa Information Service, ed., *Return to the Source: Selected Speeches of Amilcar Cabral.* New York: Monthly Review Press, 1973.

Alexander, M. Jacqui. *Pedagogies of Crossing: Meditations on Feminism, Sexual Politics, Memory, and the Sacred.* Durham and London: Duke University Press, 2005.

Andaiye. "The Angle You Look at Determines What you See: Toward a Critique of Feminist Politics in the Caribbean," Lucille Mathurin-Mair Lecture 2002, UWI, Mona, 8, March 23, 2002.

Angelou, Maya. "Still I Rise." In *The Norton Anthology of African American Literature*, 2nd ed. Edited by Henry Louis Gates Jr. and Nellie Y. McKay. New York: W. W. Norton & Company, 2004: 2156-2157.

Antwi, Phanuel and Ronald Cummings. "1865 and the Disenchantment of Empire." *Cultural Dynamics* 31, no. 3 (2019): 161–179.

ARWEE - The Working Class Speaks. "Police Officers Raided ARWEE's Office." March 1977: 7.

Austin, David. "Regarding Henry: Lessons on Autonomy from one of Montreal's Oldest Black Activists." *Hour*, July 22-29, 1993.

——. "Introduction to Walter Rodney." *Small Axe*, September 2001: 60-65

——. "All roads led to Montreal: Black Power, the Caribbean, and the Black Radical Tradition in Canada." *The Journal of African American History* 92, no. 4 (2007): 516-539.

——. "Anne Cools: Radical Feminist and Trailblazer," *MaComere* 12, no. 2 (2010): 68-76.

——. *Fear of a Black Nation: Race, Sex, and Security in Sixties Montreal.* Toronto: Between the Lines, 2013.

——. "The Black Jacobins: A Revolutionary Study of Revolution, and of a Caribbean Revolution," in Charles Forsdick and Christian Hogsbjerg (eds.), *The Black Jacobins Reader.* Durham, NC: Duke University Press, 2017: 256-277.

——. *Moving Against the System: The 1968 Congress of Black Writers and the Making of Global Consciousness.* London: Pluto, 2018.

——. "Dread Dialectics," *Small Axe* 63, 2020: 228-238.

Backhouse, Constance. *Petticoats and Prejudce: Women and the Law in Nineteenth-Century Canada*. Toronto: Women's Press, 1991.

Bagoo, Andre. *The Undiscovered Country*. Leeds, UK: Peepal Tree, 2020.

Bair, Barbara. "True Women, Real Men: Gender Ideology and Social Roles in the Garvey Movement." In *Gendered Domains: Rethinking Public and Private in Women's History*, edited by Dorothy O. Helly and Reverby, Susan M., 156-66. Ithaca: Cornell University Press, 1992.

Bakiner, Onur. *Truth Commissions: Memory, Power, and Legitimacy* (Philadelphia: University of Pennsylvania Press, 2016.

Baksh-Soodeen, Rawwida. "Issues of Difference in Contemporary Caribbean Feminism." *Feminist Review* 59(1998): 74-85.

Baldwin, James. *The Fire Next Time*. New York: Vintage International,1993.

Barriteau, Eudine V. "Issues and Challenges of Caribbean Feminisms, Keynote Address at Inaugural Workshop on Recentering Caribbean Feminisms," Centre for Gender and Development Studies, UWI, Cave Hill, Barbados, 2002.

Beckles, Hillary. *Britain's Black Debt: Reparations for Caribbean Slavery and Native Genocide*. Kingston, Jamaica: University of the West Indies Press, 2013.

Belgrave, Valerie. "The Sir George Williams Affair." In *The Black Power Revolution of 1970: A Retrospective*, edited by Selwyn Ryan and Taimoon Stewart. Kingston: University of the West Indies Press, 1995: 119-131.

——. "Confronting Power and Politics: A Feminist Theorizing of Gender in Commonwealth Caribbean Societies." *Meridians* 3, no. 2 (2003): 57-92.

——. "Memories of a Hot Winter." *The Caribbean Review*. August 3, 2017. https://www.caribbeanreview.org/2017/08/memories-hot-winter/

——. "Protecting Feminist Futures in the Caribbean's Contemporary." *Journal of Eastern Caribbean Studies* 42, no. 3 (2017): 7-25.

Benítez-Rojo, Antonio. *The Repeating Island: The Caribbean and the Postmodern Perspective*. Trans James E. Maraniss. Durham: Duke University Press, 1997.

Bernard, Jay. *Surge*. London: Chatto and Windus, 2019.

Berry, Mary Frances. *My Face is Black is True: Callie House and the Struggle for Ex-Slave Reparations*. New York: Random House, 2006.

"Black Power." *The Forum*, April 10, 1970: 13.

"Black Power in St. Vincent." *The Vincentian*, August 23, 1969: 5.

Blier, Suzanne Preston. *African Vodun: Art, Psychology, and Power*. Chicago: University of Chicago Press, 1995. 49-54.

Bobb-Smith, Yvonne. *I Know Who I Am: A Caribbean Woman's Identity in Canada*. Toronto: Women's Press, 2003.

Bolender, Keith. "When Cuban-American Terrorism Came to Canada." In *Other Diplomacies, Other Ties: Cuba and Canada in the Shadow of the US*. Edited by Luis René Fernández Tabio, Cynthia Wright, and Lana Wylie, 115-135. Toronto, Canada: University of Toronto Press, 2018.

Boyce Davies, Carole. *Black Women, Writing and Identity: Migrations of the Subject.* New York and London: Routledge, 1994.

—. "Sisters Outside: Tracing the Caribbean/Black Radical Intellectual Tradition." *Small Axe 28,* no.13.1 (2009): 217-229.

Bradley, Stefan M. *Harlem vs. Columbia University: Black Student Power in the Late 1960s.* Urbana: University of Illinois Press, 2009.

Brand, Dionne. *Bread Out of Stone.* Toronto: Coach House Press, 1994.

Brathwaite, Kamau Edward. *The Arrivants.* Oxford: Oxford University Press, 1973.

—. "History of the Voice". In *Roots,* 259-304. Ann Arbor: University of Michigan, 1993.

Breitman, George. ed., *Malcolm X Speaks: Selected Speeches and Statements.* New York Pathfinder Press, 1989.

Bristow, Peggy, Dionne Brand, Linda Carty, Afua Cooper, Sylvia Hamilton, Adrienne Shadd (eds.), *Were Rooted Here and They Cant Pull us up.* Toronto: University of Toronto Press, 1994.

Browne, V.C. *Atlantic Interactions.* Kingston: Ian Randle Publishers, 2008.

Bunce, Robin and Paul Field, *Darcus Howe: A Political Biography.* London: Bloomsbury, 2014.

Buhle, Paul. *C.L.R. James: The Artist as Revolutionary.* London: Verso, 2017

Butcher, LeRoi. "The Anderson Affair." In *Let the Niggers Burn: The Sir George Williams University Affair and Its Caribbean Aftermath,* edited by Dennis Forsythe, 76-109. Montreal: Black Rose Books, 1971.

Butler, Shelley Ruth. *Contested Representations: Revisiting Into the Heart of Africa.* Peterborough: Broadview Press, 2008.

Campbell, Horace. "Pan-Africanism and African Liberation. "In *Imagining Home: Class, Culture and Nationalism in the African Diaspora,* edited by Sidney J. Lemelle and Robin D. Kelley, 285-307. London and New York: Verso, 1994.

Campbell, Parnel, interview by Kirland Ayanna Bobb. *Mr.,* September 4, 2018.

"Canadian Justice in Operation." In *UHURU* 1, no. 15, Feb. 2, 1970.

Carew, Jan. *Ghosts in Our Blood: With Malcolm X in Africa, England, and the Caribbean.* Chicago: Lawrence Hill Books, 1994.

Carey, Beverly. *The Maroon Story.* Gordon Town: Agouti Press, 1997.

Carmichael, Stokely and Charles V. Hamilton, *Black Power: The Politics of Liberation in America.* New York: Vintage Book, 1967.

—. *Ready for Revolution. The Life and Struggles of Stokely Carmichael.* New York: Scribner, 2003.

Carson, Clayborne and Kris Shepard, eds., *A Call to Conscience: The Landmark Speeches of Dr. Martin Luther King, Jr.* New York: Grand Central Publishing, 2001.

Carter, Martin. "The Race Crisis-British Guiana:" Speech at the Inter-American, University of Puerto Rico, 1964.

Castello, June. "Where Have All the Feminists Gone: Learning the Lessons of a Long Time Passed in the Women's Movement in the Caribbean." *Caribbean Quarterly* 52, no. 2-3 (2006): 1-13.

Cececco, Leyland. "Black Toronto residents 20 times more likely to be shot dead by police, study says," *The Guardian*. December 10, 2018.

Chancy, Adeline. "Notes on the Congrès des écrivains noirs." Unpublished. October 1968.

Chantiluke, Roseanne, Brian Kwoba, and Athinangamso Nkopo, eds., *Rhodes Must Fall: The Struggle to Decolonise the Racist Heart of Empire*. London: Zed Books, 2018.

Choudry, Aziz, ed., *Activists and the Surveillance State: Learning from Repression*. London: Pluto Press, 2019.

Chung, Clairmont ed., *Walter A. Rodney: A Promise of Revolution*. New York: Monthly Review Press, 2012.

Cleaver, Eldridge. *Soul on Ice*. New York: A Delta Book, 1968.

Clouden, Anselm. "Black Power: Shadow and Substance," *The Black i* 2, no. 1, June 1973.

Coclough, Wes. "The Henry Foss Hall Building, Montreal: From Riots to Gardens in Forty Years." In *Montreal as Palimpsest III: The Dialectics of Montreal's Public Spaces*, edited by Cynthia Hammond. Department of Art History, Concordia University, 2010.

Collins, Merle. "Louise Langdon Norton Little, Mother of Malcom X," *Caribbean Quarterly* 66(43), 2020, 346-369.

Cone, James H. *Martin & Malcom & America: A Dream or Nightmare*. Maryknoll, NY: Orbis Books, 1991.

Cooper, Afua. *The Hanging of Angélique: The untold story of Canadian Slavery and the Burning of Old Montreal*. Athens: University of Georgia Press, 2007.

Cottle, Junior 'Spirit'. "Message from Spirit." *Freedom*, October 11, 1974: 3-4.

——, interview by Kirland Ayanna Bobb. *Mr.*, August 30, 2017.

Crenshaw, Kimberle. "Mapping the Margins: Intersectionality, Identity Politics, and Violence against Women of Color," *Stanford Law Review* 43, no. 6 (1991): 1241-1299.

Cudjoe, Selwyn R. ed., *Eric E. Williams Speaks: Essays on Colonialism and Independence*. Wellesley, MA: Calaloux Publications, 1993.

Cummings, Ronald. "Maroon In/Securities." *Small Axe* 57 (2018): 47–55.

Cummings, Ronald and Nalini Mohabir, "On the Poetics of a Protest: Literature and the Sir George Williams Protest," *sx salon* 33, February 2020. http://smallaxe.net/sxsalon/discussions/poetics-protest.

Currie-Williams, Kelann. Forthcoming. "In the Legacy of Marronage: The Sir George Williams Affair and Acts of Refusal, Protest, and Care." *Topia* 43 (2021).

de la Fuente, Alejandro. *A Nation for All: Race, Inequality, and Politics in Twentieth-Century Cuba*. Chapel Hill: University of North Carolina Press, 2001.

Desmond Dekker and the Aces. "The Israelites." London: Pyramid, 1969.

Depestre, René. "Lettre de Cuba." *Présence Africaine* 56.4 (1965): 105-142.

——. "Aventuras de la Negritud." *Casa de las Américas* 47 (1968): 108-111.

——. "Jean Price-Mars et le mythe de l'Orphée noir ou les aventures de la négritude." *L'Homme et la société* 7 (1968): 171-181.

Diederich, Bernard. *1959: The Year that Inflamed the Caribbean*. Princeton, NJ: Markus Wiener Publishers, 2009.

Draper, Nicholas. *The Price of Emancipation: Slave-Ownership, Compensation and British Society at the End of Slavery*. Cambridge University Press, 2013.

Eber, Dorothy. *The Computer Centre Party: Canada Meets Black Power*. Montreal: Tundra Books, 1969.

——. "Notes on the Trial of the 'Trinidad Ten,'" *Canadian Forum*, October 1974, 21-2.

Edwards, Zophia. "Racial Capitalism & COVID-19." *Monthly Review* 72(10), March 2021, 21-32.

Eltis, David, Stephen D. Behrendt, David Richardson, and Herbert S. Klein. *The Trans-Atlantic Slave Trade: A Database on CD-ROM*. Cambridge and New York: Cambridge University Press, 1999.

Fanon, Frantz. *The Wretched of the Earth*, trans. by Constance Farrington. New York: Grove Press, 1965.

Fager, Charles. *Uncertain Resurrection: The Poor People's Campaign*. Grand Rapids: Eerdmans, 1969.

Fairclough, Adam. "Was Martin Luther King a Marxist?", *History Workshop*, 15, no. 1 (1983), 117-125.

Feenberg, Andrew and Jim Freedman, *When Poetry Ruled the Streets: The French May Events of 1968*. Albany: State University of New York Press, 2001.

Ferguson, Tyrone. *To Survive Sensibly, or to Court Heroic Death*. Georgetown: Guyana National Printers, 1999.

"Focus on UHURU." *UHURU* 1, no. 12, Dec. 8, 1969.

Ford-Smith, Honor. "Women and the Garvey Movement in Jamaica." In *Garvey: His Work and Impact,* edited by Rupert Lewis and Bryan Patrick. Kingston: ISER, and UWI Extra Mural Studies Department, 1988.

——. "Unruly Virtues of the Spectacular: Performing Engendered Nationalisms in the UNIA in Jamaica." *Interventions* 6, no. 1(2004): 18-44.

Forsythe, Dennis. *Let the Niggers Burn: The Sir George Williams University Affair and Its Caribbean Aftermath*. Montreal: Black Rose Books, 1971.

——. "West Indian Radicalism Abroad." PhD dissertation, McGill University, 1973.

Foster, Cecil. *They Call Me George: The Untold Story of Black Train Porters and the Birth of Modern Canada*. Windsor, Ontario: Biblioasis, 2019.

Franko. "Black Power." *The Vincentian*, March 28, 1970: 4.

Gaffar La Guerre, John. "The Indian Response to Black Power: A Continuing Dilemma," in *Black Power Revolution*. Edited by Selwyn Ryan and Taimoon Stewart. Port of Spain: University of the West Indies, 1995: 273-307.

Garrow, David J. *The FBI and Martin Luther King, Jr.* New York: Penguin Books, 1983.

Gaye, Egbert. "Something Happened…50 Years Ago." *Montreal Community Contact*. January 24, 2019.

Genovese, Eugene. "By Way of Dedication." In *Red and Black: Marxian Explorations in Southern and Afro-American History*. New York: Pantheon Books, 1971.

Girvan, Norman. "After Rodney: The Politics of Student Protest in Jamaica," *New World Quarterly* 4, no. 3 (1968): 59-68.

Gonsalves, Ralph E. *The Making of 'The Comrade': The political journey of Ralph Gonsalves.* Kingstown: Strategy Forum Inc., 2010.

Goudsouzian, Aram. *Down to the Crossroads: Civil Rights, Black Power, and the Meredith March Against Fear.* New York: Farrar, Straus, and Giroux, 2014.

Graham, Peter and Ian McKay. *Radical Ambition: The New Left in Toronto.* Toronto: Between the Lines, 2019.

Greene, Simeon, interview by Kirland Ayanna Bobb. *Mr.*, August 24, 2017.

Grewal, Inderpal and Caren Kaplan. "Global Identities: Theorizing Transnational Studies of Sexuality." *GLQ: A Journal of Lesbian and Gay Studies* 7, no. 4(2001): 663-679.

Griffin, Phil. "SGWU and the Black Studies Program," *The Georgian*, February 7, 1969.

Grimshaw, Anna. ed., *The C. L. R. James Reader.* Oxford: Blackwell, 1992.

Guerra, Lillian. *Visions of Power in Cuba: Revolution, Redemption, and Resistance, 1959-1971.* Chapel Hill: University of North Carolina Press, 2012.

Guevara, Ernesto Che. *Guerilla Warfare.* Lincoln: University of Nebraska Press, 1998. First edition (translation) 1961.

——. *The African Dream: The Diaries of the Revolutionary War in the Congo.* London: Harvill, 2000.

Hall, Stuart and Bill Schwarz, *Familiar Stranger: A Life Between Two Islands.* Durham: Duke University Press, 2017.

Hamilton, Sylvia. *Little Black Schoolhouse.* Maroon Films, 2007.

Hampton, Rosaline. *Black Racialization and Resistance at an Elite University.* Montreal: McGill University Press, 2020.

Handyside, Richard ed., *Revolution in Guinea: Selected Texts by Amilcar Cabral.* New York: Monthly Review Press, 1969.

Haynes, Tonya. "Interrogating Approaches to Caribbean Feminist Thought" *Journal of Eastern Caribbean Studies* Vol. 42, No. 3, 2017: 26–58.

Hébert, Paul C. "A Microcosm of the General Struggle': Black Thought and Activism in Montreal, 1960-1969." PhD dissertation, University of Michigan, 2015.

Hewitt, Steve. *Spying 101: The RCMP's Secret Activities at Canadian Universities, 1917-1997.* Toronto: University of Toronto Press, 2001: 150-155.

Hill, Robert. *Walter Rodney Speaks: The Making of an African Intellectual.* Trenton: Africa World Press, 1990.

——. "From *New World* to *Abeng*: George Beckford and the Horn of Black Power in Jamaica, 1968–1970." *Small Axe*, 24 (2007): 1-15.

Hill, Sharon. "Former University of Windsor Law Dean honoured at start of Black History Month." *Windsor Star* (Windsor, ON), Feb. 03, 2020.

Horne, Gerald. *From the Barrel of a Gun: The United States and the War Against Zimbabwe, 1965-1980.* Chapel Hill: University of North Carolina Press, 2001.

Hosein, Gabrielle. "What Does Feminism Mean to Young Women?" *CAFRA News,* December 15, 2002

Hudson, Peter James. "Imperial Designs: The Royal Bank of Canada in the Caribbean," *Race & Class* 52, no. 1(2010): 33-48.

Ibrahim, Awad and Ali A. Abdi. *The Education of African Canadian Children: Critical Perspectives.* Montreal: McGill-Queen's University Press, 2016.

Ismay, John. "Rhodesia's Dead—but White Supremacist Have Given It New Life Online," *New York Times* Magazine, April 2018.

Jackson, George. *Soledad Brothers: The Prison Letters of George Jackson.* New York: Bantam Book, 1970.

Jagan, Cheddi. *The West on Trial.* New York: International Publishers, 1966.

James, C.L.R. *Dr. Eric Williams: A Biographical Sketch.* Port of Spain: P.N.M. Publishing Co., 1960.

—. *The Black Jacobins.* 2nd ed. New York: Vintage Books, 1963. First edition. 1938

—. *Nkrumah, and the Ghana Revolution.* London: Allison and Busby, 1977.

—. *You Don't Play with Revolution: The Montreal Lectures of C.L.R. James,* Edited by David Austin. Oakland: AK Press, 2009.

Jayawardena, Kumari. *Feminism and Nationalism in the Third World.* London: Zed Books, 1986.

Joachim, Benoit. "Sur l'esprit de couleur. " *Nouvelle Optique 9* (1973): 149-158.

Johnson, Linton Kwesi. *Mi Revalueshanary Fren: Selected Poems.* Port Townsend, Washington: Copper Canyon Press, 2006.

Jones, Burnley. and James W. St. G. Walker, *Burnley "Rocky" Jones, Revolutionary: An Autobiography.* Halifax: Roseway Publishing 2016.

Joseph, Peniel E. "Black Liberation without Apology: Reconceptualizing the Black Power Movement." *The Black Scholar* 31, no. 3-4 (2001): 2-19.

—. *The Sword and the Shield: The Revolutionary Lives of Malcolm X and Martin Luther King Jr.* New York: Basic Books, 2020.

Kars, Marjoleine. *Blood on the River: A Chronicle of Mutiny and Freedom on the Wild Coast.* New York and London: The New Press, 2020.

Katsiaficas, George. *The Imagination of the New Left: A Global Analysis of 1968.* Boston: South End Press, 1987.

Kaufman, Fred. *Searching for Justice: An Autobiography.* Toronto: Osgoode Society, 2005.

Kimball, Eric. "What have we to do with slavery? New Englanders and the Slave Economies of the West Indies." In *Slavery's Capitalism: A New History of American Economic Development,* edited by Sven Beckert and Seth Rockman. Philadelphia: University of Pennsylvania Press, 2016.

King, Jr., Martin Luther. "Black Power." In *The Autobiography of Martin Luther King, Jr.,* edited by Clayborne Carson. New York: Grand Central Publishing, 1998.

Knights, Robert, interview by Kirland Ayanna Bobb. *Mr.,* January 22, 2018.

Kurlansky, Mark. *1968: The Year That Rocked the World.* New York: Ballantine Books, 2004.

Kwayana, Eusi. *Walter Rodney*. Georgetown: The Catholic Standard Ltd, 1986.

Lenin, Vladimir. *What Is To Be Done?: The Burning Questions of Our Movement*. New York: International Publishers, 1929; First Edition,1902.

—. *Imperialism: The Highest Stage of Capitalism*. Moscow: Foreign Language Pub. House, 1951; First Edition, 1917.

Lewis, Gordon. "The Challenge of Independence in the Caribbean." In *Caribbean Freedom*. Edited by Hilary Beckles and Verene Shepherd. Princeton: Markus Wiener Publishers, 1996.

Lewis, Rupert. *Walter Rodney's Intellectual and Political Thought*. Kingston: The Press University of the West Indies and Detroit: Wayne State University Press, 1998.

Library and Archives Canada. "Immigration Act, Immigration Regulations, Part 1, Amended" *RG2-A-1-a*, Vol 2380, PC1967-1616, August 16 1967.

Lorde, Audre. "Learning from the 60s." In *Sister Outsider*. New York: Crossing Press, 2007.

Mamdani, Mahmood. *Citizen and Subject: Contemporary Africa and the Legacy of Late Colonialism*. Princeton: Princeton University Press, 1996.

Marable, Manning. *Malcolm X; A Life or Reinvention* New York: Viking, 2011.

Mars, Perry. "Caribbean influences in African-American political struggles." *Ethnic and Racial Studies* 27, no. 4 (2004).

Martel, Marcel. "'Riot' at Sir George Williams: Giving Meaning to Student Dissent." In *Debating Dissent: Canada and the Sixties*, edited by Lara Campbell, Dominique Clément, and Greg Kealey, 97-114. Toronto: University of Toronto Press, 2012: 97-114.

Martinez, Gil. "De l'ambiguïté du nationalisme bourgeois en Haïti." *Nouvelle Optique 9* (1973): 1-32.

Marx, Karl and Friedrich Engels. *The Communist Manifesto*. London. Verso, 1998 (first pub. 1848).

Marx, Karl. *The Eighteenth Brumaire of Louis Bonaparte: With Explanatory Notes*. New York: International Publishers, 1963. First edition, 1852.

Massiah, Joycelin. "Feminist Scholarship in the Academy." In *Gender in the 21st Century*, edited by Barbara Bailey and Elsa Leo-Rhynie, 5-34. Kingston: Ian Randle Publishers, 2004.

Mathieu, Sarah-Jane. *North of the Color Line: Migration and Black Resistance in Canada*, 1870-1955. Chapel Hill: University of North Carolina Press, 2010.

McCartney, Dale M. "Inventing international students: Exploring discourses in international student policy talk, 1945–75." *Historical Studies in Education/Revue d'histoire de l'éducation*, 28, no. 2 (Fall 2016): 1-27.

McGee, Adam M. "Haitian Vodou and voodoo: Imagined religion and popular culture." *Studies in Religion/Sciences Religieuses* 41.2 (2012): 231-256.

McKenzie, Hermione. "Shifting Centres and Moving Margins: The UWI Experience." In *Gender in the 21st Century*, edited by Barbara Bailey and Elsa Leo-Rhynie, 397-415. Kingston: Jan Randle Publishers, 2004.

McKercher, Asa. "Lifting the Sugarcane Curtain: Security, Solidarity, and Cuba's Pavilion at Expo 67." In *Other Diplomacies, Other Ties: Cuba and Canada in the Shadow of the US,* edited by Luis René Fernández Tabio, Cynthia Wright, and Lana Wylie, 85-114. Toronto, Canada: University of Toronto Press, 2018.

McLaren, Kristin. "We had no desire to be set apart': Forced Segregation of Black Students in Canada West Public Schools and the Myth of British Egalitarianism." *Socal History/Histoire Sociale* 37, 73 (2004): 1-24.

McPherson, Anne. "Colonial Matriarchs: Garveyism, Maternalism and Belize's Black Cross Nurses, 1920-1952." *Gender and History* 15, no. 3 (2003): 507-527.

Meeks, Brian. *Caribbean Revolutions and Revolutionary Theory: An Assessment of Cuba, Nicaragua and Grenada.* London: MacMillan Caribbean, 1993.

——. *Radical Caribbean: From Black Power to Abu Bakr.* Barbados: University Press of the West Indies, 1996.

——. *Narratives of Resistance: Jamaica, Trinidad, the Caribbean.* Kingston: The University of West Indies Press, 2000.

——. and Norman Girvan (eds.), *The Thought of New World: The Quest for Decolonisation.* Kingston and Miami: Ian and Randle Publishers, 2010.

——. "Black Power Forty Years On." In *Critical Interventions in Caribbean Politics and Theory,* 75-85. Jackson: University Press of Mississippi, 2014.

Mills, Sean. *The Empire Within: Postcolonial Thought and Political Activism in Sixties Montreal.* Montreal: McGill-Queen's University Press, 2010.

——. *A Place in the Sun: Haiti, Haitians, and the Remaking of Quebec.* Montreal: McGill-Queen's University Press, 2016.

Milne, June. ed., *Kwame Nkrumah, the Conakry Years: His Life and Letters.* London: PANAF, 1990.

Moggach, Douglas and Gareth Stedman Jones, eds., *The 1848 Revolutions and European Political Thought.* Cambridge: Cambridge University Press, 2018.

Mohammed, Patricia. "Towards a Caribbean Feminist Philosophy." *CAFRA News* 5, no. 2-3 (1991): 19-21.

——. "The Future of Feminism in the Caribbean. "*Feminist Review* 64 (2000): 116-119.

——. "Like sugar in coffee: Third Wave feminism and the Caribbean. "*Social and Economic Studies* (2003): 5-30.

Moore, Carlos. "Le peuple noir a-t-il sa place dans la Révolution Cubaine?" *Présence Africaine* 52.4 (1964): 177-230.

Moten, Fred and Stephano Harney, *The Undercommons: Fugitive Planning & Black Study.* New York: Minor Compositions, 2013.

Murphy, J.M. "Black religion and "Black Magic": Prejudice and projection in images of African-derived religions. *Religion* 20, 4 (1990): 323–337.

Murray, Pauli. *Song in a Weary Throat: An American Pilgrimage.* New York: Harper & Row, Publishers, 1987.

Nettleford, Rex. *Mirror Mirror: Race, Identity and Protest in Jamaica.* Kingston: W. Collins and Sangster, 1970.

Nicholls, David. "East Indians and Black Power in Trinidad," *Race* 12, no. 4 (1971): 443-459

——. *From Dessalines to Duvalier: Race, Colour, and National Independence in Haiti.* New Brunswick, NJ: Rutgers University Press, 1996. First Edition, 1979.

Nkrumah, Kwame. *Neo-colonialism: The Last Stage of Imperialism.* London: Thomas Nelson & Sons, Ltd., 1965.

——. *Challenge of the Congo.* London: Panaf Books Ltd, 1967.

——. *Dark Days in Ghana.* New York: International Publishers, 1968.

Ollivier, Émile. Documents related to the Institut cubain d'amitié avec le peuple. October 5,1975–October 14, 1977. P0349/E2,0004. Fonds Émile Ollivier. Université de Montréal. Montréal, Québec, Canada.

Oyeniran, Channon. "Sleeping Car Porters in Canada." In *The Canadian Encyclopedia.* https://www.thecanadianencyclopedia.ca/en/article/sleeping-car-porters-in-canada

Oxaal, Ivar. *Race and Revolutionary Consciousness: A Documentary Interpretation of the 1970 Black Power Revolt in Trinidad.* Cambridge, MA: Schenkman Publishing Company, Inc., 1971.

Padmore, George. *The Gold Coast Revolution: The Struggle of an African People from Slavery to Freedom.* London: Dennis Dobson Ltd, 1953.

Pajonas, Pat. "All the World Knows the Score..." *Direction One*, March 1969.

Palmer, Colin A. *Eric Williams & the Making of the Modern Caribbean.* Chapel Hill: University of North Carolina Press, 2006.

Palmer, Bryan D. *Canada's 1960s: The Ironies of Identity in a Rebellious Era.* Toronto: University of Toronto Press, 2009.

Pantin, Raoul. *Black Power Day: The February 1970 Revolution.* Santa Cruz, Trinidad and Tobago: Hatuey, 1990.

Paravisini-Gebert, Lizabeth. "Decolonizing Feminism: The Home-Grown Roots of Caribbean Women's Movements." In *Daughters of Caliban: Caribbean Women in the Twentieth Century*, edited by Consuelo López Springfield, 3-17. Bloomington Indiana University Press, 1997.

Parmasad, Ken "Ancestral Impulse, Community Formation and 1970: Bridging the Afro-Indian Divide," in *Black Power Revolution*. Edited by Selwyn Ryan and Taimoon Stewart. Port of Spain: University of the West Indies, 1995: 309-317.

Pasley, Victoria. "The Black Power Movement in Trinidad: An Exploration of Gender and Cultural Changes and the Exploration of Feminist Consciousness. *Journal of International Women's Studies* 3, no. 1 (2001): 24-40.

Payne, Anthony. "The Rodney Riots in Jamaica: The Background and Significance of the Events of October 1968," *Journal of Commonwealth and Comparative Politics* 21, no. 2 (1983):158-74.

Patil, Vrushali. "From Patriarchy to Intersectionality: A Transnational Feminist Assessment of How Far We've Really Come." *Signs* 38, no. 4(2013): 847-867.

Peake, Linda, Karen De Souza, Amanda L. Swarr, and Richa Nagar. "Feminist Academic and Activist Praxis in Service of the Transnational." In *Critical Transnational Feminist Praxis*, edited by Amanda L. Swarr and Richa Nagar, 105-123. Albany, NY: State University of New York Press, 2010.

Post, Ken. *Arise Ye Starvelings: The Jamaican Labour Rebellion of 1938 and Its Aftermath*. Boston: Nijhoff, 1978.

Protest and Pedagogy: Accessed January 02, 2021. https://protestsandpedagogy.ca.

Putnam, Lara. "To Study the Fragments/Whole: Microhistory and the Atlantic World." *Journal of Social History 39, 3* (2006): 615-630.

Qualified Barber. "Afro Hair Style Condemned." *The Vincentian*, May 20, 1972: 8.

"Quebec Separatism" In *The Canadian Encyclopedia*. Accessed January 02, 2021.

Quinn, Kate, ed., *Black Power in the Caribbean*. Gainesville, FL: University Press of Florida, 2014.

Rae, Robert. "In Defense of Student Activism: A Reply," in *Student Power and the Canadian Campus*, edited by Tim and Julyan Reid. Toronto: Peter Martin Associates Limited, 1969.

Raguette, Hugh, interview by Kirland Ayanna Bobb. *Mr.*, April 13, 2018.

Rapport, Mike. *1848: Year of Revolution*. New York: Basic Books 2009.

Reddock, Rhoda. "Contestations over National Culture in Trinidad and Tobago: Considerations of Ethnicity, Class and Gender." In *Caribbean Portraits: Essays on Gender Ideologies and Identities*, edited by Christine Barrow, 414-435. Kingston: Ian Randle Publishers, 1998.

——. "Diversity, Difference, and Caribbean Feminism: The Challenge of Racism." *Caribbean Review of Gender Studies* 1(2007): 1-24.

——. "The first Mrs. Garvey: Pan-Africanism and feminism in the early 20th century British colonial Caribbean. "*Feminist Africa 19* (2014): 58-77.

Reitan, Ruth. *The Rise and Decline of an Alliance: Cuba and African American Leaders in the 1960s*. Lansing: Michigan State University Press, 1999.

Rennie, Bukka. Interview. *Trinidad & Tobago Review*, January 31, 2010.

Richardson, Bonham C. *Igniting the Caribbean's Past: Fire in British West Indian History*. Chapel Hill and London: University of North Carolina Press, 2004.

Rodney, Walter. *The Groundings With My Brothers*. London: Bogle-L'Ouverture Publications Ltd, 1969.

——. *A History of Upper Guinea Coast, 1545-1800*. New York: Monthly Review Press, 1970.

——. *George Jackson*. 1971 (unpublished).

——. *Marxism as Third World Ideology*. Paper held at University of Guyana, 1978.

——. "Race and Class in Guyanese Politics." Speech at unknown venue, USA, 1978.

——. "Transition." *Transition*, 1, no.1 (1978).

——. *Marx in the Liberation of Africa*. Georgetown, Guyana: WPA booklet, 1981.

——. *In Defence of Arnold Rampersaud*. Georgetown, Guyana: WPA booklet, 1982.

——. *The Russian Revolution: A View from the Third World*. London, New York: Verso, 2018.

Rodriguez, Besenia. "'De la Esclavitud Yanqui a la Libertad Cubana': US Black Radicals, the Cuban Revolution, and the Formation of a Tricontinental Ideology." *Radical History Review* 2005, 92 (2005): 62-87.

Rogers, Ibram Henry. "The Black Campus Movement: An Afrocentric Narrative History of the Struggle to Diversify Higher Education, 1965-1972". PhD dissertation, Temple University, 2009.

Rose, Renwick, interview by Kirland Ayanna Bobb. *Mr.*, September 4, 2017.

Rosenthal, Michael with Pamela Ritterman and Bob Sherman. "Blacks at Brandeis." In *Essays on the Student Movement*, edited by Patrick Gleeson. Columbus: Charles E. Merrill Publishing Company, 1970.

Ryan, Selwyn and Taimoon Stewart. *The Black Power Revolution of 1970: A Retrospective*. Port of Spain: University of the West Indies, 1995.

Salkey, Andrew. *Havana Journal*. London: Penguin, 1971.

——. "Appendix D" In *Georgetown Journal: A Caribbean writer's journey from London via Port of Spain to Georgetown, Guyana, 1970*, 399-402. London: New Beacon Books, 1972.

Sansaricq, Lidia. *Traición múltiple*. Montréal: Éditions CIDIHCA, 2015.

Sawyer, Mark Q. *Racial Politics in Post-Revolutionary Cuba*. Cambridge: Cambridge University Press, 2006.

Scobie, Edward. *Black Britannia: A History of Blacks in Britain*. Chicago: Johnson Pub. Co., 1972.

Scott, David. "The Archaeology of Black Memory: An Interview with Robert A. Hill, *Small Axe*, 3(1), 1999, 100-102.

——. "The Dialectic of Defeat: An Interview with Rupert Lewis," *Small Axe*, 5(2), 2001, 98-113

——. "On the Question of Caribbean Studies." *Small Axe: A Caribbean Journal of Criticism* 17, no. 2(41), 2013: 1-7.

Seidman, Sarah. "Tricontinental Routes of Solidarity: Stokely Carmichael in Cuba." *Journal of Transnational American Studies* 4(2), 2012: 1-25.

Shah, Raffique. "Reflections on the Mutiny." In *The Black Power Revolution, 1970: A Retrospective*. Edited by Selwyn Ryan and Taimoon Stewart. Port of Spain: University of the West Indies, St. Augustine, 1995.

Shepard, R. Bruce. *Deemed Unsuitable: Black from Oklahoma Move to the Canadian Prairies in Search of Equality in the Early 20th Century Only to Find Racism in their New Home*. Toronto: Umbrella Press, 1997.

Siblin, Eric. "Rosie the Red Stops Smashing the State," *Saturday Night*. May 27, 2000: 27-34.

Makeda Silvera. *Silenced*. Toronto: Williams Wallace, 1983.

Spener, David. *We Shall Not Be Moved: Biography of a Song of Struggle*. Philadelphia: Temple University Press, 2016.

Stephens, Michelle. "Disarticulating Black Internationalisms: West Indian Radicals and the Practice of Diaspora." *Small Axe* 9, no.1(2005): 100-111.

"Still no justice." *UHURU* 1, no. 16, Feb. 16, 1970.

Swan, Quito. *Black Power in Bermuda: The Struggle for Decolonization.* Palgrave MacMillan, 2009.

Sweig, Julia. *Inside the Cuban Revolution.* Cambridge: Harvard University Press, 2002.

Taylor, Ula Y. "'Negro Women are Great Thinkers as well as Doers': Amy Jacques Garvey and Community Feminism in the United States, 1924-1927." Journal of Women's History 12, no. 2 (2000): 104-126.

Tennassee, Paul Nehru. *Guyana: A Nation in Ruins.* Toronto: Clarion Typesetting, 1982.

"The Political Trial of Bro London." *Freedom,* November 21, 1975: 4.

The Wailers. "Catch A Fire." Kingston: Island Records, 1973.

The Wailers. "Burnin." Kingston: Island Records, 1973.

Thomas, Bert. "Caribbean Black Power: from Slogan to Practical Politics." *Journal of Black Studies* 22, No. 3 (1992).

Thomas, Clive. *The Poor and the Powerless.* New York: Monthly Review Press, 1988.

Thomas, Deborah A. *Modern Blackness: Nationalism, Globalization, and the Politics of Culture in Jamaica.* Durham, NC: Duke University Press, 2004.

—. *Political Life in the Wake of the Plantation: Sovereignty, Witnessing, Repair.* Durham; London: Duke University Press, 2019.

Thomas, Jomo, interview by Kirland Ayanna Bobb. *Mr.,* August 21, 2017.

Thomas, Tony, and John Riddell. *Black Power in the Caribbean; The 1970 Upsurge in Trinidad.* New York: Pathfinder Press, 1971.

Thompson, W. Scott. *Ghana's Foreign Policy, 1957-1966: Diplomacy, Ideology, and the New State.* Princeton: Princeton University Press, 1969.

Tinson, Christopher M. "'The Voice of the Black Protest Movement:' Notes on the *Liberator Magazine* and Black Radicalism in the Early 1960s." *The Black Scholar* 37, no. 4 (2008): 3-15.

Traverso, Enzo. *Left-Wing Melancholia-Marxism, History and Memory.* New York: Columbia University Press, 2016.

Trouillot, Michel-Rolph. *Haiti: State Against Nation.* New York: New York University Press, 1990.

Trotz, Alissa D. "Going Global? Transnationality, Women/Gender Studies and Lessons from the Caribbean." *Caribbean Review of Gender Studies* 1 (2007): 1-18.

Tunteng, Kiven P. "Racism and the Montreal Computer Incident of 1969." *Race* 14, no. 3 (1973): 229-240.

"Une poupée vodou pour Me Sheppard." *La Presse,* March 11, 1969.

Verta, Taylor. "Gender and Social Movements: Gender Processes in Women's Self-help Movements." *Gender & Society* 3, no. 1 (1999): 8-33.

"Violation of Fundamental Rights." *The Forum,* March 31, 1972: 20.

UPM. "Reflections and Projections." *Justice,* January 19, 1981: 3.

Walcott, Rinaldo "Outside in Black Studies: Reading from a Queer Place in the Diaspora." In *Black Queer Studies: A Critical Anthology*, edited by E. Patrick Johnson and Mae G. Henderson, 90-105. Durham: Duke University Press, 2005.

Walcott, Rinaldo and Idil Abdillahi. *Black Life: Post BLM and the Struggle for Freedom*. Winnipeg: ARP Books, 2019.

Warren, Jean-Philippe "Le défi d'une histoire objective et inclusive. *Fear of a Black Nation: Race, Sex, and Security in Sixties Montreal* by David Austin" in *Bulletin d'histoire politique*, 23(1), 2014, 264-291.

"West Indian Domestic Scheme" (1955-1967). Parks Canada. Government of Canada.ca. https://www.canada.ca/en/parks-canada/news/2020/07/west-indian-domestic-scheme-19551967.html

West, Cornel. ed., *The Radical King: Martin Luther King Jr*. Boston: Beacon Books, 2015.

West, Michael O. "History vs. Historical Memory Rosie Douglas, Black Power on Campus, and the Canadian Color Conceit." *Palimpsest: A Journal on Women, Gender, and the Black International* 6.1 (2017): 84-100

——. "History vs. Historical Memory Rosie Douglas, Black Power on Campus, and the Canadian Color Conceit." *Palimpsest: A Journal on Women, Gender, and the Black International* 6.2 (2017): 178-224.

——. "Walter Rodney and Black Power: Jamaican Intelligence and US Diplomacy." *African Journal of Criminology and Justice Studies* 1, 2 (2005): 1-50.

——. "Seeing Darkly: Guyana, Black Power, and Walter Rodney's Expulsion from Jamaica," *Small Axe, 25* (2008): 93-104.

Westmaas, Nigel. "An Organic Activist: Eusi Kwayana, Guyana, and Global Pan-Africanism." In *Black Power in the Caribbean*, edited by Kate Quinn, 159-178. Gainesville: University Press of Florida, 2014.

Wilkins, Ivor. and Hans Strydom, *The Broederbond*. New York: Paddington Press, 1979

Williams, Dorothy W. *Blacks in Montreal: 1628-1986: An Urban Demography*. Cowansville: Éditions Yvon Blais, 1989.

——. *The Road to Now: A History of Blacks in Montreal*. Montreal: Véhicule Press, 1997.

——. "*Sankofa*: Recovering Montreal's Heterogeneous Black Print Serials," PhD dissertation, McGill University, 2006.

——. "The Free Lance." In *History of the Book in Canada/Histoire du livre et de l'imprimé au Canada, vol. III (1918-1980)*. Edited by C. Gerson & J. Michon, Toronto, University of Toronto Press. 2007.

Williams, Eric. *Capitalism & Slavery*. Chapel Hill: University of North Carolina Press, 1944.

——. *Inward Hunger: The Education of a Prime Minister*. London: Deutsch, 1969.

——. *From Columbus to Castro: The History of the Caribbean, 1492-1969*. London: Deutsch, 1970.

Williams, Roosevelt. "The Myth of White "Backlash." In *Let the Niggers Burn: The Sir George Williams University Affair and its Caribbean Aftermath*, edited by David Forsythe, 111-143. Montreal: Black Rose, 1971.

Winbush, Raymond. *Should America Pay? Slavery and the Raging Debate on Reparations*. New York: Amistad Press, 2003.

Worrell, Delisle. "Canadian Economic Involvement in the West Indies." In *Let the Niggers Burn!: The Sir George Williams University Affair and Its Caribbean Aftermath*, edited by Dennis Forsythe, 41-56. Montreal: Black Rose Books, 1971.

Wynter, Sylvia. "Black Metamorphosis: New Natives in a New World" (unpublished ms., n.d. [1970s]).

——. "1492: A New World View." In *Race, Discourse, and the Origin of the Americas*, edited by Vera Lawrence Hyatt and Rex Nettleford. Washington, DC: Smithsonian Institution Press, 1995.

X, Frederick. ""Black Power" What is it?" *The Vincentian*, May 23, 1969: 2.

Young, Cynthia A. "Havana Up in Harlem: LeRoi Jones, Harold Cruse and the Making of a Cultural Revolution." *Science & Society* 65, 1 (2001): 12-38.

YULIMO. "Education for Liberation." *Freedom*, August 1, 1974: 1.

——. "Demonstration in Chateaubelair." *Freedom*, September 26, 1975: 9.

"YULIMO Pickets Ministry, Police HQ." *The Vincentian*, July 11, 1975: 1.

CONTRIBUTORS

Christiana Abraham is Scholar in-residence, Critical Race Pedagogies, in the department of Communication Studies at Concordia University. Her teaching and research focus on critical race studies, visual representations and culture; de/post-coloniality and gender; race, ethnicity and medias.

David Austin is an educator and writer, and chronicler of Black Montreal. He is the author of *Fear of a Black Nation: Race, Sex and Security in Sixties Montreal* and of *Dread Poetry and Freedom*.

Clarence Bayne is a lifelong educator. He has a PhD in economics from McGill, and is a professor emeritus at Concordia University's John Molson School of Business.

Kirland Ayanna Bobb is currently a PhD Candidate of History at the University of the West Indies, Cave Hill campus Barbados. Her thesis is entitled *"Black Radicalism in Twentieth Century St. Vincent and the Grenadines."* She is a recipient of the Postgraduate Elsa Goveia scholarship award.

Afua Cooper is a poet and historian. The author of four books of poetry, her non-fiction book, *The Hanging of Angélique* was nominated for a Governor General's Award.

Ronald Cummings is an associate professor in the English and Cultural Studies department at McMaster University, Hamilton.

Brenda Dash is an activist and organizer. She was born and grew up in Montreal. She was one of the protestors involved in the Sir George Williams Affair, and was subject to a significant fine for her role.

Philippe Fils-Aimé is a writer of Haitian origin. He is author of various books dealing, among other things, with the problem of integrating Haitian immigrants into Canada. He was one of protestors involved in the Sir George Williams Affair.

Alexis Pauline Gumbs is a writer, scholar, poet, and activist and the granddaughter of Anguillian revolutionaries Lydia and Jeremiah Gumbs. The Anguilla Literary Festival has called her "the pride of Anguilla." She is working on her next book *The Eternal Life of Audre Lorde: Biography as Ceremony*.

Océane Jasor is an Assistant Professor in the Department of Sociology and Anthropology at Concordia University. Her research explores non-western and gendered responses to developmentalist discourses and global processes.

Kaie Kellough is a novelist, poet, and sound performer based in Montreal. His book *Magnetic Equator* won the 2020 Griffin Poetry Prize.

Rupert Lewis is a professor emeritus in the Department of Government at the University of the West Indies, Kingston, and a research fellow in the UWI's P. J. Patterson Centre for Africa-Caribbean Advocacy. For fifty years, he has been a public educator on Marcus Garvey, and is the author of *Marcus Garvey: Anti-Colonial Champion*.

Nalini Mohabir is an assistant professor in Geography, Planning, and Environment at Concordia University, Montreal.

Amanda Perry specializes in the literature and history of the Anglophone, Francophone, and Spanish-speaking Caribbean and teaches at Champlain College-Saint Lambert. She received her PhD in Comparative Literature, with distinction, from New York University in 2019.

Raffique Shah has played vital roles in Trinidadian society including as a journalist, union leader, member of parliament, military officer, and revolutionary.

Nancy Warner was born and grew up in Montreal. At the time of the Sir George Williams affair, she was a student at McGill University.

Michael O. West is professor of African American Studies, History, and African Studies at the Pennsylvania State University. His current research centers on the Black Power movement in global perspectives, including a forthcoming book on Kwame Nkrumah and Black Power.

Nigel Westmaas is an associate professor of Africana studies at Hamilton College, New York. His research interests include the history of the newspaper press in Guyana, Pan-Africanism, and the rise and impact of political and social movements, mainly in the anglophone Caribbean.

Dorothy W. Williams is a historian who specializes in Black Canadian History. She has authored three books, including *The Road to Now: A History of Blacks in Montreal*, and has contributed to other scholarly and academic publications.